Innovation Management and Growth in Emerging Economies

Heather C. Webb
Higher Colleges of Technology, Dubai, UAE

Wendy Wu
Edinburgh Napier University, UK

Hussain Al Numairy
Higher Colleges of Technology, Dubai, UAE

A volume in the Advances in Business Strategy and Competitive Advantage (ABSCA) Book Series

IGI Global
PUBLISHER of TIMELY KNOWLEDGE

Published in the United States of America by
IGI Global
Business Science Reference (an imprint of IGI Global)
701 E. Chocolate Avenue
Hershey PA, USA 17033
Tel: 717-533-8845
Fax: 717-533-8661
E-mail: cust@igi-global.com
Web site: http://www.igi-global.com

Copyright © 2021 by IGI Global. All rights reserved. No part of this publication may be reproduced, stored or distributed in any form or by any means, electronic or mechanical, including photocopying, without written permission from the publisher.
Product or company names used in this set are for identification purposes only. Inclusion of the names of the products or companies does not indicate a claim of ownership by IGI Global of the trademark or registered trademark.

Library of Congress Cataloging-in-Publication Data

Names: Webb, Heather C., 1979- editor. | Wu, Wendy, 1973- editor. | Al Numairy, Hussain, 1986- editor.
Title: Innovation management and growth in emerging economies / Heather C. Webb, Wendy Wu, and Hussain Al Numairy, editors.
Description: Hershey : Business Science Reference, 2020. | Includes bibliographical references and index. | Summary: "This book showcases how innovations from emerging economies are being developed through strategic choices and the knowledge being created is aiding practitioners and researchers as it provides fresh insights to broaden their horizons with different contextual issues , allowing them to interact to shape and define either new institutions or new industries"-- Provided by publisher.
Identifiers: LCCN 2020019402 (print) | LCCN 2020019403 (ebook) | ISBN 9781799841951 (hardcover) | ISBN 9781799858454 (paperback) | ISBN 9781799841968 (ebook)
Subjects: LCSH: Management--Technological innovations--Developing countries. | Organizational change. | Strategic planning.
Classification: LCC HD70.D44 I66 2020 (print) | LCC HD70.D44 (ebook) | DDC 658.4/063091724--dc23
LC record available at https://lccn.loc.gov/2020019402
LC ebook record available at https://lccn.loc.gov/2020019403

This book is published in the IGI Global book series Advances in Business Strategy and Competitive Advantage (ABSCA) (ISSN: 2327-3429; eISSN: 2327-3437)

British Cataloguing in Publication Data
A Cataloguing in Publication record for this book is available from the British Library.

All work contributed to this book is new, previously-unpublished material.
The views expressed in this book are those of the authors, but not necessarily of the publisher.

For electronic access to this publication, please contact: eresources@igi-global.com.

Advances in Business Strategy and Competitive Advantage (ABSCA) Book Series

ISSN:2327-3429
EISSN:2327-3437

Editor-in-Chief: Patricia Ordóñez de Pablos Universidad de Oviedo, Spain

MISSION

Business entities are constantly seeking new ways through which to gain advantage over their competitors and strengthen their position within the business environment. With competition at an all-time high due to technological advancements allowing for competition on a global scale, firms continue to seek new ways through which to improve and strengthen their business processes, procedures, and profitability.

The **Advances in Business Strategy and Competitive Advantage (ABSCA) Book Series** is a timely series responding to the high demand for state-of-the-art research on how business strategies are created, implemented and re-designed to meet the demands of globalized competitive markets. With a focus on local and global challenges, business opportunities and the needs of society, the **ABSCA** encourages scientific discourse on doing business and managing information technologies for the creation of sustainable competitive advantage.

COVERAGE

- International Business Strategy
- Balanced Scorecard
- Joint Ventures
- Business Models
- Strategy Performance Management
- Ethics and Business Strategy
- Foreign Investment Decision Process
- Co-operative Strategies
- Entrepreneurship & Innovation
- Small and Medium Enterprises

IGI Global is currently accepting manuscripts for publication within this series. To submit a proposal for a volume in this series, please contact our Acquisition Editors at Acquisitions@igi-global.com or visit: http://www.igi-global.com/publish/.

The Advances in Business Strategy and Competitive Advantage (ABSCA) Book Series (ISSN 2327-3429) is published by IGI Global, 701 E. Chocolate Avenue, Hershey, PA 17033-1240, USA, www.igi-global.com. This series is composed of titles available for purchase individually; each title is edited to be contextually exclusive from any other title within the series. For pricing and ordering information please visit http://www.igi-global.com/book-series/advances-business-strategy-competitive-advantage/73672. Postmaster: Send all address changes to above address. Copyright © 2021 IGI Global. All rights, including translation in other languages reserved by the publisher. No part of this series may be reproduced or used in any form or by any means – graphics, electronic, or mechanical, including photocopying, recording, taping, or information and retrieval systems – without written permission from the publisher, except for non commercial, educational use, including classroom teaching purposes. The views expressed in this series are those of the authors, but not necessarily of IGI Global.

Titles in this Series

For a list of additional titles in this series, please visit:
http://www.igi-global.com/book-series/advances-business-strategy-competitive-advantage/73672

Advanced Models and Tools for Effective Decision Making Under Uncertainty and Risk Contexts
Vicente González-Prida (University of Seville, Spain & UNED, Spain) and María Carmen Carnero (University of Castilla-La Mancha, Spain)
Business Science Reference • © 2021 • 423pp • H/C (ISBN: 9781799832461) • US $195.00

Knowledge Management for Corporate Social Responsibility
Gregorio Martín-de Castro (Complutense University of Madrid, Spain) and Jaime González-Masip (Rey Juan Carlos University, Spain)
Business Science Reference • © 2021 • 300pp • H/C (ISBN: 9781799848332) • US $195.00

Handbook of Research on Quality Management for Competitive Advantage in Global Markets
José Manuel Saiz-Álvarez (EGADE Business School, Tecnológico de Monterrey, Mexico & Mexican Academy of Sciences, Mexico) and Beatriz Olalla-Caballero (Pontifical University of Salamanca, Spain)
Business Science Reference • © 2021 • 400pp • H/C (ISBN: 9781799850366) • US $265.00

Applications of Soft Systems Methodology for Organizational Change
Maryam Ebrahimi (Independent Researcher, Germany)
Business Science Reference • © 2021 • 236pp • H/C (ISBN: 9781799845041) • US $195.00

Handbook of Research on Multidisciplinary Approaches to Entrepreneurship, Innovation, and ICTs
Luísa Cagica Carvalho (Instituto Politécnico de Setúbal, Portugal & CEFAGE, Universidade de Évora, Portugal) Leonilde Reis (Instituto Politécnico de Setúbal, Portugal) Alcina Prata (Instituto Polytechnic of Setúbal, Portugal) and Raquel Pereira (Instituto Polytechnic of Setúbal, Portugal)
Business Science Reference • © 2021 • 455pp • H/C (ISBN: 9781799840992) • US $295.00

For an entire list of titles in this series, please visit:
http://www.igi-global.com/book-series/advances-business-strategy-competitive-advantage/73672

IGI Global
PUBLISHER of TIMELY KNOWLEDGE

701 East Chocolate Avenue, Hershey, PA 17033, USA
Tel: 717-533-8845 x100 • Fax: 717-533-8661
E-Mail: cust@igi-global.com • www.igi-global.com

Table of Contents

Preface xii

Chapter 1
India's Entrepreneurial Path to Green Market Solutions in Waste Management: The Case of Carbon Masters 1
Heather C. Webb, Higher Colleges of Technology, Dubai, UAE

Chapter 2
Picturing the Indian Automotive Sector's Slowdown 16
Rajat Deb, Tripura University, India

Chapter 3
Corporations and Social Enterprises: Co-Creators of Social Value in Asia 26
Rob John, The Centre for the Study of Philanthropy and Public Good, University of St. Andrews, UK

Chapter 4
Policies for Science, Technology, and Innovation: A Case Study of Transitional China 54
Li He, City University of Hong Kong, China
Xukun Zhang, Shenzhen Research Institute, City University of Hong Kong, China

Chapter 5
Sustainable Innovation Management in Indonesia: Enhancing Private Sector Participation Within Innovation Management 73
Abdul Karim Mohamed Yusoff, Higher Colleges of Technology, Dubai, UAE

Chapter 6
National Innovation Systems: Comparison of Turkey and South Korea 106
Fatma Nur Karaman Kabadurmus, Yasar University, Turkey
Ceyda Senses, Pamukkale University, Turkey
Buse Turkyilmaz, Yasar University, Turkey

Chapter 7
Innovative Approaches to Building Enterprise Risk Management in Emerging Economies: The Case of Mexico's Grupo Proeza 133
Ilse Patricia Lopez de la Cruz, Grupo Proeza, Mexico
Alasdair James Marshall, University of Southhampton, UK
Udechukwu Ojiako, University of Sharjah, UAE
Serkan Ceylan, University of Southampton, UK
Fenfang Lin, University of Southampton, UK

Chapter 8
Innovation of SMEs and Their Effect on Productivity in Jalisco....................... 155
José G. Vargas-Hernández, University Center for Economic and Managerial Sciences, University of Guadalajara, Mexico

Chapter 9
Developing the First Digital Bank of Africa: The Steps Towards the Creation of a Digital Bank in a Very Challenging Environment..................................... 192
Konstantinos Tsanis, Hult International Business School, Greece
Vasilios Stouraitis, Glasgow Caledonian University, UK

Chapter 10
Risk Management: Minimizing the Triple Risks – Strategic, Financial, and Operational.. 206
Eman A. Zabalawi, Higher Colleges of Technology, Dubai, UAE
Abderazak Bakhouche, Higher Colleges of Technology, Dubai, UAE
Randa El Chaar, Higher Colleges of Technology, Dubai, UAE

Compilation of References 226

Related References 251

About the Contributors 282

Index 287

Detailed Table of Contents

Preface xii

Chapter 1
India's Entrepreneurial Path to Green Market Solutions in Waste Management: The Case of Carbon Masters 1
Heather C. Webb, Higher Colleges of Technology, Dubai, UAE

New technologies and increasing opportunities in sustainable development propel start-ups in the green economy. For an emerging economy such as India, the government is focusing heavily on creating a green economy through changes and development of its governmental policies to strengthen green practices among entrepreneurs and other businesses. Specifically, though, India is focused on creating more marketable solutions for the bottom-of-the-income population. Nonetheless, for green entrepreneurs, starting a business is not easy and even more difficult within the workings of sustainability and other external barriers. Barriers may include weak institutional frameworks, weak supply chains, lack of infrastructure, or lack of regulations, which are more problematic in emerging economies. The chapter defines green entrepreneurship and the green economy while discussing India's policy agendas and path towards green market solutions. It then presents a case study about a green start-up, Carbon Masters, and their path towards an innovative waste management solution.

Chapter 2
Picturing the Indian Automotive Sector's Slowdown 16
Rajat Deb, Tripura University, India

The Indian automotive industry has remained a significant driver of the manufacturing sector and contributed to the GDP around 7% in 2018, but it is confronting its biggest slump in last 19 years with a double digit downfall in revenues across all segments. Such slowdown has caused job cuts of around 0.2 million workers, particularly contractual labourers, and shut down of around 300 dealers' shops in the last few months. A number of cyclical and structural contributing factors for the slowdown have been identified. Measures for turnaround are suggested, highlighting a recently announced stimulus package for reviving the industry.

Chapter 3
Corporations and Social Enterprises: Co-Creators of Social Value in Asia........26
Rob John, The Centre for the Study of Philanthropy and Public Good, University of St. Andrews, UK

This chapter describes how corporations and social enterprises in Asia can co-create social value. The traditional role of corporate philanthropy is transactional in nature, where the donation of resources from a corporation allows a non-profit organisation to create social value through its mission. The rise of social entrepreneurship as an alternative for creating social value through hybrid business models has given rise to novel opportunities for corporate philanthropy. Corporations can use their discretionary finances to support social enterprises across the spectrum of their organisational development from ideation and early stage ventures to later stages of maturity. The chapter offers case studies from Singapore, India, and Hong Kong that exemplify the co-creation of social value through small enterprise acceleration, angel investing, corporate venture capital, and business process outsourcing.

Chapter 4
Policies for Science, Technology, and Innovation: A Case Study of Transitional China..54
Li He, City University of Hong Kong, China
Xukun Zhang, Shenzhen Research Institute, City University of Hong Kong, China

Although there is plenty of research in the science, technology, and innovation (STI) policy studies, the trend and process of government regulations in a transition economy is underexplored. Empirical data such as central government laws, regulations, and policies for STI are collected from 1978 to 2018. Qualitative analysis software is adopted to facilitate the documentary analysis process. After a temporal examination of the government policies, the authors unearthed four stages in the evolution of STI policy: recovery and reconstruction of science and technology, transformation and market-led science and technology development, adjustment and innovation of science and technology, and promotion of science and technology and development of independent innovation. They found that the policy system has gradually changed and improved in continuous exploration and practice. First, the focus of the national policies has changed from science and technology to innovation. Second, the regulations are closely relevant to the political economy environment and central objectives.

Chapter 5
Sustainable Innovation Management in Indonesia: Enhancing Private Sector Participation Within Innovation Management 73
Abdul Karim Mohamed Yusoff, Higher Colleges of Technology, Dubai, UAE

Indonesia's National Innovation Policy requires consistent support from the private sector participation to raise its knowledge-based economic growth and become one of the top 15 powerful countries in the world by 2045, as declared by the Presidential decree. The low participation rate of private industries in R&D activities is a cause for concern for the government, as an effort to improve the country's social and economic performance must be a shared responsibility. This chapter looks into how the private sector participation in innovative effort plays an essential role in improving the country's economic performance. The challenges that lie ahead in achieving the goals of National Innovation Policy rest with both the government and the private sector.

Chapter 6
National Innovation Systems: Comparison of Turkey and South Korea 106
Fatma Nur Karaman Kabadurmus, Yasar University, Turkey
Ceyda Senses, Pamukkale University, Turkey
Buse Turkyilmaz, Yasar University, Turkey

Since innovation is central to the success of firms in the 21st century, policymakers in many countries try to achieve sustained competitive advantage by promoting technological innovations. However, achieving this goal requires coordination of all actors in the economy including governments, industries, and national institutions. Although each individual actor has unique capabilities and strategic resources, how well the economy performs depends on the strengths of the network as a whole. National Innovation Systems (NIS) approach considers all these interdependent actors within a country to increase national competitiveness. A good example in this regard is South Korea, an innovation leader, which could be a role model for developing countries with its well-established NIS. This chapter studies the elements of the NIS of this country and compares them with that of an emerging economy, Turkey, by using data from the Global Innovation Index and the Global Competitiveness Index. The analysis reveals the strengths and weaknesses of Turkey and helps to draw concrete policy conclusions.

Chapter 7
Innovative Approaches to Building Enterprise Risk Management in Emerging Economies: The Case of Mexico's Grupo Proeza............................133
Ilse Patricia Lopez de la Cruz, Grupo Proeza, Mexico
Alasdair James Marshall, University of Southhampton, UK
Udechukwu Ojiako, University of Sharjah, UAE
Serkan Ceylan, University of Southampton, UK
Fenfang Lin, University of Southampton, UK

This chapter explores a very positive example of enterprise risk management (ERM) development in Mexico, set by the firm Grupo Proeza, from which valuable and highly generalisable lessons can be learned. These lessons will pertain most centrally to Grupo Proeza's techniques of ERM building, where risk management practices are used to enhance the cultural and other foundations for ERM. Of particular interest is the notion that various risk assessment techniques can be used for this purpose, which may seem counter-intuitive by reversing the formative relationship between risk culture and risk assessment practice that is more typically the focus for attention.

Chapter 8
Innovation of SMEs and Their Effect on Productivity in Jalisco.......................155
José G. Vargas-Hernández, University Center for Economic and Managerial Sciences, University of Guadalajara, Mexico

Small and medium enterprises (SMEs) in Jalisco represent one of the main entities of economic activity that supports the bulk of the population living in the state; using statistics as a fundamental tool for conducting studies in the economic, natural, health sciences, among others, allows one to have proactive foundations for decision making within companies by senior executives and in the field public by officials responsible for promoting the growth of the industry in the State of Jalisco. This research tries to represent, under a statistical scheme, the use and disposition of information and communication technologies (ICTs) as a tool to increase average productivity levels within companies and under the Cobb production function. Douglas determines the ICT impact.

Chapter 9
Developing the First Digital Bank of Africa: The Steps Towards the Creation of a Digital Bank in a Very Challenging Environment....................................192
Konstantinos Tsanis, Hult International Business School, Greece
Vasilios Stouraitis, Glasgow Caledonian University, UK

The following case study overviews the steps followed to develop the first Digital Bank in Africa. Following a case study method, the crucial decisions made over a 2-year period is analyzed. The challenges of each different phase are described, as well as the outcomes and the impact they had in the bank's digital transformation journey. The case study is accompanied by illustrative strategy tools used during development to make the reader more familiar with the decision made. The case study concludes by highlighting success and failures in digital transformation and lessons for other banks.

Chapter 10
Risk Management: Minimizing the Triple Risks – Strategic, Financial, and Operational 206
Eman A. Zabalawi, Higher Colleges of Technology, Dubai, UAE
Abderazak Bakhouche, Higher Colleges of Technology, Dubai, UAE
Randa El Chaar, Higher Colleges of Technology, Dubai, UAE

The chapter covers practical risk managers' points during the planning stage of entrepreneurship to integrate into decision making and core business processes. The chapter includes three risks and how to improve the integration of risk management into organizational culture grouped into three high-level objectives. First, strategic risks include the study of competitors, macroeconomics with its industry changes. Second, financial risks such as the business return of investment and forecasting, customer payments, loan interest charges, and liquidity. Access to finance featured prominently in several studies as a constraint on SME development. The third is the operational risks and internal analysis that includes legal compliance, breakdown of essential equipment, employee mismatch, partnership, information technology, external events, and supply chain reliability. It is vital to establish an organizational culture where risk management is a daily component activity.

Compilation of References 226

Related References 251

About the Contributors 282

Index 287

Preface

The term emerging economy was first used back in 1981 by the World Bank to mean an emerging market economy. It is a loosely used term to describe a country's economy having low to middle per capita income. Countries vary in size, population, and economic strength depending on governmental, economic development policies, and reform programs. It is with the hope that countries that are categorized as emerging economies will eventually be more reliable and more efficient in the market to be categorized as a developed country. Only time will tell as political and country leaders try to balance political and social factors locally as well as globally.

Emerging economies have had tremendous growth because of innovations. Despite any kind of innovation's economic impact, understanding what shaped these emerging economies' success seems enigmatic. Thus, the impact and development of various innovations from emerging economies need to be told. Technologies and innovative capabilities have a social impact. However, it is how the unforeseen or uncontrollable external factors in which other individuals or even other countries can learn and gain knowledge.

Businesses and start-ups are creative activities from mobilizing resources, such as people and finances, to meet an identified need before someone else does. Anti-business rhetoric is not going to help society nor develop innovation. Indeed, this book's central message is seeing how innovations develop from the perspective of a developing country. Individuals from developing countries or emerging economies see up close the realities of poverty and the influence of government or corporate development. The role of businesses, whether established into eventual big corporations or a small business of fewer than 25 employees, in society, are often embraced, and other times, criticized. However, individuals also have to deal with a lack of certain institutions that can impact innovation development.

In emerging economies, the absence of institutional support and arrangements are more considerable. Institutional arrangements shape innovation. Therefore, it becomes even more essential to study the innovation process from these kinds of countries. Research is taking place in how companies overcome the lack of institutional support to function as well as how innovation takes shape. Therefore, it becomes a question of how actors or firms interact to shape and define either new institutions or new industries in such contexts in avoiding institutional arrangements.

Our hope with this book is that people, whether in academic or business settings, learn from the presented cases. Additionally, we want people to continue the sustainability and development discussion, where future research can most certainly arise. There are always outside variables to consider for any kind of business, but reviewing businesses from these emerging markets can help even developed countries.

The chapters presented in the book include such topics as sustainability, the automotive industry's impact on the economy, social enterprising and co-creating social value, corporate philanthropy, governmental policy impact on innovation development, national innovation systems, enterprise risk management, productivity impact on SMEs, and digital banking transformation. Therefore, this book showcases how businesses and country policies are developing innovation from emerging economies. Innovation can transform individual lives and national power development, but it is not without risks that need to be managed. Additionally, the book presents the benefits and drawbacks, the processes, characteristics, and the management practices of private/public organizations. The chapters identify the trends and approaches to innovation development as well as the strategies of adapting and converting threats/challenges into opportunities. We aim to present solutions useful for start-ups, businesses, and societies overall. Some chapters are organized as case studies, whereas others present government policies' concepts and the impact on businesses.

APPROACH TO THE CHAPTERS

Chapter 1, "India's Entrepreneurial Path to Green Market Solutions in Waste Management: The Case of Carbon Masters," presents a case about a British university spinout company working in India's sustainability field. The chapter gives a snapshot as to what Indian policies are in terms of environmental impact and how India is changing her policies to reflect the impact of climate change to allow for more entrepreneurs. The government is strengthening green practice policies, and the chapter tells a story about how Carbon Masters has developed marketable solutions. The company has finally found success by overcoming struggles, such as financing or adapting to updated governmental policies. However, Carbon Masters are on their way to becoming India's premier innovative waste management provider.

Chapter 2, "Picturing Indian Automotive Sector's Slowdown: Automobile Slowdown," continues with India's other case. This chapter looks at the automotive industry in India, which has been a significant economic driver. The industry has had a slump, which has caused job cuts. The chapter focuses on identifying the factors for the slowdown, and it highlights suggestions for reviving the industry.

Chapter 3, "Corporations and Social Enterprises: Co-Creators of Social Value in Asia," presents multiple mini-cases from Singapore, India, and Hong Kong that exemplifies the co-creation of social value through small enterprise acceleration, angel investing, corporate venture capital and business process outsourcing. The chapter describes how corporations and social enterprises in certain Asian countries can co-create value. Additionally, it defines the role of corporate philanthropy and the rise of the social entrepreneur as an alternative for creating social value through hybrid business models. Thus, corporations can use their discretionary finances to support social enterprises.

Chapter 4, "Policies for Science, Technology, and Innovation: A Case Study of Transitional China," discusses the trend and process of government regulations within China's transitioning economy. Data from central government laws, regulations, and policies from science, technology and innovation (STI) are collected from 1978 to 2018. Analysis software is applied and analyzed to unearth four stages of evolution in China's STI policies. The first stage is the recovery and reconstruction of science and technology. The second stage is transformation and market-led science and technology development. The third stage is the adjustment and innovation of science and technology. While the fourth stage is the promotion of science and technology and the development of independent innovation. The chapter finds that the STI policy system has gradually changed and improved in continuous exploration and practice.

Chapter 5, "Sustainable Innovation Management in Indonesia: Enhancing Private Sector Participation Within Innovation Management," looks at Indonesia's national innovation policy. It gives a historical description of what led to the various government reforms, critiques the impact of these reforms, and offers suggestions on what can be improved. It presents how the government and private sector need to forge a strong partnership and the impact of the essential role of the private sector.

Chapter 6, "National Innovation Systems: Comparison of Turkey and South Korea," looks at how policymakers need to support innovation to have successful, competitive firms. Economic success will depend on the relationship by all the actors within the national innovation systems. The chapter focuses on South Korea's success in using a template for Turkey. It also uses data from the Global Innovation Index and the Global Competitiveness Index. South Korea is used as an example of success to rise from being an emerging economy to a developed economy with the hopes that Turkey can learn. The chapter reveals the strengths and weaknesses of Turkey and helps to draw concrete policy conclusions.

Chapter 7, "Innovative Approaches to Building Enterprise Risk Management in Emerging Economies: The Case of Mexico's Grupo Proeza," uses a case study on the company Grupo Proeza. This case study explores enterprise risk management development in Mexico. Lessons to learn from this central to Grupo Proeza's ERM building techniques include where risk management practices are used to enhance the cultural and other foundations for ERM. The chapter also discusses the notion that various risk assessment techniques can be utilized by reversing the formative relationship between risk culture and risk assessment practice.

Chapter 8, "Innovation of SMEs and Their Effect on Productivity in Jalisco," discusses how small and medium enterprises (SMEs) in Jalisco are among the main economic activities for the population of this Mexican state. It uses statistics as a fundamental tool for conducting studies in the economic, natural, health sciences, among others, allows to have proactive foundations for decision making within companies by senior executives and in the field public by officials responsible for promoting the growth of the industry in the State of Jalisco. This research tries to represent, under a statistical scheme, the use and disposition of Information and Communication Technologies (ICTs) to increase average productivity levels within companies and under the Cobb production function. -Douglas determines the ICT impact.

Chapter 9, "Developing the First Digital Bank of Africa: The Steps Towards the Creation of a Digital Bank in a Very Challenging Environment," presents a case about the first digital bank in Africa, specifically Nigeria. The case is written up following two years discussing the challenges at each phase of development. It also describes the outcomes and impacts the bank had on the bank's digital transformation journey. The case uses illustrative strategy tools used during development, to make the reader more familiar with the decision made. It concludes by highlighting success and failures in digital transformation, and lessons for other banks.

Chapter 10, "Risk Management: Minimizing the Triple Risks – Strategic, Financial, and Operational," presents from a perspective of a risk manager during the planning stage of entrepreneurship. It includes discussion on three risks and how to improve the integration of risk management into organizational culture grouped into three high-level objectives. First, strategic risks include the study of competitors, macroeconomics with its industry changes. Second, financial risks include the business return of investment and forecasting, customer payments, loan interest charges, and liquidity. Access to finance featured prominently in several studies as a constraint on SME development. The third is the operational risks and internal analysis that includes legal compliance, breakdown of essential equipment, employee mismatch, partnership, information technology, external events, and supply chain reliability. Also, it offers some discussion on the impact in the United Arab Emirates.

Heather C. Webb
Higher Colleges of Technology, Dubai, UAE

Wendy Wu
Edinburgh Napier University, UK

Hussain Al Numairy
Higher Colleges of Technology, Dubai, UAE

Chapter 1
India's Entrepreneurial Path to Green Market Solutions in Waste Management:
The Case of Carbon Masters

Heather C. Webb
Higher Colleges of Technology, Dubai, UAE

ABSTRACT

New technologies and increasing opportunities in sustainable development propel start-ups in the green economy. For an emerging economy such as India, the government is focusing heavily on creating a green economy through changes and development of its governmental policies to strengthen green practices among entrepreneurs and other businesses. Specifically, though, India is focused on creating more marketable solutions for the bottom-of-the-income population. Nonetheless, for green entrepreneurs, starting a business is not easy and even more difficult within the workings of sustainability and other external barriers. Barriers may include weak institutional frameworks, weak supply chains, lack of infrastructure, or lack of regulations, which are more problematic in emerging economies. The chapter defines green entrepreneurship and the green economy while discussing India's policy agendas and path towards green market solutions. It then presents a case study about a green start-up, Carbon Masters, and their path towards an innovative waste management solution.

DOI: 10.4018/978-1-7998-4195-1.ch001

Copyright © 2021, IGI Global. Copying or distributing in print or electronic forms without written permission of IGI Global is prohibited.

INTRODUCTION

Individuals become entrepreneurs when they identify an unsolved problem or an unmet need and turn it into an opportunity. Thus, how opportunities are recognized and grow from an idea to an entity is a central theme to entrepreneurship. Nevertheless, entrepreneurs are focusing on solving sustainability issues and turning climate change problems into opportunities. These entrepreneurs are known as 'green entrepreneurs.' Entrepreneurs are agents of innovation, but, individually, green entrepreneurs are driven not only by profitability but also by improving the environment. Indeed, as a paraphrased lyric from Kermit the Frog: "It's not easy being green!" (Raposo, 1970:87).

Without a doubt, a 'green' start-up has more obstacles to overcome than any other kind of venture, especially in a developing country such as India. With her massive population, India is known for having an entrepreneurial culture (Gupta, 1994). Individuals make a living by selling anything from used parts to soap sachets to anyone who passes by. Most people think of Indian entrepreneurs as call centers, or IT-focused companies. Rarely do people connect green entrepreneurs to India. However, Indians have been able to identify opportunities and combine resources in unique ways to create value, which is the essence of being an entrepreneur (Gartner, 1990).

As entrepreneurs develop their businesses in environments where institutional uncertainties are more considerable, start-ups have to build trust with potential customers more-so in order to create value and fill institutional voids (Palepu et al., 2010). Institutional voids are more common in emerging economy countries such as India. As a result, start-ups rely more heavily on informal relations with key institutional stakeholders to reduce institutional uncertainty (Uzo and Mair, 2014). Institutional uncertainty arises from the difficulty some start-ups face when navigating in a weak, formal institutional environment which is a common characteristic in addition to higher levels of poverty (Dorobantu, et al., 2016). Therefore, to find success, potential entrepreneurs have to increase their networks (London and Hart, 2010), whether formal or informal. With that said, emerging economies offer tremendous opportunities for start-ups willing to radically change their practices (Bylund and McCaffrey, 2017).

While entrepreneurship is not a new concept, green entrepreneurship is a recent phenomenon. Within the last century, there has been an overbearing need for sustainable consumption and production practices. Indeed, environmental problems are nothing new, but the traditional efforts to be a corporate socially responsible company is to be innovative for the so-called green economy. Consequently, there has been a paradigm shift of changing priorities for start-ups to focus on sustainability from the very beginning of company inception. Nevertheless, most research has focused its attention on how and why existing companies can become greener. By first considering the environmental needs, this can create a niche market, yet does not necessarily equate to success. There are constant barriers to survival that evolve as the company operates and expands.

One of the significant barriers is financing, but other barriers include a lack of intellectual property rights to protect one's innovation. Intellectual property policies and regulations need to be strong in countries to support entrepreneurs because if it is weak or lacking, then entrepreneurs will not risk losing their ideas or concepts to others. Thus, once the market opportunity presents itself, and the team of people is in place, it becomes a matter of securing the finances and protecting one's innovation.

One such green, innovative start-up is Carbon Masters, currently based in Bangalore, India. They work in a niche industry of carbon consulting, which is challenging to secure continuing financing. There are various options to finance one's start-up, but how Carbon Masters was able to start and expand is worth analyzing for future start-ups in either a developed or developing country context. In reality, more often than not, Carbon Masters spends more time educating businesses and governments about the impact of the environment in order to convince potential investors how their innovation can help create more sustainable communities.

Therefore, this chapter will define a green entrepreneur and briefly discuss the meaning behind a green economy. The next section showcases India's path to green market solutions that presents India's policies that support green innovation, especially within waste management systems. Finally, this chapter presents a case study about Carbon Masters and their innovative ways to solve waste management issues. The chapter concludes by offering possible research ideas for the future.

GREEN ENTREPRENEURSHIP

Becoming an entrepreneur is not an easy task, but it seems there is a greater focus to be a so-called "green" entrepreneur with a concentration on sustainable development. Schumpeter defines an entrepreneur as an innovator and visionary because one is a change creator who forms new value out of existing resources (Schumpeter, 1934). Berle (1991) first coined the term "green entrepreneurship" as a way to explain a variance from conventional entrepreneurship. A green entrepreneur requires savviness with innovative ideas and a willingness to take on additional risk. Generally, though, all potential entrepreneurs, whether green or not, identify new commercial businesses, incubate ideas, and accumulate resources into commercial realities to obtain profitability (Haldar, 2019; Hendrickson and Tuttle, 1997).

Green entrepreneurs have not been warmly welcomed by other groups, such as Small-to-Medium-Enterprises (SMEs) entrepreneurs (Ahmad et al., 2015). A green entrepreneur is different from an SME entrepreneur who may implement green practices in their business activities but does not thoroughly look at sustainability issues as their primary business model. However, environmental problems are increasingly becoming an integral part of the business without being recognized as such (Ndubisi et al., 2009). At times, it becomes more difficult for green start-ups to gain a competitive advantage and find success. Undeniably, the perception is that green entrepreneurs have an extra cost, which could be a factor as to why there are not more green start-ups. Other factors, or challenges, include financing from venture capitalists, banks, governments, or any other kinds of investors where green entrepreneurs have to be more convincing about environmental impact. Additionally, government regulations that impact potential innovations and the ability to market the need for potential customers can prevent start-ups from being successful. Therefore, timing is another factor because if potential customers do not know or understand the innovation, then entrepreneurs need to ask themselves what is the point of starting the business.

The Green Economy

The concept of green economy evolved from discussions at the United Nations 1992 Rio Conference Summit (UNRISD, 2012). The green economy is an intersection of the environment and the economy. It is an accounting term that focuses on additional performance measurements of companies besides purely measuring it in terms of profitability (Elkington, 1998). These performance measurement terms include the traditional financial bottom line plus social/ethical and environmental performances (Norman and MacDonald, 2004).

Policies and governmental agendas are always central to the development of any economy. However, in order for an economy to become a green economy, it has to overcome resource constraints. Unfortunately, resources such as natural resources are becoming depleted (Cabezas and Diwekar, 2012). Governments regulate business behaviors, and businesses react to changes, but for a green economy, time and money costs are higher (Webb and Liu, 2019). Nowadays, the general public is becoming more knowledgeable about sustainability issues and the environment. Globally, most governments have committed to environmental policies and regulations to create environmentally friendly businesses and green start-ups because of pressure from the masses. In other words, a much stronger collective, compelling force of individuals are pressuring governments to become economically greener.

INDIA'S PATH TO GREEN MARKET SOLUTIONS

India is a dynamic country with a diverse, populous society. There is a certain level of optimism about India's future because of their young, and ever-increasing workforce. India, with one of the world's fastest-growing, major economies, is a population of 1.4 billion; thus, India is vital for the future of a cleaner environment (IEA, 2020). Consequently, India is ripe to become a global leader for green growth strategies and poverty reduction, or all together poverty eradication. Therefore, the Government of India has been committed to sustainable development goals to fulfill their commitment to social progress, accelerated economic growth, and increased environmental conservation (Agarchand and Laishram, 2017).

Policy Agendas

At the Paris Agreement in 2015 and under its Nationally Determined Contributions (NDC) (PTI, 2019), India made four commitments that included reducing greenhouse gas emission intensity by 33-35% below 2005 levels by 2030; and that 40% of India's power capacity will remain on non-fossil fuel sources. The country would create a so-called 'carbon sink' of 2.5 to 3 billion tonnes of carbon dioxide equivalent by planting new trees and forests (The Indian Times, 2019). India has multiple objectives, and precisely 17 sustainable development goals under "The 2030 Sustainable Development Agenda" (Global Green Growth Institute, 2015). However, achieving these objectives makes for a complex balancing act while overseeing how different ministries and levels of government cohesively acting on these agendas. The overall goals mainly focus on climate mitigation and adaptation while achieving economic growth that is socially all-encompassing.

The Indian government has been prioritizing to make India clean or what the scheme is known as "Swachh Bharat Abhiyan" (Department of Drinking Water & Sanitation, 2020). The concept of 'Clean India' is where every person is to have access to sanitation facilities, clean and adequate drinking water, and other cleanliness aspects. Once cleanliness can be achieved, the next step is to preserve and conserve the greenery through mass participation. 'Green India' is an initiative under India's National Action Plan on Climate Change (NAPCC) launched in 2008 (Rattani et al., 2018). The action plan aims at responding to climate change by combining adaptation and mitigation measures such as enhancing carbon sinks. Thus, one of the main objectives of these agendas is to focus on technological fixes in fossil fuels that can spur innovation, which can then equate to profits.

Green Indian Innovation

In the absence of government interactions, green innovation has existed throughout the last century, even before it became a trendy term (Silverthorne, 2011). For India, the innovative focus has not necessarily been on the environment, but on trying to find ways to address the needs of the poor (Prahalad, 2004). A concept termed as that of frugal innovation: an idea raised by Prahalad and Hammond (2002) and later developed by Collier (2007) and Prahalad and Mashelkar (2010) to suggest low-cost product development, creating low-cost products addressing bottom-of-the-pyramid consumers. As Tata's Nano and Huawei washing machines demonstrate, frugal products can then migrate into internationally competitive products. These innovative examples developed from the 45 million entrepreneurs that drive India's growth (The Economist, 2010). Innovations are always non-linear and frequently (Hartford, 2011) the unintended results of trial and error or improvisation (Eisenhardt, 1989). Increasingly, innovation processes are open to ideas from the market and networks (Chesbrough, 2006); often-emergent technologies create an array of new products until a dominant logic (Prahalad and Bettis, 1995) wins out.

Waste Management System Solutions

India wants to convey the beauty of the country. However, unfortunately, historically, there has been uncontrolled dumping of waste on the outskirts of towns and cities, which has created overflowing landfills (Gupta et al., 1998). These overflows not only create a negative image, but it also has serious environmental implications for the population in terms of groundwater pollution and global warming because burning waste leads to air pollution (Gupta et al., 1998). Although recycling helps, especially cardboard and plastic, enough is not collected to make an actual impact, and, on some levels, it has become an outdated concept.

Therefore, for India's diverse society, day-to-day issues become problematic, especially with waste management. Waste development technology is crucial to India's green policies as technologies convert waste into renewable energy and other biodegradable components. Currently, a holistic approach to waste management is to solve current problems through social science tools while working towards preventing further complications in the future (D'Cunha, 2017). Devadula et al. (2015) reviews other countries' framework on waste management and proposes a technological approach for India, such as utilizing less water-intensive toilets and improving sewage transportation methods. This approach reduces waste in homes and on an overall societal scale. For the most part, solid waste management is a challenge, especially in urban areas. Thus, considering rising populations and rates of waste production, this places stress on governmental budgets (Guerrero et al.,

2013), especially in countries with limited resources. Whereas most would see this as an obstacle, entrepreneurs see this as a challenge.

In 2016, India started to allow new players from the private sector to tackle waste management (Kumar, 2019). These new players are a symbol of India's drive towards innovation to mainstream and re-organize a more efficient and sustainable waste management system. Indeed, innovative approaches have been explored from a Western-centric lens and not necessarily from an Asian-centric perspective. For India, innovation development suffers more-so from weak infrastructures, lack of reliable supply-chains, and inefficient institutions or burdensome regulations (Farinelli et al., 2011). However, Boston Consulting Group (BCG) has found that some of these innovative green start-ups are using unique practices for doing business in resource-constrained and population-stressed environments (Farinelli et al., 2011). One such player is the green start-up, Carbon Masters, who seems to be finding success within waste management innovation through their brand name of Carbonlites.

CARBON MASTERS

Carbon Masters is a UK based consulting company of experienced carbon management professionals. It was founded in 2009 by two partners, Kevin Houston and Som Narayan. Kevin and Som met at the University of Edinburgh Business School, where they completed their MSc in Carbon Management. Carbon Masters provides carbon mitigation services and software solutions to measure business and people in both developed and developing countries. They analyze one's carbon impact through measuring carbon footprint, and present ideas to reduce the carbon impact. They find the appropriate strategy for businesses that are now starting to adapt to climate change impacts. Their "CarbonGuru" is a web-based software program created to measure carbon footprints, including energy in buildings and homes, the emissions arising from food choices, and travel and transport. Their "Financial Impacts Calculator" was created to measure businesses' or people's energy usage. Overall, Carbon Masters is trying to raise awareness of the environment and develop a low carbon economy.

Access to Financing

Financial capital is a crucial element and resource for any company's growth. Accessing finance can often be the deciding factor of any entrepreneurial venture and time-consuming for the start-ups (Choi and Gray, 2008). With green entrepreneurs, raising capital can be even more complicated and challenging because of their commitment to a social mission. Professional investors with their traditional views about business could impede their ability to pursue non-financial objectives. Green start-ups have to pick the right strategy and, when expanding the business, have to ensure that capabilities also grow in place to support international businesses. Relationships with local governments and communities are sometimes a vital resource for expanding the business. Although not easy being 'green,' it, thus, becomes a more significant challenge to take on.

Financing to start Carbon Masters was through an invested shared capital of £9,000 by the two partners. Kevin and Som were also able to use an interest-free loan of £10,000 provided as part of the Edinburgh Pre Incubator Scheme (EPIS) project in conjunction with the University of Edinburgh, Scottish Enterprise, and the European Regional Development Fund to promote and support innovation. Further support was also sought from the Scottish Enterprise's Investors Ready program to cover costs incurred in seeking more external investment to staff the business. Like any green start-up, Carbon Masters is not just about being profitable. Most socially responsible entrepreneurs perceive the start-up business as a vehicle for not only achieving their personal financial goals but also for accommodating their strong social and environmental values. Carbon Masters has furthermore created the Carbon Masters Trust as a wholly-owned subsidiary charity. Carbon Masters Trust assists communities predominantly in developing countries. The founding partners have agreed that the percentage of profits made by Carbon Masters will fund the Carbon Masters Trust.

In regards to starting a small business in the UK, Carbon Masters wants to see the government provide financial assistant in the form of loans, grants, and VAT exemption to people in the early stages of a start-up. Various hidden costs become quite onerous and act as a disincentive. Individual costs should combine since a proper shareholder agreement and articles of association are around £3,000. Legal fees to trademark brand names and logos locally and internationally are a further £10,000. Although the costs are legitimate for businesses, looking for better assistance from the government would allow start-up companies to spend what limited capital they have on areas that can build the business and create new jobs. Their most significant investment is in software programs. Carbon Masters' critical turning point in creating the company was when the European Commission hired them as an advisor on a three-year study to help reduce carbon emissions in the information and communication technology sector. This advisement role has given them access to over 4,000 companies and help Carbon Masters generate license and services revenue.

Carbon Masters is no longer able to receive any more grant money from the Edinburgh Environmental Partnership Grant. Therefore, Carbon Masters looks for other ways to increase their capital, like through networking. Som is part of the Hindu community and attends the Hindu temple on the edge of Leith Links. His connection with the Hindu community and involvement with the Cultural Centre has led the temple to receive a £49,895 grant from the Climate Change Fund. Som is the project manager for this initiative. The Carbon Reduction Initiative aims to educate and support changes in the Hindu community lifestyle changes in Edinburgh with three key areas to focus on: energy consumption, transport, and food. The grant money does not allow for usage of building materials, but it is for educating people about the benefits of solar panels and double glazing. A portion of the money will study the feasibility of solar panels on the roof of the Mandir.

Carbon Masters has looked at the likely impact of the CRC carbon tax in the United Kingdom and developed a CRC financial Impacts Calculator to allow companies to quickly assess the full carbon and energy cost implication under two scenarios over the next five years of the CRC scheme. These scenarios are as follows: 'business as usual' (BAU) and 'carbon management' where carbon emission reduction strategy is in place. This calculator will help companies facing a carbon tax bill to understand the impacts under both scenarios. Companies can accurately account for their energy-related carbon emissions and, more importantly, identify ways to reduce carbon emissions. Using the CRC Financial Impacts Calculator, it has found that cash-strapped places face potential bills of £990,000 for Edinburgh City Council, £325,000 for Glasgow University, and £187,000 for Edinburgh Airport, respectively. These figures are a significant impact on most businesses. This carbon tax, though, should increase Carbon Masters cliental base.

Waste Management System: Carbonlites

The carbon management industry is still in its infancy, but waste management is not. As a result of India's allowance of private organizations to tackle waste management, by December 2010, Carbon Masters was able to open their first office in Bangalore, India. Som's visa had run out in the UK at that time, which became a good time for Carbon Masters to start their expansion. They always knew they would expand into India since Som is from there, and by the end of 2010, the opportunity presented itself. However, Carbon Masters knew it was going to be an even more challenge in setting up their new office in Bangalore, India. They also knew they were up for this challenge as their success in the UK was giving them more confidence to apply their knowledge to India.

Therefore, they took an opportunity presented to them by becoming a complete end-to-end waste management solutions provider. Consequently, they have radically changed the way one looks at waste for India (Revathy, 2020). Additionally, Carbon Masters has been able to create India's first bottled bio-compressed natural gas (CNG) and be a driving force in the "Clean India, Clean Energy" movement under their brand name of Carbonlites.

The Carbonlites biogas facility is located in Malur, India, which is just outside Bengaluru (Chakraborty, 2018). The biogas facility is in partnership with Mahindra & Mahindra, where Carbon Masters produces high-purity compressed methane from food waste collected from farms and homes, and then sells it to restaurants. Organizations in the food industry are abandoning liquefied petroleum gas (LPG) in favor of an alternative to fossil fuels. The Carbonlite cylinder releases only the CO2 levels found in the original organic, collected food waste. Therefore, their production plant turns waste into renewable energy (Campsie, 2017).

CONCLUSION

Successful entrepreneurs can clear growth hurdles by recognizing and addressing their limitations as well as, at times, having the ability to come up with solutions with minimal applications. Green Entrepreneurship is vital since new ventures have the potential to be a significant force in the overall adoption of green business practices. The nature of climate change demands that businesses and people make an effort to reduce their environmental impact. By having patience and resilience is a must for starting a new business because it is always challenging, especially in an emerging economy such as India. However, to start a business in a relatively new market like carbon management is even more challenging. The freedom to start a venture, take risks, and to be fully responsible for the outcome can be an exciting prospect.

Carbon Masters' consultancy side has evolved into a product to produce and run renewable energy facilities. Furthermore, they continue to be in the business of advising clients on reducing their carbon footprint. However, Carbon Masters' biggest hurdle has been to be taken seriously by clients and convincing clients that carbon management should be businesses' most pressing priorities. It has not been an easy path to becoming a green, innovative start-up, but Carbon Masters continues to educate companies on the concept of what it means to be sustainable. As Kermit the Frog sings:

When green is all there is to be

It could make you wonder why, but why wonder why

Wonder, I am green and it'll do fine, it's beautiful

And I think it's what I want to be (Raposo, 1970:87)

By demonstrating the economic benefits that come from being green, Carbon Masters can be a catalyst for green entrepreneurs, green start-ups, and green innovation. One of the main lessons to learn from Carbon Masters is maintaining continued motivation. It has not been an easy path to their success, but Carbon Masters has a focused agenda and strategy. Plus, their priority is to help people at the end of the day, and they have never lost sight of this.

FUTURE RESEARCH

To be truly green and sustainable is not only a challenge but a pipe dream because it requires complete cooperation at all levels of government as well as producer and consumer responsibility. However, through education and involving the community, levels of sustainability can be achieved and modeled. As green energy becomes popular, future research should continue to be from an entrepreneurial perspective within the sustainability segment. Possible research on green entrepreneurship can influence reducing environmental deregulation if researchers find a need or cause for such a case. Additionally, though, for such places as developing countries, lack of institutional mechanisms can impact entrepreneurs; thus, this should entice more investigative research.

The Government of India has had ambitious plans to bring affordable and sustainable energy to all its citizens. Therefore, another focus for future research is the success of business models within waste management and the influence of artificial intelligence technologies. Globally, countries are looking at developing more "smart city" initiatives, and whatever India develops can be a prime research focus. Only time will tell if India has had success with these plans, and future research can look at whether start-ups have found success and the effects of policies that have focused on green initiatives. This way, future decision-makers can understand what policies worked and which ones need tweaking.

REFERENCES

Agarchand, N., & Laishram, B. (2017). Sustainable infrastructure development challenges through PPP procurement process: Indian perspective. *International Journal of Managing Projects in Business*, *10*(3), 642–662. doi:10.1108/IJMPB-10-2016-0078

Ahmad, N., Abdul Halim, H., Ramayah, T., & Rahman, S. A. (2015). Green Entrepreneurship inclination among Generation Y: The road towards a green economy. *Problems and Perspectives in Management*, *13*(2).

Berle, G. (1991). The Green Entrepreneur: Business Opportunities that can Save the Earth and Make You Money. *Journal of Business Venturing*, *32*(5), 461–475.

Bylund, P., & McCaffrey, M. (2017). A theory of entrepreneurship and institutional uncertainty. *Journal of Business Venturing*, *32*(5), 461–475. doi:10.1016/j.jbusvent.2017.05.006

Cabezas, H., & Diwekar, U. (2012). Sustainability: Multi-disciplinary perspectives. Sharjah, UAE: Bentham Science Publishers Ltd. doi:10.2174/97816080510381120101

Campsie, A. (2017 August 6). Indian chefs enlisted in climate change battle. *Scotland on Sunday*, 28.

Carbon Masters Ltd. (2011). *Carbon Masters.* Retrieved from http://www.carbonmasters.co.uk/

Chakraborty, S. (2018). Carbon Masters: Fueling new possibilities. *Forbes India.* Retrieved from http://www.forbesindia.com/article/social-impact-special-2017/carbon-masters-fuelling new-possibilities/49105/1

Chesbrough, H. W. (2006). *Open Innovation.* Harvard Business School Press.

Choi, D. Y., & Gray, E. R. (2008). Socially responsible entrepreneurs: What do they do to create and build their companies? *Business Horizons*, *51*(4), 341–352. doi:10.1016/j.bushor.2008.02.010

Collier, P. (2007). *The Bottom Billion: Why the Poorest Countries are Failing and What Can Be Done About It.* OUP.

D'Cunha, S. D. (2017 June 21). This Start-up Is Making India's Garbage Its Business. *Forbes.* Retrieved from https://www.forbes.com/sites/suparnadutt/2017/06/21/this-startup-is- making-indias-garbage-its-business/#78beb8e55124

Department of Drinking Water & Sanitation. (2020, June 9). *Swachh Bharat Mission – Gramin*. Retrieved from https://swachhbharatmission.gov.in/sbmcms/index.htm

Devadula, S., Gurumoorthy, B., & Chakrabarti, A. (2015). Design for sustainability: Case of designing an urban household organic waste management system. *Current Science*, *109*(9), 1622–1629.

Dorobantu, S., Kaul, A., & Zelner, B. (2017). Nonmarket strategy research through the lens of new institutional economics: An integrative review and future directions. *Strategic Management Journal*, *38*(1), 114–140. doi:10.1002mj.2590

Economist. (2010, Oct. 2). A Bumpier but Freer Road. *The Economist,* 58-60.

Eisenhardt, K. M. (1989). Making Fast Strategic Decisions in High-Velocity Environments. *Academy of Management Journal*, *32*(September), 543–576.

Elkington, J. (1998). Cannibals With Forks: The Triple Bottom Line. In 21st *Century Business*. Stony Creek, CT: New Society Publishers.

Farinelli, F., Bottini, M., Akkoyunlu, S., & Aerno, P. (2011). Green Entrepreneurship: The Missing Link Towards a Greener Economy. *ATDF Journal, 8*(3/4).

Gartner, W. B. (1990). What Are We Talking About When We Talk About Entrepreneurship? *Journal of Business Venturing*, *5*(1), 15–28. doi:10.1016/0883-9026(90)90023-M

Global Green Growth Institute. (2015). *Green Growth and Sustainable Development in India: Towards the 2030 Development Agenda*. Retrieved from https://www.teriin.org/projects/green/pdf/National_SPM.pdf

Guerrero, L. A., Maas, G., & Hogland, W. (2013). Solid waste management challenges for cities in developing countries. *Waste Management (New York, N.Y.)*, *33*(1), 220–232. doi:10.1016/j.wasman.2012.09.008 PMID:23098815

Gupta, A. (1994). *Indian Entrepreneurial Culture: Its Many Paradoxes*. Wishwa Prakshan.

Gupta, S., Mohan, K., Prasad, R., Gupta, S., & Kansal, A. (1998). Solid waste management in India: Options and opportunities. *Resources, Conservation and Recycling*, *24*(2), 137–154. doi:10.1016/S0921-3449(98)00033-0

Haldar, S. (2019). Green entrepreneurship in the renewable energy sector – a case study of Gujarat. *Journal of Science and Technology Policy Management*, *10*(1), 234–250. doi:10.1108/JSTPM-12-2017-0070

Hardford, T. (2011). *Adapt: Why success always starts with failure*. Macmillan.

Hendrickson, L., & Tuttle, D. B. (1997). Dynamic management of the environmental enterprise: A qualitative analysis. *Journal of Organizational Change Management*, *10*(4), 363–382. doi:10.1108/09534819710175875

IEA. (2020). India 2020. *IEA*. Retrieved from https://www.iea.org/reports/india-2020

Kumar, R. (2019 May 9). Waste controlling in India – Is it really happening? *Business Today India*. Retrieved from https://www.businesstoday.in/opinion/columns/waste-controlling-india-waste-management-plastic-recycling/story/344945

London, T., & Hart, S. (2010). *Next Generation Business Strategies for the Base of the Pyramid: New Approaches for Building Mutual Value* (1st ed.). FT Press.

Ndubisi, N., & Nair, S. (2009). Green entrepreneurship (GE) and Green Value Added (GVA): A conceptual framework. *International Journal of Entrepreneurship*, *13*, 21–34.

Norman, W., & MacDonald, C. (2004). Getting to the bottom of "Triple Bottom Line.". *Business Ethics Quarterly*, *14*(2), 243–262. doi:10.5840/beq200414211

Palepu, K. G., Bullock, R. J., & Khanna, T. (2001). *Winning in Emerging Markets: A Road Map for Strategy and Execution*. Harvard Business Press.

Prahalad, C. K. (2004). *The Fortune at the Bottom of the Pyramid: Eradicating Poverty Through Profits*. Wharton School Publishing.

Prahalad, C. K., & Bettis, R. A. (1995). The Dominant Logic: A New Linkage Between Diversity and Performance. *Strategic Management Journal*, *16*, 5–14.

Prahalad, C. K., & Hammond, A. (2002). Serving the World's Poor, profitably. *Harvard Business Review*, (September), 4–11. PMID:12227146

Prahalad, C. K., & Mashelkar, R. A. (2010). Innovation's Holy Grail. *Harvard Business Review*, (July-August), 1–10.

PTI. (2019 August 23). India to achieve most of COP21 climate change goals in next 1.5 years: Modi. *The Economic Times of India*. Retrieved from https://economictimes.indiatimes.com/news/politics-and-nation/india-to-achieve-most-of- cop-21-climate-change-goals-in-next-1-5-years- modi/articleshow/70809788.cms?from=mdr

Raposo, J. (1970, Jan. 20). Bein' Green. [Recorded by Jim Henson as Kermit the Frog]. On Sesame Street [television]. Los Angeles, US: Jonico Music Inc.

Rattani, V., Venkatesh, S., Pandey, K., Kukreti, I., Somvanshi, A., & Sangomla, A. (2018 October 18). India's National Action Plan on Climate Change needs desperate repair. *DownToEarth.* Retrieved from https://www.downtoearth.org.in/news/climate- change/india-s-national-action-plan-on-climate-change-needs-desperate-repair-61884

Revathy, L. N. (2020 January 30). Renewable energy start-up Carbon Masters receives second round of funding. *The Hindu*. Retrieved from https://www.thehindubusinessline.com/companies/renewable-energy-start-up-carbon masters-receives-second-round-of-funding/article30685467.ece#

Schumpeter, J.A. (1934). The theory of economic development: an inquiry into profits, capital, credit, interest and the business cycle. *Harvard Economic Studies, 46.*

Silverthorne, S. (2011). The Untold Story of 'Green' Entrepreneurs. *HBS Working Knowledge*. Retrieved from https://hbswk.hbs.edu/item/6561.html

UNRISD. (2012). United Nations Research Institute for Social Development. In Social Dimensions of Green Economy. UNRISD.

Uzo, U., & Mair, J. (2014). Source and patterns of organizational defiance of formal institutions: Insights from Nollywood, the Nigerian movie industry. *Strategic Entrepreneurship Journal*, *8*(1), 56–74. doi:10.1002ej.1171

Webb, H., & Liu, S. (2020). The Sustainable Falcon: Dubai's Path to Becoming a Green Economic Leader. In H. C. Webb & H. A. Al Numairy (Eds.), *Entrepreneurial Innovation and Economic Development in Dubai and Comparisons to Its Sister Cities* (pp. 1–16). IGI Global. doi:10.4018/978-1-5225-9377-5.ch001

Wright, M. (2001). Creating and growing wealth: Sue Birley on entrepreneurship and wealth creation. *The Academy of Management Executive*, *15*(1).

Chapter 2
Picturing the Indian Automotive Sector's Slowdown

Rajat Deb
https://orcid.org/0000-0002-7009-0051
Tripura University, India

ABSTRACT

The Indian automotive industry has remained a significant driver of the manufacturing sector and contributed to the GDP around 7% in 2018, but it is confronting its biggest slump in last 19 years with a double digit downfall in revenues across all segments. Such slowdown has caused job cuts of around 0.2 million workers, particularly contractual labourers, and shut down of around 300 dealers' shops in the last few months. A number of cyclical and structural contributing factors for the slowdown have been identified. Measures for turnaround are suggested, highlighting a recently announced stimulus package for reviving the industry.

THE CONTEXT

Indian business newspapers since July have been consistently reporting about the worst automotive slump emerged in the last quarter of a century leading to double-digit decline in top line, layoff of more than 0.2 million jobs, de-growth in the insurance premium collections and in the ancillary firms. The Society of Indian Automobile Manufacturers (SIAM) has empathically shown that vehicle wholesale across the categories have significantly dropped by 18.71 percent in July, 2019 vis-à-vis the corresponding period on year-on-year (y-o-y) comparison, a steepest downfall in last 19 years (Bhargava, 2019). Interestingly, the cascading effect of the slump has also adversely impacted the tyre, steel steering producers and the

DOI: 10.4018/978-1-7998-4195-1.ch002

Copyright © 2021, IGI Global. Copying or distributing in print or electronic forms without written permission of IGI Global is prohibited.

general insurance companies. The automobile industry has been contributing almost 8 percent in India's Gross Domestic Production (GDP) and around 49 percent of her manufacturing GDP. The Annual Survey of Industries (ASI) has reported the automotive industry has employed around 8 percent of total employment across industries (around 1.4 million) and highest number of contractual laborers (Vyas, 2019). Further, it has created direct and indirect employment as it has forward and backward linkage with other industries (EPW Editorial, 2019). Interestingly, the ASI figure has not considered the employees engaged with unorganized manufacturing sector, in the roadside garages, with dealers and distributors and according to the Automotive Component Manufacturers Association (ACMA) around 5 million workers have been engaged. The Federation of Automobile Dealers Association (FADA) has estimated that around 0.2 million front-end jobs have been cut by auto dealers during May-July in the current fiscal and it has been apprehended that such retrenchments likely be extended to technical jobs unless any stimulus package is offered. The National Accounts Statistics (NSA) has revealed the current slowdown and its continuation in near future is likely to adversely impact the investments and exports which, earlier was combated through abound consumer-credits (Mahendra & Goyel, 2019). Edelweiss Securities in a recent report has shown that the industry is currently passing through a down cycle stage and unlikely the volume recovery would be materialized without fiscal stimulus. The report has categorically mentioned the current slowdown is differed from the earlier slowdowns in a multiple ways. The automotive slowdown has driven by domestic factors rather by global factors, tough competition with the growing organized pre-owned vehicle markets and high margin pressures from the distribution members have also significantly contributed. Further, the downturn has likely to persist for an average period of 4-22 quarters as opposed to 7-11 quarters. Adding to this the implementation of Bharat Stage (BS VI) norms from April, 2020 has likely impacted the complexity as well (Wadhwa & Koorgaonkar, 2019). The credit rating agency Investment Information and Credit Rating agency (ICRA) has estimated that the auto industry's slowdown would adversely affect the tyre industry's revenues which is likely to curtail by around 4 percent in the current fiscal (Majumder, 2019). Furthermore, the slowdown has created a shadow on general insurance business inasmuch the auto insurance having the highest share in non-life insurance segment up to 38 percent and in the first quarter of the 2019-20 it has reported the lowest growth rate among the last five quarters. The analysts have shown that insurance from new vehicles have been significantly contributed in overall premium collections and the slowdown in sales has adversely affected the auto insurance business (Panda, 2019).

THE DEBATE

Literature has vehemently shown boom and bust has remained a coherent feature for developing economies (Temple, 1999, Pritchett, 2000) and India's slowdown primarily has been driven by domestic factors rather global events (Mehrotra, 2010). The strand of studies prior to global sub-prime crisis have documented that the fundamentals of Indian economy were strong and it had potential to register growth in midterm (Oura, 2007, Poddar & Yi, 2007, Ranjan, Jain & Dhal, 2007). Macro economists have been divided in two schools of thought for labeling the appropriate nomenclature to this current slowdown and have identified it as 'structural' as opposed to 'cyclical'. By structural slowdown, the first group of economists have argued that the auto industry has consistently and significantly contributed in the GDP notwithstanding in last few months has been confronting industry specific impediments (Roy, 2019). On the other hand, during cyclical slowdown entire economy is affected causing the downturn of the concerned sector as well. Interestingly, the current slowdown has two parts- a part is cyclical while a major structural part has as well. The cyclical slowdown has started in 2013-14 while the structural part has emerged post demonitisation and rolling out of the Goods and Services Tax (GST). Surprisingly, the current demand in the economy in general has been largely contributed by households from their incomes derived directly or indirectly from the formal sector rather from the informal sector (Sen, 2019). The informal sector such as auto ancillary manufacturing units were struggling post demonitisation and the demand of the sector has been shifted to the formal sector.

THE CAUSES

The contribution of Indian manufacturing sector in her GDP has remained static around 17 percent since last two decades impeding to create global competitiveness and to serve the domestic market with low cost of production (Dewangan, Agarwal & Sharma, 2015). Innovation has remained the corner stone for India's competitiveness in the manufacturing sector (Porter, 1966; Burgelman & Sayles, 1988) and traditional factors *viz.* quality, cost, price, services and flexibility have unlikely to contribute in the competitiveness (Bierly & Daly, 2007; Liu, 2013). Literature has indicated the slowdown of Chinese economy during 2015-16 caused by external structural factors such as slow growth of the world economy (Lin, Guanghua & Morgan, 2016). Unsustainable long run growth likely has to be reported inasmuch economies such as in China having no comprehensive reforms, following old model and practicing credit-fuelled economic strategy (Elliott, 2017). Economists have conceded slowdown in least developing economies have their country-specific factors like high growth rate of labour force, lower levels of education and even political turmoil (Eichengreen, Park & Shin, 2014). On the other hand, slowdown in emerging economies have emerged due to reaching the saturation level in shifting the labour force from agriculture to manufacturing sector (Agénor, 2017). As far as slowdown in the Indian automobile industry has concerned, the government should bear responsibility especially for its regulatory uncertainty. The aggressive propaganda for electrification of personal vehicles has created confusion for the producers in their investment, lease or buying decisions. The troubled financial sector has badly hit the sector in twin manners- the exorbitant financing costs as Reserve Bank of India (RBI) has cut the interest rate which has been transmitted in the form higher costs of capital. Further, the crisis of Non-Banking Financial Companies (NBFCs) has also adversely affected the auto-ancillary companies as well as consumers inasmuch traditionally the sector has remained as credit-fuelled sector. The liquidity crunch faced by the NBFCs has hit the domestic demand inasmuch a significant portion of automobile sales have been financed by them. High shoot up in inventory costs and piling up of inventory have also compelled a good number of auto shops to lay off employees and even shut down their operations (Kripalani, 2019). Moreover, adverse monsoon effects and sluggish rural demand have also added in the automotive downturns. Adding to the woes, banks have been putting stringent conditions such as demanding collateral up to 25 percent for the newly sanctioned loans and extended loans to the auto dealers due to the non performing asset (NPA) phobia. Interestingly, the fear of dealers' shut down rather liquidity crunch has become cause of concerns for many auto companies e.g., Maruti Suzuki and Hyundai Motor India. Such shut down has not only created panic amongst the banks and auto companies nut even around 0.003 million employees have lost their jobs (Majumder, 2019). The average inventory for the Passenger Vehicles (PVs), Commercial Vehicles (CVs) and two-wheelers have been substantially increased due to dealers' inadequate liquidity to 30-35 days, 55-60 days and 65-65 days respectively for these three categories of automobiles. Notwithstanding macro economists have conflicting opinions regarding the causes of current slumps in automotive industry, and broadly they have been in consensus that high real interest rates have adversely affected the sector. It has been argued that past growth has been excessively debt-fuelled and currently the domestic consumers have been exhausted by such over-borrowing. Further, lower rural demands and dampened sentiments with animal spirits from aggressive government policies to enhance tax revenues have been identified as the prime contributing factors for the slowdown (Kohli, 2019; Roy, 2019). The demand for PVs by middle class and government employees have also been fallen as potential customers likely is waiting for deep discounts at the end of current fiscal as was allowed at the during transition to BS-IV. Further, it has been expected that auto dealers would offer heavy discounts while transiting to BS-VI in April 2020 hence they have likely preferred to delay the purchases. The central government employees have been demanding hike in their salaries beyond the Seventh Central Pay Commission (SCPC) recommendations which yet not been materialized and has adversely impacted the sales of PVs. Surprisingly, the demand from the shared mobility providers such as Ola and Ubber has also reported downfall which earlier had helped the sector from turn around such downfalls. The budget announcement of levying higher surcharges on the super rich has also adversely hit the sale of luxurious and expensive PVs. The three-wheeler market has also been confronting tough challenges both domestically and in export markets. Many Indian states have been aggressively working on their electric vehicle (EV) policies and a few e.g., Karnataka has planned to phase out the two-stroke and diesel autos from Bangaluru. Further, the cheaper operating costs in compared to conventional Internal Combustion Engine (ICE) based three-wheelers have been significantly affecting the auto sector. The volatile global economic environment and regulatory developments in prime export markets such as Nigeria and Sri Lanka have also declined the export sales during the 2018-19 fiscal (Ravichandran, 2019).

Tata Nano: A Failure of Innovation

Innovation has been crucial in addressing the largest portion of the problems of mankind. The researchers have been providing several definitions of innovation in different disciplines i.e., psychology, business and education as problem-solving process, execution of new ideas to construct value to the society and implementation of the creative ideas (Soleas, 2020). In relation to business, innovation has depicted a strong correlation among economic value creation, firm's growth and a country's economic development (Okumu, Bbaale & Guloba, 2019). Similarly, the automotive industry which has been inclined towards research and development (R&D) for new product development is likely to be successful depending on the rate of its innovation. However, innovation could have been turned as a bad experience when companies fail to recognise the best idea to execute among the available alternatives (Burkus, 2013). Each time it has become critical for the automotive companies to understand whether a new innovative product will find its place in the market or the product is likey to fail in the competitive market (Gerhard, Brem & Voigt, 2008). Nevertheless, the automotive industry through its robust investment in R&D continously paving the way for introducing new and innovative products. The Indian automobile sector is expected to reach USD 6.7 trillion in total size in the year 2030 and almost 30 percent revenue is expected from the lastest innovation in forthcoming days with major changes in the product design, features and driving engines as four wheelers equiped with electric engines are likely to be the next generation automotives (Desjardins, 2018).

Indian giant automotive company Tata Motors has been granted 57 patents in between the year 2011-2018 (Miglani, 2019) and which is likely to indicate the thrust of the company to innovate and serve latest technologies to its customers. Notwithstanding, a major failure to the innovation has been witnessed by the Tata Motors when Tata Nano four wheeler which has been introduced in January, 2008 as “people's car” failed to cater to the targeted customers and that has forced the company to stop its production since November, 2019 (PTI, 2020). Innovation strategy is crucial to bring the product in the market as novel and understanding the market requirements such as the market demand, targeted customers, and under what conditions people will use the product is the important part of innovation strategy and probably TATA Motors has likely failed to understand such market requirements (Eyring, 2011). Despite of the fact that the claim has been made on the car that it has modern technologies, international safety standards, high fuel efficiency and light weight, it has failed to attract the potential buyers and factors that has hindered the prospective customers perception are likely to be its stigma in connotation i.e., “cheapest” car, delay of 18 months in production which has made demand gap by shifting of its manufacturing unit from West Bengal to Gujarat due to land acquisition controversy and the unmatched features and standards of the car as promised by the company. However, the proper formulation of value propositions and product differentiation from competitors along with better identification and analysis of targeted customers are likely to be a lesson for the company in the process of new product development (Roy, 2018).

THE WAY FORWARD

The potential synergy between growth, social investment and job creations should be explored as advised by scholars (Mehrotra & Delamonica, 2007). For addressing the auto dealers' liquidity problems, banks should adopt ‘case-by-case approach’ ensuring bonafide dealers should not have been deprived of the credit. The auto manufacturers should initiate close cooperation and negotiations between the banks and dealers for smooth lending to the dealers. It has been argued that in the short run NBFC lending unlikely to revive hence Public Sector Banks (PSBs) should bear the onus of reducing the liquidity crunch of the informal sectors (Ram Mohan, 2019). Further, adequate recapitalization of banks coupled with counter-cyclical fiscal and monetary policies likely to arrest the liquidity problems of the automotive sector to a greater extent. To accelerate the three-wheeler market, the abolition of permit regime in larger markets such as Maharashtra, Gujarat and Delhi vis-à-vis issuance of fresh permits in other states have been identified as the need of the hour. The structural changes in the business models driven by dynamic business environment should be explored taking into cognizance that demand for transportation is an instance of derived demand, i.e., users access the transportation service not directly to use its associated benefits rather to access other services (Jain, 2019). Subscription, leasing and shared mobility solutions likely to be explored extensively to cross over the slowdown tides. Instead of relying exclusively on dealers and distributors, the automotive sector has been using the subscription model against a specified monthly rental where the users can use a brand new car without actually buying it and after the end of the lock-in period the customer either may purchase the same car or may quit by exercising opt-out clause. Furthermore, the shared mobility has identified as another high potential business model in the auto sector and few industry leaders e.g., Hyundai Motors have been exploring the model in collaboration with Ola by offering range of financial services and maintenance. Industry experts have pointed out that ownership as a method for accessing the services of cars has been losing its shine and instead young India has preferred subscription model inasmuch it has no upfront expenses, insurance payments, repairs and maintenance expenses and convenience for anytime opt-out (Narasimhan, 2019). The transition to Electric Vehicles (EV) even though on the cards, should be implemented in phased manner as such mammoth transformation would impact on the allied sectors, require re-skilling and re-modeling of the production and likely to have replacement of 70-80 percent of the current workforce. Multiple EV issues such as huge initial investment, mileage, pulling, cost, maintenance and sustainability should be addressed with due diligence. It would be very crucial for conventional auto manufacturers to assess how far the Faster Adoption and Manufacturing of Electric Vehicles (FAME II) policy initiated in April 2019 for 3 years get success in its implementation since the experience of EV has remained a lukewarm affair. Finally, breaking the stigma of 'Black Friday' the Finance Minister's stimulus package announced on 23rd August has shown some sort of reliefs for the auto sector. As a pre-Diwali bonanza it has offered plethora of boosters ranging from allowing higher depreciation of 30 percent on all vehicles, waving of registration free of cost till June 2020, lifting ban on government departments' new purchase and to extending the registration time of BS-IV vehicles beyond March 2020 would most likely to revive the sector and soon it will turn around to dominate the Indian economy.

REFERENCES

Agénor, P. R. (2017). Caught in the middle? The economics of the middle-income traps. *Journal of Economic Surveys*, *31*(3), 771–791. doi:10.1111/joes.12175

Bierly, P. E., & Daly, P. S. (2007). Alternative knowledge strategies, competitive environment, and organizational performance in small manufacturing firms. *Entrepreneurship Theory and Practice*, *31*(4), 493–516. doi:10.1111/j.1540-6520.2007.00185.x

Burgelman, R. A., & Sayles, L. R. (1988). *Inside corporate innovation*. Simon and Schuster.

Burkus, D. (2013, July 23). *Innovation Isn't an Idea Problem*. Retrieved June 04, 2020, from Harvard Business Review: https://hbr.org/2013/07/innovation-isnt-an-idea-proble

Desjardins, J. (2018, February 15). *The Future of Automotive Innovation*. Retrieved June 04, 2020, from Visual capitalist: https://www.visualcapitalist.com/future-automobile-innovation/

Dewangan, D. K., Agarwal, R., & Sharma, V. (2015). Enablers for Competitiveness of Indian Manufacturing Sector: An ISM-Fuzzy MICMAC Analysis. *Procedia: Social and Behavioral Sciences*, *189*, 416–432. doi:10.1016/j.sbspro.2015.03.200

Editorial. (2019, August 17). Crisis in the Automobile Industry. *Economic and Political Weekly, 54*(33), 8.

Eichengreen, B., Park, D., & Shin, K. (2014). Growth Slowdown redux. *Japan and the World Economy*, *32*, 65–84. doi:10.1016/j.japwor.2014.07.003

Elliott, L. (2017, August 15). IMF warns China over 'dangerous' growth in debt. *The Guardian*. Retrieved from https://www.theguardian.com/business/2017/aug/15/imf-warns-china-debt-slowdown-financialcrisis

Eyring, M. (2011, January 11). *Learning from Tata's Nano Mistakes*. https://hbr.org/2011/01/learning-from-tatas-nano-mista?registration=success

Gerhard, D., Brem, A., & Voigt, K.-I. (2008). Product development in the automotive industry: Crucial success drivers for technological innovations. *International Journal of Technology Marketing*, *2*(2), 203–222. doi:10.1504/IJTMKT.2008.019922

Jain, A. K. (2019, August 20). Demand for transportation is falling first. *The Business Line*, p. 7.

Kohli, R. (2019, August 20). What to do about the slowdown? *The Financial Express*, p. 8.

Kripalani, J. (2019, August 15). Auto stocks lose favor among FIIs, fund houses. *The Business Standard*, p. 9.

Lin, J., Wan, G., & Morgan, P. J. (2016). Prospects for a re-acceleration of economic growth in the PRC. *Journal of Comparative Economics*, *44*(4), 842–853. doi:10.1016/j.jce.2016.08.006

Liu, Y. (2013). Sustainable competitive advantage in turbulent business environments. *International Journal of Production Research*, *51*(10), 2821–2841. doi:10.1080/00207543.2012.720392

Mahendra, S., & Goyel, A. (2019, August 21). GDP measurement and the slowdown. *The Business Standard*, p. 9.

Majumder, A. (2019, August 22). Maruti seeks better terms of lending for dealers. *The Business Standard*, p. 3.

Mehrotra, S. (2010). India and the global economic crisis. *Journal of Asian Public Policy*, *3*(2), 122–134. doi:10.1080/17516234.2010.504326

Mehrotra, S., & Delamonica, E. (2007). *Eliminating human poverty. Macro-economic and social policies for equitable growth.* Zed Press.

Miglani, S. (2019). The Growth of the Indian Automobile Industry: Analysis of the Roles of Government Policy and Other Enabling Factors. In Innovation, Economic Development, and Intellectual Property in India and China. Springer.

Narasimhan, T. E. (2019, August 8). Carmakers drive market disruption for growth. *The Business Standard*, p. 8.

Nhargava, Y. (2019, August 18). Why is the auto industry facing trouble? *The Hindu*, p. 2.

Okumu, I. M., Bbaale, E., & Guloba, M. M. (2019). Innovation and employment growth: Evidence from manufacturing firms in Africa. *Journal of Innovation and Entrepreneurship*, *8*(7), 1–27. doi:10.118613731-019-0102-2

Oura, H. (2007). *Wild or tamed? India's potential growth.* IMF Working Paper WP/07/224.

Panda, S. (2019, August 4). Auto slowdown hits insurers. *The Business Standard*, p. 3.

Poddar, T., & Yi, E. (2007). *India's rising growth potential.* Goldman Sachs Global Economics Paper No. 152. https.gs.com

Porter, M. (1996). *America's green strategy. In Business and the Environment.* Earthscan.

Pritchett, L. (2000). Understanding patterns of economic growth: Searching for hills among plateaus, mountains and plains. *The World Bank Economic Review, 14*(2), 221–250. doi:10.1093/wber/14.2.221

PTI. (2020, January 6). *Tata Nano ends 2019 with zero production; sales of 1 unit.* https://timesofindia.indiatimes.com/business/india-business/tata-nano-ends-2019-with-zero-production-sales-of-1-unit/articleshow/73119753.cms

Ram Mohan, T. T. (2019, August 23). Fix credit growth to fix the slowdown. *The Business Standard*, p. 9.

Ranjan, R., Jain, R., & Dhal, S. C. (2007). India's potential economic growth, measurement issues and policy implications. *Economic and Political Weekly, 28*(April).

Ravichandran, R. (2019, July 27). 3-wheeler sales dip 11.64% in first quarter. *The Financial Express*, p. 7.

Roy, R. (2019, August 9). Structural slowdown and home market demand. *The Business Standard*, p. 11.

Roy, S. (2018, July 17). *Tata Nano – Why Did the People Not Want the People's Car?* Retrieved June 04, 2020, from The Wire: https://thewire.in/business/tata-nano-why-did-the-people-not-want-the-peoples-car

Sen, P. (2019, August 10). Rural investment best way to revive economy. *The Business Standard*, p. 6.

Soleas, E. K. (2020). Leader strategies for motivating innovation in individuals: A systematic review. *Journal of Innovation and Entrepreneurship, 9*(9), 1–28. doi:10.118613731-020-00120-w PMID:32685342

Temple, J. (1999). A positive effect of human capital on growth. *Economics Letters, 65*(1), 131–134. doi:10.1016/S0165-1765(99)00120-2

Vyas, M. (2019, July 30). Worry about informal employment. *The Business Standard*, p. 8.

Wadhwa, P., & Koorgaonkar, D. (2019, July 20). Auto indices hit 3-year low. *The Business Standard*, p. 10.

Chapter 3
Corporations and Social Enterprises:
Co-Creators of Social Value in Asia

Rob John
The Centre for the Study of Philanthropy and Public Good, University of St. Andrews, UK

ABSTRACT

This chapter describes how corporations and social enterprises in Asia can co-create social value. The traditional role of corporate philanthropy is transactional in nature, where the donation of resources from a corporation allows a non-profit organisation to create social value through its mission. The rise of social entrepreneurship as an alternative for creating social value through hybrid business models has given rise to novel opportunities for corporate philanthropy. Corporations can use their discretionary finances to support social enterprises across the spectrum of their organisational development from ideation and early stage ventures to later stages of maturity. The chapter offers case studies from Singapore, India, and Hong Kong that exemplify the co-creation of social value through small enterprise acceleration, angel investing, corporate venture capital, and business process outsourcing.

INTRODUCTION

The early stages of developing an idea into a viable business, whether an explicitly social or purely commercial enterprise, are fragile and usually rely on access to concessionary funding such as ‘family and friends’, personal savings, low interest loans, enterprise grants and awards, or prizes from business plan competitions.

DOI: 10.4018/978-1-7998-4195-1.ch003

Copyright © 2021, IGI Global. Copying or distributing in print or electronic forms without written permission of IGI Global is prohibited.

Subsidy through grants is a vital source of funds for both social enterprises and nonprofits in the conception and infancy stages. In a series of studies at the National University of Singapore Business School from 2012 to 2017 we explored how philanthropy and social investment is innovating and evolving to meet the needs of Asia's social entrepreneurs. This chapter draws upon research during this period in a collection of working papers published internally by NUS Business School, Singapore, principally our study on corporate philanthropy (John, Chia & Ito, 2107). We introduced the term 'Entrepreneurial Social Finance' (ESF) to capture a growing number of financing models that focus on providing capital and non-financial support to social entrepreneurs and entrepreneurial social ventures. ESF is a canopy of financing practices that include venture philanthropy and impact investing, characterised by an investment-minded approach that is focused on helping build a well-managed, resilient organisation rather than simply supporting discrete projects. Venture philanthropists and impact investors actively work alongside an organisation's management team, providing technical advice and mentoring as well as finance. A social entrepreneur is an individual with the skill, outlook and ability to build an organisation that creates social value. The entrepreneur's choice to use the medium of a social enterprise or a nonprofit to deliver impact is generally pragmatic and situational rather than ideological. Even so, the potential for a business to deliver impact sustainably through trading without the long-term need for grant subsidy is a compelling reason to explore the trading model when building an organisation that seeks to have social impact. Throughout our studies, we have viewed ESF models as deploying financial, intellectual and human capital for primarily social impact. Therefore, the sharing of skills, know-how and volunteering time are as much acts of philanthropy as giving a grant; venture philanthropy and related models emphasise the synergy of combining finance and non-financial advisory to support the organisational development of nonprofits and social enterprises. In our series of studies, we explored a diverse range of capital-providing players in the philanthropy ecosystem, including individuals, collectives such as giving circles, family and private grantmaking foundations, angel networks, governments and corporations. The corporation, either publicly or privately owned, is also an actor in this space selected as the focus of this chapter. We wanted to understand how corporations in Asia are adapting traditional models of grantmaking and volunteerism to serve the region's social entrepreneurs. We also wanted to move beyond what are commonly thought of as philanthropy practices to business models usually associated with commercial operations that support social enterprise to co-create social value – angel investing, corporate venture capital and business process outsourcing.

The objectives of this chapter are to illustrate, through case studies in three Asian countries, new opportunities for corporate philanthropy to co-create social value together with social enterprises. This co-creation of value differs from more traditional expressions of discretionary corporate philanthropy by being more engaged, relational and utilising a more comprehensive toolbox of financial, human and intellectual resources.

CORPORATE PHILANTHROPY

Corporate philanthropy is plagued by definitional ambiguity and inconsistency. Order been brought to the chaotic terminology of giving by companies in the review of the academic literature of corporate philanthropy by Gautier and Pache (2013). Even so, their sample of research literature is biased towards the study of North American and British businesses with very little on the Asian corporate environment (two percent of the papers are by Hong Kong-based researchers and one percent from Australia, with no other Asian countries represented). The review reveals terms are used loosely and interchangeably – corporate philanthropy, corporate social responsibility, corporate responsibility, community engagement, community investment, strategic philanthropy (as applied to corporations), cause-related marketing, corporate social performance, Creating Shared Value, sustainability, corporate citizenship, as well as terms related to the donation of employee skills and time with or without a financial contribution. At the root of this complex lexicon is the unresolved understanding about the very nature or essence of corporate philanthropy. Individuals, acting alone or in an organised group or institution, act altruistically in the act of giving, but can a corporation with its fiduciary responsibility to shareholders have the capacity for philanthropy? The assertion that discretionary giving or CSR is a distraction from the primary purpose of creating shareholder wealth was propagated by Milton Friedman nearly half a century ago, but over the last decade this neoclassical approach has not been viewed so dogmatically. Indeed, some now argue that corporate generosity is a legitimate avenue for increasing profits, with long-term benefit outweighing short-term cost (Abzug & Webb, 1996). The literature review by Gautier and Pache suggests a broad consensus that corporate philanthropy can and does serve a company's business interests, directly or indirectly. This is evident when a business invests in the community in which it operates; the logic being an educated and healthy workforce living within an effective community infrastructure contributes to the well-being of the company. It is not uncommon for a business to make philanthropic donations to create goodwill and enhance its standing with consumers, regulators and other stakeholders who hold the key to its licence to operate and ultimately impact its profitability. In 1979 Carroll proposed what is generally considered today the classical pyramidal conceptualisation of corporate social responsibility in which a business has three obligatory responsibilities. A company has an economic responsibility to create and trade goods and services and thus maximise profitability to shareholders; society expects it to pursue this economic mission within a framework of laws and regulations; and to exhibit ethical behaviour even though this is unlikely to be codified in law. Beyond these three, the company can engage in discretionary activities – desirable but not mandatory – such as philanthropy and other forms of community engagement (Carroll, 1979).

Our working definition of corporate philanthropy is the use of discretionary financial and human resources for primarily public benefit, while recognising that impact might also accrue for the company's shareholders and employees. Carroll completes his conceptual model by introducing "corporate social responsiveness" to address the degree of managerial action in response to social issues on a continuum from "no response" to "proactive" – a pragmatic framework that works around the preoccupation with ethical or moral threads inherent in CSR. A corporation's managers are clearly key in the execution of CSR, including philanthropy. Scholars of corporate philanthropy have noted is the inherent tension between a corporation's owners and managers, the corporate area conceptualised as 'agency theory' as applied to the discretionary actions of corporate philanthropy (Jensen & Meckling, 1976). In a narrow sense, corporate philanthropy is a diversion of a company's resources from its owners to activities that might enhance its executives' standing as business leaders amongst their peers or wider society. The 2008 financial crisis and its perceived lack of moral restraint by market participants has generated a renewed interest in the ethical dimension of financial sector actors and a call to 'restore trust' in global finance (Menzies, Simpson, Hay & Vines, 2019).

The businesses profiled here represent a variety of ownership/manager models, including privately held (owner or executive managed), partnerships, and public companies. While it was beyond the scope of our studies to compare a company's philanthropic activity with ownership structure, we consistently see that owners and owners/managers play a key role in setting a culture of giving and operational style.

In the following sections, we explore examples of the corporation as philanthropic actor supporting nonprofits and social enterprises by utilising financial, human and intellectual capital. Enterprise accelerators help social entrepreneurs grow their ideas into early stage social enterprises or non-profit organisations. Angel investors seeking social impact work alongside entrepreneurs to offer commercial acumen coupled to equity investment at a critical stage in the lifecycle of a young organisation. Corporate venture capital, an investment tool long used by businesses to develop new products or enter new markets is becoming a way in which a company can co-create social value with social entrepreneurs. Business Process Outsourcing is a growing opportunity for co-creation as company purchasing managers include social enterprises to their roster of contractors.

ENTERPRISE ACCELERATORS

The terms *accelerator* and *incubator* are often used interchangeably, perhaps more so in the social enterprise sector than in the commercial world where they originated. Both business incubators and accelerators help enterprises at the earliest stages of their development, providing seed capital, working space and networking. The most fundamental difference between the two is "the limited duration of accelerator programmes as compared to the continuous nature of incubators and angel investments" (Cohen, 2013). The differences that stem from this distinction are generally less pronounced in the social enterprise sector, so the term accelerator is adopted here. While the role that accelerators play in nurturing for-profit ventures has been documented, particularly in the U.S. and European technology sector (Hackett & Dilts, 2004), there is less independent research on developing economies and the body of knowledge especially thin on enterprises focused on social impact.

Since 2013 there has been interest in accelerators that nurture young social enterprises that are believed to have the potential to reach scale and thus greater social impact. The key players in studying the role for impact-focused accelerators and promoting their use are the Aspen Network of Development Entrepreneurs (ANDE) in collaboration with Village Capital, and Monitor Deloitte in partnership with the Rockefeller Foundation. Monitor and Rockefeller mapped 165 accelerators globally, including 36 in Asia (Monitor Deloitte, 2015), that typically offered early stage social enterprises office space, pro bono professional advice, introduction to investors, and seed funding. From information available on a selection of the Asia-based accelerators in the Monitor study, the role for corporates appears to be largely limited to sponsorship. For example, the Center for Social Initiatives Promotion (CSIP) in Vietnam, which provides incubation and acceleration for Vietnamese social enterprises, lists several multinational corporate partners on its website. Other accelerators are linked to philanthropic funds or family offices, indicating they are subsidised by grants in addition to assessing fees on social enterprises that are their clients.

ANDE and Village Capital surveyed 52 "impact-focused accelerators worldwide" (Baird, Bowles, & Lall, 2013) – including 34 percent located in Asia and Oceania – in one of the first attempts to collect and interpret data on accelerator inputs and enterprise outcomes in the impact ecosystem. The findings of the study reveal three interesting characteristics of impact-focused accelerators. A report by the European Venture Philanthropy Association (EVPA, 2019) into ways to increase the pipeline of investable social enterprises in Europe highlights the importance of accelerators and incubators:

Organisational Structure: Perhaps counterintuitively, impact accelerators were more likely than their business-oriented peers to develop earned revenue streams beyond grants. Thirty-eight percent were structured as for-profits, 44 percent as nonprofits, with the remainder constituted as hybrids.

Funding Sources: Nearly three quarters of accelerators relied on philanthropic support for their operations with 54 percent of the capital they deployed as seed funding philanthropic in origin. Earned income streams included fee levied on entrepreneurs, consulting contracts, returns from investment, and success fees for brokering investment by external investors.

Partnerships: Accelerators typically have multiple partnerships with investors, universities, government, foundations and corporations. These partnerships may take the form of help with the deal flow, investments in social enterprises, or financial support for the accelerator. The report is not explicit about the role that corporations play in their partnership with accelerators, but it is likely that some of this support is given as grants for the operational costs of the accelerator.

The ANDE/Village Capital study takes the first evidential steps in determining the factors that are most likely to lead an accelerator to help early stage enterprises flourish sustainably. Monitor Deloitte's study, funded by the Rockefeller Foundation, identified the best practices for impact-focused accelerators:

- Develop customised services that meet the non-generic needs of early stage ventures from specific geographies or industries.
- Operate in a strong ecosystem of support utilising partnerships with mentors and investors.
- Carefully screen enterprises to ensure enterprise needs meet accelerator resources.
- Foster collaboration among social enterprises for peer-to-peer support and sharing of best practices.
- Remain engaged with an enterprise for as long as possible, recognising that testing and scaling can be a long and unpredictable process.

Many corporations engage with accelerators across the globe, providing financial resources through grants and sponsorship, or access to employee volunteering time. Accelerators can also offer start-up enterprises access to corporations as potential investors or clients. In such engagement with accelerators, corporations most usually act as strategic partners rather than active managers of the accelerator. Villgro is India's longest established social enterprise incubator, having helped more than 300 ventures accelerate their growth over the last 20 years. Corporate partnership is a key strategy that enables Villgro to deliver advice, mentoring and operational support to the social enterprises it supports. The professional services firm Accenture assists in scaling up ventures operating in the skills and employability sector; Hindustan Unilever's corporate foundation provides advice to start-ups managing water use in agriculture or improving yield and efficiency in the farming sector. Partnership with Rabobank enables Villgro's ventures to improve supply chain and food waste efficiencies.

A minority of corporations choose to manage their own accelerator projects for start-up enterprises across the commercial and social impact spectrum. In 2016 UBS, the Swiss-headquartered private bank and wealth manager, launched UBS Social Innovators across three of the bank's operating regions, including Asia-Pacific. In each region a dozen or so social enterprise start-ups participate in a 'boot camp' designed by Ashoka, the social entrepreneurship network, where the ventures interact with each other and bank employees. The social enterprises pitch their ideas during these residential events before a panel of judges, with winning ventures invited to enrol in a year-long accelerator programme of funding and mentoring aimed at helping them become ready for impact investment.

Another corporation that manages its own accelerator is Singtel, an Asian telecommunications corporation whose accelerator, *Future Makers*, aims to address the 'fragmented ecosystem' for social innovation. The initiative provides acceleration for either nonprofits or social enterprises seeking to address a social problem by leveraging technology, Singtel's core expertise.

CASE STUDY: SINGTEL FUTURE MAKERS

Singtel is one of the largest Singapore companies by market capitalisation. The communications group employs more than 23,000 people worldwide in a network of offices throughout Asia Pacific, Europe and the United States, which includes Optus, a major subsidiary in Australia. The company has more than 130 years of operating experience and played a pivotal role in Singapore's development as a global communications hub.

The Singtel Group is committed to responsible corporate citizenship in all the markets where it operates and does so by "driving positive and sustainable changes in disadvantaged communities", especially among vulnerable children and youth, through corporate and workplace giving, staff volunteering, and leveraging its skills and ICT innovations.

Singtel Touching Lives Fund (STLF) is the company's internal philanthropic grant programme that raises funds for charities helping children and youth with special needs in Singapore. The fund has given over S$33 million (US$24 million) since its launch in 2002. In Australia, the Optus Community Grant programme has given to projects supporting the inclusion and wellbeing of underprivileged youths through more than 200 grants totalling over A$1 million (US$750,000). In 2015 Singtel extended its philanthropic support of children with special needs by funding the establishment of the Singtel Enabling Innovation Centre in Singapore to provide training for people with disabilities that prepares them to join the workforce.

The Singtel Group's approach to corporate citizenship is evolving "beyond philanthropy" towards 'Shared Value Creation'. One step in this process was the launch of *Future Makers* in 2016. The initiative was born when Singtel drew several conclusions about the state of organisations creating social value in Singapore; many nonprofits (including those that provide social welfare programmes) did not fully utilise innovations and technology; start-up social enterprises struggled to sustain growth due to lack of capacity; and little collaboration and connectivity existed among players in the broader ecosystem of corporates, nonprofits, social services agencies and social entrepreneurs.

Future Makers is Singtel's response to the fragmented 'social start-up ecosystem' and builds on the company's experience of mentoring and funding support for social entrepreneurs in Singapore and Australia. *Future Makers* is a six-month long accelerator programme for start-ups, both social enterprises and nonprofits, which leverages technological or other innovative solutions that address challenges in the social sector in Singapore, Australia and potentially the wider region.

The programme funds start-ups whose products and service enable the 'wellbeing of vulnerable communities', including people with disabilities, the vulnerable elderly or children, and youths at risk. In the 2016 first round of selections, more than 70 start-up enterprises applied for funding online. These were then narrowed down to a dozen ventures for consideration. A panel comprising Singtel staff, community partners, social entrepreneurs, venture capital and social funders chose the final seven candidates who were enrolled as the accelerator programme's first cohort.

Over six months the start-ups participate in monthly workshops run by a mix of Singtel employees and external experts from its partner community. Monthly coaching sessions and regular mentoring will further strengthen the enterprises' capacity during the six months of intense acceleration. Singtel volunteers are drawn from mid to senior management who commit up to four hours each month to face-to-face meetings, and phone and video conferencing with the staff of social enterprises.

Unlike their commercial counterparts, *Future Makers* does not charge a fee for the acceleration service or take equity positions in the supported ventures, so is a philanthropic contribution to preparing selected enterprises for future investment readiness and growth. At the end of the accelerator programme some of the ventures may be invited to continue their relationship with Singtel, including additional funding rounds or collaboration with the business.

The total number of Singtel and Optus employee hours volunteered grew 21 percent in the financial years 2015 and 2016 from 26,614 to 32,175 hours. The company sees skilled volunteering as a core component of developing staff leadership and reinforced this commitment by becoming the first Asia-Pacific corporate partner to join Impact 2030 – the global initiative to leverage workforce volunteering in support of the UN Sustainable Development Goals. *Future Makers* has grown in scope to involve Singtel's other regional subsidiaries – AIS (Thailand), Globe (Philippines, and Telkomsel (Indonesia).

In 2020 *Future Makers* responded to the coronavirus pandemic by launching a Special Pandemic Support Grant for promising start-ups that utilised technology in the global campaign to tackle challenges posed by the infection.

IMPACT ANGELS

Angels invest both their money and time into early stage businesses with the objectives of financial return and the personal fulfilment of helping small ventures grow. They do so by acting either alone or in formal or informal syndicates called angel groups or networks. Angels are typically wealthy individuals; many are successful entrepreneurs with first-hand knowledge of launching and growing companies and help to cultivate entrepreneurship around them by drawing on their own business acumen and experience. Some angels are returning diaspora who become key enablers of entrepreneurship in countries such as Cambodia, India or Vietnam after having built enterprises in the United States or Europe. Other angels come from successful corporate business background whose capital and business connections are a resource for entrepreneurs starting their own ventures. But funding is not the only critical asset business angels bring. Their business acumen, patience and understanding of the length of time required before a new business develops into a thriving venture are qualities valued by entrepreneurs. To these, mentoring, expertise and access to business networks can be more valuable than cash.

The business angel investment model is being extended to support social enterprises in Asia (John, 2015), a development we termed *impact angel investing*. Our 2015 study offered an exploratory categorisation of angel models based on its initial observations. We observed the *migration* by traditional business angel groups into impact investing. We found *impact angel networks* (either independent or embedded within other organisations) and *individual angels* investing alone or in ad hoc association with others. Corporate involvement in impact angel investing is somewhat tangential and indirect, but most angels have a corporate or entrepreneurial background. Their investing is usually made on a personal basis, as individuals, within or outside of angel networks. Such networks may also comprise institutional investors, with more direct corporate involvement.

The Indian Angel Network (IAN) was formed in 2006 and has grown to over 400 individual angels and eight institutional investors who look for opportunities to invest up to US$1 million in scalable business. The institutional investors are venture capital funds, a family office and business intermediaries. The angel network works in partnership with corporate bodies including India's National Association of Software and Service Companies (NASSCOM) and the Indian Venture Capital Association.

The growing interest by angels in supporting businesses with social objectives led to the network launching its impact group, IAN Impact, in 2013. The network screens over 400 deals a month, of which up to 75 are eligible for impact investment by IAN Impact. Seven investments were made during the first year with up to 40 angels collaborating to invest in some of the ventures. In 2014 IAN Impact partnered with the German official development agency and the Small Industries Development Bank of India to launch *iArise* – an incubator of 200 social enterprises that focus on the base of the economic pyramid – with angels providing mentoring to entrepreneurs as they become investment ready.

While strictly speaking an independent network body, IAN is ultimately a part of the Indian corporate environment as reflected by the professional backgrounds of its members and through strategic partnerships with corporations. IAN Impact draws on the corporate expertise and networks of individuals and is an example of indirect corporate philanthropy by investing in scalable social businesses. Angel investing (whether targeted at purely commercial or social enterprises) is largely the domain of individuals rather than an institution like a corporate, so it is not straightforward for a company to directly engage in angel investing. But as the following case study of IAN Impact shows, it is possible for corporate bodies to partner with angels in providing non-financial and ecosystem support to fledgling enterprises.

Kolkata Angels and Mumbai Angels are other Indian networks that are migrating from exclusively commercial to social and environmental ventures, although not yet exhibiting the direct corporate collaborations of the larger and longer established Indian Impact Network. Such angel networks, as well as others exclusively focused on impact such as in B Current Impact Investment (Taiwan) and Invest2Innovate (Pakistan) have the potential to collaborate with corporate partners as investors or service providers as their portfolios grow.

CASE STUDY: INDIAN ANGEL NETWORK – IAN IMPACT

The Indian Angel Network was founded in 2006 by entrepreneurs who rode the first wave of entrepreneurship that followed the liberalisation of the Indian economy 15 – 20 years earlier. These individuals, including creators of the Indian technology industry, wanted to invest close to the spirit of entrepreneurship, and were committed to creating jobs and wanting to improve the lives of the many Indians living at the base of the economic pyramid. Today, the network has international coverage and comprises 432 business angels and eight institutions investing in start-up and early stage ventures as individuals and syndicates. IAN's investors are based in 10 countries and have invested in seven.

The institutional investors include venture capital funds, the family office of a major Indian conglomerate and corporate intermediaries.

IAN angels typically invest up to US$1 million over a three- to five-year investment period. IAN's President Padmaja Ruparel said "two conversations were happening in recent years amongst many of the network's angels." The first was around how the most talented entrepreneurs could use their industry-building skills to improve the lives of the poorest. The other was about the sustainability of philanthropy – "good work stops when good money stops." Over the last seven years IAN has built a substantial resource of individual entrepreneurial talent, business know-how, capital and networks that can be leveraged for the underdeveloped sector of "businesses with a social cause."

In July 2013 the network announced the setting up of IAN Impact – a subgroup of angels seeking investments in businesses that would serve the base of India's economic pyramid. The impact group includes experienced angels; among them two of IAN's original founders and others who are active across the spectrum from purely commercial to impact investing and philanthropy. Ruparel said the pipeline of potential social investments is strong despite the relative infancy of social business in India, adding that "in a batch of typically 400 potential ventures screened every month, 75 or so are candidates for impact investment." While it is still too early to fully understand how the angels will balance financial and social return on their investments, Ruparel believes the initiative can "divert money from 'champagne and diamonds' into something useful for reaching India's poor."

Aaditeshwar Seth was an academic at the Indian Institute of Technology (IIT) and an entrepreneur who wanted to harness technology to empower millions of the rural poor. Using a grant from an American foundation in 2009, Seth co-founded Gram Vaani (*voice of the village*) – a low-cost technology provider for communities and rural NGOs. Gram Vaani has grown to more than two million users in India, Afghanistan, Namibia, Pakistan and South Africa. Thirty rural radio stations are able to manage and share content over mobiles and the web; corrupt ration shop officials were arrested due to citizen complaints; women's groups in Uttar Pradesh can share learning and opinions; and Delhi citizens monitor waste management.

While the early pioneering activities could use grant finance, Seth said "the only way we could grow the scale of our impact was by transforming the organisation into a media company." Before meeting IAN Impact angels at an event for entrepreneurs, Seth had spoken with well-known social investors like the Omidyar and Acumen funds, only to find Gram Vaani was not yet the kind of 'big ticket' investment they were seeking. Seth found that most venture capital type investors were "focused on verticals like education, health or sanitation whereas our company provides technology solutions horizontally across several sectors."

Gram Vaani became the first publicised investment of IAN Impact with 24 individuals pooling their capital and co-investing with the Digital News Ventures in a round totalling US$500,000. Gram Vaani and its investors have agreed on social impact metrics, which are presented and discussed at regular investor meetings alongside the more traditional reporting on business growth and profitability. Seth values the angels' involvement in his business as they are "entrepreneurs who know how to grow a company, whose inputs are very useful in helping us overcome bottlenecks in our growth, and who open up their networks to bring us new business." The IAN Impact angels are represented on Gram Vaani's board by Srikant Sastri, an established media entrepreneur, who also drives *Growth-for-All*, a movement that seeks to include all in India's development and prosperity.

In 2013 IAN Impact and Unitus Seed Fund, India's most active seed stage impact investor, announced an undisclosed investment in GoCoop Solutions and Services Pvt. Ltd., a Bangalore-based venture that provides a social marketplace for co-operatives and community-based enterprises to list and sell their produce online. India has over 600,000 co-ops with more than 240 million members, but they are exploited by middlemen offering poor terms and low payments. GoCoop developed a technology platform and marketing services that provide co-ops in India and around the globe with market access and fair trading.

After its first year as a niche group within the angel network, IAN Impact had a portfolio of seven social businesses which engaged 40 angels as active investors. In June 2014 IAN collaborated with GIZ (the German development agency) and SIDBI (the bank serving Indian small and medium enterprises) to launch the iArise Incubator – an initiative to incubate close to 200 social enterprises that serve the bottom of the economic pyramid. IAN's intention through this incubator is to help guide entrepreneurs through the process of business scale up to ensure the widest possible geography and population are touched by social impact. The nine-month incubation programme will see IAN mentors help refine business plans and sales strategies and assist with access to angel investors and other sources of capital.

During our interviews we found that none of the entrepreneurs we interviewed felt that equity investment by a corporate had distorted the social mission embedded in their ventures. But one experienced angel investor in Asian social businesses cautioned that corporate venture capital investments in base-of-the-pyramid enterprises "are hard to pull off, as conflicts around mission arise. It's hard for corporates not to interfere negatively, unless they make such investments philanthropically and are completely disengaged."

CORPORATE VENTURE CAPITAL

As social enterprises grow and develop organisationally only a very small number will operate a business model that may be of direct interest to commercial investors, including corporations. But, for a subset of enterprises, direct investment by a company using a venture capital model will offer a significant opportunity to create social value at scale. In two case studies from India we illustrate the practice of corporate venture capital when directed towards investment in businesses that provide affordable healthcare or educational services.

Corporate venture capital (CVC) is an equity investment by a company in an external, independent venture that is typically in the early stages of business development. A company may make such an investment to earn a substantial financial return if the venture is successful; for example, through the sale of shares after an Initial Public Offering or by acquiring a profitable venture outright. Financial reward, however, is not the sole driver for a company to utilise a venture capital model. Knowledge that drives innovation often resides outside the intellectual resources of an individual company. A company uses CVC to invest in an entrepreneurial start-up as the means by which knowledge transfer can take place (Dushnitsky & Lenox, 2005). Such knowledge may be technical – perhaps relating to the design of new products or services – or it may help a company break into new consumer segments or geographical markets. Investment in an early stage venture thus meets one or more strategic requirements of the company. The venture receives capital and management support from the investing company typical of the venture capital model.

With growth in the number of new CVC funds and new ventures that promise financial return and social value, we may now have arrived at a point of convergence. The potential for CVC to "invest with impact" has been explored only recently, most notably by Volans, a certified B Corporation, and by Impact Economy, a Swiss-based strategy firm that coined the phrase "Corporate Impact Venturing" to describe CVC directed towards social impact (Martin, 2014).

In 2014 Volans collaborated with Global Corporate Venturing in a research project – *Investing in Breakthrough: Corporate Venture Capital* – to better understand how some CVC funds were investing in deals with the potential to yield both financial return and social impact, and to encourage more activity in this space. Their initial findings (Volans, 2014) were tested before an audience of global firms with active CVC programmes boasting an aggregated value of "more than US$20 billion" in order to build the business case for partnership between CVC funds and impact investors.

The Volans report described the historical waves in the development of CVC since it emerged as a subsector of the venture capital industry in the 1960s. Sustainability became a new motivation for CVC from 2007 onwards. Volans argued that this heralded the "Breakthrough Decade" when forward-looking companies became responsive to market trends and open to new kinds of partnership, driven by a combination of forces: evolving consumer demand for ethical products, new market opportunity at the base of the pyramid, market-based public services, the pressure on natural resources, and the imbedding of social responsibility into the core of business strategy.

Volans identified six sectors that represent a common ground for corporate and impact investors where co-investment would lead to a potentially fertile partnership, including several examples of well-known multinational corporations using this venture capital approach. The energy company Shell invests, through its Foundation, in Husk Power Systems to expand rural biomass in India; Google co-invests with private foundations in the Eye-Q Indian eye care hospitals; and Unilever Pakistan has invested in Micro Drip, a business providing affordable, small scale irrigation systems.

The Volans' study notes the ambition of corporations to enter new and underserved markets, either intentionally or serendipitously as in the case of Medipass, an Italian company founded in 1995, and the subject of our first case study. A chance introduction led to Medipass investing in the Indian cancer treatment sector through a joint equity venture with Clearview Healthcare, an entrepreneurial start-up. Clearview's founders wanted to provide high quality nuclear medicine at affordable prices to low-income populations served by smaller tier 2 and tier 3 cities. This business model was unfamiliar to Medipass, which was used to the European pricing model for cancer diagnostic equipment. Clearview's business case rested on low operating costs, strategic partnerships, and high volume to provide affordable services. Despite the fact that the Italian company was not seeking expansion into Asia, it saw the potential and committed to a 49 percent equity position in a joint venture company named ClearMedi. The investment provided an opportunity for Medipass to learn about the economics of nuclear medicine at the base of the pyramid, and the company is now considering expansion into other emerging markets. Clearview was created by its socially-minded founders with an intentional social purpose – affordable cancer diagnostics for low-income families without the costs associated with travel to distant health facilities. To expand the business the start-up needed an investor who understood the technical field. Medipass does not describe its business in terms of social impact, but through CVC has learned to serve the base of the pyramid sector profitably with social impact .

The second case study features Pearson PLC, one world's largest education companies. Nearly 15 percent of its 2015 sales revenue came from growth markets including China and India. The company believes that "commercial solutions can accelerate access to quality education … especially in places where education standards fall well behind the best in the world, [and] require us to challenge the way we think about our business." In 2012 Pearson launched a US$15 million Affordable

Learning Fund (PALF) which was topped up with an additional US$50 million in 2015 to invest in "novel educational innovations with commercial potential". PALF has invested in 11 start-up ventures in South Africa, Ghana, India, and the Philippines; half of which are led by female entrepreneurs. Our case study features PALF's investment in Sudiksha, an Indian enterprise providing affordable pre-school service as a franchise run by female entrepreneurs.

The role of private enterprise in delivering affordable education – directly through privately owned, fee-paying schools or contracted by government to provide services in the public sector – is growing. There may be an ideological edge to the role of business in education, and the burgeoning number and models of private-public partnership in education in developed and developing countries is an area of intense debate and experimentation (Patrinos & Sosale, 2007).

PALF is an active venture capital investor taking double-digit equity positions and a board seat in the ventures. The fund is too young to have made an *exit* from an investment and Pearson does not want to second guess the trajectory of its experimentation in this space, but the firm appears to be committed to building a more robust ecosystem for private education in the long term rather than simply identifying potential for financial return on investment. PALF partners with ecosystem builders and impact funders like Village Capital and Omidyar Network.

The founding entrepreneurs of Sudiksha and Clearview drew on their own savings and funding from family and friends for their start-ups before accessing investment by external investors. As the business grew, it needed access to capital at different stages of its development. For Clearview and Sudiksha, venture capital investment by corporations aligned to their respective core business came at the right time to fuel growth. Pearson is open minded about the exit options that may materialise once the PALF portfolio matures. Medipass chose the route of gradual acquisition as early shareholders divested.

CASE STUDY: CLEARMEDI HEALTHCARE

Shashi Baliyan is an Indian-trained physician and entrepreneur who built his career in the National Health Service in the United Kingdom and founded his own health services company. A family visit to India set in motion a chain of events that would enable him to bring low cost, high quality cancer diagnosis and treatment to the poorest communities in India. Baliyan was attending a medical conference in Hisar – India's "City of Steel," the country's largest producer of galvanised steel products and a fast-growing industrial city to the west of New Delhi. Visiting the local hospital, built and maintained by the city's oldest steel company, Baliyan realised that "across hundreds of kilometres from Delhi to the Pakistan border there was not a single piece of equipment for the treatment of cancer."

"This was a stark reminder of the gaps in Indian healthcare I had so easily forgotten about after spending so many years in the United Kingdom," he said. Even if cancer facilities exist in the capital city, a person living in the small towns and rural areas will have to travel hundreds of kilometres with family members and live for lengthy periods far from home. These observations remained with Baliyan after he returned to the United Kingdom. Driven by the desire to "make a difference," he discussed with friends and colleagues in the health service the notion of setting up an Indian company to provide cancer treatment in small towns and cities. After a year of research, shuttling between London and Delhi, he established Clearview Healthcare in 2010, with several British colleagues providing him with start-up capital.

Baliyan's new venture won a contract with Hisar Hospital to provide radiology facilities for cancer treatment. The hospital constructed a radiotherapy suite and Clearview supplied, operated and maintained specialist equipment under a revenue-sharing arrangement in a project to provide low cost cancer treatment at provincial level. Despite this early success Baliyan realised that this was not a problem isolated to Hisar, but a nationwide lack of provision in cancer care. He knew that real impact meant scaling up from a single city to many. That would require investment far beyond what he and his colleagues could personally provide. An unexpected introduction to an Italian health care corporation provided just such an opportunity.

Medipass is an Italian company founded in 1995 which has operated within the KOS healthcare group since 2006. Friends introduced Baliyan to representatives of Medipass at a time when the company was looking to expand its cancer care into the United Kingdom health system. Baliyan argued that the Indian market could provide Medipass with a business opportunity where scale would compensate for much lower treatment fees. In 2010 Medipass and Clearview created the joint venture ClearMedi as a means to enter the Indian cancer treatment sector at a much larger scale with advanced turnkey financing, planning, development and management services for complex medical equipment provided to hospitals and public and private healthcare facilities. The business model, based on treatment fees 20 times lower than the European market, was unfamiliar to Medipass but the company recognised that the innovative model would have lower operating costs in India and would benefit from a volume of patients not found in a European setting.

Baliyan met with the Managing Director of Medipass Guglielmo Brayda di Soleto to present his business case. Following the meeting and after its own research, Brayda found the argument compelling. "We realised that Dr Baliyan's service model for India was similar to the recent European growth of Medipass. Importantly we saw the growth potential in India ... especially in cities with populations from 700,000 to 10 million." Baliyan and his private investors controlled 51 percent of the new company and by September 2011 it had won its first hospital contract. In the following four years ClearMedi expanded to 16 facilities across India and diversified from radiotherapy to diagnostic nuclear medicine, including locating the first Positron Emission Tomography–Computed Tomography machine (PET/CT) in Bihar, India's poorest state.

ClearMedi's revenue model was adapted entrepreneurially according to local market and institutional needs. A contract with a teaching hospital in Delhi was negotiated with a 20-year term, charging patients a small fee and recouping the investment over a long time period. "In this hospital, 90 percent of patients are living in Delhi's slums," said Baliyan. Over time the company developed bargaining power with instrument suppliers because of the volume of sales as the business expanded across India. Even Medipass' own European operations benefitted in this way from the volume of orders its joint venture placed for India.

Within four years ClearMedi grew new market for high quality cancer diagnostics and treatment, and a full-service offering to charitable and public hospitals, mostly serving low income populations in tier 2 and tier 3 cities and surrounding rural districts. This expansion was made without a marketing team but "by word of mouth and through the instrument supplier networks," said Baliyan. With Medipass seeing reasonable returns on investment and continued market potential in India, Baliyan and his initial investors began to disinvest. For Baliyan this cashing out yielded the capital needed for new entrepreneurial healthcare ventures he has started up with family members. Brayda described the joint venture as "a very satisfactory experience for Medipass, with great potential for growth in the areas of oncology diagnostic imaging and therapy and a virtuous impact on the population." The collaboration with Clearview provided a learning opportunity for Medipass in considering potential business in other emerging markets. "The high clinical and technical levels of the Indian health service contributed to enriching the corporate know-how of Medipass so that we now feel ready to address some of the health markets of countries in the Middle East and South Asia," said Brayda. Baliyan is confident that Medipass' ownership of the business will continue to uphold its inherent social mission. His business plan has demonstrated that serving low income communities is no barrier to a return on investment when delivered at scale and low-cost base.

CASE STUDY: PEARSON AFFORDABLE LEARNING FUND

Pearson PLC is one of the world's largest education companies. Founded in 1844 and headquartered in London, the company has been strategically focused on global education since 2015. In 2016, it organised into a single coursework product organisation. The company's sales revenue of £4.78 billion (US$6.66 billion) in

2015 was derived from three markets: North America (its largest market, accounting for 62 percent of sales), "Core" including the United Kingdom, Italy and Australia (17.5 percent), and "Growth" including Brazil, China, India and South Africa (14.5 percent). As a founder signatory of the UN Global Compact, Pearson has committed to a responsible supply chain on over £2 billion (US$2.9 billion) of goods and services purchased annually. The Pearson Charitable Foundation had been the avenue for the company's philanthropy, but following a major business review in 2014, funding of the foundation ceased and the charity wound down its operations. In 2014 the company announced that its major commitment to community investment would be implemented through Project Literacy, a five-year anchor social impact campaign to improve literacy globally. Pearson's 2014 Annual Report states, "Key to our social innovation approach is our belief that commercial solutions can accelerate access to quality education. Uncovering, developing and scaling solutions, especially in places where education standards fall well behind the best in the world, can require us to challenge the way we think about our business." In 2012 the company launched the Pearson Affordable Learning Fund with US$15 million of capital to explore novel educational innovations with commercial potential. In 2015 a further US$50 million was injected into this corporate venture capital fund focused on "education for students from the poorest and most marginalised families." PALF has invested in education start-ups in South Africa, Ghana, India and the Philippines. Half of the fund is currently invested in companies with female founders.

Arvind Nagarajan is investment director for PALF based in New York City. He identifies two key individuals whose thought leadership led to the creation of PALF. Sir Michael Barber was head of the education practice at management consultants McKinsey with experience of education policy and reform in developing countries. Professor C. K. Prahalad, the Indian academic and author of *The Fortune at the Bottom of the Pyramid,* sat on Pearson's board before his death in 2010.

Prahalad's insights inspired Pearson and many other companies to find profits and growth by serving the world's five billion poorest people. When Barber joined Pearson in 2011, he and colleague, Katelyn Donnelly, spearheaded the creation of PALF, drawing on their experience of delivering radical education reform in the Punjab, Pakistan. "We worked with the Punjab government to focus on improving educational outcomes amongst the 70 percent of students who attended small, private schools, and learnt that such schools can potentially be a real solution for governments to overcome enormous educational challenges," said Donnelly.

Punjab now runs the largest school voucher system in the world with 1.5 million learners placed into the school system where "vouchers cost government one-third the price per pupil in a state school yet learning outcomes as much as doubled. In creating PALF we were responding to the fact that low-cost private schools meet parent demand. We believed that chains of private schools could benefit from economies of scale and global best practice in proven educational methods," Donnelly said.

Nagarajan views PALF "as like a venture capital fund with a seven- to 10-year investment horizon, backing products, services or schools that 'deliver efficacy' or measurable outcomes in the lives of learners. We want the fund to reach more than a million learners during this time horizon." And pragmatically, Nagarajan wants the fund to help move beyond "ideological debate" about public and private education to "transforming how emerging markets see the role of private players in delivering a quality education for all citizens." By early 2016 PALF has invested in a portfolio of 11 educational ventures in Africa and Asia (see Table 1 for the list of Asia-based investments). As with any venture capital fund, a healthy pipeline of potential investments is essential. Nagarajan said, "PALF identifies investment opportunities in three ways. First, by on the ground meetings with entrepreneurs, angels and other investors. Second, at ecosystem building events like accelerators, summits, one-day events that we convene or do so in partnership with other funds like Village Capital or Omidyar Network. And third, by referrals through our networks."

The selection of shortlisted businesses takes place in Pearson's investment committee composed of several of the company's senior executives, including the CEO, Chief Education Advisor, and heads of growth markets, corporate affairs, finance and legal. "Due diligence focuses on three areas: 'profitability' to catalyse the sector more broadly; 'efficacy' evidenced by data that demonstrates the journey of improvement; and 'reach' giving low income learners access to quality education," said Nagarajan.

Table 1. PALF portfolio investments in Asia

Venture	Country	Description
APEC Schools	Philippines	Affordable secondary schools focusing on employment readiness. A joint venture with Ayala Corporation.
Karadi Path	India	Language learning.
Zaya	India	An adaptive learning product delivering digital content.
Experifun	India	Low-cost interactive science learning products.
Sudiksha	India	Affordable pre-schools.
Avanti	India	Science and mathematics education for college entrance.

Once the investment decision is made, PALF becomes an active investor, taking a board seat and a "substantive double-digit" minority equity stake in the venture. "We spend time on the ground," said Nagarajan, "offering both operational support and a thought partner for strategic decisions and governance." While "closeness to the investee" is a key value for PALF, it poses a challenge for global team members who are constantly on the road supporting the entrepreneurs they back and keeping the pipeline of potential ventures healthy. Pearson PLC is a large company and there are sometimes opportunities for local staff to support PALF portfolio companies by mentoring or taking a board seat. In South Africa the CEO of Pearson South Africa sat on the board of a PALF investee business.

At the time of writing, PALF had not yet exited from an investment. Nagarajan believes exit strategies will vary from one business and context to another. "We envisage some will be acquired by specialist education companies; in India there is an active private equity space looking for growth companies. But, we don't want to over-define the end game too early on," he said.

One of PALF's Indian investments is Sudiksha, an educational business located in Hyderabad. Sudiksha was started up in 2010/2011 by entrepreneurs who wanted to offer a high quality, affordable pre-school service to low-income families for just US$8 a month per child. There are now 23 schools in the Hyderabad area, of which six are franchisees. Most are already operationally breaking even at the school level. The founders relied on their own financing at start up, followed by angel investment (John, 2015, p. 36). Within two years, Sudiksha had attracted investment from two U.S.-based impact investment funds.

The PALF team identified Sudiksha as an investment not through the typical sourcing routes but through an accelerator programme held in India over a three-month period in partnership with Village Capital. Twelve teams from across India attended intensive training on weekends ending with a review of each other's business model and peer selection of three winning ventures. Sudiksha was chosen and received a grant from PALF and Village Capital, eventually joining the PALF portfolio as an equity investment.

Sudiksha is PALF's first investment in the early childhood sector which Nagarajan said, "has huge potential from an educational point of view while the brain is still developing - we liked that the Sudiksha model was very affordable, utilised female entrepreneurs, and had strong community buy-in." PALF views these as a strong foundation for long-term success despite the financial challenge of early years schooling being a service for which people are less willing to pay. "Despite it being a tough area financially, we are keen that Sudiksha gets on top of the unit economics to find a model that can be successfully scaled," he added.

While half of PALF's current portfolio is in India, it is looking to expand over time into other parts of Asia, including Southeast Asia and China. In the meantime, PALF is building its brand in India and Nagarajan sees the "vocational space in India [as] a huge opportunity with a rising population of workers, but under educated and underutilised. The upskilling of these many is a once-in-a-generation opportunity for the country." Donnelly says, "Being close to the portfolio companies and working with them day in day out means we can feed learning back throughout the company. Investing in an early-stage company helps Pearson understand the risks of operating a sustainable business in that environment and is a cost-effective way for us to be exposed to new markets."

BUSINESS PROCESS OUTSOURCING

The previous section on corporate venture capital describes an *investor* relationship with a social enterprise – the corporation or its foundation offers funds to the social enterprise to seek a return on that investment that is purely social (philanthropy) or blends social and financial return (venture capital for impact). An alternative relationship is that of *client* – when a corporation purchases goods or services from a social enterprise. This is a potentially important development for the social enterprise sector in its attempt to become mainstream and compete openly with traditional business for customers among corporate clientele.

For supply chain managers who are sourcing goods or business processes from outside their company, there is seldom any incentive to consider social enterprises as potential suppliers. Social enterprises seldom have the track record or profile of their traditional competitors and are likely to be prejudicially viewed as risky or unreliable. For corporations that are already sensitised to social enterprises through, for example, their CSR programmes, there is potential to enter into a purchasing relationship.

In 2016, Social Enterprise UK launched the *Buy Social Corporate Challenge* as part of which a group of well-known corporations agreed to contact social enterprises for goods and services to the amount of £1 billion (US$1.3 billion) by 2020. The founding corporate partners are Interserve, Johnson & Johnson, PwC, RBS Group, Santander, Wates, and Zurich, but the plan was to draw in many other businesses across diverse sectors to open their supply chains to the 70,000 social enterprises in the United Kingdom.

Social Enterprise UK offers the following support to participating corporations to help them overcome barriers to sourcing from social enterprises:

- A review of supply chain and benchmarking existing social enterprise spend.
- Training for procurement teams.
- Brokerage support.
- Advice and support on how to measure the impact of outsource spending with social enterprises, and how to use this in sustainability reporting/bid writing.

Among the benefits accruing to companies outsourcing to social enterprises include “the opportunity to be a force for good in the communities in which they operate” and a means to “meet their supplier diversity aims” with social enterprises that “bring with them innovation and creativity,” argues this British initiative.

In Singapore, Bizlink, provides training for people with disabilities. Originally an initiative within a government ministry, Bizlink is now an independent non-profit organisation with a wholly-owned social enterprise division. The enterprise utilises a roster of individuals with disabilities to offer business services, including data entry, cleaning and order fulfilment, to corporate clients. One of these clients is DBS, a major banking group that integrates its banking services and corporate philanthropy in support of social enterprises. Corporate purchasing departments that have a prior understanding of social enterprises, such as DBS, are more likely to consider them as potential vendors and outsourcing partners. A survey in 2013 by Singapore’s Social Enterprise Association found that 66 percent of purchasing managers were not yet prepared to purchase services from social enterprises either because of a lack of familiarity with their business models or because social enterprises could not yet offer what clients required.

Hong Kong Broadband Network is the island’s largest supplier of residential high-speed fibre broadband and is experimenting with outsourcing some of its business processes to social enterprises. A publicly owned company since 2015, it retains a strong entrepreneurial culture and has made the support of social enterprise the primary theme of its corporate social investment. HKBN’s strategy for supporting social enterprise is guided by the *MOVE* programme – marketing social mission, outsourcing business activities, skills-based volunteering, and ethical consumption. Since 2014 the technology company has started to experiment with outsourcing business processes as a means to reach its social investment objectives as illustrated in the following case study.

The purchasing power of corporations and the desire of many to find new and creative ways to support social enterprises make outsourcing an attractive opportunity. For social enterprises that are well managed and able to offer services in a competitive environment, there is no reason for such outsourcing to involve any sacrifice in quality. Campaigns like *Buy Social Corporate Challenge* in the United Kingdom, if run in Asia and targeted not only at CSR executives but also purchasing managers, would help raise awareness of the potential to outsource corporate business processes to social enterprises. This outsourcing could help position social enterprises as real businesses in corporate supply chains and establish them as vendors rather than grantees.

CASE STUDY: HONG KONG BROADBAND NETWORK

Hong Kong Broadband Network (HKBN) was established in 1999 out of the former City Telecom and grew rapidly to be the largest supplier of fibre high-speed residential broadband in Hong Kong SAR. The private equity fund CVC Capital Partners bought the company in 2012, leading to a broadly based management buyout later that year when 63 manager/co-owners acquired 14 percent of the firm's equity. HKBN retains a relatively flat management structure and articulates its core purpose as *Make our Hong Kong a Better Place to Live.* The company's entrepreneurial style guided its commitment to what it calls 'corporate social investment' – the framework for the company's strategic support for Hong Kong's social enterprise sector. "A few years back we had a long list of quite diverse projects and volunteering," says Director of Talent Engagement and Corporate Social Investment (CSI) and Co-Owner Ivy Lau. "But when we heard about social enterprise it was a light-bulb moment for us – we knew this is where we should focus our resources in corporate social investment."

Since 2014, HKBN has channelled this commitment to social enterprise through the MOVE programme – Marketing social mission, Outsourcing business activities, skills-based Volunteering, and Ethical consumption. HKBN's outsourcing of a customer service call centre and in-house catering to social enterprises marked the move from a sponsorship model towards a business-based relationship with social enterprises.

HKBN's customer service helplines have long been offshored to neighbouring Guangzhou on mainland China in line with common industry practice. Since February 2014 the social enterprise iEnterprise has augmented the company's 1083 telephone customer enquiry service. iEnterprise was founded in 2012 as a privately owned work integration social enterprise to create employment opportunities for people with disabilities. Out of principle it did not seek government subsidy or donations but relied on private share capital and a sustainable, commercially minded business model. The enterprise tested an e-commerce consumer model for the sale of floristry products to the public. With a modest capital base of only HK$40,000 (US$5,000), iEnterprise initiated a call centre with 13 employees with physical or mental disabilities or other employability challenges. The operation reached breakeven after three months and generated a profit of HK$2,000 after six months although the business did benefit from hidden subsidies such as free technology services provided by HKBN that lowered its costs. To improve the telephone skills of iEnterprise call handlers, HKBN's Talent Development Department provided free training and guidance. Lau said that "around half of the calls to 1083 are handled by iEnterprise, and all performance targets for this service have been met." She is adamant that contracting out to a social enterprise does not compromise the quality of helpline services even though its staff members are offered flexible working hours to best cater to their needs. Employee surveys before and after six months of employment revealed a significant improvement in overall well-being, financial capability and self image (Lam, 2013).

The positive experience of outsourcing call centre activity to a social enterprise encouraged the HKBN team to nominate other potential opportunities. This led to the awarding of the contract for in-house catering at HKBN's office to Hong Kong Joyking Enterprise, which employs the hearing-impaired, semi-retired and the long-term unemployed. Broadband Delight, the in-house canteen, sources the majority of its supplies responsibly and works with HKBN on ethical consumption – one of the components of the firm's MOVE programme.

The second platform for supporting social enterprise is skills-based volunteering. Knowledge Volunteers for the Community initially recruited 40 volunteers from HKBN's top and middle management who are placed into social enterprises to offer business advice and coaching to social enterprises over a six-month period.

In its second year the programme has been opened to a wider mix of company staff, including many at more junior levels. Teams of three to four staff drawn from a variety of departments offer practical advice and coaching on presentational skills. HKBN staff typically volunteer four hours of their time a month. Lau believes that social enterprises are not the only ones to benefit, suggesting that "the engagement with social enterprises enhances staff creativity and is a team-building exercise."

Elinor Shiu, associate director for marketing and a co-owner, was a part of a three-person team advising the environmental enterprise, HK Recycles. Through her experience, she found that topics such as finance, sales & marketing, operations and logistics gave her the "opportunity to further consolidate the learning from my EMBA and take it to the next level."

Each volunteering assignment begins with the HKBN staff and the social enterprise agreeing on quantifiable targets for six months with progress being regularly monitored. Feedback from early trials of the programme resulted in volunteers being selected for best fit rather than self nominating.

By its third year, the Knowledge Volunteers for the Community Programme has extended to offer assistance to both social enterprises and non-profit organisations. Apart from the inaugural model of providing business guidance and sharing experience with social enterprises through the course of each six- to 12-month phase, HKBN also welcomes project-based requests that directly address specific needs identified by the organisations.

HKBN seeks multiple opportunities for supporting social enterprises, either directly through outsourcing and volunteer engagement, or indirectly by promoting the concept of social enterprise amongst its customers.

Corporations and Social Enterprises Create Social Value Together

Our case studies from Singapore, India and Hong Kong, summarised in Table 2, serve to illustrate that corporate philanthropy can add a value to social enterprises that is beyond a transactional, traditional, grantmaking model. Singtel supports the incubation of early stage social enterprises by directly managing its own accelerator programme to provide grants and the leveraged business skills of its workforce. Investors in India's largest angel network, with a track record of investing in purely commercial deals are now migrating into the space where investment by individual and corporate members seeks to create sustainable social and financial value. Pearson and Medipass are businesses that deploy the tools of corporate venture capital to build their own capacity to offer new products and enter new markets by investing in social enterprises. Purchasing managers, like those at Hong Kong Broadband Network, accept that social enterprises are potential outsourcing contractors that are competitive and align with the company's corporate philanthropy strategy and values. In all of the case studies the corporate brings financial resources coupled to non-financial advisory services that adds value to their investment. Engaging a company's employees to provide skilled volunteering to social enterprises can enhance professional development and give team building opportunities, as we saw with HKBN. The case studies may be harbingers of a broader movement away from passive, transactional corporate philanthropy towards the engaged, relational co-creation of social value.

Table 2. Comparison of case studies

	Singtel Futuremakers	IAN Impact	Clearmedi Healthcare	Pearson Affordable Learning Fund	Hong Kong Broadband Network
Country	Singapore & Australia	India.	India	India & Philippines	Hong Kong
Case Type	Accelerator	Angel investing.	Corporate venture capital.	Corporate venture capital.	Business process outsourcing.
Organisation Type	Social enterprise; non-profit (charity).	Social enterprise; business with social objectives.	Business with social objectives.	Business with social objectives.	Social enterprise.
Organisation Stage	Ideation; early stage.	Early stage.	Mid stage with commercial growth potential..	Mid stage with commercial growth potential.	Mid stage.
Social impact area	Multiple social areas with focus on technology solutions.	Multiple social areas with focus on enterprises serving customers at the base of the economic pyramid.	Affordable healthcare diagnostics.	Affordable education.	Inclusive employment for adults with learning and physical disabilities, and long term unemployed.
Finance instrument	Grant	Equity	Equity	Equity	Fee for service.
Non-financial services - format	Workshops and regular coaching.	Regular advice at board and operational levels; plus, a structured incubation programme.	Regular advice at board and operational levels.	Regular advice at board and operational levels.	Ad hoc; separate programmes for staff volunteering with social enterprises and community organisations.
Non-financial services - supplier	Company volunteer employees; external consultants.	Individual angel investors; external consultants.	Company executives.	Fund executives and external consultants.	Company staff.
Outcome for corporation	Staff volunteering; visible community engagement.	Potential return on investment; visible community engagement.	Entry into a new geographic market; potential return on investment.	Develop new affordable products; intelligence on geographic sectors of strategic importance.	Fulfilment of business processes; staff volunteering; staff creativity and team building
Outcome for social enterprise/non-profit	Grant funding; professional advice and mentoring; recognition and visibility.	Investment with hands-on professional advice and coaching; leading to business expansion.	Investment and joint venture leading to service development, scale up and potential exit for founders.	Investment leading to service development, scale up and potential exit for founders..	Fee based income route to sustainability and growth leading to increased social impact.

REFERENCES

Abzug, R., & Webb, N. J. (1996). Rational and extra-rational motivations for corporate giving: Complementing economic theory with organization science. *New York Law School Law Review. New York Law School, 41*, 1035.

Baird, R., Bowles, L., & Lall, S. (2013). *Bridging the pioneer gap: The role for accelerators in launching high-impact enterprises. Innovations, 8(3/4).*

Carroll, A. B. (1979). A three-dimensional conceptual model of corporate performance. *Academy of Management Review*, *4*(4), 497–505. doi:10.5465/amr.1979.4498296

Cohen, S. (2013). *What do accelerators do? Insights from incubators and angels. Innovations, 8(3/4).*

Dushnitsky, G., & Lenox, M. J. (2005). When do incumbents learn from entrepreneurial ventures? *Research Policy*, *34*(5), 615–639. doi:10.1016/j.respol.2005.01.017

EVPA. (2019). *Policy Brief. Incubators and Accelerators: Bridging the Gap for New Impact Ventures in Europe.* Accessed 20th March 2020 at https://evpa.eu.com/knowledge-centre/publications/incubators-and-accelerators-bridging-the-gap-for-new-impact-ventures-in-europe

Gautier, A., & Pache, A.-C. (2015). Research on corporate philanthropy: A review and assessment. *Journal of Business Ethics*, *126*(3), 343–369. doi:10.100710551-013-1969-7

Hackett, S., & Dilts, D. M. (2004). A systematic review of business incubation research. *The Journal of Technology Transfer*, *29*(1), 55–82. doi:10.1023/B:JOTT.0000011181.11952.0f

Jensen, M. C., & Meckling, W. H. (1976). Theory of the firm: Managerial behavior, agency costs and ownership structure. *Journal of Financial Economics*, *3*(4), 305–360. doi:10.1016/0304-405X(76)90026-X

John, R. (2015). *Asia's impact angels: How business angel investing can support social enterprises in Asia.* Entrepreneurial social finance in Asia: Working paper no. 4. Singapore: Asia Centre for Social Entrepreneurship & Philanthropy, NUS Business School.

John, R., Chia, A., & Ito, K. (2017). *Corporate Philanthropy in Asia.* Entrepreneurial social finance in Asia: Working paper no. 5. Singapore: Asia Centre for Social Entrepreneurship & Philanthropy, NUS Business School.

Lam, I. (2013). *Social Enterprise: Mission Analysis and Practice of Value Creation*. Dissertation of Doctor of Business Administration, United Business Institute (UBI), Belgium.

Martin, M. (2014). *Driving innovation through corporate impact venturing: A primer on business transformation*. Impact Economy Primer Series, Vol. 3. The Italian language version can be downloaded for free at https://www.impacteconomy.com/en/primer3.php

Menzies, G., Simpson, T., Hay, D., & Vines, D. (2019). Restoring Trust in Finance: From Principal–Agent to Principled Agent. *The Economic Record*, *95*(311), 497–509. doi:10.1111/1475-4932.12494

Monitor Deloitte. (2015). *Accelerating impact: Exploring best practices, challenges and innovations in impact enterprise acceleration*. New York, NY: Rockefeller Foundation. Retrieved September 21, 2016, from https://www.rockefellerfoundation.org/report/accelerating-impact-exploring-best-practices-challenges-and-innovations-in-impact-enterprise-acceleration/

Patrinos, H. A., & Sosale, S. (Eds.). (2007). *Mobilizing the private sector for public education. A view from the trenches*. World Bank. doi:10.1596/978-0-8213-7199-2

Volans. (2014). *Investing in breakthrough: Corporate venture capital*. Retrieved March 7, 2016, from http://volans.com/project/investing-in-breakthrough-corporate-venture-capital/

Chapter 4
Policies for Science, Technology, and Innovation:
A Case Study of Transitional China

Li He
City University of Hong Kong, China

Xukun Zhang
Shenzhen Research Institute, City University of Hong Kong, China

ABSTRACT

Although there is plenty of research in the science, technology, and innovation (STI) policy studies, the trend and process of government regulations in a transition economy is underexplored. Empirical data such as central government laws, regulations, and policies for STI are collected from 1978 to 2018. Qualitative analysis software is adopted to facilitate the documentary analysis process. After a temporal examination of the government policies, the authors unearthed four stages in the evolution of STI policy: recovery and reconstruction of science and technology, transformation and market-led science and technology development, adjustment and innovation of science and technology, and promotion of science and technology and development of independent innovation. They found that the policy system has gradually changed and improved in continuous exploration and practice. First, the focus of the national policies has changed from science and technology to innovation. Second, the regulations are closely relevant to the political economy environment and central objectives.

DOI: 10.4018/978-1-7998-4195-1.ch004

Copyright © 2021, IGI Global. Copying or distributing in print or electronic forms without written permission of IGI Global is prohibited.

INTRODUCTION

China, with other emerging economies, are playing an increasingly vital role in global innovation, as they move from imitating technology to producing genuine innovation. Ever since opening up to foreign trade and investment and implementing market reforms in 1979, innovation has been listed as a priority in the country's agenda. In recent years, the country, as a key global player, issued several high-profile initiatives, such as "Made in China 2025" to upgrade and modernize its manufacturing to earn a place in the global market. Therefore, China offers a fertile setting to scrutinize this issue. Against this backdrop, this purpose of this chapter is to evaluate the progress and trends of the central government's science, technology, and innovation (STI) policy in China. It is found that this kind of case-specific and context-specific analysis can provide strong and rich insights for this issue Through a historical examination of government rules and regulations, we identify critical junctures in the evolution of STI policy. To be specific, we aim to explain patterns and underlying logic in government policies, as well as the role of the state in promoting and boosting innovation policies.

Although there is plenty of research in the STI policy literature, the evolution of government policies in a transition economy is underexplored. Putting research on innovation in China into a global perspective, this chapter sheds light on what and how other emerging and developing economies can learn from the Chinese experience, and how China's rise to a significant player in the field of global innovation implies for other developing countries' innovation and industrial policies.

The rest of chapter is balanced as follows: section 2 provides an overview of extant pieces of literatures of STI policy studies from several perspectives; section 4 analysis the development and trends of Chinese STI policies; and identified its critical junctures; section 5 focus on the underlying mechanism behind the adjustments and trends; section 6 state the concluding remarks.

LITERATURE REVIEW

The field of science policy and innovation studies began in the 1950s (Martin, 2012). The earliest research in this field covering diverse disciplines including economics (Solow, 1954), sociology (Coleman et al., 1957; 1966); management (Woodward, 1958); organizational studies (Burns and Stalker, 1961); political science (Walker, 1969), and psychology (Pelz and Andrews, 1966). Since the 1970s and 1980s, there was a substantial surge in the pond dedicated to the study of the STI system itself, especially in the United States and the United Kingdom.

Although plenty of research has been done in the innovation field, its policy studies are at a crossroads (Flanagan and Uyarra, 2016; Morlacchi and Martin, 2009). STI policy research can be defined as the application of social science to the study of policy for STI (Morlacchi and Martin, 2009). Over the years, STI researchers have developed several methodological tools for empirical research. Some scholars are focusing on the definition and measurement of the STI system, as it is continuously and rapidly evolving. For instance, Wu (2007; 2010) reviewed and compared the definitions of science policy, technology policy and innovation policy. Therefore, Freeman and Soete (2009) examined the commonly used indicators to measure STI. They caution that scholars must update these indicators, because some of them are significant in the last century, and may not be so relevant today. The selection of indicators may even be misleading. Moreover, Fan et al. (2012) reviewed the literature on the definitions, classifications, evolutions, evaluations of innovation policies in China and other countries, and concluded that till 2012 there was lack of research (especially empirical research) on the quality of innovation policy and its effect on performance of such policy, the coordination mechanisms of innovation policies, and simulation studies of innovation policies.

Governments, in all countries, are responsible for policy formulation and implementation. Existing studies argue that the government can both act as a facilitator and become a barrier. On the one hand, the government intervenes in scientific research and increases research and development (R&D) investment are considered as the strong support for realizing revival of science and technology in the history of some developed countries such as the U.S., South Korea, Japan, etc. (Chen and Gan, 1997; Deng and Zhang, 2000; Li, 2009; Li and Li, 2009; Liu et al., 2013; Liu, 2014). With power and adequate information and resources, the government can provide proper environment and enough funding for conducting research and developing science and technology, which is quite crucial for small and medium-sized enterprises (SME) (Liu et al., 2013). Besides, the government and its relevant policies are the guidance or even guarantee of basic research, which is the foundation of both innovation and application of high and frontier technology (Fang, 1989; Deng and Zhang, 2000; Ru and Su, 2010). On the other hand, various small and developing countries across the world have shared some obstacles. Some common barriers for the design and the implementation of the policies are summarized as: shortage of funding; lack of long-term planning and constant implementation; lack of higher-level political support and coordination between various departments; failure to monitor and evaluate the policy implementation; weak demand of the private sector for new policies and complex products and services; weak education system and information infrastructure (Aubert, 2004; Hadjimanolis and Dickson, 2001; Lall and Pietrobelli, 2005; Luthria, 2002; Padilla-Pérez and Gaudin, 2013; World Bank, 2010;). Furthermore, in China, some issues such as insufficient independent innovation capacity of enterprises, inefficient transformation of science and technology achievements, misallocation of science and technology resources, and defects in property rights structure also existed (Hu, 2009).

During the past decade, global policymakers have recognized the central importance of STI for inclusive social development and sustainable economic growth. In practice, some countries have established government institutions, research institutions, and public organizations to promote STI development. Therefore, scholars began to focus on the policy formulation and implementation and the development of STI policies system. Padilla-Pérez and Gaudin (2013) studied the STI policies in six Central American countries, including Nicaragua, Panama, Honduras, Costa Rica, El Salvador, and Guatemala. They found that although a variety of government regulations have been enacted and implemented to support STI, there lack valid technological-capability indicators to illustrate the results. Zhang and Chen (2013) analyzed the convergence trend of science and technology policy in eleven countries with relatively high innovation capacity and emphasized the roles of R&D investment, overseas talents, international cooperation and the combination of production, study and research, which are also summarized in other related research (Xu, 2005; Zhou, 2010; Liu et al., 2013). Amankwah-Amoah (2016) uncovered three development stages based on a sequential model in Ghana. At the same time, the newly industrializing states and emerging economies in the Asia Pacific region have also attracted the attention of the academic community. Some scholars have attributed the greater success to governmental ability to formulate practical STI policies and foster innovation (Aghion et al., 2009; Dodgson, 2000a, 2000b; Vitta, 1990).

Studies on China as an emerging economy started to blossom in the last decade. Wu and Li (1998) reviewed the evolution of STI policies from the planned economy to marketization and innovation across three phases (the 1980s, the 1990s, and after 1995). Liu and Sun (2007) found that most innovation policies were science and technology policies by classified 289 innovation policies in 1980-2005 and divided this period into three phases: 1980-1984, 1985-1994 and 1995-2005 according to the number of innovation policy. Peng et al. (2008) quantified power and potential effects of 423 STI policies based on their forms and goals. They revealed that in 1979-1992 the number and power of policy were both less and weaker than those in 1993-2006, while in 1993-2006 more emphases were put on innovation than previous period. Hu (2009) compared the aims and objectives of national-level science and technology policies of China among three periods, 1978-1985 for reconstruction, 1985-1993 for marketization, and after 1993 for innovation. Sun and Du (2010) proposed that since 1949 China's national innovation system (NIS) had experienced two significant periods of development. The year 1978 is a watershed, before 1978, with state as the driving force and the planned economy as background; while after 1978 the NIS focused on promoting technology transfer in the 1980s and then shifted to innovation. This is similar to the findings of Suttmeier (2002). Huang et al. (2015) employed co-word analysis and cluster analysis to examine the change of the focus of STI policies on the basis of 4707 policy documents, and proposed that the policies had changed significantly in terms of human resource, structural reform, international cooperation and research development throughout the initial stage (1949-1977), the recovery stage (1978-1984), the reform stage (1985-1994), the stage of deepening reform (1995-2005), and the stage of strategic development (2006-2010). Such a phase division was supported by Li and Li (2009) through reviewing the dynamic of STI policy. Cao and Yuan (2019) defined four stages of the policy development based on the contents and goals of the STI policies in 1949-2019, whose evolution presented the distinctive characteristics of switching from serving politics and military to serving economic development. Zhang (2019) divided the evolution of STI policies into reconstruction stage (1978-1985), systematic development stage (1986-1994), adjustment stage (1995-2005), and promotion stage (2006-2018), with the shifts from a single instruction to the multiple policy set together with economic and talent policies, from government-led to the combination of government-led and market-regulation, and from imitation to integrated innovation and independent innovation. In addition, Cheng (2008) uncovered three phases of the central-level STI strategy and policy of international cooperation, with the characteristics of recovery, all-round development, and win-win development respectively. From the perspective of the policy for the transformation of scientific and technological achievements, Du and Zhang (2018) revealed the three stages of development, and Zhang et al. (2016) examined the process and characteristics of policy diffusion in terms of quantitative analysis of documents.

Another stream of literature focusing on the evaluation and analyses of the performance and effects of the STI policies in China. After referring to the index measuring the legal change first conducted by Gray (1978) and constructing the indicators reflecting the power of policy, Peng et al. (2008) concluded that the national STI policies, especially the policy goal of absorbing STI could significantly improve both technical performance and economic performance based on Cobb-Douglas production function and the regression results. Cheng and Qian (2013) adopted similar models and 454 policies with relevant panel data in 2000-2009 revealed that the power of policy had a significant impact on the technological performance but not on the economic performance, while the instability of policy had a negative effect. Furthermore, the supply policy affects the technological performance more importantly, and environmental policy has a lagged positive effect on the technological and economic performance, and the demand policy is highly influenced on the economic performance. Such models and analyses on the power and goals of STI policies are also employed in other research (Sun et al.,

2007; Xiao et al., 2009). Moreover, Tan and Tong (2004) introduced the evaluation system of scientific plans applied in Korea employing the methods such as peer review, survey, cost-benefit method, and case study for different purposes and types of research and development.

METHODOLOGY

Empirical data are derived from the government website, news reports and other online websites. National-level policies for STI are collected from 1978 to 2018. Documentary analysis has been widely used in the policy analysis (Shaw et al., 2004). It has advantages in terms of less time-consuming, less costly and availability (Bowen, 2009). Moreover, documents are usually unobtrusive' and 'non-reactive. We use qualitative data analysis software NVivo 12 to facilitate data analysis. Considering the dynamic of characteristics and focuses of the policies (Peng, 2006) and referring to four milestones of the development STI policy summarized by Liu (2008) as the recovery from the National Conference on Science, the structural reform starting from releasing *the Decision on the Reform of Science and Technology System,* the Strategy of Developing the Country through Science and Education, and independent innovation highlighted in *the Decision on Implementing the Planning of Science and Technology and Enhancing the Independent Innovation.* All the themes were collected and coded for explanation and interpretation.

THE DEVELOPMENT OF POLICIES FOR SCIENCE, TECHNOLOGY AND INNOVATION IN CHINA

To evaluate the progress and trends of STI policy issued by the central government in China, this chapter first collects the national-level policies relevant to STI from 1978 to 2018. The national-level policies include laws, regulations, plans, decisions, and other documents. Then, this chapter divides the development stages into four phases based on their patterns and themes. Different from previous studies (Wu and Li, 1998; Liu and Sun, 2007; Peng et al., 2008; Hu, 2009; Sun and Du, 2010; Huang et al., 2015; Cao and Yuan, 2019; Zhang, 2019), we divide the national-level policies for STI into four phases: recovery and reconstruction stage, competition and transformation stage, adjustment and innovation stage, and promotion stage.

Phase 1: Recovery and Reconstruction of Science and Technology, 1978-1984

After the ending of the Cultural Revolution, a relatively stable and united political situation has recovered in China together with the resumption of the College Entrance Examination in the late 1970s. As a milestone in the science development history of China, the National Conference on Science was held in Beijing in 1978, with the aim to restore the respect of intellectuals, adjust the strategy of science and technology development, and initiate the reform of relevant system. At this conference, 'Science and technology are the primary productive forces' (*kexue jishu shi diyi shengchanli*) was declared by the then Vice Premier Xiaoping Deng. This motto has been praised as the fundamental theoretical and ideological basis for the formulation of science and technology development strategy in the new era of China. Moreover, with the emphasis on the crucial role of science and technology in economic growth and realizing the so-called "four modernizations" (including modernization of agriculture, modernization of industry, modernization of national defense and science, and modernization of technology), the conference has proposed and enacted the '1978-1985 National Plan for Science and Technology Development'. After that, scientific and technological development and innovation activities in China have boomed to revitalize the national economy. In the nationwide, innovation in the scientific and technological field has become a consensus.

To achieve national planning, the Chinese government has consecutively implemented several significant scientific and technological planning, industrial planning, and national-level regulations. Those include macro planning such as *the National Technological Transformation Plan, the National Key Scientific and Technological Research Plan* (the most prominent national science and technology plan in the 20th century), *the National Key Technological Development Project Plan, the National Key Laboratory Construction Plan, the National Key Industrial Test Plan,* and *the Major Technical Equipment Development Plan,* and formal regulations and law such as *the Regulations on Awards for Inventions, the Regulations on Awards for Natural Science, the Regulations on Awards for Technology Improvement* (which was revised in 1986), and *the Patent Law.*

In general, after the ten-year Cultural Revolution, China's economic growth has been severely hindered. Moreover, the role of science and technology has been questioned and criticized, and scientific research institutions, experimental bases, technical facilities, and data have been severely damaged. Thus, during this period, there were abundant science and technology policies and plans, which restored the development of not only science and technology but also industrial, technological innovation to a certain extent. In contrast, the policies for innovation were relatively few.

Phase 2: Transformation and the Market-Led Development of Science and Technology, 1985-1991

The planned economy has its own structural loopholes; one prominent issue is the staff in each research institution seldom communicate with others, which leads to the duplications in the research projects, the low conversion rate of research results, inefficiency of scientific research, and waste of scientific research funds. To improve efficiency and better development, the government considered introducing economic leverage and the market mechanism. Therefore, the government proposed *the Decision on the Reform of Science and Technology System* in the mid-1980s. This regulation includes the reform of science and technology appropriation system, the policy of science and technology personnel management, the policy of basic scientific research, the policy of exploring the technology market, and the policy of enhancing the transformation of technological achievements. Then, the State Council promulgated *the Provisions on Further Promoting the Reform of the Science and Technology system* and *the Decision on Deepening the Reform of the Science and Technology system* in 1987 and 1988 respectively, to streamline the research institutions and encourage them to focus on economic development.

The focus of policies and regulations is shifted to promoting the macro-structural reform for science and technology development. To be specific, as the supporting policies of science and technology system reform, STI plans played an increasingly crucial role both in this phase and in the whole development history. The principal regulations in this period include *the National Science and Technology Research Plan, the National Major Science and Engineering Plan, the National Research and Development Plan of High Technology (i.e., 863 Program), the National Key Projects on Basic and Applied Research (i.e., Pandeng Program), the National Technology Innovation Project Plan,* and *the Plan of Promoting Rural Economic Development through Science and Technology (i.e., Spark Program), the Guiding Plan of China's High and New Technology Industry (i.e., Torch Program)*, and the formulation and implementation of a series of plans above were accompanied by and also guided the reform of the science and technology system. Furthermore, *the Technical Contract Law* has clearly defined the basic norms and guidelines for technology development and trading in 1987, which was implemented with *the Measures for the Achievements Appraisal of Science and Technology* for further regulation and better development of the technology market in China.

In this phase, the national-level policies for STI have also adjusted. We summarized six trends: from planned economy to market economy, or commodity-market economy; from government-led development to enterprise-led development; from the construction of science and technology system to the reform of science and technology system, from serving production and national defense construction to serving economic development; from promoting national prestige to enhancing national economic level; from safeguarding national security to improving people's quality of life.

Phase 3: Adjustment and Innovation of Science and Technology, 1992-2005

Before 1992, a series of national science and technology plans were designed for scientific research projects, which have largely promoted the competition and development of STI but seemed a little isolated. After 1992, the central government began to provide auxiliary policies including industrial policies, fiscal policies, supportive policies for enterprises, talent cultivation programs to support the science, technology and innovation development. The next development phase is from establishing the goal of the structural reform in 1992 to releasing *the Decision on Implementing the Planning of Science and Technology and Enhancing the Independent Innovation* in 2006. This period can be briefly summarized as the strategic stage of driving economic development via science and education. Some scholars believe that the primary trend of China's science, technology and innovation policies in this phase is to implement the national-level Strategy of Developing the Country through Science and Education and strengthen the national innovation system construction (Fang, 2007; Cao and Yuan, 2019).

It should be noted that relevant official laws and regulations such as the Law of Science and Technology Progress, the Law of Enhancing the Transformation of Scientific and Technological Achievements, the Law of Science and Technology Popularization, the Regulations on Awards for Scientific and Technological Progress, and the Regulations on National Awards of Science and Technology, together with the Decision on Accelerating the Progress of Science and Technology, the Decision on Strengthening the Development of Technological Innovation and the Industrialization of High and New Technology, the Development Outline of the Construction of Scientific Research Conditions, the Development Plan of National Key Basic Research (i.e., 973 Program), and 2004-2010 Development Outline of the Construction of Basic Conditions Platform for the National Award of Science and Technology were enacted in this period.

Among which, the Law of Science and Technology Progress has been viewed as the basic law in the realm of science and technology and constructed the framework of science and technology legal system in China since 1993. The Regulations on Awards for the Progress of Science and Technology which was replaced by the Regulations on National Awards of Science and Technology after 1999. The Decision on Accelerating the Progress of Science and Technology proposed that the economic development should rely on scientific and technological progress and improvements in the quality of workers, and decided to implement the Strategy of Developing the Country through Science and Education in 1995. The Law of Enhancing the Transformation of Scientific and Technological Achievements was issued in 1996 to boost the scientific achievement conversion and the science and technology progress in a formal way. The Development Plan of National Key Basic Research was set up in 1997, aiming to solve the major scientific topics for the national strategic needs, and the scientific frontier issues that would play a key role in human understanding of the world. Focusing on the awards, in 1999, the Regulations on National Awards of Science and Technology established the National Top Award of Science and Technology, improved four influential national awards (including the National Award for Natural Science, the National Award for Technological Invention, the National Award for Science and Technology Progress, and the Award for International Science and Technology Cooperation), raised not only the rewards but also the standard of the National Awards of Science and Technology, and also established the National Science and Technology Award Committee. Then as the primary initiative to implement the Strategy of Developing the Country through Science and Education, the Decision on Strengthening the Development of Technological Innovation and the Industrialization of High and New Technology instituted a national knowledge innovation system with the emphases on promoting the technological innovation, and promoting the commercialization and industrialization of technological innovation in better and more efficient policy settings. And then, the Law of Science and Technology Popularization defined and highlighted the significance of science popularization and the relevant responsibilities and obligations of the government and other social subjects for the first time in 2002, which was a significant fundamental advance in enhancing the national innovation capacity.

Moreover, for better construction of research institutions and innovation system, other related national policies for science, technology and innovation, such as *the Technology Innovation Program* (for enterprises), *the Knowledge Innovation Project of the Chinese Academy of Sciences, 21st Century Education Revitalization Plan and World Class University Plan (i.e., 985 Project), 211 Project* and so on, were also put into practice in this period. What is more, after the National Conference on Technological Innovation was held in 1999, the technology innovation policy became the leading direction of China's science and technology policy, by formulating the industrial policies of the high and new technology development zone, accelerating the transformation of scientific and technological achievements, developing high technology, realizing industrialization, and finally forming a national innovation system with Chinese characteristics.

Overall, the guidelines of policies in this period are the Strategy of Developing the Country through Science and Education. In addition, the focus of national STI policies in China has turned to promote the mutual connection and combination between science and technology, economy, and society. Meanwhile, the change of system paid more attention to the coordination and matching among the reforms of the economic system, political system, science and technology system, and education system. Through further improvements of the science and technology system, national-level policies for STI focused on developing industrial and agricultural scientific research and technology, promoting the development of basic research and high-tech industries, and improving the scientific and technological quality of citizens. Thus, the contribution of progress in the scientific and technological fields to economic development has increased significantly.

Phase 4: Promotion of Science and Technology and Development of Independent Innovation, 2006-2018

After the construction of the STI system, the relevant laws and regulations in China were improving while the policies became more and more open and inclusive with more forms, more extensive coverage and more profound impacts. Although the Strategy of Developing the Country through Science and Education has made initial progress, the shortage of scientific and technological talents, especially in the key fields, has become a short board in the development of science and technology. In addition, it lacks a mechanism to stimulate and encourage independent innovation in the policies for science and technology, especially in the aspects of major technological inventions and significant scientific discoveries. In 2006, the problems of low self-sufficiency rate of key technologies, lack of independent innovation, and the weak competitiveness of enterprises were proposed at the National Conference on Science and Technology in 2006. Consequently, the policies for STI in this period emphasized on enhancing the independent innovation capacity as the strategic basis for the development of science and technology. China strived to build an innovative country with Chinese characteristics.

In this phase, *the Decision on Implementing the Outline of Science and Technology Plan and Enhancing the Independent Innovation Capacity* is an important policy. This policy stressed that the core of becoming an innovative country, the central link for adjusting the industrial structure and shifting the growth mode, and the national strategy, mainly through strengthening the dominant position of enterprises in technological innovation in 2006. *The National Long-term Scientific and Technological Development Plan (2006-2020)*, which has realized the major strategic change of national science and technology development, from imitation to independent innovation, and the new stage of national innovation system construction at the national level. *Opinions on Deepening the Reform of Science and Technology System and Accelerating the Construction of National Innovation System*, which set the goal of basically building a national innovation system in the special context of China by 2020 that adapted to the socialist market economy system, improved the independent innovation capacity and innovation benefits, achieved a major breakthrough in key fields, optimized the innovation environment, etc. in 2012. *Opinions on Policies of Promoting Mass Entrepreneurship and Innovation*, which was a systematic and inclusive policy document to promote both entrepreneurship and innovation with the purpose of reforming and improve relevant mechanisms and build the policy support system. In 2016, *the National Innovation-driven Development Strategy*, which provided the top-level design and systematic planning for the future development of science, technology and innovation in China, and proposed the goals, directions and focuses of the innovation-driven development by 2050 as well. Then, *Opinions on Strengthening the Basic Scientific Research*, which focused more on further strengthening the basic scientific research, aiming to lay a solid foundation for building an innovative country with high-level development of science and technology. And *Opinions on Enhancing High-quality Development of Innovation and Entrepreneurship and Creating an Upgraded Version of Mass Entrepreneurship and Innovation,* which was also proposed in 2018 to upgrade innovation and entrepreneurship services, enhance the transformation and application of scientific and technological achievements, and encourage the integration of the value chain and resources among international and domestic enterprises of different sizes.

Furthermore, to promote the role of colleges and research institutions in the innovation system through supporting talents and promoting knowledge innovation, *the Training Program for Top Students in the Basic Subjects (i.e., Zhufeng Program)* and *2011 Plan* also been carried out at this stage.

Generally, in this period, there are two national policies have significant implications: one is *the National Long-term Scientific and Technological Development Plan (2006-2020)*, as monumental work of China's medium and long-term science and technology planning; and another is *the National Innovation-driven Development Strategy,* as a leading programmatic document of policy for science and technology in the new era. After 2006, independent innovation has become the theme of national-level policies for STI. In other words, the significance of innovation and innovative talents has been highlighted in the development of not only science and technology but also the country.

POLICY ASSESSMENT

According to the release date, this section summaries the 36 national-level policies for STI in China after 1978 as follows:

Table 1. Summary of China's national-level policies for science, technology and innovation after 1978

#	Time	Major national policies for science, technology and innovation	Phase divisions
1	Mar, 1978	1978-1985 National Plan for Science and Technology Development	Phase 1
2	Dec, 1978	the Regulations on Awards for Inventions	
3	Nov, 1979	the Regulations on Awards for Natural Science	
4	1982	the National Key Scientific and Technological Research Plan	
5	Mar, 1982	the Regulations on Awards for Technology Improvement	
6	1984	the National Key Laboratory Construction Plan	
7	1984	the National Key Industrial Test Plan	
8	Mar, 1984	the Patent Law	
9	Mar, 1985	the Decision on the Reform of Science and Technology System	Phase 2
10	May, 1985	the Plan of Promoting Rural Economic Development through Science and Technology (i.e. Spark Program)	
11	Mar, 1986	the National Research and Development Plan of High Technology (i.e. 863 Program)	
12	Jan, 1987	the Provisions on Further Promoting the Reform of the Science and Technology System	
13	June, 1987	the Technical Contract Law	
14	Dec, 1987	the Measures for the Achievements Appraisal of Science and Technology	
15	May, 1988	the Decision on Deepening the Reform of the Science and Technology System	
16	Aug, 1988	the Guiding Plan of China's High and New Technology Industry (i.e. Torch Program)	
17	July, 1991	the National Key Projects on Basic and Applied Research (i.e. Pandeng Program)	
18	June, 1993	the Regulations on Awards for Scientific and Technological Progress	Phase 3
19	July, 1993	the Law of Science and Technology Progress	
20	May, 1995	the Decision on Accelerating the Progress of Science and Technology	
21	Nov, 1995	211 Project	
22	May, 1996	the Law of Enhancing the Transformation of Scientific and Technological Achievements	
23	1997	the Development Plan of National Key Basic Research (i.e., 973 Program)	
24	May, 1998	21st Century Education Revitalization Plan and World Class University Plan (i.e. 985 Project)	
25	May, 1999	the Regulations on National Awards of Science and Technology	
26	Aug, 1999	the Decision on Strengthening the Development of Technological Innovation and the Industrialization of High and New Technology	
27	June, 2002	the Law of Science and Technology Popularization	
28	Jan, 2006	the Decision on Implementing the Outline of Science and Technology Plan and Enhancing the Independent Innovation Capacity	Phase 4
29	Feb, 2006	the National Long-term Scientific and Technological Development Plan (2006-2020)	
30	2009	the Training Program for Top Students in the Basic Subjects (i.e. Zhufeng Program)	
31	May, 2012	2011 Plan	
32	Sep, 2012	Opinions on Deepening the Reform of Science and Technology System and Accelerating the Construction of National Innovation System	
33	June, 2015	Opinions on Policies of Promoting Mass Entrepreneurship and Innovation	
34	May, 2016	the National Innovation-driven Development Strategy	
35	Jan, 2018	Opinions on Strengthening the Basic Scientific Research	
36	Sep, 2018	Opinions on Enhancing High-quality Development of Innovation and Entrepreneurship and Creating an Upgraded Version of Mass Entrepreneurship and Innovation	

Source: collected and organized by the authors

Through the analysis of the development trend of the policies for STI in China after 1978, several findings are presented:

1. The focuses of the relevant national policies have shifted from science and technology to innovation (such as independent innovation, knowledge innovation, etc.), especially after the National Technology Innovation Conference held in 1999. In other words, Hu (2009) summarized the development of technology in China had experienced four stages characteristic with introduction, imitation, exploration, and innovation since 1978, respectively;
2. The emphases of national-level policies for STI are highly influenced by the political economy environment and central task. Specifically, after the severe political and social unrest in China, relevant policies first concentrated on recovery and reconstruction, and then on adjustment to both economic and social development through the efficient system and independent innovation capacity for better, systematic and sustainable development;
3. The national-level science and technology policy system in China has gradually established, changed, adjusted, and improved in continuous exploration and practice. Firstly, the function of national policies for STI has evolved from the early auxiliary means of science and technology management to the important guarantee of science and technology system and mechanism, which has also been supplementing with economic policies, especially industrial policies and fiscal policies for synergetic development and management. Secondly, to regulate and guide the science and technology management and activities, the form of the regulations for STI has been enriched in practice to laws, regulations, rules, and many other types of normative documents. Besides, the policy system has also formed by policies focusing on planning, finance or awards, talents, and popularization in the field of science and technology. The combination of policies has gradually replaced the single policy implementation in China. Thirdly, the national policies for STI have shifted from government-oriented to the combination of government-oriented and market adjustment, which is the result of reforms and lays emphasis on the interactions among enterprises, research institutions, and markets.

DISCUSSION AND CONCLUSION

Since the beginning of the 21st century, the innovation in China faced with a low self-sufficiency rate of crucial technologies, weak independent innovation ability, a small proportion of high-tech industry in the whole national economy, significant dependence on foreign technology in some critical areas of industrial technology, lack of outstanding top talents and other problems. Thus, independent innovation has become an inevitable policy in the new era, the national innovation system construction, innovation-driven development strategy in the top-level design layout.

Through a policy analysis of in the past four decades, this chapter unearthed four stages in the process and trends of science and technology policy: recovery and reconstruction of science and technology, 1978-1984; market-led science and technology development, 1985-1991; adjustment and innovation of science and technology, 1992-2005; and promotion of science and technology and development of independent innovation, 2006-2018. Through the trends and assessment, we found that the focus of the relevant national policies has changed from science and technology to innovation. Meanwhile, the change and adjustment of the national level regulations are closely relevant to the political economy environment and central objectives. Besides, the policy system in China has gradually established, changed and improved in continuous exploration and practice.

Nowadays, socialism with Chinese characteristics has entered a new era. General secretary Xi Jinping has proposed that "innovation is the primary driving force for development." China's science and technology policies are facing new demands. In response, China has adopted a three-step strategy for scientific and technological innovation. By 2020, China will become an innovation-oriented country, and by 2035, it will be one of the most innovation-oriented countries in the world. By 2050, China aims to become a world leader in science and technology.

In the future, STI will play an increasingly important supporting, driving, and guiding role for development. Science, technology and innovation policies should be based on the inherent laws of its development, and strive to meet the needs of the world's cutting-edge science and technology development.

REFERENCES

Aghion, P., David, P. A., & Foray, D. (2009). Science, technology and innovation for economic growth: Linking policy research and practice in 'STIG Systems'. *Research Policy*, *38*(4), 681–693. doi:10.1016/j.respol.2009.01.016

Amankwah-Amoah, J. (2016). The evolution of science, technology and innovation policies: A review of the Ghanaian experience. *Technological Forecasting and Social Change*, *110*, 134–142. doi:10.1016/j.techfore.2015.11.022

Aubert, J. E. (2004). *Promoting innovation in developing countries: a conceptual framework*. The World Bank.

Bowen, G. A. (2009). Document analysis as a qualitative research method. *Qualitative Research Journal*, *9*(2), 27–40. doi:10.3316/QRJ0902027

Burns, T., & Stalker, G.M. (1061). *The management of Innovation.* Tavistock.

Cao, X., & Yuan, Z. (2019). Overview of the important science and technology policies of new China in 70 years. *Science & Technology Review*, *37*(18), 20–30.

Cassiolato, J. E., & Vitorino, V. (Eds.). (2009). *BRICS and development alternatives: innovation systems and policies* (Vol. 1). Anthem Press.

Cheng, H., & Qian, F. (2013). Research on the relationship between innovation performance and the power, stability and instruments of policy—Empirical analysis based on 2000-2009 industry panel data. *Science Research Management*, *34*(10), 103–108.

Cheng. (2008). The evolution of China's science and technology strategy and policy of international cooperation in the past 30 years. *Forum on Science and Technology in China*, *2008*(7), 7-11.

Coleman, J., Katz, E., & Menzel, H. (1957). The diffusion of an innovation among physicians. *Sociometry*, *20*(4), 253–270. doi:10.2307/2785979

Coleman, J. S., Katz, E., & Menzel, H. (1966). *Medical innovation: A diffusion study*. Bobbs-Merrill Co.

Dodgson, M. (2000a). Innovation policies in East Asia. *Science, technology and innovation Policy: Opportunities and Challenges for the Knowledge Economy*, (8), 399.

Dodgson, M. (2000b). Policies for science, technology and innovation in Asian newly industrializing economies. *Technology, learning, and innovation: Experiences of newly industrializing economies*, 229-268.

Du, B., & Zhang, H. (2018). An Analysis of the Policy System for the Transformation of Scientific and Technological Achievements in China Based on the 'Three-Dimensional'. *Perspective. Science of Science and Management of S.& T.*, *39*(9), 36–49.

Fan, B., Duan, Z., & Jiang, L. (2012). Literature Review on Innovation Policy. *China Soft Science*, *26*(11), 43–47.

Flanagan, K., & Uyarra, E. (2016). Four dangers in innovation policy studies–and how to avoid them. *Industry and Innovation*, *23*(2), 177–188. doi:10.1080/13662716.2016.1146126

Freeman, C., & Soete, L. (2009). Developing science, technology and innovation indicators: What we can learn from the past. *Research Policy, 38*(4), 583–589. doi:10.1016/j.respol.2009.01.018

Hadjimanolis, A., & Dickson, K. (2001). Development of national innovation policy in small developing countries: The case of Cyprus. *Research Policy, 30*(5), 805–817. doi:10.1016/S0048-7333(00)00123-2

Hu, C. (2009). Review of the development of China's Science and Technology Policy since the Reform and Opening Up. *Productivity Research, 2009*(12), 5-8.

Huang, C., Zhao, P., & Li, J. (2015). Research on China's Science and Technology Policy Changes based on Co-word Cluster Analysis. *Chinese Public Administration, 363*(9), 115–122.

Lall, S., & Pietrobelli, C. (2005). National technology systems in sub-Saharan Africa. *International Journal of Technology and Globalisation, 1*(3/4), 311. doi:10.1504/IJTG.2005.008746

Laranja, M., Uyarra, E., & Flanagan, K. (2008). Policies for science, technology and innovation: Translating rationales into regional policies in a multi-level setting. *Research Policy, 37*(5), 823–835. doi:10.1016/j.respol.2008.03.006

Lemola, T. (2002). Convergence of national science and technology policies: The case of Finland. *Research Policy, 31*(8-9), 1481–1490. doi:10.1016/S0048-7333(02)00077-X

Liu, F., & Sun, Y. (2007). The Course of, Trend in and Proposal for Evolution from S&T Policies to Innovation Policies—Based on the Empirical Analysis of China's 289 Innovation Policy Documents. *China Soft Science, 2007*(5), 34–42.

Liu, L. (2008). Four milestones of China's science and technology policy since the reform and opening up. *Forum on Science and Technology in China, 2008*(10), 3-5.

Liu, X., & Liu, J. (2011). *Science and technology and innovation policy in China*. Anthem Press.

Liu, Y. (2014). The evolution of technology policy in Britain, France and Germany and their inspiration to our count. *Scientific Management Research, 32*(4), 113–116.

Liu, Y., Fu, Z., & Liu, Z. (2012). Evolution of Technology Policy in the United States, Japan, Korea and their Inspiration to our Count. *Science and Technology Management Research, 2013*(2), 31–35.

Lu, L., & Etzkowitz, H. (2008). Strategic challenges for creating knowledge-based innovation in China. *Journal of Technology management in China.*

Lundvall, B. Å., & Borrás, S. (2005). Science, technology and innovation policy. The Oxford handbook of innovation, 599-631.

Luthria, M. (2002). Supporting technology generation and diffusion at the firm level. *Building Competitive Firms*, 98.

Martin, B. R. (2012). The evolution of science policy and innovation studies. *Research Policy*, *41*(7), 1219–1239. doi:10.1016/j.respol.2012.03.012

Millar, C. C., Choi, C. J., & Chu, R. T. (2005). The state in science, technology and innovation districts: Conceptual models for China. *Technology Analysis and Strategic Management*, *17*(3), 367–373. doi:10.1080/09537320500211722

Morlacchi, P., & Martin, B. R. (2009). *Emerging challenges for science, technology and innovation policy research: a reflexive overview*. Academic Press.

Padilla-Pérez, R., & Gaudin, Y. (2014). Science, technology and innovation policies in small and developing economies: The case of Central America. *Research Policy*, *43*(4), 749–759. doi:10.1016/j.respol.2013.10.011

Pelz, D. C., & Andrews, F. M. (1966). *Scientists in organizations: Productive climates for research and development*. Academic Press.

Peng, J., Sun, W., & Zhong, W. (2008). The evolution of Chinese technological and innovational policies and the empirical research on the performance (1978 -2006). *Science Research Management*, *29*(4), 134–150.

Rehn, D., & Simon, D. F. (1988). *Technological Innovation in China: The Case of the Shanghai Semiconductor Industry*. Ballinger.

Rothwell, R. (1992). Industrial innovation and government environmental regulation: Some lessons from the past. *Technovation*, *12*(7), 447–458. doi:10.1016/0166-4972(92)90050-R

Salazar, M., & Holbrook, A. (2007). Canadian science, technology and innovation policy: The product of regional networking? *Regional Studies*, *41*(8), 1129–1141. doi:10.1080/00343400701530865

Shaw, S., Elston, J., & Abbott, S. (2004). Comparative analysis of health policy implementation: The use of documentary analysis. *Policy Studies*, *25*(4), 259–266. doi:10.1080/0144287042000288451

Solow, R. M. (1956). A contribution to the theory of economic growth. *The Quarterly Journal of Economics*, *70*(1), 65–94. doi:10.2307/1884513

Sun, Y., & Du, D. (2010). Determinants of industrial innovation in China: Evidence from its recent economic census. *Technovation*, *30*(9-10), 540–550. doi:10.1016/j.technovation.2010.05.003

Turpin, T., & Liu, X. (2000). Balanced Development: The Challenge for Science, Technology and Innovation Policy. In Contemporary Developments and Issues in China's Economic Transition (pp. 191-211). Palgrave Macmillan.

Vitta, P. B. (1990). Technology policy in sub-Saharan Africa: Why the dream remains unfulfilled. *World Development*, *18*(11), 1471–1480. doi:10.1016/0305-750X(90)90037-X

Walker, J. L. (1969). The diffusion of innovations among the American states. *The American Political Science Review*, *63*(3), 880–899. doi:10.1017/S0003055400258644

Woodward, J. (1958). *Management and technology* (No. 3). HM Stationery Off.

Zhang, J., Huang, C., Ye, X., Shi, K., & Su, J. (2016). Study on China's Public Policy Diffusion Based on the Quantitative Analysis of Policy Documents: A Case Study on Policies Promoting Commercialization of Scientific and Technological Achievements. *China Soft Science*, *2016*(2), 145–155.

Zhang, Y. (2019). Evolution of China's Science and Technology Policy since the Reform and Opening Up. *Forum on Science and Technology in China*, *2019*(4), 1–7.

Zhang, Y., & Chen, R. (2012). The Convergence Trend of Science and Technology Policy in Technological Power and Its Countermeasure. *Science & Technology Progress and Policy*, *30*(2), 108–111.

Chapter 5
Sustainable Innovation Management in Indonesia:
Enhancing Private Sector Participation Within Innovation Management

Abdul Karim Mohamed Yusoff
Higher Colleges of Technology, Dubai, UAE

ABSTRACT

Indonesia's National Innovation Policy requires consistent support from the private sector participation to raise its knowledge-based economic growth and become one of the top 15 powerful countries in the world by 2045, as declared by the Presidential decree. The low participation rate of private industries in R&D activities is a cause for concern for the government, as an effort to improve the country's social and economic performance must be a shared responsibility. This chapter looks into how the private sector participation in innovative effort plays an essential role in improving the country's economic performance. The challenges that lie ahead in achieving the goals of National Innovation Policy rest with both the government and the private sector.

INTRODUCTION

The economist Joseph Schumpeter (1947) once said that "Innovation process was significantly relevant for emerging countries to undertake the path to industrialization" (Aghion, P et al., 2005).

DOI: 10.4018/978-1-7998-4195-1.ch005

Copyright © 2021, IGI Global. Copying or distributing in print or electronic forms without written permission of IGI Global is prohibited.

This statement has a ring of truths as Indonesia has been focusing its development on the industrialization pathway for the last three decades. The largest economy in South East Asia, Indonesia, with a population of 273 million (worldometer.com, 2020), has had stable growth in the gross domestic product (GDP) of more than 6.4% in 2014. Anticipated that by 2013, Indonesia would have achieved economic growth of 5.9%, and by 2020, from 6 to 8%. The GDP per capita in 2010 was USD 3,015 and has risen to USD 3,952 in 2012. GDP per capita could reach up to USD 9,000 through knowledge-based competitiveness by 2020. Poised to be among the 15 countries in South East Asian and the Pacific, according to Goldman Sachs research (2010), Indonesia should be the most extensive GDP worldwide by 2030. Its young and active population is under the median age of 30, which comprises almost 43% of the population. Thus, this creates the potential to be the 10th most significant market globally (GIPA, 2005). This chapter looks into how the private sector participation in innovative effort plays an essential role in improving the country's economic performance. This chapter also presents the challenges that lie ahead in achieving the goals of national innovation policy in coordination with both the government and the private sector.

POLITICAL ECONOMY THAT UNDERLIES NATIONAL INNOVATION POLICY

Indonesia's economy has gone through rapid transitions from being dominated by the purely agricultural sector in the early 1960s to oil and import substitution in the 1980s, and labor-intensive and export-oriented activities in the 1990s. Throughout the thirty years, many economic and social reforms from 1966 to 1998 induced stability and unity within its society.

Immediately after independence from Dutch administration in 1819, the Indonesian Republic under the "Old Order" faced economic stagnation and severe budget deficits. Back then, it traded on commodities and natural raw resources as the main economic activities and source of income. However, the Indonesian economy has been vulnerable to the instability of the world's prices of natural resources and agricultural produce.

When President Suharto came into power in 1966, severe economic and social reforms were needed to stabilize its economic return and provide the younger population with jobs. When oil prices were going down, and economic return was minimal, the New Order under President Suharto sought to open up the economy to foreign investors in order to liberalize trade from 1966 to 1973. From 1974 to 1985 onwards, they increased oil revenue and set up Indonesia's pace to develop its domestic industries, supported by its import substitution strategies. There was an air of anti-foreign investment during this period. Due to imbalanced economic development between regions in Indonesia, and in order to centralize power and administration in the capital, political reform was adjudicated for the allocation of revenues and redistribute earnings.

During these years, Indonesia was still dependent on the trading of natural resources and small capital-intensive industries of questionable efficiency. (Soesastro and Pangestu, 1998). Unlike other countries in South East Asia, (example, Singapore and Malaysia), Indonesia did not have a full focus on building industrial development during this period. Imbalanced economic development between regions in the young Republic was the source of political upheavals and contempt. The strong military supported this centralization of power in order to unify the country.

As the country's political order stabilized, its economic activities had also changed. Decentralization of power became the norm as regional developments came into effect. Regional governments with subsidiary legislative powers were accorded recognition under the new order of President Suharto. From 1986 to 1996, the effects of globalization and deregulation set in. Trading partners demanded openness and liberalization of trading activities with Indonesia. It, therefore, had to step up its economic activities towards a more export-oriented strategy. Indonesia once again had to open its borders to foreign investment but at this period, with only a few import restrictions. (Bhattacharya & Pangestu, 1993)

In sync with its trading partners, in the 1990s, Indonesia saw a substantial reduction of most of its tariffs and non-tariff barriers. In May 1994, Indonesia removed further restrictions on foreign investments. 100% of foreign ownership was allowed and created its own "superhighway facilities (more accessible custom gateway, reduced procedures for banking, easy calculation on taxes) and even allowed foreign companies to sell products in the domestic market up to wholesaler level (Aminulla et al., 2006). However, there was not a strong strategy for industrial upgrading still. There was a structure of protection for infant industries, but it favored the production of final consumer goods and disfavored capital and intermediate goods for manufacturing (Soesastro & Pangestu, 1993). The heavy dependence on its trading legacy and small capital-intensive industries, as the primary income earner for the country, will be a setback for transformation to the next stage of the knowledge-based economy. Without a high value-added industrial component of its own, technology capacity building will be highly dependent on foreign direct investments (Soesastro & Pangestu, 1993).

As Indonesia has learned from its experience with foreign direct investments, capacity building for technological progress could not be that reliable when future economic crisis sets in. It has to bear the enormous cost of getting this technology using foreign direct investment as a strategy.

Ethnic Issues and Isolation from National Innovation Policy

With 360 ethnic groups, 34 provinces,415 regencies, and 92 cities, challenges in coordinating its national policies, communicating its utmost priorities in innovation activities, and fundings are not easily surmountable. Thus ethnic loyalties, regional power politics, large government bureaucracies, and the magnitude of corruption, which are still prevailing among the civil servants, will hamper its success towards achieving the goal.

The Chinese immigrants had lived in Indonesia since the 13th Century, when trade missions came from China to the Javanese kingdom were conducted. During the period of the Dutch Colonial Administration, around 1815, the Chinese migrants were made to be the intermediaries between the Dutch Administration and the indigenous population. Today, the Indonesian-Chinese population comprises almost 6 million out of the 250 Million. In 1993, 204 of the top 300 companies, with 80% of total equivalent national assets, were owned by the ethnic Chinese origin (Pangestu & Harianto, 1999).

Per Credit Suisse Research Institute's 2016 Global Wealth Report, the top 1% of the wealthiest Indonesians owned 49.3% of national wealth, "making Indonesia an unequal nation in the world" (Reuters, 2017). The wealthiest Indonesians here are presumably that of ethnic Chinese origins. Heightened by the economic crisis in1997, the inequality had brought about racial riots in 1998 that toppled President Suharto. In 2001, the subsequent government addressed the social tensions by passing laws that canceled the ban on the right to practice Chinese culture and language and making the Lunar New Year an official holiday (Hutton, 2018).

Despite all the recent government attempts to redress this divisive national issue, racial cleavage and distrust between the indigenous population known as the "Pribumi" and the Indonesians of Chinese origin are still felt. Several notable efforts have been made to reduce this cleavage that includes co-optation of the Indonesian-Chinese managerial elites, into the Pribumi controlled State-Owned- enterprises (SOEs), as the board of directors and vice versa. However, to change the situation, little effect was done. (Aminullah et al., 2003). The mistrust with the Chinese heritage individuals and their Dutch intermediaries simply rested upon one perception; these individuals are only seeking to build family interest and self-profit-seeking, not national interest, persists up to this day.

Hence, private industries controlled by the Indonesians of Chinese origin are isolated from the national innovation policy. Consequently, these private industries would preferably depend on their foreign partners or purchase directly through foreign vendors, to bring in their required advanced technology to achieve their corporate goals. The isolation of the private industries from national innovation policy is causing severe repercussions to the already highly segmented national innovation policy. In order for Indonesia's national innovation strategy to be competitive economically, these issues need to be addressed.

INNOVATION AS A NATIONAL STRATEGY FOR COMPETITIVENESS

For it to leap ahead in competitiveness and growth into a knowledge-based economy, innovation will be the key to this drive.

Innovation is critical for developing countries like Indonesia to avoid the middle-income trap and achieve much-needed industrial, productivity, and technological upgrading. Attaining sustainable, competitive, and substantial economic growth requires accumulating more labor and capital and new technology and innovation (Yose Damuri et al., 2018).

The word "innovation" has many definitions. "Innovation means turning bold ideas into reality and changing lives for the better" (nesta.org, 2019). Riederer et al. (2005), said: "Innovation is the economic application of ideas, processes, and technology in a new way to gain a competitive advantage." However, what Indonesia needs is the whole gamut of innovation management. Innovation management is not only concerned with the commercial application of ideas, processes, and technology in a new way for organizational purposes, but it also involves developing and sustaining innovation strategies, culture, idea management, and implementation of innovation processes towards obtaining the result (Riederer et al., 2005).

Both the pubic and private sector organizations need to develop and sustain and implement innovation management in its entirety in order to compete economically with other nations in these turbulent times. It has to reduce its dependence on growth by trading its depleting natural resources and embrace technological innovations.

Organizations must innovate to achieve revenue growth through new products and services, and improve their response to customer demands. Thus, to innovate successfully and efficiently, the process of innovation must be managed (Deloitte, 2005).

Therefore a national policy and strategy on innovation management with commitment from both public and private sectors is imminent and timely. Indonesia has to face several challenges as a nation in implanting the seeds for innovation management.

The Global Innovation Index

In the Global Innovation Index, Indonesia ranked 87th out of 128 countries in 2016, and in technology readiness, it ranked 80th. (GIPA, 2005). The Global Innovation Index measures the national inputs and outputs in the innovation management process. According to GIPA (2005), Indonesia ranked 36th place in the macro indicator, "Global Competitive Index." This measures how well Indonesia could survive in global competitiveness by innovating.

Indonesia then has a long way to go towards using innovation as a competitive tool. It needs a coherent innovation management strategy, improve its education system, especially in Science and Technology, and increase its research and development spending for both public and private sectors to achieve competitiveness. During the 1980s, productivity was gained purely by massive labor-intensive productions and trading of natural resources. Innovation activities were minimal. Research and development spending that reflects Indonesia's innovation activities has improved, but it accounted for only 0.2% of gross domestic products compared to 1.0% spent by other emerging countries in 2016.

The National Innovation Policy and Actors in the Framework

In the year 2010, the previous President SBY set up a National Committee of Innovation, but this was disbanded by 2014. The present President Jokowi merged the Ministry of Education and Culture with the Ministry of Research Technology and Higher Education in 2014, which became known as "Ristekdikti." He opened up the centre of excellence and 100 technoparks empowered to do innovation activities and programs. Thus the government is still the leading player that controls the fundings for innovation programs. Four leading agencies represent the innovation ecosystem in Indonesia now. These are:

1. Ristekdikti (Ministry of research technology and Ministry of Higher education)
2. Bappenas (Ministry of national development)
3. Kemenperin (Ministry of Industry)
4. Kemenkeu (Ministry of finance)
5. Kementan (Ministry of Agriculture)

The Kemenkeu (Ministry of Finance) has the power to decide how budgets are allocated and whether budgets need to be revised yearly since the budget is an indicator of government agencies' performance in innovation activities. Thus, this makes the Kemenkeu the most potent and influential agency in innovation spending and sets them apart among the other ministries in decision-making status. Ristekdikti

(Ministry of research technology and Ministry of Higher Education) looks after the budget allocations among the government institutions of higher education, namely the universities' research laboratories and centers as well as public research laboratories. The Kemenperin (Ministry of industry) looks after the budgets and direction of innovation activities in the industry, namely the private sector participation. The Kementan (Ministry of Agriculture) looks after the agriculture-sector innovation policies and spendings. Balitbantang, a public research institution related to Kementan, received the highest government budget allocation for research and development in Indonesia (GIPA, 2005).

In research and development activities, the Minister of Research and Technology has been given a clear mandate to formulate the national Research and Development (R&D) strategic policy and has the power to coordinate all institutions in conducting research and application of technology. R&D activities are conducted in all ministries by their respective R&D agencies (Lakitan, 2011). There are many non-ministerial government institutions, universities, provincial governments that conduct their R&D activities. The provincial R&D agencies report to the respective governors, and they, in turn, report to the Minister of internal affairs.

Challenges in Indonesia's Innovation Management System

Currently, most of the research funds are allocated to the universities and the public R&D institutes. Only a trickle goes to other research public institutions or non-ministerial agencies.

The mandate given by the presidential decree to the Minister of Research and Technology to formulate and maintain R&D activities were not implemented because the mandate was not backed by the financial authority (Lakitan, 2011). Initiatives will remain in the house due to financial constraints.

Despite the bulk of the government funds given to universities, there is still a low percentage of academicians that have registered themselves as researchers. Out of 150,000 academicians in Indonesia, only 17,000 researchers are registered at the R&D Institutes (Lakitan, 2011). There has been a lack of coordination among the various institutions and ministerial agencies that govern innovation activities. This unfortunate state of coordination is hampering synergies that hamper R&D activities within the institutions (GIPA 2005).

The Indonesian Institute of Science (Pappitek-LIPI) conducted a study in 2009 and found that its overall R & D expenditure was 0.08% of GDP. Out of these total, 0.04% contributed by the government, and only 0.02% was from higher education and manufacturing industries. Pappitek-LIPI surveyed collaborations between private companies and R & D institutions in 2009 and found that only 17% of respondents (private companies) have R & D collaborations, and the majority of companies (83%)

have no collaborations at all. It is assumed that they conducted their R&D activities themselves within their capacity. The low participation of the R & D activities of private companies within the national policy framework is a severe cause. The study also found that the agenda of the R&D activities conducted by the Universities and public R&D institutions are not the motivating factors for private industries to go into R&D (Soenarso et al., 2013).

Table 1.

Country	Ranking of company spending on R&D
Singapore	8
Malaysia	17
Indonesia	23
Philippines	51
Vietnam	59
Thailand	62
Brunei Darrusalam	67

The low company spending on R&D activities, as per table 1, explains that the Indonesian private sector has yet to commit to innovation activities as a core corporate strategy in their businesses. Benjamin Lakitan (2011) highlights the following challenging issues facing the innovation system as follows:

1. There should be lower dependence among public institutions (including government) and industries on domestic R & D institutions that could develop reliable technologies. Historically, buying foreign technologies have always been cheaper than developing using R&D funds. These foreign technologies have had successful track records, already tested, have higher reliability, and could reduce waiting time.
2. The absorption by domestic firms of technologies developed by local R&D Institutions is low. The buy-in of local domestic firms on locally produced technologies was but a dismal proportion. However, this has something to do with the state of the economy of the time. Indonesia has depended on its trading activities of natural resources and light manufacturing. There was little progress made to go into heavy manufacturing and high value-added economic activities using advanced technologies. The R&D activities evolved from academic goals but did not match the needs of the domestic industries. There is a mismatch of goals and needs between technology developers and potential users.

3. Insufficient funding for R&D activities in Indonesia is the most perplexing problem. Indonesia was spending only less than 1% of the GDP to fund this R&D. In 2013, insufficient funding was recorded far below that of the middle-income country average of 1% (Yose Damuri et al., 2018).
4. The lack of funds for local R&D activities means that Indonesia has to depend on the foreign inflow of technologies brought by foreign investments.
5. Existing policies and regulations have yet to contribute to developing a sustainable ecosystem for innovation. There have been regulations and Presidential decrees for tax incentives for firms undertaking R&D activities, namely, Regulations 35/2007 and 93/2010, but so far, none of the domestic firms were fully aware and interested. Some of the policies and regulations have not been adequately communicated to the intended target groups.

Apart from the above challenges, GIPA (2005) have highlighted several existing issues that need to be developed, namely:

1. The R & D system and innovation governance structure were still highly fragmented, and the lack of coordination dissipates interest in the R & D activities by the public and private sectors.
2. The allocation of research funds needs to be further improved. Deserving institutions, especially members of the private sector industries, should gain access to these funds to develop a higher rate of absorption of local R & D technologies by the domestic firms.
3. Flexibility in design and disbursements of the research funding has to be maintained. Red tape and bureaucratic approvals need to be reduced for the system to be efficient.
4. The number of researchers in R&D activities has to be increased. Indonesia has 89,597 researchers per million population up to recent years. This is far from adequate for the size of the population it has now.
5. The quality of human resources does not match the size of the population. Indonesia needs to have educational reforms and improve further the quality of its human resources. Improved Curriculum should focus more on Science, Technology, and Innovation (STI) in its universities and colleges.
6. Inefficient bureaucracy and high corruption levels will always plague the national system with inordinate consequences in service and reputation.
7. Many regions that suffer underdeveloped Information and Computer technology (ICT) infrastructure are still unable to access information on the available technologies. Thus, a setback because future technopark centers that will bring R&D activities will have to be sited on some of these regions to reduce the over-focused development in developed cities and maintain regional balance.

Recent Efforts Undertaken by the Government to Improve Innovation Management

There are, however, recent efforts by the government undertaken to eradicate these challenges. The government has formed the Directorate -General (DG) to strengthen the innovation policy in 2015. The directorate will ensure that proper coordination among innovation agencies and R&D institutes are conducted and that the present bureaucratic channels that hamper funding activities be reduced effectively.

The DG shall also attempt to focus on innovation-led growth of the economy using advanced technologies. The government has also identified potential philanthropic funds that could be used for innovation-related education and training initiatives, and this will help to commercialize innovative ideas from R&D agencies faster.

The government has also improved the patent system with decrees 13/2016 that will improve the patent system and registration. Ristekdikti (Ministry of Research Technology and Higher Education) has set up a center of Data and Information for Science, Technology, and Higher Education. This center will integrate data in Science and Technology as well as Higher Education for innovation management purposes.

The sustaining economic growth in recent years, supported by Indonesia's trading partnership with the United States and China, will also produce a positive environment for innovation. The most recent government plan is to spend at least 2% of the GDP is a good start (GIPA, 2005).

Presidential Decrees in 2011, 2013 and 2015

This decrees reviewed government regulations enacted in 2003 that provide incentives to encourage private firms to conduct R&D activities, innovation, and diffusion of technologies. The decrees plan to increase funding within the next five years as the country moves towards science and technology-driven economic competitiveness. The new funding instruments were developed from the RPJMN (2015) decrees. These decrees include debt financing and risk sharing, tax incentives, corporate income tax benefits, VAT exemption on technology-based products, and tax reliefs for local production based on 50% local resources. The revised funding schemes also include public procurement arrangements to make it flexible and accessible to public organizations and private industries. Known as the Electronic Procurement Agency (LPSE), it supports procurement procedures for public organizations, state-owned companies, and private industries.

The Presidential decree of 32/2011 focuses on the so-called "Masterplan for the Acceleration and Expansion of Economic Development of Indonesia" (MP3EI) until the year 2025. The masterplan contains Indonesia's development process to become a developed country as the top 12th powerful country by 2025. It also aspires Indonesia to be among the top powerful countries in the world by 2045 through sustainable economic growth that achieves economic targets using Science, Technology, and Innovation (Soenarso et al.,2013).

Decentralization Process

A roadmap for regional innovation systems to improve and strengthen regional competitiveness has been created. It is also meant for regional R&D institutions to address basic needs. It will be a stimulus to regional universities and research departments to improve its innovation, further improve its innovation activities.

Indonesian Firms and International best practices in innovation management

Indonesia firms need to learn from international best practices in innovation management to benchmark their progress. It needs to distinguish what types of innovation strategies and how these strategies could be implemented. Innovation -led growth has to develop following the varying stages of its economic development, demands of the millennial population, and in tandem with educational reforms.

Innovation management is not only about generating commercially viable ideas that are put on the market, but successful innovation management requires the implementation of an innovation culture within the organization, developing the appropriate structures within the organization, and lastly, measuring the innovation output itself (Deloitte, 2005). Innovation has to be part of the organization's business strategy (Turrell & Lindow, 2003). It is stressed that innovation is not an invention unless the invention is sold in the market, but the invention itself has no value to add (Riederer et al., 2005). Innovation thus far has to be distinguished in terms of products and processes. There have been researchers who merged the two concepts into "hybrid" innovation (Accenture, 2005).

LITERATURE REVIEW

Technology Push and Demand-Pull Innovations

Schumpeter (1912), in his Theory of Economic Development, states that creative disruption will occur when one technological invention that is brought to the market, disrupts existing technologies. Thus, the new technology will rein control the market until new technology will, in turn, disrupt the existing ones. This is called "Technology push innovation. The "demand-pull innovation" happens when demand forces within the market, pull innovations, and inventions into it (Schmookler, 1966). The "lead-user -concept" type of innovation happens when product users facilitate new ideas for better performance or new applications. Due to the close cooperation with customers, innovation can become more market-oriented and successful (Hippel, 1988; Riederer et al. 2018).

Process Innovation

Indonesia's innovation management should also look into process innovations, especially in the manufacturing sector or service industries, to heighten its competitiveness. This involves the reduction of product costs, delivery of products, and optimizing the customer experience. Technological process innovation is defined as the adoption of technologically new improved production methods, including product delivery. It significantly involves changes in equipment, production organization, or a combination of these changes (OECD, 1997).

On the broader scale, process innovation includes the planning, steering, and support processes in the organization. Imhausen (2005) states the broader and supportive process innovation that includes; strategic planning and implementation, customer use optimization, product and services allocation, logistics, maintenance, quality assurance, capacity planning, and personnel training and motivation.

Some examples are Just-in-time management's development to reduce product costs, e-stores like Amazon to deliver product available to the market in a short time and supply chain efficiencies and Lean Manufacturing. In the banking sector, digital banking, online customer service, and communication apps are likely outcomes of process innovations.

FOUR LEVELS OF INNOVATION ACTIVITIES

Riederer et al. (2005) state that organizations that undertake innovation management needs to further distinguish the four levels of innovation for their own. These are namely:

1. **Sustaining Innovation:** This involves innovating incrementally, where small improvements in products, services, or the organization's processes are made using existing technology. These examples include altering packagings, offering different flavors or sizes or colors to improve customer experience, or offering flexible timing and schedules for services.

2. **Technological Substitution:** These innovations are using new technology development to create new products that fill existing market categories. Examples are cordless phones and power tools.
3. **Market Innovation:** These innovations are done by combining and presenting existing technologies that is unprecedented to the market. The output is creating a new market segment. An example of this innovation type is Sony Walkman. It combines existing audio-headphone technology with a cassette recorder.
4. **Radical Innovation:** This is a type of disruptive innovation that is facilitated by technologically advanced products or services that create an entirely new market segment. It is very risky, most rare, and with the highest rewards.

Disruptive innovation will result in higher potential rewards, even though accompanied by high risks, due to the organization's temporary monopolistic status (Burmester et al., 2005).

INNOVATION MANAGEMENT AS A BUSINESS STRATEGY

Firms that have successful programs in innovation management have clear R&D distinct strategies which types of innovation pathways to choose. The top management of these organizations should ensure that once they have decided on the strategy, it must be clearly understood by all within the organization. Therefore, whether it is solely a product innovation strategy, process innovation, or the hybrid innovation strategy, Indonesian organizations must decide its core strategy. (Viki, 2017)

A study was conducted in Europe and USA by IBM, Economist and Nikkie Research in 2004, with more than 400 CEOs of various global corporations, to establish the role of Innovation management as a concept within the organizations.

It was found that successful organizations use their innovation management as a core of their competitive strategy. 90% of the CEOs interviewed said that they expected to transform their organization to be more responsive to their customers. Almost 70% expected that their organization's revenue growth would come from new products and services. The study also found that 61.4% of consumers in Germany were willing to spend more if they could find better products. Thus product innovation is critical for business even during an economic downturn. "However, we know that recessions are times of opportunity. Many successful start-ups began during recessions. Habits change, customers adapt new practices. This all means opportunity for the nimble". (Sloane P, 2020)

Revisiting Strategies for Innovation Management

Indonesian policymakers for both the public and private sector innovation management might need to focus their strategies in stages or choose either sustaining or radical innovation. Sustaining or incremental innovation, i.e. creating small improvements, minor additions to existing products or services, finding new uses for existing products or using less expensive materials for products, might just be as profitable and safer in the long term pursuing disruptive or radical innovation (Deloitte, 2005).

[I]t is an irony that the bureaucrats, officials, academics, and entrepreneurs give more attention to the riskiest form of innovation due to the blinding appeal of disruptive innovation that comes from the glamour of R&D activities and opportunities for large grants and tax credits. Breakthroughs such as these come only once or twice in a company's lifetime. (Bergmann et al., 2005; Valery, 1999; Riederer et al., 2005).

A study done by Accenture in 2005 in Germany found that companies that implemented process innovations had achieved annual revenue growth of 15% and a reduction in the cost of goods sold by 13%. The strengths of process innovation will remain within the company, and it will be difficult for competitors to replicate new process improvements. Unlike process innovation, the outcome of product innovation is placed on the market with the new product for competitors to copy them. " Without an innovation strategy, different part of an organization can easily wind up pursuing conflicting priorities - even if there is a clear business strategy". (Pisano, GD, 2015)

When deciding to choose innovation strategy, organizations should study their strengths and weaknesses, i.e., analyze their assets, human capital, market competition, and culture. It is just the same as they were doing strategic management exercise. Overstraining the organization by going too far away from innate competencies will not pay off (Zyman et al., 2000; Powers, 2004).

The timing of entering a specific market is also the competency of an innovator. The innovator must know when to enter and exit the market. Therefore, the timing for leader-innovator," "follower-innovator," and "lead user strategy" has significant implications for the business. For organizations to be leader-innovators, they require substantial R & D budgets and the ability to take the risks of failure. At times it will be best for organizations to be "follower-Innovator" just like Microsoft, who comes into the market with their "window-standard," following Apple Macintosh's first graphical user interface (Burmester et al., 2005). However, "late-follower" will be at a disadvantage due to the high industry barrier that includes complex technological inputs, costly after-sales service, and high switching costs faced by the customer, put up by the "leader innovator" (Gerpott, 1999).

The Different Stages of Innovation Process

Organizations usually will go through undertake to study their innate competencies, understanding the boundaries of their capacity to do innovation. The ability to innovate will be affected by their past experiences. The whole process will generate new ideas and, lastly, the critical assessment of total projects. Therefore, the idea management system is at the core of the innovation system. This involves the generation, collection, development, evaluation, and selection of business ideas (Turrell &Lindow, 2003).

The Stage-Gate Model

Cooper (1993) initiated the "Stage-Gate Model" of the entire innovation process after a series of studies on the successes and failures of firms' innovation process. The table below shows the different stages or "gates" under which ideas are screened and given value. The project owner will evaluate the ideas at each "gate" with a "go" or "no-go" decision. It is evident that some predefined "must-meet criteria" and some "should -meet criteria."

Table 2.

The Stage-Gate Model	
Gate 1	Idea screening and commitment of resources
Stage 1	Preliminary market and technical assessments of the project
Gate 2	More vigorous screening concerning market attractiveness, technical advantages of the product
Stage 2	Development of the business case (Incl.legal and financial analysis.)
Gate 3	Yield a "sign-off" on the product definition.
Stage 3	Technical development; deliverable; lab-tested prototype of the product
Gate 4	Check the attractiveness and quality of the product.
Stage 4	Testing and validation of the entire project concerning all dimensions (marketing; engineering and accounting)
Gate 5	Appropriateness of production, launch and finance plan
Stage 5	Market launch
Review	Evaluation of the project after commercialization

However, to emphasize that the stage-gate model will only apply for new product development and the overlapping of some phases, which is expected (Cooper & Kleinschmidt, 1993; Dejong et al., 2003).

Developing the Innovation Culture

Organizations in Indonesia may require to undergo a transformation that fosters flexibility for its employees to be creative and disband the fear of failures in engaging with innovation activities. Although there is no hard and fast rule about successful innovation activities, there are some common traits found in organizations that are generally able to achieve their goals in various innovation activities. These are namely below.

Leadership

Leaders in the organizations at all levels play a role in creating a conducive internal environment for employees to take risks in creative activities. Therefore leaders at all levels are responsible for steering the organization's attitudes and behavior towards innovation. Top management, which fails to recognize employees' contributions to new ideas, rewards them, and provides continuing support until fruition may block innovation (Karlsberg & Adler, 2005; Deloitte 2005; Sherman 2005; Riederer et al., 2005).

Employees Adding Needed Value

Organizations that pay adequate compensations and treat their employees fairly may create a conducive internal climate where employees' creativity can be easily accessed. Innovation is an output of non-traditional thinking. Thus firms that are tolerant, flexible, and allow personal space for creative thinking have a supportive structure for innovative work (Sherman, 2005).

Cross-Functional Teams

New ideas that are forthcoming as innovative might arise from cross-functional teams. These are diverse groups of employees formed from different backgrounds and occupations within the organization to solve workplace problems. Diversity is the key and an asset in this team. Hence a higher number of ideas and solutions can be generated from this diverse team (Amabile et al., 1998).

Open Communication and Collaboration

Organizations that encourage inter-division or department forum will foster the culture of openness that will generate new ideas and innovative collaborations. This enhanced collaboration will result in applications of new technologies and problem-solving opportunities (Deloitte 2004; Breen, 2005; Sherman 2005).

Trust and Autonomy

Organizations that empower employees to use a portion of their work time for creative and innovative pursuits within the organization without supervision will provide their employees with personal space to be creative and generate new ideas. Companies that include 3M, Toyota, and Clariant Gbh provide time for employees to come out with new ideas that will later be the innovations to be commercialized by them. "Most of the inventions that 3M depends on today came out of ... individual initiative. You don't make a difference by just following orders" (3M, 2002).

Tolerance of Risk-Taking and Fear of Failure

Organizations that create an internal environment where employees could take risks in their search for new solutions and ideas will indeed erase the fear of failure. A higher degree of tolerance for risk-taking activities will steer the way for employees to try out new innovative ideas without this fear (A.T Kearney, 2005b). "The learning friendly workplace uses the diversity of ideas as a rich source of connectivity and relationship to foster innovation, and provide breakthrough thinking to arrive at creative outcome that would otherwise be very unlikely" Pearl Zhu, (2020)

Learning from Customers and Users

Following Verworn et al. (2005) and Riederer et al. (2005), almost half of the innovative ideas are sourced from customers, as explained by Figure 1 below.

In a survey conducted by Booz Allen Hamilton in 2005 of European companies, more than half of the surveyed executives mentioned that most of the new ideas to improve existing products and services would come from customers and users. (Booz Allen Hamilton, 2005)

Figure 1. Most essential sources for innovation ideas (Verworn et al. 2000) (Adapted in C-LAB-TR-2005-3, pp 18 by Riederer et al. 2005)

The Whirlpool Company, a large home appliance manufacturer in North America, began focusing on design and used customer observation to develop products that were distinct and easy to use. Despite high prices, their new products are selling extremely well (Salter, 2005).

When organizations convert employees to become "customers" of the products, that employees will have the first-hand experience with the products, and they will be able to provide rich sources of new ideas of the existing products. The Harley Davidson company's employees are their customers, and the company was able to generate new ideas from the first-hand experiences (Verworn et al., 2000). "Innovation is more than generating the next big idea. It involves how you implement the ideas that make it out of the gate, and how you build the culture to sustain the creativity of ideas. Innovation's ability to modify strategy is critical". (Brands, 2015)

CURRENT INDONESIAN MANUFACTURING FIRMS' EXPERIENCES WITH INNOVATION MANAGEMENT

One of the most insidious problems with innovation management in the country is the low participation of local domestic firms in collaborative innovation activities. Okamoto and Sjöholm (2001) said that the lack of technological development due to the low level of R & D budget and education is the first setback Indonesia has faced in implementing innovation activities. Indonesia's technological capacity has to rely heavily on foreign direct investments." However researchers, Van Geenhuizen and Indarti (2005) state that "financial constraints found to be the most important barrier that the small and medium companies faced in accessing knowledge to be used in innovation process."

There was an instance whereby technology transfer in the turbine industry was severely hampered by the lack of knowledge and skills of Indonesian personnel (Soekarno et al., 2009). A study conducted by an Indonesian researcher, Arif Hartono (2017), based on data of a survey of 1179 manufacturing firms, completed in 2011, which covers the period 2009 to 2010, revealed some common significant barrier perceptions faced by Indonesian manufacturing firms in performing innovation. These barrier perceptions are namely: Market and institutions, employee and organization, financial and risks, and knowledge and cooperation. The study also studies the impact of innovation barriers to both innovative firms and non-innovative firms.

Market and institution barriers are related to factors that include market domination, demand uncertainty, market information, cooperation, and availability of technical information. Employee and organization barriers are related to factors that include employee resistance, managers' resistance to change, and organizational rigidities. Financial and risk barriers are related to factors on the availability of financial support both internally and externally, easy access to fundings, cost of innovation, and risks to firm performing innovation activities. Knowledge and cooperation barriers are related to factors concerning the sharing of knowledge and cooperation among firms performing innovation activities.

The second Indonesian Innovation survey conducted in 2011, using the guidelines stated by the OECD & Eurostat (2005), defined innovation "as the implementation of a new or significantly improved product (goods or services) or progress, a new marketing method, or a new organizational method in business practices or workplace organization or external relations". The survey found that the types of innovation predominantly adopted by Indonesian manufacturing firms are marketing innovation, product innovation, process innovation, and organizational innovation. Marketing innovation receives the highest mean score of 43%, and the lowest is organizational innovation, which receives 31%. This indicates that manufacturing firms focus more on marketing innovation than other types of innovation activities (Hartono, 2017). "Innovation activities in developing countries focus more on the market rather than on technology" Wamae (2009).

Barriers That Influence the Types of Innovation

The study found that the most significant influence among Indonesia's manufacturing firms' perception is the financial and risk barriers. It has a mean score of almost 3 (from 0 to 4). Market and institution received the score of average, 2.65, knowledge and cooperation received an average score of 2.24 and employee and organization received an average score of 1.78

The researcher also noted that the financial and risk barriers have a negative direction on the various types of innovation. Firstly, this means that the more financial and risk barriers the firm faces, the more reluctant it is to engage in various types of innovation activity. Secondly, this is the knowledge and cooperation of barrier perception. The more the firm encounters the lack of knowledge or cooperation in the innovation activities, the more reluctant it will be the firm's behavior to engage in innovation activities. Interestingly, the market and institution barriers have no significant relationship between the barriers and any innovation types. As far as the employee and organization barrier, it has a positive association with the type of innovation the firm is going to undertake.

The Relationship of Barriers to Innovation Success

The survey also studied the strengths and weaknesses of the relationship between barriers to innovation success. Using the Tobit regression, the researcher found out that market and innovation factors, and employee and organization factors, have a direct positive influence on innovation success. In contrast, financial and risk, as well as knowledge and cooperation factors, have a negative direct association with innovation success. Thus, this means that the lack of financial support or the considerable cost of R&D activities and the high risk of the market factors, faced by the firm, will likely act as a severe deterrence to the firm to undertake any innovation activities.

Strategies of Open Innovation to Counter Barriers

Indonesian manufacturing firms do have strategies to overcome some of these innovation barriers. Following the same study as mentioned, open innovation might be a way for these firms to seek external sources of knowledge or expertise to overcome the setback of these barriers (Hartono, 2017). Dahlander and Gann (2010) state that a single organization cannot innovate in isolation. To win the competition, firms should engage external partners (e.g. customers, foreign partners, suppliers, public or private R & D institutions, consultants, or commercial laboratories) for expertise or specialized knowledge (Chesbrough, 2006; Laursen and Salter, 2006; Hartono 2017).

Chesbrough (2006) defines open innovation as seeking an external source of knowledge and expertise. Therefore, open innovation is the purposive inflows and outflows of knowledge to accelerate internal innovation and expand the market for external use of innovation (Chesbrough, 2006). In the open innovation concept, the study investigates the breadth and depth of the external knowledge sought by Indonesian manufacturing firms. The breadth of knowledge conceptually views how widely the firm seeks more external knowledge, whereas the depth means how in-depth the knowledge is. For Laursen and Salters, (2006), the width of external knowledge represents the breadth aspect and how deeply external knowledge is sought represents the depth aspect of open innovation. The study found that not all internal or external barriers were responded to by adopting open innovation concepts. Only the internal barrier to innovation (i.e. employee and organization barriers) have a definite link to both the firm's breadth and depth of openness. (Hartono, 2017).

Internal barriers, namely, staff resistance, managers' resistance, and organizational rigidities, categorized as employee and organization, responded positively to open innovation strategy. Thus, this means that when Indonesian manufacturing firms face these three types of barriers, they would be more likely to respond by seeking external knowledge "widely" (breadth) and "deeply" (depth). When the firm faces market and institution barriers, they will seek external knowledge more intensely (depth). Barriers such as financial and risk have no positive relationship with Open Innovation. The firm will likely seek help from banks and venture capitalists externally. The smaller the firm, the higher the firm's efforts that tend to seek external knowledge widely (breadth) (Hartono, 2017). Open innovation often faces a backlash because ideas that are not adopted are due to cultural and political biases. Non-adoption of these ideas are not necessarily technical in nature. Innovators in the organization need to forge consensus and create a large network of supporters at every layer. A large network of supporters will help reduce silo thinking and increase the odds of creating a more holistic acceptance of equal ownership of these ideas. (Dirk et al, 2017)

BENCHMARKING OTHERS COUNTRIES' INNOVATION STRATEGIES

Indonesia could learn how Germany and Netherlands developed its national innovation models and implement the whole system of innovation management strategies. Despite Germany's domination in the world's automobile and auto engineering and vehicle technology sectors, to remain competitive, Germany has to re-assess its innovation management policy annually. Germany's innovation management policies had a critical underpinning, namely the reliable vocational education training system and the establishment of higher education research-based institutions. The vocational education training system provides the skilled workforce with its complex industrial infrastructure to remain competitive in its dominance, i.e. motor vehicles and mechanical engineering. The research institutions, both public and private R&D

institutes, and universities conduct R&D activities linked to their private industries. As such, Germany's innovation strategy framework is the following:

1. Innovation activities that stem from R & D institutes receive funding from Federal and State governments and private industries. Private industries' fundings have been increasing over the years.
2. All public and private R & D institutions, including universities and colleges, undertake basic research and innovation-oriented R & D activities.
3. The R & D institutions' linkage is strongly motivated by the federal and state governments through its funding activities and collaborative efforts among the R&D institutions themselves.
4. Major Universities and colleges that conduct R & D activities have one primary aim: to focus on advanced areas that are primary strategic and programmatic importance to society, science, and industry.
5. The federal government efforts in promoting technology commercialization have the following objectives, namely:
    a. The exploitation of research results into commercial products and services to boost future value adds and creating new jobs.
    b. Spin-offs - increase in the number of research-related startups or Small and Medium-sized firms (SMEs).
    c. Partnerships - heighten collaboration between research institutions and private sectors.
    d. Competence- facilitate the use of research results in private firms' innovation activities. Private or public research institutions can perform further research on the results of a private firm's innovation activities for scaling up products or services.

There is an added incentive as of now to motivate researchers to achieve their goals. The universities, however, own the inventions originated by these researchers in the respective universities. If this invention is patented and when the patents generate money, the university researcher will receive 30% of the gross income. In this way, the government supports researchers to open their businesses and speed up innovation. Experienced researchers have now become Technological consultants to offer their expertise to SMEs and corporate bodies.

Industry Cluster Research

The Federal and State governments are also encouraging its affiliated research agencies, including the German Research Foundations, Max Plank Society, Fraunhofer Society, to create industry cluster research. The aim is to widen its reach and specialize in research into various new technological fields in more depths within the private industries. Hence, fields that include nanotechnology, information and communication technology, and medical and pharmaceutical technologies have formed clusters for government-funded research.

RECOMMENDATIONS FOR INDONESIA'S INNOVATION STRATEGIES

Indonesia needs to develop new strategies and revisit its policies at both the micro and macro levels to achieve more significant synergies and collaboration of all actors in the innovation arena. Indonesia's private sector has to collaborate with the government and public R&D institutions to be useful for national innovation management.

Firms' Roles

Improve the Efficiency of Innovation Activities

Going forward is to improve the efficiency of the firm's internal innovation strategies by reducing the hierarchal effects that nullify the efforts to achieve measurable achievement in innovation. These hierarchical barriers are ingrained in the culture and communication styles within society. Employees are only to be seen at work and not to speak up. New idea generations will be difficult under this circumstance. The knowledge that is tacit within the employee will remain hidden, and diffusion of knowledge across the workplace gained through experience from work is nullified. Diversity in ideas must be encouraged with the objective of improving the firm's competitiveness. Technology itself will not bring about innovation. Tacit knowledge has to be shared, and ideas have to be diffused, and "learning" of how to use diverse ideas for improvements must exist organically within the firm. Learning can transform existing technology into innovative results. Firms could develop their idea generation model or innovation management system that includes the "Stage-Gate Model" initially and further improves its innovation management system.

Top Management Support for Innovation Activities

Without top management support in innovation activities, innovation activities will be disadvantaged. A positive and enabling environment within the firm for innovation activities has to be created by top management. The lack of key stakeholder's participation that includes the top management or CEO is indeed becoming one of the most significant barriers to innovation. (Day, 2016)

Develop Cross-Functional Teams and On-the-Job Training

It is known throughout organizational development research that cross-functional team will be able to generate new ideas. A cross-functional team is a team that is comprised of employees from different backgrounds, disciplines, and departments that could generate ideas for problem-solving. Firms that encourage the formation of cross-functional teams regularly benefit from this exercise. Learning and tacit exchange of ideas will spur on the transformation of existing technology and knowledge into innovations. Extensive on the job training schemes within the firm could also encourage "knowledge transfer and technology diffusion" with the firm.

Improve Vocational Training Scheme

Improvement of vocational training scheme within the firm that is directly connected to the firm's products and services will increase the stock of knowledge ready-made for the transfer of technology from direct foreign investment. It will be difficult for firms to adopt, adapt, and imitate new technology through foreign direct investment or technology licensing when they do not have a skilled workforce. Government support for this vocational training scheme at a public or private level must be enhanced. Government innovation agencies that are responsible for coordinating for the upgrading of vocation skills within private industries must be created to have a strong linkage with the private industries.

Equal Contribution from Government and Private Industries

Government collaboration efforts in innovation should also devise a policy whereby private industries should contribute towards workers' vocational upgrading. Equal contributions from the government and the private industries could be made to sustain the cost of continual improvements of skills directly needed for firms or specialized industries. Tax incentives for firms that participate in this scheme should be allowed. Future innovation activities do not grow in a vacuum. Previous stocks of knowledge created will enhance future innovation activities of the firm.

Document and Journalize Firm's Innovation Activities

Numerous innovative activities were conducted by small firms or enterprises that were rarely covered by scholarly research. The formal segment of national innovation policy rarely covers these aspects too. Small incremental innovations of these enterprises will count towards the stock of knowledge that has to be diffused across the economy. There is a need to capture these incremental innovations that were done informally. Government agencies like the Techno Parks or regional R&D Institutes should capture these innovations by documenting and journalizing them for further, and higher value adds the transformation to be done. Each firm or enterprise must be linked to the Techno Park agencies or regional R&D institutes for collaboration to document these innovations or knowledge stock.

Enhance the Industry Clusters' Absorptive Capacity

Private industries cluster should be formed to focus on its specific needs for a skilled workforce and logistical support to achieve their innovation goals. Each firm shall endeavor to collaborate within the niche and requirements within the specific industry cluster. Movement of labor within the specific cluster should be allowed. Linkages of this specific cluster with the R&D institutions of various universities should be maintained. Within the cluster, these R & D institutions could do essential research work for the entire cluster because the specific industry needs might be the same, thus reducing the firm's cost within the cluster. The R&D institutions that serve the industry cluster must foster adoptive capacity by encouraging learning and transfer of skills within the clusters.

Incentivize or Reward New Idea Sources at Firm Level

The firm's Human resource management shall take into account the employees' contribution to innovation activities. Rewarding employees for their ideas when the innovation goal is achieved could set a new pace for educational support for innovation activities. Additionally, HRM plays an integral part in transforming the culture of the organization. An organization that empowers line managers to encourage employees to engage in innovation activities may overcome barriers to innovation effectively and sustain the generation of ideas consistently. (Gupta, 2017)

Enhancing the "Adopt, Adapt and Imitate" Strategies

For emerging economies and developing countries, going into radical innovation will be quite a difficult task. The most suitable strategy for developing countries is to adopt, adapt, and imitate foreign technologies. Indonesia's innovative firms could do this by collaborating with the Techno parks research facilities and public R & D institutions. Collaborative efforts and suitable linkages between the firms,

R&D institutions in this direction to gain the advantage of acquiring technologies from direct investments will enhance the "learning process" within the local firms.

GOVERNMENT'S ROLE IN ENHANCING PRIVATE SECTOR PARTICIPATION

Improve Social, Legal, and Political Reforms to Rid of Racial Divide

While Indonesia's economy is improving, substantial social, legal, and political reforms need to solve the divisive racial tension and mistrusts between the Pribumi and Chinese ethnic groups. The government and the leadership could do these societal reforms within the political system. Divisive political and social cleavage should be avoided, and the innovation system could reach a more comprehensive level of performance.

Linkages with Research Local Institutes and Universities

The German and Netherlands innovation agencies create emphasis on linkages and collaborations among R&D institutions and universities with the private industries. This effort is unavoidable if the output of the national innovation policy is to bear fruits. Government effort to set up and intensify linkages and collaborations must be supported by all actors/stakeholders. The DG Strengthening Innovation must be empowered to raise the linkages and collaborations across the board up to a higher performance level. Evaluations of these linkages and collaborations must be made into a factor in assessing the annual allocation of fundings to each institution.

Incentivize Collaborations between R&D Institutes and Individual Firms or Industry Clusters

Industry clusters in innovation activities could provide a mechanism to evaluate the success of the innovation work of R&D institutes. The pairing of R&D Institutes with each firm, or within the cluster, provides the necessary linkages for the diffusion of technology. Hence, the government should incentivize this collaboration by providing more fundings when evaluating each R & D institute's performance. R & D institutes provide a more significant performance in specialized research that improves innovation; private industries' innovation should get funding bonuses from the government. The result should be a better product, process, or organizational innovations that will provide the competitiveness of the firms or strategic industry the country needs.

Improve Curriculum for Science, Technology, and Innovation for Higher Level of Absorptive Capacity

Improving the curriculum for science, technology, and innovation education at the national level will help Indonesia achieve milestone progress in innovation activities and the "catching-up" rate of absorptive capacity with new technology from advanced economies. Acquisition of new technology from direct foreign investment or foreign technology licensing could be enhanced when 'absorptive capacity" to adapt, adopt, and imitate these technologies.

International Linkages and Collaborations with local R&D Institutions and Universities

Linkages and collaborations with international R & D institutions and research Universities with local R & D institutions would positively influence local R & D institutions' performance. Government to government bilateral diplomatic relations could help in this collaboration. This will improve the diffusion of knowledge, knowledge transfer, and exposure for local researchers to International benchmarking of research activities.

Improve International Competitiveness by Subsidizing Wages of Scientists or Researchers

In Germany, the federal and state governments sponsor the firm's innovation activities by paying the scientists and engineers the necessary R & D activities in specific technology that the government has earmarked to improve overall economic competitiveness. This will reduce the cost burden of private firms and entice them to create innovations that will achieve international competitiveness.

Tax Incentives and Legalities of Registered Patents

The government should give private firms tax incentives if they can show innovation work using registered patents. Indonesia's tax regimes and patent registration system should be revamped to enable this effort. Active legal institutions must back recent improvements in patent and copyright registrations. When the court administration involves long, lengthy, and costly procedures, it will not help the patent owner or the copyright owner seek legal redress. Instead, it will become a disincentive. Indonesia might want to establish good arbitration centers as a recourse for patent and copyright enforcement apart from the court system as a less costly and efficient alternative.

Incentivize Individual Researcher or Firm

Individual researchers in research laboratories and from universities and R&D institutes should earn specific percentages of income generated from new patented innovations. The patents of these innovative efforts shall remain with the respective universities or R&D institutions. Individual inventions might contain the benefits of externalities. This means that the result of the individual researcher or firm's innovation might be copied by other competitive firms or organizations or researchers. There are social benefits attached to the product of the innovation itself. Hence, this is why there is less incentive for individual researchers or firms to commit to innovation activities. Incentives for the individual researcher or firm to come out with innovation should be protected by sufficient patent rights or copyrights framework and given adequate monetary incentives and social recognitions.

Open Innovation, Learning and Technology Transfer

Open innovation that allows learning of new technology from external sources of the organizations or the firm should be encouraged. This will help technology transfer, learning, and development of new researchers. The government should encourage experienced researchers or foreign technology consultants to set up businesses as consultants to undertake research work with private industries. This will speed up the process of innovation and competitiveness of the specific private industries.

Spin-offs from Industry Clusters for SMEs

The government agencies or technopark's research management should coordinate and incubate technology-based SMEs to absorb and learn new technologies from spin-offs of foreign technologies. This could come from industry clusters or foreign direct investments. The technopark's management should also liaise with venture capitals or banks for these SMEs to gain access to fundings. SMEs that are technology-based might have the requirements for readily trained and skilled workforce to absorb these technologies. However, without funding, these SMEs might not have the resources to gain an advantage from the new technologies.

Enhancing Multiple Funding Sources by Building Financial Ecosystem

The government should enhance the current funding sources for innovation activities. Efforts to get fundings from international philanthropies and venture capitals should be intensified. Besides the present bank fundings, private stakeholder fundings should be made available to SMEs and private industries to get into innovation activities. SMEs with a good track record shall be assisted via a crowdfunding mechanism to get into the growth stage. Besides direct funding by government, banks, schemes such as Debt financing, public-private sector financing collaboration, risk reduction funding, and venture capital seed funding, it will also enhance the funding environment for SMEs and private firms.

Service-Based Industry

The service-based industry that represents the hospitality, tourism, and retail sectors have not been featured due to lack of data. Government agencies could survey their innovation plans and strategies that would highlight innovation activities conducted within the industry. This will significantly help the public and private sector innovation agencies to plan and assist them in improving their financial competitiveness.

CONCLUSION

Indonesian firms and government agencies involved in innovation activities need to enhance their collaboration and synchronize their strategies to achieve economic competitiveness. Systemic coordination and linkages by all actors in the national innovation management system will result in the efficient management of innovation activities. Government initiatives to entice private companies to engage in innovation activities must be reviewed and improved from time to time. Enhancing employees' learning skills will improve the firms' absorptive capacity to engage in adapting and adopting the technologies they acquired. This will improve participation within the industry. The government cannot avoid focusing on helping SMEs with science-based capabilities in its growth stage to innovate new technologies and to help develop Indonesia's dream of becoming among the top powerful countries in the world by 2045, using its science and technology capabilities.

REFERENCES

Accenture. (2005). What Makes Innovation Successful? In *Accenture Report on European Companies*. Accenture Publishing.

Aghion, P., & Akcigit, U. (2017). Innovation and Growth. The Schumpeterian Perspective. In Economics without Borders, Economic Research for European Policy Challenges (pp. 29-72). Cambridge University Press. doi:10.1017/9781316636404.003

Allen, M. M. C. (2009). Germany's National Innovation System. In *Encyclopaedia of Technology & Innovation* (pp. 375–389). Basil Blackwell Ltd.

Amabile, T (1998). How to kill creativity. *Harvard Business Review, 76*, 77-87.

Aminulla, E., & Gammeltoft, P. (2006). *The Indonesian Innovation System at a Crossroads, Research papers in economics*. http://www.dieas.repec.org

Bergmann. (2005). Jesu Ein and Alles. *Brandeius, 9*, 94-99.

Bhattacharya, A., & Pangestu, M. (1993). *The Lessons of East Asia. Indonesian Development, Transformation and Public Policy*. The World Bank.

Booz Allen Hamilton. (2005). *How Companies Turn Customer's Big Ideas into Innovation*. Strategy & Business. http/:www.strategy-business.com/sbkw article/ sbkw050112/pg=3&id=230(status.06.12.2005

Brands, R. F. (2015). *The Key to Successful Innovation is Proper Implementation*. The Chief Executive. http://www.chiefeexcutive.net

Breen. (2004). *The 6 Myths of Creativity*. Fast Company. https://www.fastcompany.com/magazine/89/creativity.html

Chesbrough, H., Vanhaverbeke, W., & West, J. (Eds.). (2006). Open Innovation: Researching a new Paradigm. Oxford University Press.

Cooper & Kleinshmidt. (1992). Stage Gate System for New Product Success. Marketing Management, 7, 20-29.

Dahlander, L., & Gann, D. (2010). *How Open is Innovation?* http://www.sciencedirect.com

Day, J. (2016), *Overcoming 10 Barriers to Innovation*. http://www.ideascale.com

Dejong. (2003). *Innovation in Service Firms explored: What, How and Why?* EIM Business Policy Research. http://www.eim.net/pdf-ez/B200205

Deloitte. (2005). *Glittering Price, How Financial Institution can drive growth through process and service innovation*. Author.

Dirk, D., Leva, R., & Barnhorn, R. (2017). Open Innovation Generates Great Ideas, So Why aren't Companies adopting them? *Harvard Business Review*. http://hbr.org.org

Gerpott. (1999). *Strategie-Technologie-und Innovation Management*. Auflage.

GIPA. (2019). *Understanding Indonesia's Innovation system*. GIPA.

Gupta, M. (2017). *How to Overcome Barriers to Innovation in Your Organization*. Customer Think. http://www.customerthink.com

Hartono, A. (2017). What Hampers Innovation of Indonesian Manufacturing Firms? Insight from the Indonesian Innovation Survey, In *CIE 2017-Proceedings of the 5th International Conference on Innovation and Entrepreneurship* (p. 33). Academic Conferences and Publishing Ltd.

Hippel, E. V. (2005). The Sources of Innovation. Oxford University Press.

Hutton, J. (2018). *Corruption 101: An Insider's guide to graft in Indonesia*. http://www.international.the news.com

Imhausen. (2005). *Haus-Peta-Herausfor derung und Zeid*. PFIF 2005. http://www.pfif.de/herausfordeng.html

Karslberg, R., & Adler, J. (2005). *Strategies for Sustained Innovation*. http://www.innovationtools.com/Articles/EnterpriseDetails.asap?a=185

Kearney, A. T. (2005). *European Best innovators, in: The New frontiers*. http://www.atkearney.com/shared.pdf/European-Bestinnovator.pdf

Kramer, E., & Maharajh, R. (2010). *Innovation Strategies in Developing Countries*. https://www.resarchgate.net/publications/1231182504

Lakitan, B. (2013). *Connecting all the dots: Identifying the "actor level" Challenges in establishing effective Innovation System in Indonesia*. Science Direct. http://www.elservier.com/locate/techsoc35

Laursen, K., & Salter, A. (2006). Open for Innovation: The role of Openness in Explaining Innovation Performances among UK Manufacturing Firms. *Strategic Management Journal*, *27*(2), pp131–pp150. doi:10.1002mj.507

LIPI. (2010). *Current Conditions, Research and Development of State University survey R and D of Higher Education Sector in 2010*. http://www.Pappiptek.lipi.go.id/id/node/48

Nesta. (2019). *Understanding Policymakers in Indonesia*. http:/www.nesta.org.uk

OECD. (2016). Indonesia. In *SMEs, Entrepreneurship and Innovation*. OECD Publishing.

OECD & Eurostat. (2005). Oslo Manual: Guidelines for Collecting & Interpreting Innovation data (3rd Ed). Paris: Author.

Okamoto, Y., & Sjoholm, F. (2001). *Technological Development in Indonesia*. ELJS. (Working paper no: 124)

Pangestu, M., & Hrianto, F. (1999). *Corporate Governance in Indonesia. Prognosis and Way Ahead*. Submitted for International Conference on Democracy, Market Economy and Development, Feb 1999, Soeul, South Korea.

Pisano, G. P. (2015). You Need an Innovation Strategy. *Harvard Business Review*. http://www.hbr.org

Powers. (2004). *What Innovation Can't Do*. Business 2.0. http://www.business2.com/b2/web articles/0.17863,68312300.html

Riederer. (2005). *Innovation Management- An Overview and some Best Practices* (Report volume 4, No 3). Paderborn University.

Salter. (2005). *Whirlpool finds its Cool*. Fast Company. http://www.fast company.com/magazine/95/open-design-Jones-html

Schmookler, J. (1966). *Invention and Economic Growth*. Harvard University Press. http://www.philpapers.org

Schumpeter, J. (1912). Theorie der Wirtschaftlichen Ent Wickhng. Academic Press.

Schumpeter, J. (1947). The Creative Response in Economic History. *The Journal of Economic History*, *7*(2), 149–159. doi:10.1017/S0022050700054279

Sherman. (2005). *The Innovative Organization; Lessons from Most Admired Companies*. Hay Insight Selection. http://www.haygroup.com/mediafiles/downloads/Hay_Insight_selection_April_2005

Sloane, P. (2020). *Recessions, Innovation and Survival- A Lesson from Kellogg's*. http//www. innovationmanagement.se

Soekarno. (2009). Technology transfer Challenges in Indonesia; An experience from Industry Turbine Overhaul. *Asian Journal of Technology Management*, *2*(1), 2009.

Soenarso, W. S., & Saderno, H. (2014). *A Strategy to Increase Indonesian Private R and D Investment*. Asia Pacific Tech Monitor.

Soesastro, H., & Pengestu, M. (1988). Indonesia's Electronic Industry. In The Effects of Liberalization in Asia's Textiles, Clothings and Electronics Industries. Australian Pacific economic Cooperation Committee.

Turrell, M., & Lindow, Y. (2003). *The innovation Pipeline*. Imginatik Research White paper.

Vahs, D., & Burmester, R. (2005). *Vahs, Dietmari; Burmester, Ralf: Innovation Management,Auflage, Scahaeffer*. Poeschel.

Valery. (1999). Innovation in Industry: Industry Gets Religion. *Economist, 350*(8107).

Van Geenhuizen, M., & Indarti, N. (2005). Knowledge as a Critical Resource in Innovation among Small Furniture Companies in Indonesia. *Gadjah Mada International Journal of Business, 7*(3), 371–390. doi:10.22146/gamaijb.5581

Verworn. (2000). *Innovation Management in Kleinen und Mittleren*. Academic Press.

Viki, T. (2017). Why Companies must align Innovation Strategy with Business Strategy. *Innovation as a Corporate Mission/Business Goals*. http://www.forbes.com

Wamae, W. (2009). Enhancing the role of knowledge and innovation for Development. *International Journal of Technology Management & Sustainable Development, 8*(3), 199–228. doi:10.1386/ijtm.8.3.199/1

Yose Damuri, R., Aswicahyona, H., & Christian, D. (2018). *Innovation Policy in Indonesia*. Innovation Policy in ASEAN. http://www.sematic.sch

Zhu, P. (2020). Five Innovation Practices for Building and Managing all Innovation Program. *Collaborative Innovation- Leadership, Organization Culture, Strategies, Support for SMEs*. http://www.innovationmanagement.se

Zyman, S., & Brott, A. (2004). *Renovate Before You Innovate: Why doing New Thing Might Not be the Right thing*. Penguin Group USA.

Chapter 6
National Innovation Systems:
Comparison of Turkey and South Korea

Fatma Nur Karaman Kabadurmus
https://orcid.org/0000-0002-2206-8669
Yasar University, Turkey

Ceyda Senses
Pamukkale University, Turkey

Buse Turkyilmaz
Yasar University, Turkey

ABSTRACT

Since innovation is central to the success of firms in the 21st century, policymakers in many countries try to achieve sustained competitive advantage by promoting technological innovations. However, achieving this goal requires coordination of all actors in the economy including governments, industries, and national institutions. Although each individual actor has unique capabilities and strategic resources, how well the economy performs depends on the strengths of the network as a whole. National Innovation Systems (NIS) approach considers all these interdependent actors within a country to increase national competitiveness. A good example in this regard is South Korea, an innovation leader, which could be a role model for developing countries with its well-established NIS. This chapter studies the elements of the NIS of this country and compares them with that of an emerging economy, Turkey, by using data from the Global Innovation Index and the Global Competitiveness Index. The analysis reveals the strengths and weaknesses of Turkey and helps to draw concrete policy conclusions.

DOI: 10.4018/978-1-7998-4195-1.ch006

Copyright © 2021, IGI Global. Copying or distributing in print or electronic forms without written permission of IGI Global is prohibited.

INTRODUCTION

National innovation systems (NIS) approach depends on understanding the relationships between performers of innovation in order to promote economic development and growth (Freeman and Soete, 1982; Lundvall, 1992) and thus, has attracted the attention of both researchers and policymakers (Rakas and Hain, 2019). Innovation performers/actors include universities, firms, private or public research institutes, and the government. Unlike the linear model of innovation, the national innovation system is a very complicated and interrelated system (Figure 1). In knowledge-based societies, these actors contribute to achieving countries' innovation performance targets. For example, universities conduct research, commercialize the results and also educate people. The role for the industry is to transform ideas and inventions. And finally, the government's role is to set policies and provide the necessary funding for investments (Wilson et. al. 2020).

Figure 1. Components of NIS (Adapted from Betz et al., 2016)

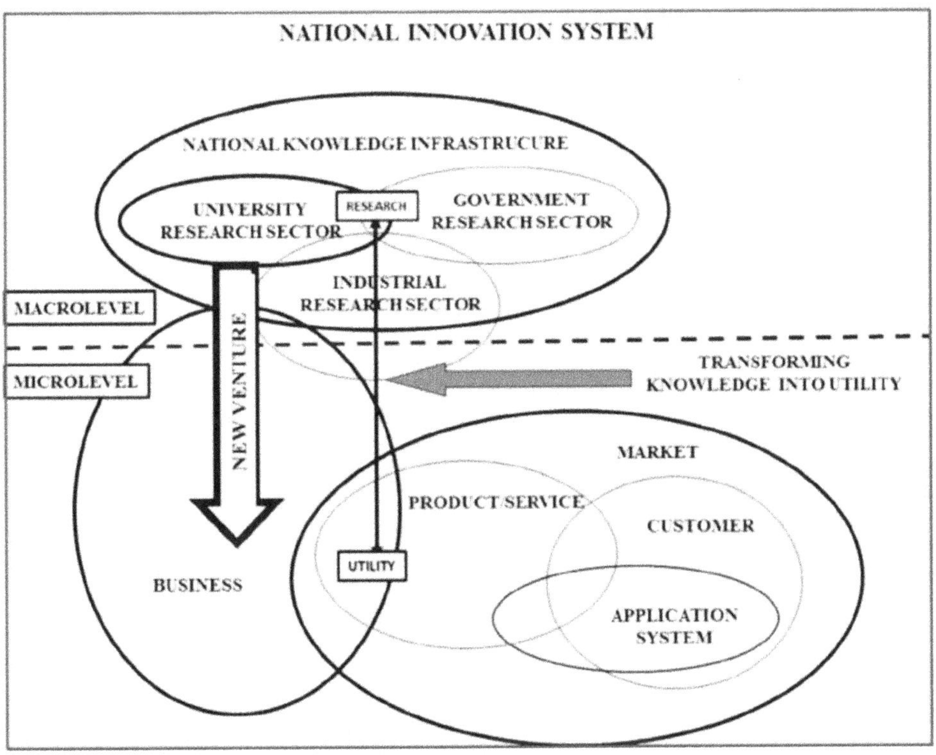

The core of the NIS consists of firms. In the wider setting, the education system, labor market, financial market, macroeconomic conditions, and government policies are included in the system since the performance of firms depends on these socio-economic conditions within a country (Lundvall, 1992). To understand the relationships between firms and institutions, Lundvall (2016) proposes a 4-step method. The first step involves analyzing the organizational structure and human resources in a firm with the consideration of sector specialization. In the second step, linkages of firms to each other (at both national and international level) and to knowledge infrastructure is analyzed. In the third step, characteristics of socioeconomic conditions that are peculiar to the nation are determined. The final and fourth step involves identifying the performance of the NIS based on firm organization and global network positioning.

South Korea is one of the leading performers of the NIS approach. In its development process, the country heavily invested in R&D, science, technology, and education. Today, the country is one of the world's major economies. On the other hand, Turkey, which had similar levels of per capita gross domestic product (GDP) as that of South Korea in the 1980s, is still a developing country, with a per capita GDP of $9370 (Figure 2).

Figure 2. GDP per capita (current US$) (1960-2018), World Bank

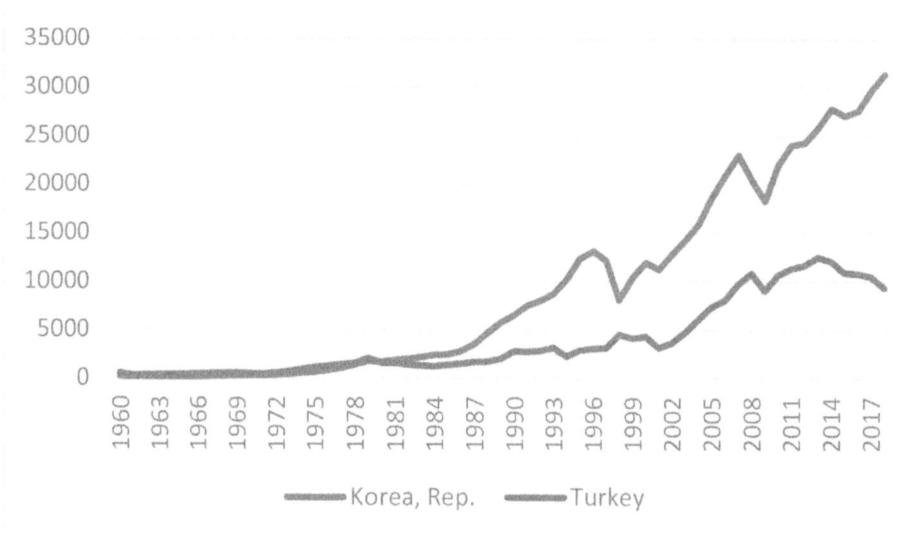

For developed countries like South Korea, the NIS helps to maintain national competitiveness, while for developing countries like Turkey, the NIS approach can be used as a means of 'catching up' (Wilson et.al., 2020). Therefore, the purpose of this study is to examine the NIS of Turkey and South Korea in order to draw implications for innovation policy in Turkey.

To this end, we will use data from the Global Competitiveness Index (GCI) and the Global Innovation Index (GII) pillars to identify the strengths and weaknesses of Turkey in terms of its national innovation system. Our analysis reveals that macroeconomic stability, institutional quality (business environment, political stability, and safety), lack of innovation linkages and knowledge diffusion and are among the major weaknesses. As for strengths, Turkey is doing better than South Korea in terms of labor market policies, business dynamism (attitudes toward risk, willingness to delegate authority, FDI new inflows), and market sophistication (measured by applied tariff rates and complexity of tariffs).

BACKGROUND

National Innovation Systems View

One of the first studies to introduce the concept of national innovation systems view is List (1841). In his pioneering work, the author discussed the importance of national systems of production and its ties with national institutions. In a later work, Freeman (1987) introduced the concept of national innovation systems. The author argued that the national innovation system is the network of public and private sector organizations that form new technologies with their activities and interactions. In another study, Lundvall (1992) discussed the importance of higher education as a source of innovation generation, and also knowledge and learning as drivers of economic performance. According to the author, such systems include 'all parts and aspects of the economic structure and the institutional set-up (of a country) affecting learning as well as searching and exploring'. Later on, innovation system perspective was developed further by many economists and took the attention of policy makers (Lundvall, 2016).

Brief Country Profiles

Innovation is the key driver of economic growth and national economic wellbeing and that is why many nations are investing in innovation to gain competitive advantages (Grossman and Helpman, 1991; Atkinson and Ezell, 2012; Bloom et al., 2019)

Innovation is defined as the development of a new or improved product, a new marketing method or a new organizational method. The transformation of innovation into an economic value-added is a general feature of innovation. Innovation is also a source of dynamism for economies, since it increases productivity, competitiveness, and the standard of living and prosperity within a country (Tomizawa et al., 2020).

South Korea is one of the most innovative countries in the world and is considered to be a knowledge-based economy (OECD, 2014). Although South Korea and Turkey had similar levels of income at the beginning of 1980s, Korea outpaced Turkey quickly first with its industrial policies in 1980s and later its innovation policies in 1990s (Table 1).

South Korea prioritized technology-intensive sectors in the 70s and 80s and, also placed high emphasis on accumulating human capital. In 1999, the South Korean government established the National Science and Technology Council (NSTC) to strengthen the Coordination of National Science and technology policies. The aim of establishing the NSTC was to increase the number of young people who choose to pursue careers in fields related to science and technology (Oguzturk, 2017).

Table 1. Macroeconomic Indicators: Turkey & South Korea

SOUTH KOREA	**1980**	**1990**	**2010**	**2014**	**2016**	**2018**	**2019**
GDP per capita (current US$)(thousand)	1.76	6.73	23.09	29.25	29.3	33.32	31.43
GDP growth (annual %)	-1.7	9.8	6.8	3.2	2.9	2.7	2
Total investment (% of GDP)	34.4	37.1	30.9	29.1	28.9	31	29.6
Gross savings (% of GDP)	23.84	38.64	32.13	35.02	36.52	34.90	34.19
Inflation %	28.7	8.6	2.9	1.3	1	1.5	0.5
Unemployment %	5.1	2.4	3.7	3.5	3.6	3.8	4
Current account balance (%of GDP)	-10.3	-1	2.4	5.6	6.5	4.4	3.2
TURKEY	**1980**	**1990**	**2010**	**2014**	**2016**	**2018**	**2019**
GDP per capita (current US$)(thousand)	2.13	3.74	10.48	12.02	10.82	9.41	8.96
GDP growth (annual %)	-0.8	9.3	8.5	5.2	3.2	2.8	0.2
Total investment (% of GDP)	26.7	23	23	29.7	28.2	29.1	24.47
Gross savings (% of GDP)	22.70	22.69	21.43	23.18	24.78	26.60	25.29
Inflation %	110.6	60.3	8.6	8.9	7.8	16.3	15.7
Unemployment %	7.2	8	11.1	9.9	10.9	11	13.8
Current account balance (%of GDP)	-3.2	-1.3	-5.8	-4.7	-3.8	-3.5	-0.6

Source: IMF

Turkey followed import-substituion policies in the 1960s and 70s, and later on shifted to export-oriented growth strategies in the 1980s (Andic, 2016). Altough the start of the export-oriented industrial strategy in Turkey and S. Korea started at similar periods, Turkey's main transition from low-tech sectors to technology-intensive sectors started very late, only at the beginning of the 2000s, during the accession process to the European Union. Turkish Industrial Strategy Document 2011-2014 (Towards EU Membership) states that in this process, Turkey focused on various organizational and structural transformations to create efficiently functioning market mechanisms. As a result, share of labor-intensive sectors in exports declined as the shares of medium-level technology products such as automotives, machinery, and electronics in the total manufacturing industry rose through out the years (Republic of Turkey Ministry of Industry and Trade, 2010). However, support programs for R&D were very limited until recently (Atiyas and Bakis, 2015). Thus, Turkey has very low levels of R&D intensity compared to Korea (Figure 3).

Figure 3. R&D expenditures (% of GDP) (World Bank)

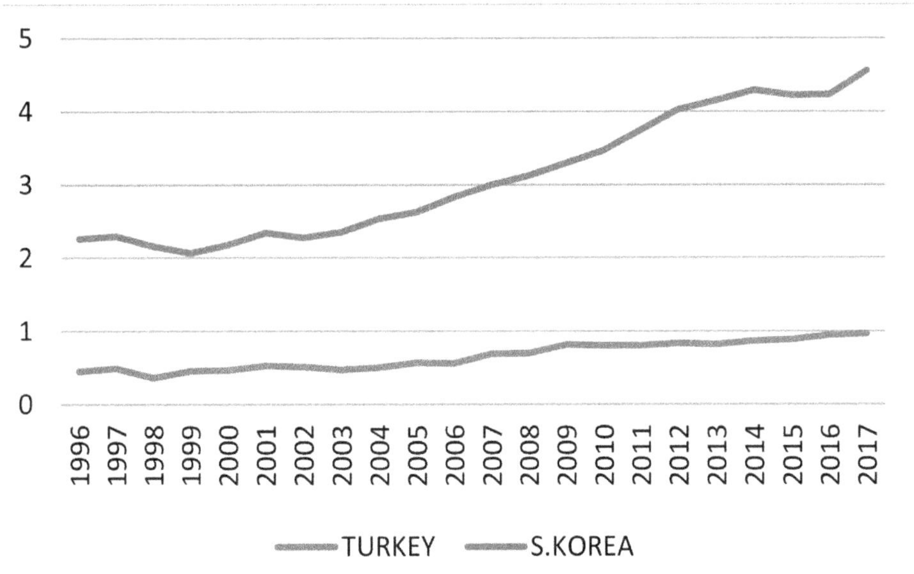

METHODOLOGY

Lundvall (2016) proposes a 4-step method to study NIS:

1. First step; analyzing the organizational structure and human resources in a firm with the consideration of sector specialization.
2. Second step; analyzing both national and international linkages of firms in the base of knowledge.

3. Third step; determining characteristics of education system, labor market, financial market, welfare government, intellectual property systems which are peculiar to the nation.
4. Fourth step; to understand efficiency level of the national innovation system looking at firms' organizational structure and network.

To compare innovation performances of South Korea and Turkey, we will follow Lundvall's 4-step method. To this end, we use data from Global Competitiveness Index (GCI) and Global Innovation Index (GII).

Global Competitiveness Index

Global competitiveness report is issued by the World Economic Forum annually since 2004. The report ranks countries according to their Global Competitiveness Index (GCI) values.

The GCI divides nations into three development stages by using information about their economic conditions, their production process and their competitiveness level. First stage includes factor driven countries; second stage includes efficiency driven countries; and finally, third stage consist of innovation driven countries. According to this development classification, Turkey is currently in the second stage and South Korea is in the third stage (GCI, 2018).

The index consists of the following twelve pillars:

1- Institutions, 2- Infrastructure, 3- ICT Adoption, 4- Macroeconomic Stability, 5- Health, 6- Skills, 7- Product Market, 8- Labour Market, 9- Financial System, 10- Market Size, 11- Business Dynamism and 12- Innovation Capability.

The GCI evaluates the main factors that determine improvement in the long-term growth and competitiveness of countries. The first five items listed above meet basic requirements and are essential for factor-driven economies. On the other hand, pillars from 6 to 10 increase efficiency and are essential for efficiency driven economies. The last two including Business Dynamism and Innovation Capability are required for innovation driven economies (Onsel et al., 2019).

Figure 4. Comparison of GCI rankings for Turkey and Korea (Global Competitiveness Report 2018)

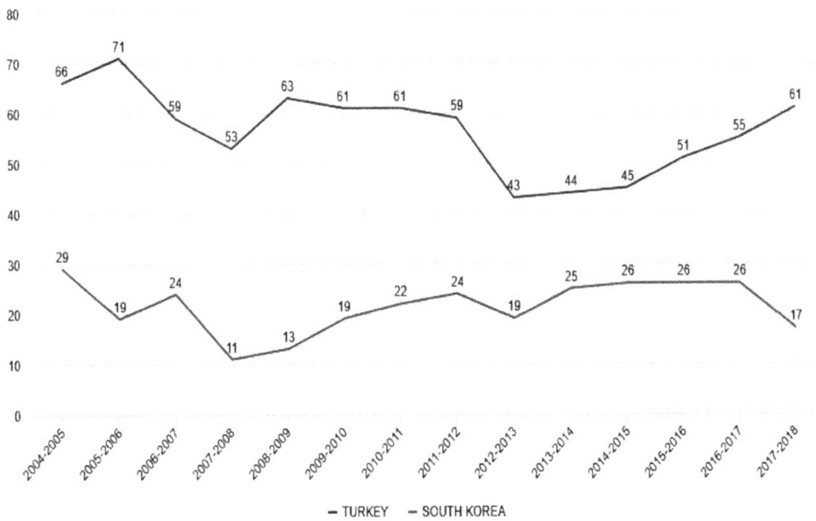

As can be seen from Figure 4, Turkey is far behind of South Korea in GCI rankings. According to the 2018 GCI, Turkey's rank is 55 and Korea's is 26.

Table 2. 2018 GCI rankings

GCI Pillars	Korea	Turkey	Difference
Institutions	27	71	44
Infrastructure	6	50	44
ICT adoption	1	71	70
Macroeconomic stability	1	116	115
Health	19	48	29
Skills	27	77	50
Product market	67	76	9
Labour market	48	111	63
Financial system	19	65	46
Market size	14	13	-1
Business dynamism	22	76	54
Innovation Capability	8	47	39

Source: Global Competitiveness Report 2018

Table 2 presents Turkey's and South Korea's GCI rankings in different pillars. We can see that Turkey's competitive advantage lies in her market size but the economy is doing worse in every other aspect of competitiveness when compared to South Korea.

Global Innovation Index

The use of indices and rankings is the most collective approach to compare the performances of different innovation systems since the late 1990s (Menna, et.al. 2019). Global Innovation Index collects data from 126 countries, representing 96.3% of global GDP. The aim of the index is to provide countries information about their innovation performance in order to help them to improve their innovation policies by identifying their strengths and weaknesses. Recent studies document that the GII is a good indicator of economic growth and innovation performance of countries (Pence et al., 2019.)

Figure 5. GII Overall Rank (2009-2018)

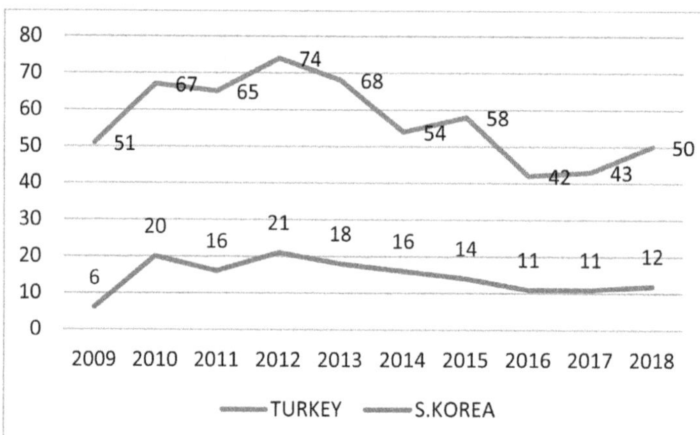

According to 2018 GII, South Korea ranked 12 and Turkey ranked 50 (Figure 5). GII also provides an input sub-index and an output sub-index. GII's input index ranking is based on data from the components in five pillars. Namely, institutions, human capital and research, infrastructure, market sophistication, and business sophistication (Figure 6). GII's output ranking is based on data from two pillars: knowledge and technology outputs and creative outputs. Again, Turkey is doing worse than South Korea in these pillars (Figure 7). Looking at both figures together, we can deduce that Turkey's innovation policies should target those pillars which constitute the input index.

Figure 6. GII input rank (2009-2018)

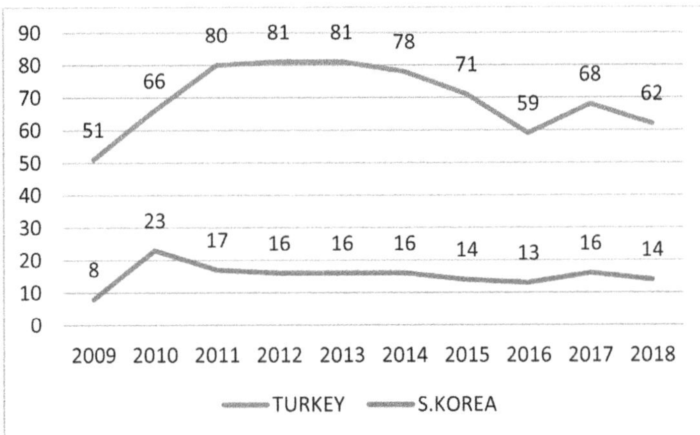

Figure 7. GII output rank (2009-2018)

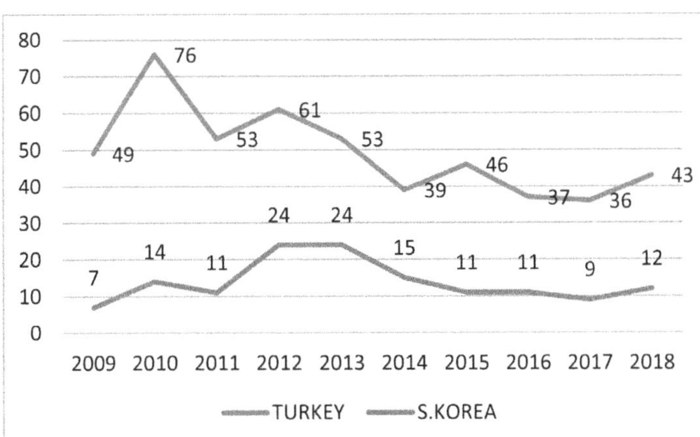

Analysis of the Central Motors and Knowledge Infrastructure

Next, following Lundvall's 4-step method, we will compare Turkey's and South Korea's NIS components as measured by the pillars of GCI and GII.

In the first and second step; we need to analyze the central motors of the NIS. These include firms' internal capabilities and their use of knowledge infrastructure. Thus, we can use data from the components in GCI Skills and ICT adoption pillars and also GII business sophistication, human capital and research, innovation capability, knowledge & technological outputs, and creative outputs pillars. To determine Turkey's strengths and weaknesses with respect to Korea, we will calculate the difference of the two countries' rankings in each relevant pillar and its components. For example, in 'ease of finding skilled employees' component under GCI skills pillar, Turkey ranks 117 and South Korea ranks 27, thus the difference in rankings is 90.

In each figure, red bars (negative values) represent the components that Turkey performs better than South Korea. Likewise, the blue bars (positive values) represent the components that Turkey performs worse than South Korea.

We first look at rankings of Turkey and South Korea in GCI innovation capability pillar, which reveals that Turkey is much behind Korea in terms on innovation capabilities (Figure 8).

Figure 8. GII innovation capability pillar (2018)

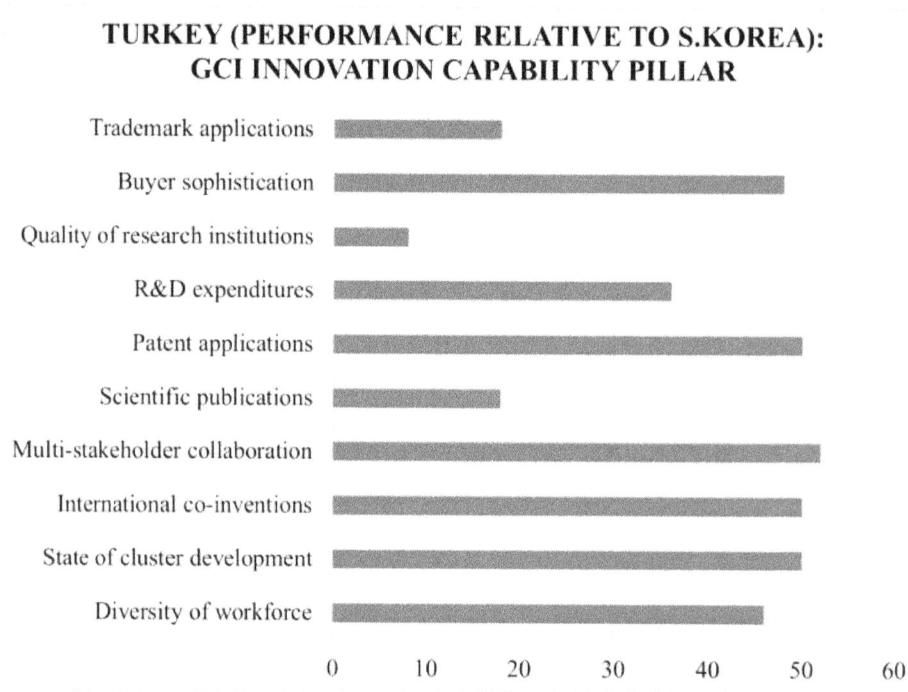

Building higher levels of collaborative innovation capabilities stimulates creativity and improves the quality of an organization's performance (Swink, 2006). However, Turkey has a low number of patent applications, collaborations and international co-inventions (Figure 8).

Figure 9. GII knowledge & technological outputs pillar (2018)

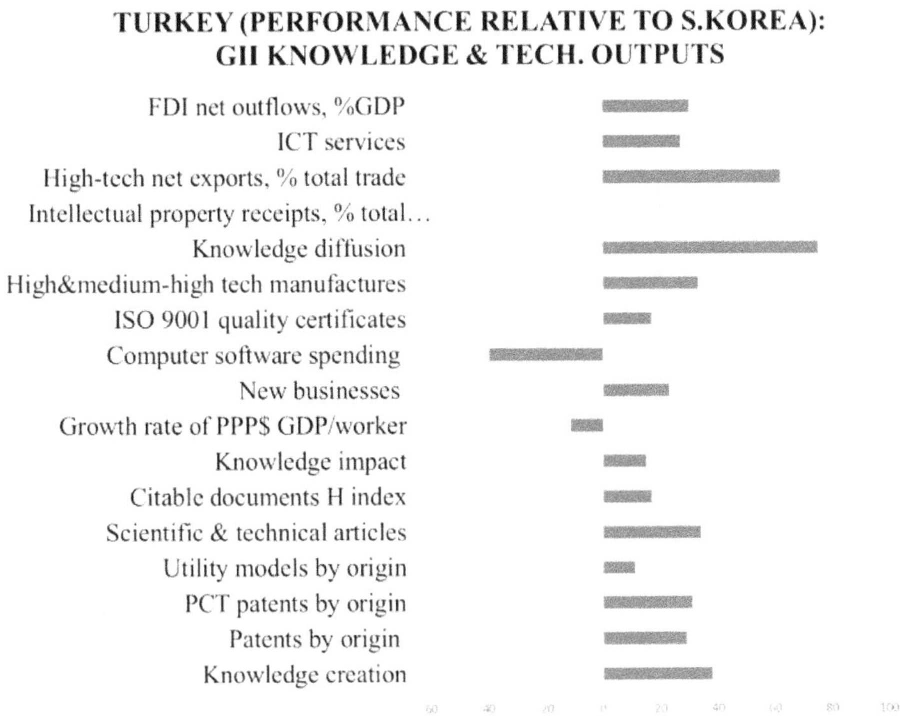

Moreover, Turkey's lack of diversity of workforce (as measured by gender, ethnicity, sexual orientation or religion) and a low level of cluster development (geographic concentrations of firms, suppliers, producers of related products and services, and specialized institutions) generates problems in creating innovation linkages (Figure 8). Therefore, Turkey's exports still depend on low-middle technology goods & services (Figure 9). Another problem lies in knowledge generation as can be seen from lower umber of patents, scientific articles, quality certificates, and intellectual property receipts (Figure 9). As a result, compared to S. Korea, percentages of ICT-enabled new organizational models (e.g., virtual teams, remote working, and telecommuting) within companies are lower in Turkey. In addition, Turkey also has a low performance in producing creative outputs such as films, entertainment, and publications (Figure 10).

Figure 10. GII creative outputs pillar (2018)

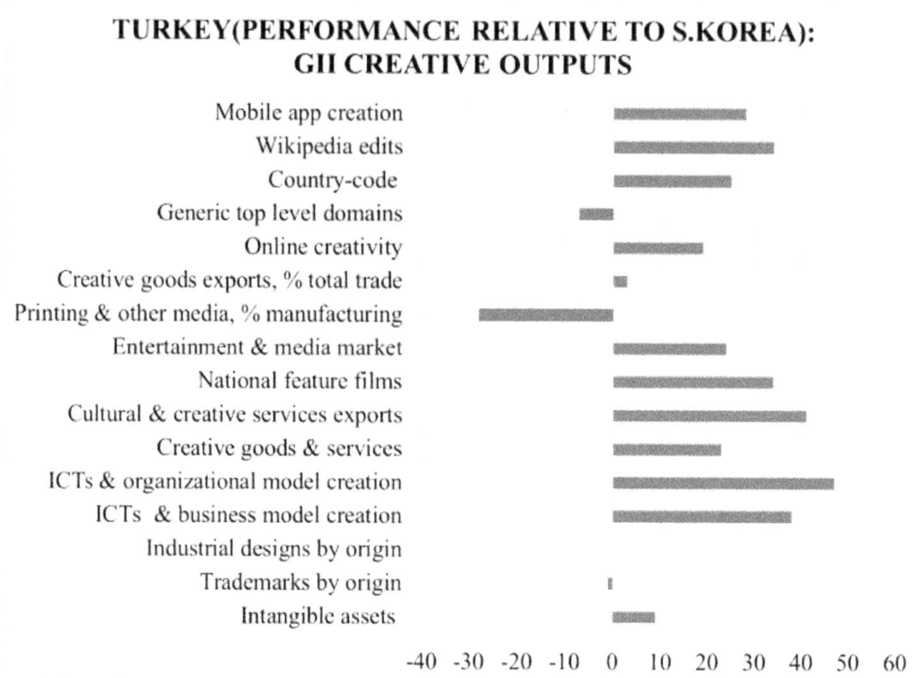

Figure 11 shows the differences in rankings of South Korea and Turkey for GCI Skills pillar. Human capital is an important driver of endogenous growth theories as a country with a high level of skilled labor force can more easily acquire and adapt technologies that have been developed by advanced economies. It is widely acknowledged that South Korea invested highly in education through its development process (Chung, 2011). Korea has a very strong knowledge production system where higher education plays an important role (Jung, 2019).

Looking at human capital indicators, Turkey is performing slightly better in school life expectancy compared to South Korea, and performing poorly in all other indicators (Figures 11 and 12). Recent studies also document that Turkey needs to improve its educational quality and increase years of schooling in order to improve its level of technology (Yilmaz and Saracoglu, 2016).

Figure 11. GCI skills pillar (2018)

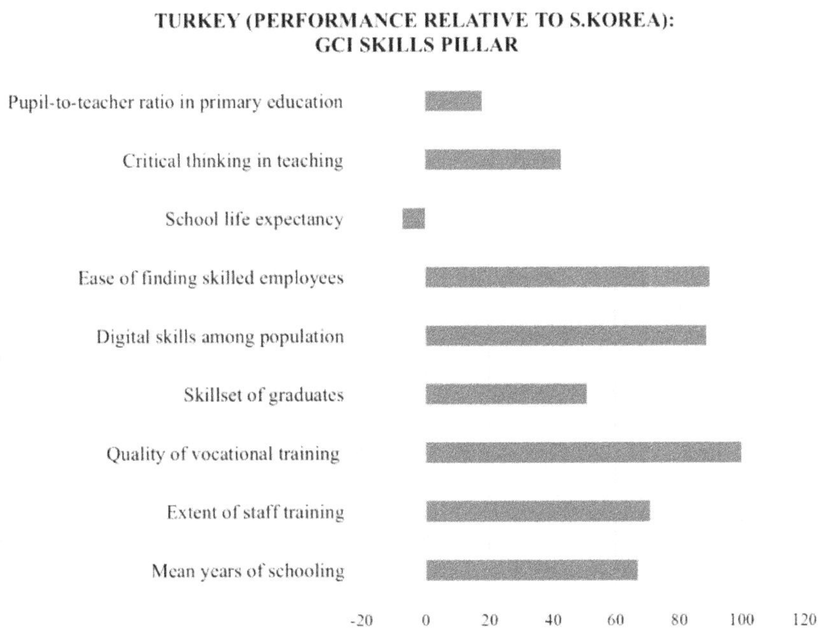

Figure 12. GII Human Capital and Research Pillar (2018)

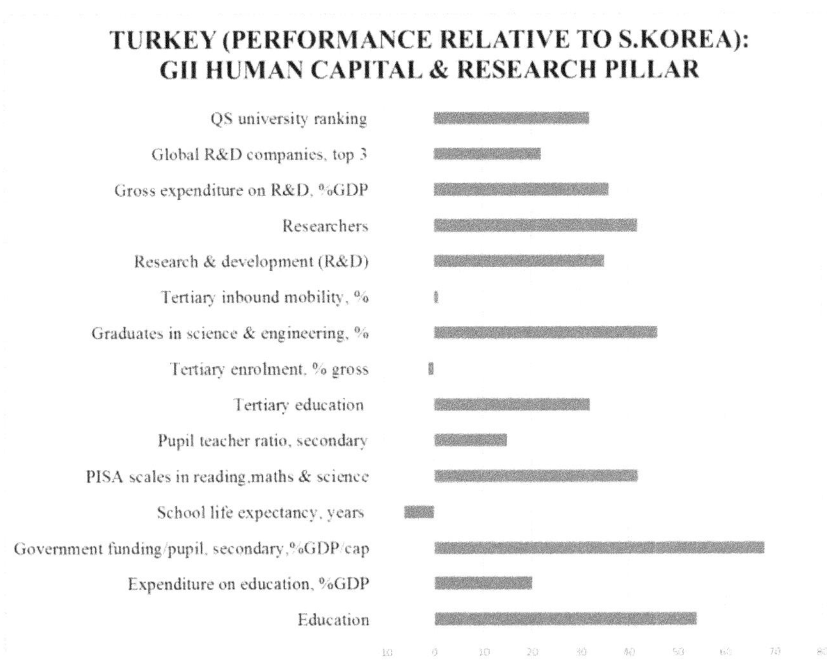

Figure 13. GII Business Sophistication Pillar (2018)

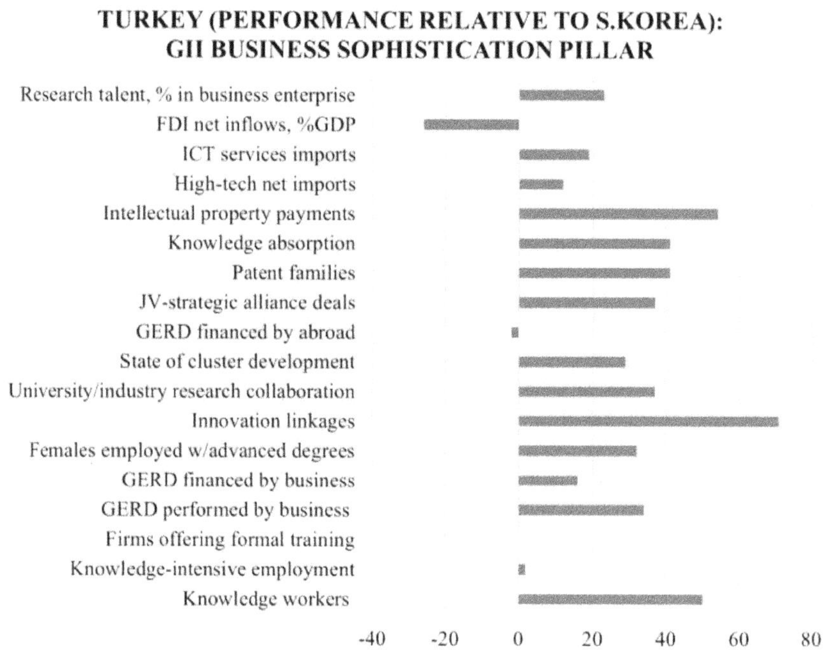

Figures 13 suggests that Turkish private sector also lacks innovation networks including those with higher education institutions. On the other hand, Korea put a lot of effort in fostering innovation linkages to reform the research system and strengthen the NIS. For example, the government established the Industry–Academy–Research Institute Cooperative Research Center (IARCRC) between 1992-1994. In order to increase industry-university collobaration, several science research centers, national research labs, and regional research centers were established. Universities also received major support through Brain Korea project in 2000s to reinforce human resources in S&T. As a result of these policies, individual organizations and researchers have become more connected and innovation outputs have increased (Shapiro et al., 2010).

An important driver of innovation is information and communication technology (ICT), which increases cooperation between various actors in the economy, including firms and customers. The ICT sector is one of the most important success factors behind South Korea's industrial revolution. Korea speacilized in and thus have high exports of ICT goods and services (Shin and Park, 2007). When we look at the ICT adoption pillar, we can see that Turkey is performing worse than South Korea in all ICT components (Figure 14). Therefore, the Turkish policy makers need to

Figure 14. GCI ICT Adoption Pillar (2018)

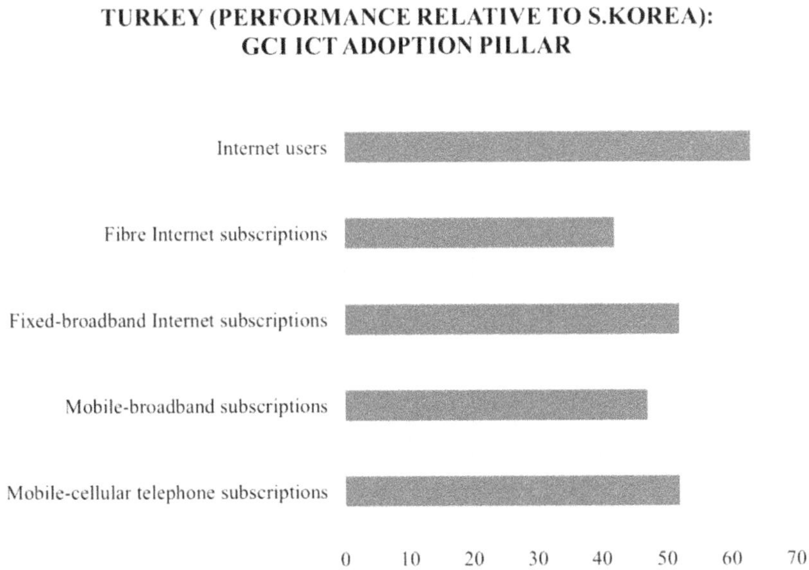

promote investments in technology infrastructure. A well-established and integrated telecommunications system ensures reliable and efficient information flows among all actors in the economy, creating better inter-organizational relationships (Singh et al., 2019).

Analysis of the Socioeconomic Systems

For the third step; we focus on national specifies, especially the socioeconomic system of the countries. Prior literature has already established that good governance and instutional quality have positive impacts on long-term economic growth (Acemoglu et al., 2005; Nawaz, 2015). Therefore, we first compare the two countries' rankings in the institutions pillar of GCI and GII (Figures 15 and 16).

Compared to South Korea, Turkey is performing slightly better in shareholder governance and burden of government regulations indicators. However, the differences in rankings for freedom of press and terrorism incidence signal a weak business environment. Moreover, Turkey also experinces problems in other important factors such as intellectual property protection, efficiency of legal framework, and corruption which negatively affect both internal and external investors' incentives for investment (Shleifer and Vishny 1993; Anokhin and Schulze, 2009).

Figure 15. GCI institutions pillar (2018)

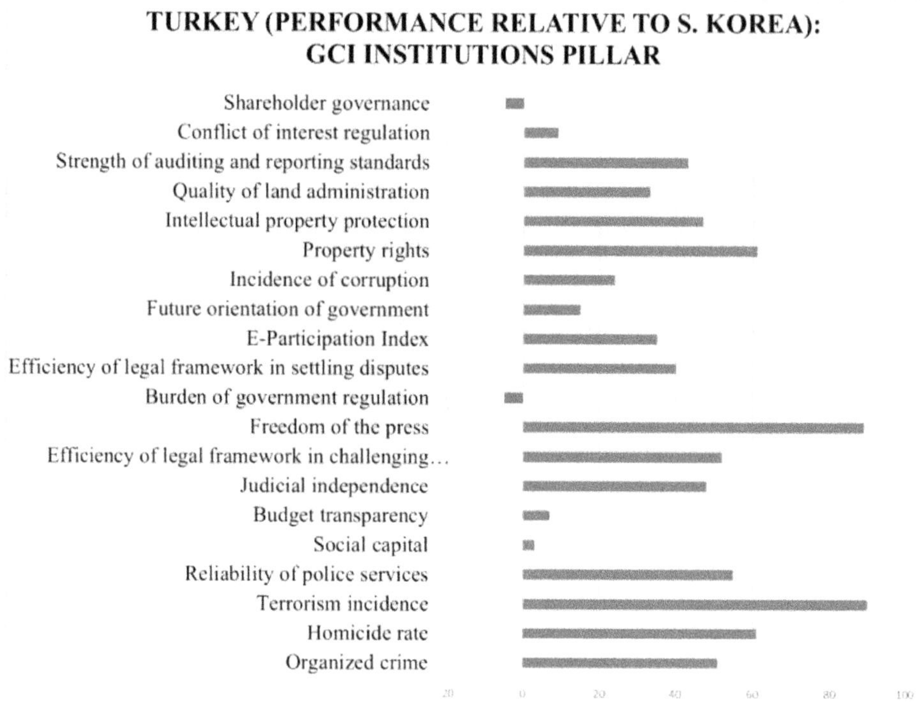

Figure 16. GII institutions pillar (2018)

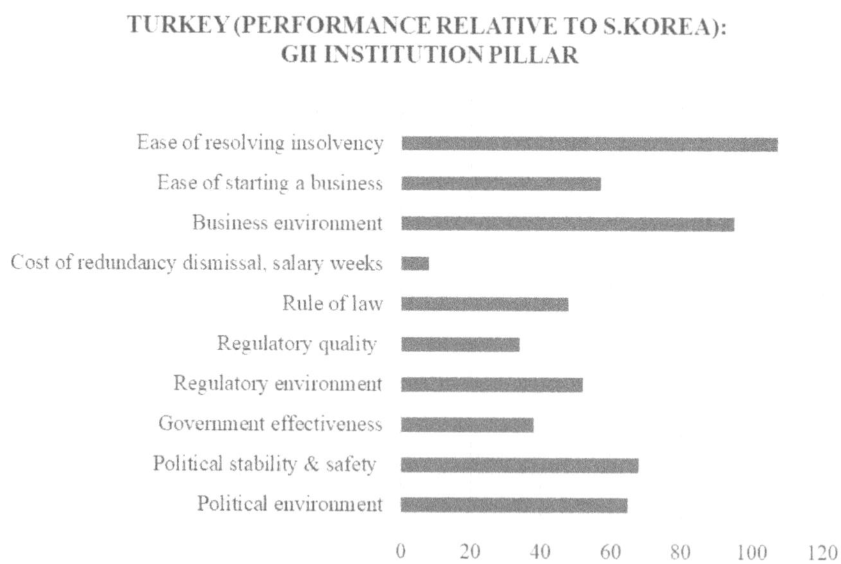

Figure 17. GCI macroeconomic stability pillar (2018)

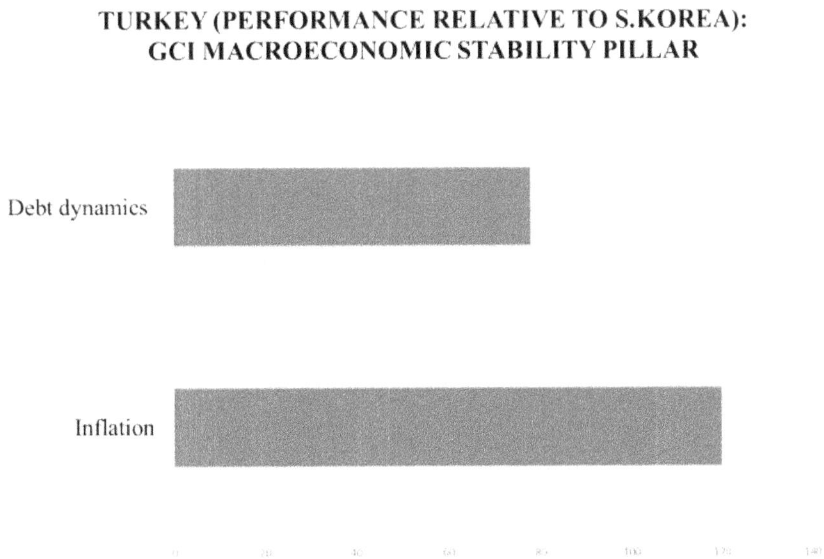

Turkey's most important problem lies in macroeconomic stability, which is calculated using indicators of debt dynamics (public debt to GDP ratio) and inflation rates. A wide body of literature has documented the adverse effects of high inflation rates on economic growth as high rates of inflation decreases the willingness of the private sector to invest (Barro, 2013). According to World Bank statistics, South Korea's annual inflation rate for 2018 was 1.48%, compared to a very high rate of 15.79% for Turkey.

Another factor which affects the level of investment in a country is the quality of infrastructure. Greater investment of the government in electricity, water, and transportation infrastructure positively affects productivity and output (Easterly and Rebelo, 1993). According to GCI and GII 2018 infrastructure pillars, Turkey's level of infrastructure is far from adequate compared to South Korea. Access to electricity (Figure 18) and ICT infrastructure (Figure 19) are the two most problematic areas.

Organization of labor is one of the external factors that affect firms' innovation decisions. Heavy labor regulations can adversely affect innovation and productivity due to high labor adjustment costs (Tressel and Scarpetta, 2004). On the other hand, labor regulations may also promote sustainability through improving the working environment, i.e., health and safety conditions for employees (Blind, 2012). The biggest differences regarding the labor markets of Turkey and South Korea are market pay and productivity, female participation in labor force, and labor tax rates (Figure 20).

Figure 18. GCI infrastructure pillar (2018)

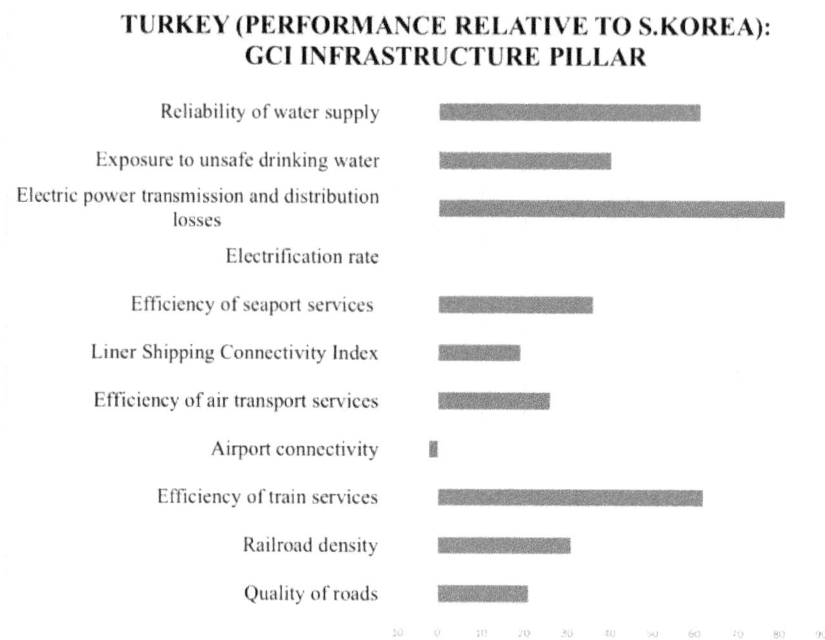

Figure 19. GII infrastructure pillar (2018)

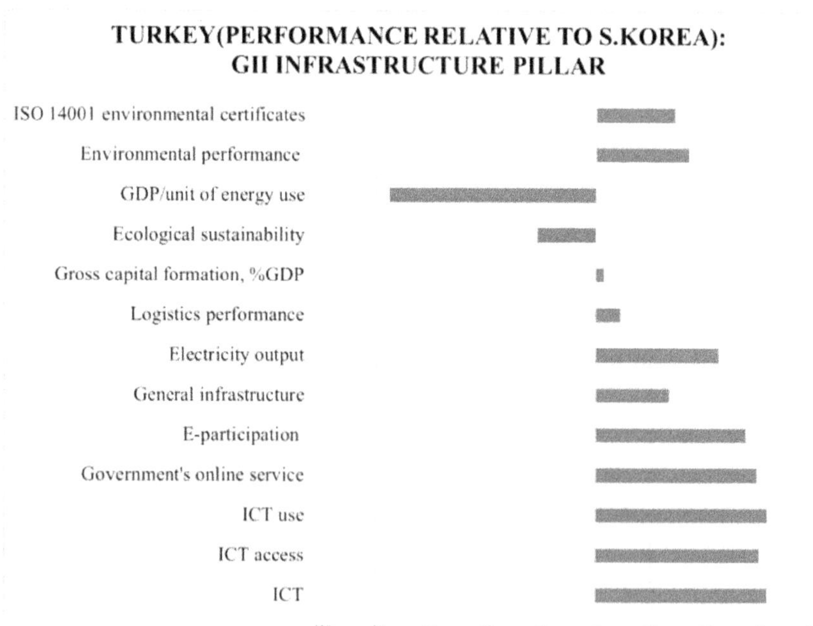

Figure 20. GCI labor market pillar (2018)

Figure 21. GCI financial market pillar (2018)

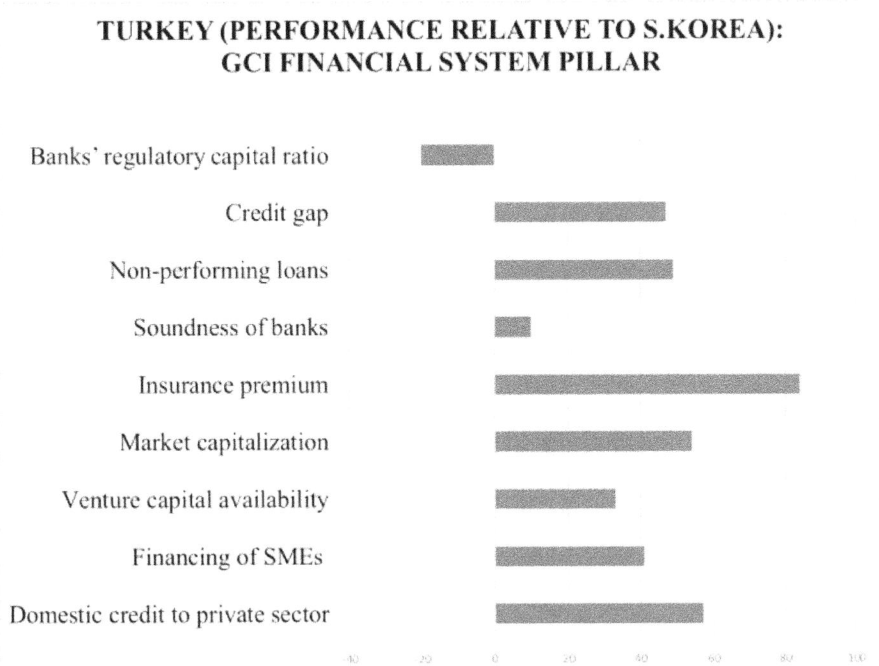

Figure 22. GII market sophistication pillar (2018)

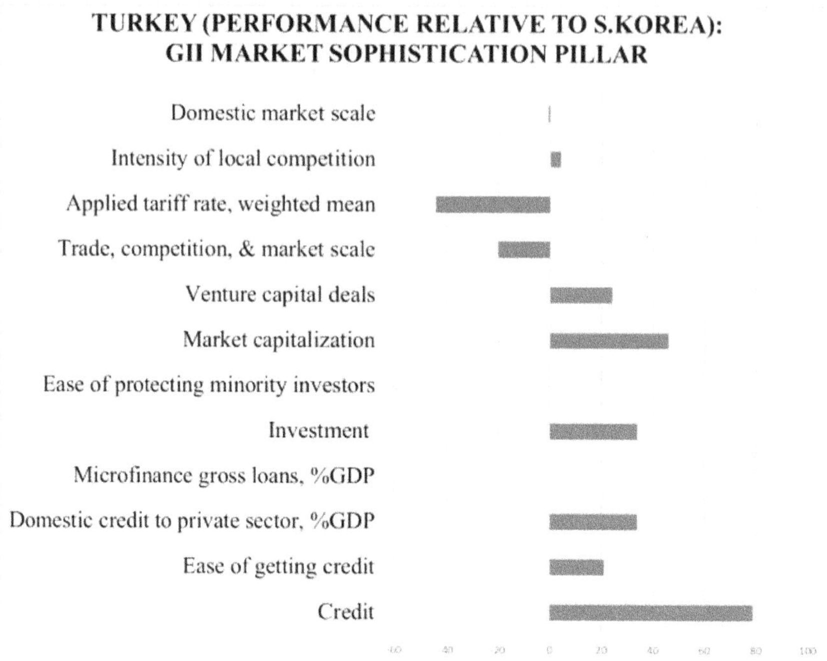

Financing of innovation is especially important and for new and small firms as it is harder to find financing for innovation investments which are more risky in nature (Hall and Lerner, 2010). For example, Zimmermann (2020) shows that as innovation expenditures go up, share of bank loans increases comparatively little due to the uncertainty about the success of innovation projects. We see that Turkey is also performing poorly in financial system pillar (Figure 21). GII market sophistication pillar also shows that access to credit is a major problem in Turkey (Figure 22).

Analysis of the Performance of NIS

Our analysis of Turkey's NIS based on GII and GCI indicators helps us to implement the performance of Turkish NIS (compared to S. Korea) which is the final step of Lundvall's 4-step method. Figures 23 and 24 report the top 10 strenghts and weaknesses of Turkey.

Turkey's strengths in components of GII lies in GDP/unit of energy use, applied tariff rates, and computer spending. On the other hand, the country is doing worse than Korea in terms of instutional quality, ease of getting credit, and knowledge generation & diffusion.

Figure 23. GII comparison of Turkey & South Korea

Turkey's strengths in components of competitiveness pillars lies in attitudes toward risk, wage determination, and ease of hiring foreign labor. Overall, labor market seems to work more efficiently in Turkey. On the other hand, the country is doing worse than Korea in insolvency regulatory framework, quality of education, and instutions. In addition, a detailed look at other components of GCI indicate the poor financial market conditions in Turkey.

CONCLUSION

Turkey has recently started to implement innovation policies and although R&D intensity is still very low, there is an upward trend in the recent years. However, in order to achieve an appropriate policy mix that strengthens all aspects of the national innovation system, Turkey should first identify its strong and weak areas. Therefore, our study aims to create a road-map for policy makers.

Figure 24. GCI comparison of Turkey & South Korea

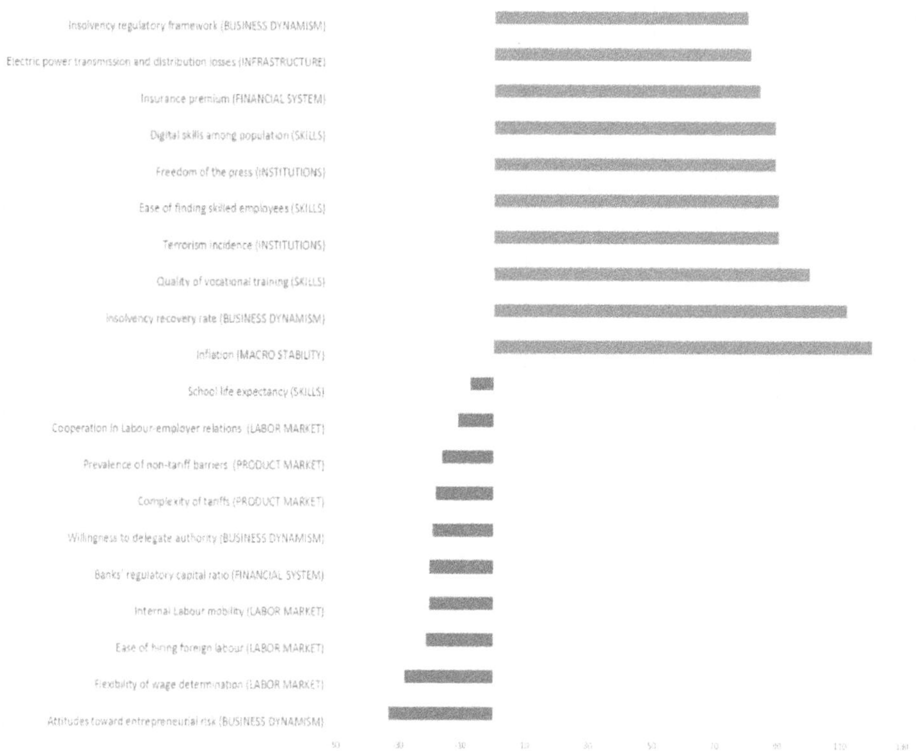

Our analysis reveals that policy makers should focus on developing innovation linkages between key actors in the economy. To foster its innovation ecosystems, Turkey can learn from the Korean experience in terms of forming innovation clusters, establishing regional research centers, and supporting optimal knowledge infrastructure.

In addition, to promote investments in innovative activities, business environment should be improved through greater macroeconomic stability and ease of access to financial markets.

REFERENCES

Acemoglu, D., Johnson, S., & Robinson, J. A. (2005). Institutions as a fundamental cause of long-run growth. In P. Aghion & S. D. Durlauf (Eds.), *Handbook of economic growth* (pp. 385–472). North-Holland.

Andic, S. (2016). The Composition of Growth Matters: South Korea vs. Turkey (No. 1629). Research and Monetary Policy Department, Central Bank of the Republic of Turkey.

Anokhin, S., & Schulze, W. S. (2009). Entrepreneurship, innovation, and corruption. *Journal of Business Venturing*, *24*(5), 465–476. doi:10.1016/j.jbusvent.2008.06.001

Atiyas, İ., & Bakis, O. (2015). Structural change and industrial policy in Turkey. *Emerging Markets Finance & Trade*, *51*(6), 1209–1229. doi:10.1080/1540496X.2015.1080523

Barro, R. J. (2013). Inflation and Economic Growth. *Annals of Economics and Finance. Society for AEF*, *14*(1), 121–144.

Betz, F., Carayannis, E., Jetter, A., Min, W., Phillips, F., & Shin, D. W. (2016). Modeling an innovation intermediary system within a helix. *Journal of the Knowledge Economy*, *7*(2), 587–599. doi:10.100713132-014-0230-7

Blind, K. (2012). The influence of regulations on innovation: A quantitative assessment for OECD countries. *Research Policy*, *41*(2), 391–400. doi:10.1016/j.respol.2011.08.008

Bloom, N., Van Reenen, J., & Williams, H. (2019). A toolkit of policies to promote innovation. *The Journal of Economic Perspectives*, *33*(3), 163–184. doi:10.1257/jep.33.3.163

Chung, S. (2011). Innovation, competitiveness, and growth: Korean experiences. In J.Y. Lin & B. Pleskovic (Eds.), *Lessons from East Asia and the global financial crisis: Annual World Bank Conference on Development Economics- Global* (pp. 333-357). Washington, DC: World Bank.

Easterly, W., & Rebelo, S. (1993). Fiscal policy and economic growth: An empirical investigation. *Journal of Monetary Economics*, *32*(3), 417–458. doi:10.1016/0304-3932(93)90025-B

Freeman, C., & Soete, L. (1982). *The Economics of Industrial Innovation*. Routledge.

Freeman, C., & Soete, L. (Eds.). (1987). *Technical Change and Full Employment*. Basil Blackwell.

Global Innovation Index. (2007-2018). Retrieved April 4,2019 from https://www.globalinnovationindex.org/Home

Grossman, G. M., & Helpman, E. (1991). *Innovation and Growth in the Global Economy*. MIT press.

Hall, B. H., & Lerner, J. (2010). *Handbook of the Economics of Innovation*. North-Holland.

Jung, J. (2019). The Fourth Industrial Revolution, Knowledge Production and Higher Education in South Korea. *Journal of Higher Education Policy and Management*, *42*(2), 134–156. doi:10.1080/1360080X.2019.1660047

List, F. (1841). *The National System of Political Economy*. Routledge.

Lundvall, B. A. (Ed.). (1992). *National Systems of Innovation: Towards a Theory of Innovation and Interactive learning*. Anthem Press.

Lundvall, B. A. (2016). *The Learning Economy and the Economics of Hope*. Anthem Press. doi:10.26530/OAPEN_626406

Menna, A., Walsh, P. R., & Ekhtari, H. (2019). Identifying enablers of innovation in developed economies: A National Innovation Systems approach. *Journal of Innovation Management*, *7*(1), 108–128. doi:10.24840/2183-0606_007.001_0007

Nawaz, S. (2015). Growth effects of institutions: A disaggregated analysis. *Economic Modelling*, *45*(1), 118–126. doi:10.1016/j.econmod.2014.11.017

OECD. (1997). *National Innovation Systems*. Retrieved March 20,2019 from https://www.oecd.org/science/inno/2101733.pdf

OECD. (2014). *Industry and Technology Policies in Korea*. Retrieved from https://read.oecd-ilibrary.org/industry-and-services/industry-and-technology-policies-in-korea_9789264213227-en#page1

Oguzturk, S. (2017). The Role of Innovation in Growth Process of South Korea: An Econometric Analysis. *Suleyman Demirel University The Journal of Faculty of Economics and Administrative Sciences*, *22*(4), 1203–1222.

Onsel Ekici, S., Kabak, O., & Ulengin, F. (2019). Improving logistics performance by reforming the pillars of Global Competitiveness Index. *Transport Policy*, *81*, 197–207. doi:10.1016/j.tranpol.2019.06.014

Pence, I., Kalkan, A., & Cesmeli, M. S. (2019). Estimation of the Country Ranking Scores on the Global Innovation Index 2016 Using the Artificial Neural Network Method. *International Journal of Innovation and Technology Management*, *16*(4), 1940007. doi:10.1142/S0219877019400078

Rakas, M., & Hain, D. S. (2019). The state of innovation system research: What happens beneath the surface? *Research Policy*, *48*(9), 103787. doi:10.1016/j.respol.2019.04.011

Republic of Turkey Ministry of Industry and Trade. (2010). *Turkish industrial strategy document (towards EU membership) 2011-2014*. Retrieved from https://www.sanayi.gov.tr/Files/Documents/TurkiyeSanayiStratejisiIngilizce.pdf

Shapiro, M. A., So, M., & Woo Park, H. (2010). Quantifying the national innovation system: Inter-regional collaboration networks in South Korea. *Technology Analysis and Strategic Management*, *22*(7), 845–857. doi:10.1080/09537325.2010.511158

Shin, J., & Park, Y. (2007). Building the national ICT frontier: The case of Korea. *Information Economics and Policy*, *19*(2), 249–277. doi:10.1016/j.infoecopol.2007.01.003

Shleifer, A., & Vishny, R. W. (1993). Corruption. *The Quarterly Journal of Economics*, *108*(3), 599–617. doi:10.2307/2118402

Singh, R. K., Luthra, S., Mangla, S. K., & Uniyal, S. (2019). Applications of information and communication technology for sustainable growth of SMEs in India food industry. *Resources, Conservation and Recycling*, *147*, 10–18. doi:10.1016/j.resconrec.2019.04.014

Swink, M. (2006). Building collaborative innovation capability. *Research Technology Management*, *49*(2), 37–47. doi:10.1080/08956308.2006.11657367

The World Bank. (2018a). *GDP (current US $) of Korea and Turkey: 1980-2017*. Retrieved from https://data.worldbank.org/indicator/NY.GDP.MKTP.CD?end=2017&locations=KR-TR&start=1980&view=chart

The World Bank. (2018b). *High-tech export % of manufactured good of South Korea and Turkey: 1980-2017*. Retrieved from https://data.worldbank.org/indicator/TX.VAL.TECH.MF.ZS?locations=KR-TR&view=chart

The World Bank. (2018c). *Researchers in R&D per million people of South Korea and Turkey: 1980-2017*. Retrieved from https://data.worldbank.org/indicator/SP.POP.SCIE.RD.P6?end=2018&locations=KR-TR&start=1980

The World Bank. (2018d). *Patent applications, residents of South Korea and Turkey: 1980-2017*. Retrieved from https://data.worldbank.org/indicator/IP.PAT.RESD?end=2016&locations=KR-TR&start=1980&view=chart

The World Bank. (2018e). *Patent applications, nonresidents of South Korea and Turkey: 1980-2017*. Retrieved from https://data.worldbank.org/indicator/IP.PAT.NRES?end=2016&locations=KR-TR&start=1980&view=chart

The World Bank. (2018f). *Government expenditure on education (%GDP) of South Korea and Turkey: 1980-2017*. Retrieved from https://data.worldbank.org/indicator/SE.XPD.TOTL.GD.ZS?end=2018&locations=KR-TR&start=1980

The World Bank. (2018g). *Scientific and technical journal articles (thousand) of South Korea and Turkey: 1980-2017*. Retrieved from https://data.worldbank.org/indicator/IP.JRN.ARTC.SC?locations=KR-TR&view=chart

Tomizawa, A., Zhao, L., Bassellier, G., & Ahlstrom, D. (2020). Economic growth, innovation, institutions, and the Great Enrichment. *Asia Pacific Journal of Management*, *37*(1), 7–31. doi:10.100710490-019-09648-2

Tressel, T., & Scarpetta, S. (2004). *Boosting productivity via innovation and adoption of new technologies: any role for labor market institutions?* Retrieved from https://documents.worldbank.org/curated/en/101151468762892644/Boosting-productivity-via-innovation-and-adoption-of-new-technologies-any-role-for-labor-market-institutions

UNDP. (2018a). *Mean years of schooling*. Retrieved from http://hdr.undp.org/en/data

UNDP. (2018b). *Expected years of schooling*. Retrieced from http://hdr.undp.org/en/data

Wilson, S., Maharaj, C. S., & Maharaj, R. (2020). Formalising the National Innovation System in a Developing Country. *The West Indian Journal of Engineering*, *42*(2), 4–16.

World Economic Forum. (2018). *Global Competitiveness Report*. Retrieved March 20,2019 from https://www.weforum.org/reports/the-global-competitveness-report-2018

Yilmaz, G., & Saracoglu, D. S. (2016). Technological change, human capital, and absorptive capacity: Can Turkey escape the Middle Income Trap? *ODTÜ Gelisme Dergisi*, *43*(1), 391–424.

Zimmermann, V. (2020). Innovation and Investment Finance in Comparison. In *Contemporary Developments in Entrepreneurial Finance* (pp. 59–79). Springer. doi:10.1007/978-3-030-17612-9_3

Chapter 7
Innovative Approaches to Building Enterprise Risk Management in Emerging Economies:
The Case of Mexico's Grupo Proeza

Ilse Patricia Lopez de la Cruz
Grupo Proeza, Mexico

Alasdair James Marshall
University of Southhampton, UK

Udechukwu Ojiako
University of Sharjah, UAE

Serkan Ceylan
University of Southampton, UK

Fenfang Lin
University of Southampton, UK

ABSTRACT

This chapter explores a very positive example of enterprise risk management (ERM) development in Mexico, set by the firm Grupo Proeza, from which valuable and highly generalisable lessons can be learned. These lessons will pertain most centrally to Grupo Proeza's techniques of ERM building, where risk management practices are used to enhance the cultural and other foundations for ERM. Of particular interest is the notion that various risk assessment techniques can be used for this purpose, which may seem counter-intuitive by reversing the formative relationship between risk culture and risk assessment practice that is more typically the focus for attention.

DOI: 10.4018/978-1-7998-4195-1.ch007

Copyright © 2021, IGI Global. Copying or distributing in print or electronic forms without written permission of IGI Global is prohibited.

INTRODUCTION

Success stories of strong and growing firms within emerging economies can be expected to attract investment capital and set important regional examples. For such firms, the pursuit of ongoing growth and innovation can also be expected to manifest within increasing complexities of organisational structures, relationships and processes. These combined complexities will of course present as problematic, and yet they can also be valued as establishing organisational crucibles wherein further growth and innovation opportunities can be explored. Such growth might well be anteceded, for example, by ever more ambidextrous (exploitative and exploratory) management practices that thrive amidst complexity, and indeed more generally by ever more hybridised management practices that pool information from amidst complexity. And, of course, ERM becomes important within that context as spontaneous, fluid and heterarchically organised management practice that harnesses complex information flows to permit the firm to continue to grow and innovate, especially via strategic agility aligned to performance management within ever more complex (internal and external) risk environments (see, in particular, the recent (2017) update of the COSO ERM guidance).

The broad mechanisms at play here can be summarised very generally, in order to more fully introduce the analytical framework for this chapter, as ones where firms within emerging economies respond to their complexity challenges through a range of business practices often focused on ERM and characterised by co-enhancements to culture, communication and coordination, both internally and, albeit to a lesser extent, within further contexts of external stakeholder engagement. Ongoing improvements to knowledge management become important here too. These can be viewed as enabling ongoing enhancements to culture, communication and coordination while locking in at least some of the gains. In general overview, however, our analytical framework will be one that fundamentally envisions ongoing synergy between increasing organisational complexity, improved business practice focused on ERM, and increasing growth and innovation.

We will use this framework to understand and evaluate certain innovative ERM building practices used by *Grupo Proeza* in Mexico. This case study illustration will, in turn, permit us to conclude with advocacy of some highly practical and straightforward management routes to growth and innovation for firms within emerging economies – especially yet not exclusively for such firms that have already embarked upon ERM programmes, or which are experimenting with basic ERM tenets as a means to produce management improvements. The basic tenets we have in mind here, to underscore this point at the outset while also focusing more within our general theoretical framework, will pertain to the key ERM themes of culture, communication and heterarchical coordination, which we will regard as fundamental considerations for complex entities seeking to innovate and grow within complex environments.

We take as our single case study, *Grupo Proeza*, an international Group headquartered in Monterrey, Mexico. Rooted in the automotive industry of the 1950s, it boasts a long history of successful diversification into fruit processing, real estate industry and communications technologies. A commitment to humanistic culture and cultivation of long-term stakeholder relationships has both shaped and consolidated within this history. Taken together, these combined factors of growth and diversification trajectory on the one hand, and humanistic, stakeholder-oriented business practice on the other hand, render *Grupo Proeza* of particular academic and practitioner interest as a case study of propitious circumstance where ERM developments can fit well and make a positive difference.

Drawing on action research undertaken within the firm in 2019, this book chapter will explore how *Grupo Proeza's* targeted deployment of a range of risk assessment tools can serve as a focal point for building an ethical risk culture and associated risk communication and coordination infrastructure, with these in turn supplying solid foundations for ERM while also enhancing knowledge management. The underlying notion here, that firms should aspire to make broader and more creative use of risk management techniques, derives in part from suggestions made by a risk management consultant and educator, Matthew Leitch, in a (2016) Centre for Risk Research Guide (written within Southampton Business School at the University of Southampton in the UK) which took the 'Directors' eye view' upon opportunities for developing corporate risk management. The Enterprise Risk Management Specialist at *Grupo Proeza,* and first author of the present chapter, came into contact with these ideas while studying MSc Risk Management modules taught by Matthew Leitch in 2018 at Southampton University.

What will emerge from this action research, particularly clearly, is that Grupo Proeza's longstanding emphasis upon ethical stakeholdership has provided foundations whereby its ERM developments in the closely interlinked areas of culture, communication and coordination, can be viewed as natural extensions to existing management practices aligned to firm values and identity.

The recommendations which we will move towards throughout our chapter will also include that other firms should seek to learn from *Grupo Proeza's* inventive use of a broad range of risk management techniques for purposes of improving both risk communication and knowledge management more broadly conceived, throughout internal teamwork and broader external stakeholder collaboration. We will advocate such practice as constituting a simple but possibly highly effective cultural engineering technique supporting endogenous knowledge capture and exploitation across emerging market economies.

To reiterate, *Grupo Proeza's* commitment to humanistic culture and cultivation of long-term stakeholder relationships has both shaped and emerged from its history. Furthermore, its high degree of amenability to innovative cultural engineering practices geared towards building strategic enterprise-wide risk management (ERM) further render it of particular academic interest. A brief introduction to the firm will follow next. That will be followed by a more extended examination of the action research process which took stock of its ongoing efforts to co-develop ERM alongside ethical risk culture, looking in particular at what a detailed and flexible understanding of contemporary risk assessment techniques might bring to the table.

Grupo Proeza

Grupo Proeza is more commonly referred to as *Proeza*. It is a private, diversified Mexican multinational with four subsidiaries: *Metalsa, Citrofrut, Astrum* and *Areya*. Metalsa is a tier 1 automotive supplier with operations in 11 countries and 60 years of history behind it (Metalsa, 2019). Citrofrut is a producer and processor of citrus and tropical fruits. While it is located in 3 countries, it does business within over 40 countries. Like Metalsa, it boasts 60 years of trading (Citrofrut, 2012). Astrum has traded for over 35 years in the Mexican market. It provides communication and satellite tracking solutions to industries such as petroleum and gas, electricity, maritime and logistics (Astrum, no date). Areya, the youngest subsidiary with just 3 years in the Mexican market, provides real estate developers with land clearance and semi-urbanization of macro- and microplots (Proeza, no date). These diversified subsidiaries share some core characteristics. All have a business-to-business operation mechanism. Most of their operations are manufacturing-based. Culturally speaking, their strategies are centralised in a portfolio vision under the Mexican-based Headquarters.

Due to the inherent diversity across the subsidiaries, communication and co-ordination are often regarded as challenging. However, as we explained at the start of the chapter, such challenges also bring opportunities. *Proeza's* Risk Management department, which first evolved from an insurance management role, is currently in the process of maturing through a focus on ERM development. Accordingly, it makes sense to focus on the ERM development process as basic context, both for understanding *Proeza's* communications and co-ordination challenges in general, and for scoping the associated solutions and further opportunities arising.

Action Research

The research drew on extensive collaboration with managers at the firm who were directly involved in developing the firm's risk management. Most notably, and as is particularly fitting for a firm pursuing a human-centric approach to ERM, interviews were conducted not just with the Corporate Risk Management Team, but also with the Human Resources and Culture Coordinator. Comprising the Corporate Risk Management Team were a Property and Casualty Senior Consultant, a Benefits Senior Consultant, an Enterprise Risk Management Specialist, a Corporate Risk Manager and a Portfolio Management and Optimisation specialist who reports directly to the CFO.

The main aim of the research was to engage with the above issues in a particular way: by exploring *Proeza's* cultural characteristics, giving critical thought in particular to how they align with Risk Management objectives (focused towards ERM development), so that a tailor-made risk communication and co-ordination infrastructure could be built from the cultural base that already exists. Structuring from pragmatism, a value-driven axiology recognising *Proeza*'s strengths was combined with an inductive and exploratory multi-method approach towards determining what the cultural base comprises and what the associated practical possibilities were for developing the risk management infrastructure.

First, *Proeza's* organizational identity was explored from various angles, including through interviews and examination of corporate documentation. Taking that approach, the firm's main cultural characteristics, objectives and values were considered and analysed with a view to distilling the core themes (which were found in particular to relate to a cultural trajectory of deepening stakeholder engagement). We describe this cultural research in more detail in the next section dealing with what we call the 'cultural base' for risk management communication and coordination. Then, a more detailed exploratory process was conducted which looked across the pre-existing organisational facilitators for communicating risk-related information towards effective end usage. Through the semi-structured interviews involving the risk management team and other participants in the firm's risk management, particular attention was paid to interviewee preferences regarding centralisation *vs* decentralisation of information flows. Emphasis was also placed upon exploring the information burdens and challenges associated with strategic objectives. Hence, for example, one interview with the Corporate Human Resources and Culture Coordinator linked issues of culture, information flows, and strategy, by looking at current mechanisms for promoting accountability for each employee's objectives – considering also how such accountabilities bear upon proactive participation in risk communication activities.

Crucially, a range of currently used risk management techniques were explored as facilitators of such communication. Added to that, a range of possible alternative risk management mechanisms (e.g. scenario analysis, war gaming and intelligence analysis) were critically explored for their potential to add further boosts. The action research concluded with a presentation to the Risk Management team, covering both current and possible alternative means. Taking into account feedback elicited at that session, final recommendations were sent to the Risk Management team, encouraging wider use of risk management techniques to improve the communication of risk information and the coordination of its end use. These final recommendations emphasised the importance of making creative use of existing meeting opportunities, and of creating new ones, where managers can be drawn into shared risk management discussions that are disciplined through use of structured risk management techniques.

Cultural Base for Risk Management Communication/Coordination

Culture is a contestable abstract concept and semantically difficult to enclose in a specific classification; nonetheless, for the purpose of the present study it was framed under the broad social anthropological definition of the way in which people live (Williams, 1967, p. 16; Jenks, 2005, p. 12; Kuper and Kuper, 2007, p. 683). Thus, individual personalities and associated behaviours are resolved within prevailing collective tendencies, expressed in terms of some combined specification of descriptive cultural attributes and context where lives unfold (Giles and Middleton, 1999). Looking at organisational culture, which takes organisational life as its limiting contextual focus, a further important requirement is to recognise the complexity and dynamism which cultural researchers typically attribute to organisational life (Slocum and Hellriegel, 2009, p. 458; Schein and Schein, 2017, p. 14). One approach is to focus on the experiences shaping a group which has learned, endured and developed whilst interacting with the outside environment (Schein and Schein, 2017, p. 14), entailing that external stakeholder contexts become significant.

The cultural analysis for the present research was focused in three areas: 1) the observable procedures, organisational arrangements and behaviours; 2) the embraced philosophies, values and principles; and 3) the fundamental assumptions and silent understandings (Deal and Kennedy, 1982, pp. 129-134; Ott, 1989, pp. 24-45; Slocum and Hellriegel, 2009, p. 459; Schein and Schein, 2017, pp. 17-21) that pervade management activity. An obvious qualification to this was the need to avoid monocultural assumptions and instead look for subcultural variation. Hence, for example, we heeded Waring and Glendon's (1998, p. 71) point that localisation should be taken as another dimension of organisational culture, by giving particular regard to the localisation of the Corporate Headquarters. More fully, we considered that the need for strategy setting at Headquarters to be sensitive to cultural differences at subsidiary level might feed into the positive dynamic of growing external stakeholder engagement which we discerned.

We further viewed culture as adjustable to achieve risk benefits while dealing with the unexpected through mindfulness (Weick and Sutclliffe, 2001, p. 150). Emerging from the early 1970s from sociological spheres of study, mindfulness within this risk psychology context has to do with the iterative process of contrasting expectations with current experience, and above all with responding urgently to disruptive and non-routine situations in the making (Langer and Moldoveanu, 2000; Weick and Sutclliffe, 2001, p. 42; Butler and Gray, 2006). We focused on this aspect of culture due to its particular relevance as a psycho-cultural foundation for that spontaneity of heterarchical management co-ordination that ERM requires. A firm that recognises and advocates mindfulness will be more resilient and adaptable (Weick and Sutclliffe, 2001, p. 124), we reasoned, through its ERM activity.

We were also concerned with aspects of culture that support knowledge management. Many cultural researchers have advocated the promotion of learning cultures (Reason, 1997, p. 218; Marsick and Watkins, 2003; Bauer and Gruber, 2007). Learning cultures are commonly reckoned to support open communication, recognising in particular the reporting, justice and flexibility issues that arise within a firm wherever developing and retaining knowledge becomes important (Reason, 1997, pp. 195-220). This means cultures for learning and for proactive risk communication (sometimes involving ethical candour) will all overlap to some significant extent and can be encouraged to co-evolve. Moreover, the flexibility foundation for effective communication strongly implies a need for culturally intelligent individuals who can efficiently work together, disregarding their respective cultural backgrounds and differences (Ang and Van Dyne, 2009, 375; Schein and Schein, 2017, p. 107). This clearly also matters if ERM communicativity and coordination are to span cultural diversity. In general, then, our exploration of *Proeza's* culture was predicated to some extent upon the assumption that an organisational culture that is mindful, keen to learn and retain what it has learned, and culturally intelligent, will most likely positively impact not just risk communication but ERM activity more broadly.

To base the cultural analysis on a sensitising template, Schein and Schein's analytic model (2017, pp. 17-21) which famously differentiates between tangible artifacts, espoused values, and underlying assumptions, proved useful. Essentially, this enables looking down through the tangibles to become more sensitive to the intangibles that really matter within the culture. Hence, for example, artifactually speaking, the organisation can immediately be recognised as an industrial private family-owned international business. More specifically, though, its north Mexican localization proved to be particularly significant by pointing towards US cultural influence. For example, one interviewee contrasted being a *Proeza* employee with her previous experience with several Mexican global organisations headquartered in Mexico City. She pointed out that besides consideration of cultural influence factors such as habitual interaction with American companies (clients and providers), there is also the cultural trajectory factor whereby it is also common for firms in North Mexico to aspire to expand into the United States or to European countries, instead of into Latin American ones. An important underlying management assumption at play within this world open stance, discerned within the interviews, is the idea that having subsidiaries, or simply trying to have business operations in more developed countries, is likely to allow for the sharing of more and better practices in future.

Espoused ideology inside the firm (comprising beliefs, values and code of conduct) is notably consistent with expectations and preferences for this cultural growth trajectory. Values promoted within firm documentation emphasise a combination of respect, dignity and trust, alongside more notably humanistic assumptions pertaining to integral human development and happiness at work. This establishes clearly that *Proeza* aspires to be a human-sensible organisation overall, whose concern for the integral development of workers is closely related to the forging of long-lasting relationships between clients, providers and employees. A less tangible value, commonly linked to risk culture debate, is that of leadership 'tone at the top' whereby leaders demonstrate through their own participation in risk management, both that such practice matters and that it is acceptable to have candid discussions and ask difficult questions about the risks. Consistent with this, most interviewees considered that the cultural characteristic that best supports the risk management process is indeed the enthusiastic participation of senior leaders. On the other hand, this was nonetheless discerned to remain a work in progress; it was felt by some interviewees that the lack of a common risk culture (based on clear specifications of content) across the organisation may have a restraining effect on the firm's risk management objectives.

Risk Communication/Co-Ordination

Effective risk communication is typically regarded as fundamental for risk management processes, these always being social in character and often reliant on proactive, non-routine inputs from those who produce, or are exposed to, many different types of information (Thompson, 2002; French, Maule and Mythen, 2005; Maule, 2008, p. 518). It follows that widespread understanding, among participants, of the social and individual processes involved, is itself an important ingredient of effective risk communication (Maule, 2008, p. 528). An appreciation of common risk communication problems, entailing a need for a flexible and mixed risk ontology that is familiar with differing understandings of risk itself, is also widely reckoned to be important (see Costa Sperb & Marshall, 2020, pp. 1-2).

For example, imbalances between qualitative and quantitative representations of risk can be highly problematic by inviting subjective interpretations (Jardine and Hurdey, 1997; Renooija and Witteman, 1999; Theil, 2002). The solution here might be framed in terms of the benefits of a more balanced risk ontology that combines both qualitative and quantitative representations. One particularly salient example of imbalance is where simplifying graphical aids can make the risk communication recipient think in relative rather than absolute terms about the risk (Lipkus and Hollands, 1999) and can misrepresent extreme probabilities (Keller et al., 2006). Commonly recommended solutions include relying, where possible, on natural frequencies instead of single event and conditional probabilities (Gigerenzer and Edwards, 2003). However, solutions can also usefully be framed in terms of promoting awareness across organisations, of the importance of more complex risk ontologies where risk is communicated flexibly through mixed and balanced approaches (Costa Sperb and Marshall, 2020). This places a premium on intensive risk management training, and likewise on learning-by-doing where wider use of a growing assortment of risk management techniques is overseen by the risk management department – which came to be the approach favoured within the present action research.

It is also well known that risk communication is easily influenced by heuristics such as representativeness, availability, feelings, and by what is often termed 'system 1' or 'experiential system' thinking in general (Maule, 2008, pp. 521-523) whose effects are likely to increase for risks that are more alarming and unknown (Maule, 2008, p. 523). A working assumption made within the present action research, in response to this problem, was that promotion of a flexible and mixed risk ontology through exposure to a range of risk assessment techniques, may help to mitigate a broad range of these biases - specifically by making risk management participants more mindful of divergence between how they feel about the risk, how other risk assessment participants feel about the risk, and what the outputs from various risk assessment techniques indicate about the risk.

It is also commonly argued that to ensure effective corporate risk communication, the firm should develop a shared risk vocabulary to avoid wasting time resolving communicational issues (Deloach, 2000, p. 43; Hopkin, 2010, p. 112). Nonetheless, an important problem arising here is that the richness of different points of view and ideas might be lost in the process. Some diversity is inevitable, given the desirability within ERM systems, and within risk management systems more generally, of encouraging novel, disconsonant and critical informational inputs that change expectations and assumptions to keep pace with changing risk environments. Moreover, the use of resources that are already part of the organisation such as corporate intranets, can be used to brief those with delegated risk management across the organisation and offer detailed support for use of risk assessment techniques (Hopkin, 2010, p. 113). Increasingly, risk management information systems (RMIS) can further assist risk owners with their risk assessment (Hopkin, 2010, p. 113). Notably, then, in promoting awareness of the need for a flexible and mixed risk ontology, through the use of various risk assessment techniques, the present research was, in effect, responding to the problem which recognises that simple and inflexible risk ontologies may often do more harm than good. We envisioned that effective risk communication solutions for making ERM work across cultural diversity and in sometimes volatile risk environments are likely to involve some combination of intensive (and often on-the-job) training and technical support for moving beyond the strictures imposed by simplistic risk ontologies.

There remain closely related issues of risk management co-ordination to be considered here. However, it will be seen that our solutions to the challenges arising are essentially the same, which is why the present section takes risk communication and coordination together. The intelligence system for risk management is sometimes represented as infrastructure needed to "connect the dots" to paint a coherent and comprehensive picture (Arad, 2008, p. 71) in firms that are already awash with information flows both within and between the various functions. Likewise, effective preparation for crisis management is commonly understood to imply the need for employee empowerment through specific infrastructural provisions that enable them to speak out prior to and amidst disruptive events (Ruff and Aziz, 2003, p. 35; Johansen, Aggerholm and Frandsen, 2012). One way of viewing the coordination challenge, then, involves recognising the need for both routine forms of risk management co-ordination that help achieve governance compliance, whilst also providing for non-routine forms of co-ordination that are more appropriate for dealing with contingencies (Harris-Jones and Bergin, 1998, p. 79).

This might also be phrased in terms of a need for formal organisational *risk hubs* and more informal *risk huddles* (irrespective of what they are actually called in organisations). Risk Hubs can be theorised as tending to operate at committee cycle pace, transacting risk information between multiple parties (e.g. functional units) from across the firm and beyond (i.e. between internal and external stakeholders). By contrast, informal Risk Huddles can be theorised as set up on an *ad hoc*, and perhaps *per risk* or crisis basis, to operate at clock speed and deliver the spontaneous and heterarchical management upon which ERM depends. This is likely to entail that Risk Huddles will be faster, and yet by that token also weaker than Risk Hubs, in terms of breadth of stakeholder input and consultation amidst their operation. Crucially, the present research looked to exploit management meeting opportunities where, through new requirements placed upon participants to participate in risk assessment techniques, minds could be focused more upon the need for such *hubs* and *huddles*, and indeed on what forms they should take, who should participate, when and where they should meet, etc. Furthermore, it was reasoned, such meeting opportunities are likely to facilitate greater awareness of cross-cutting risk in particular, which by its nature requires an enterprise-wide risk management approach through the sourcing of management expertise and capability from across the firm.

These coordination challenges do, of course, raise further practical issues of incentivisation for participation, especially for non-routine forms of coordination that, by their nature, are hard to plan for and write into job descriptions. One salient consideration here is that the principal-agent problem might bear upon broadly participative risk management by giving rise to varying risk perspectives and priorities (Besley and Ghatak, 2005, p. 149). Hence the risk management role might be theorised to include working to harmonise the incentives by which people co-ordinate during the process of managing risk, recognising in particular the varying performance management and measurement imperatives and reward structures at play (Besley and Ghatak, 2005, pp. 149-155).

There are also non-economic policies that an organisation can put in place to improve employee accountability (Besley and Ghatak, 2005, p. 158). This might involve, for example, recognising and showcasing the good examples set by individuals who evidence that they relate to the mission of the organisation and feel motivated in what they do (Besley and Ghatak, 2005, p. 159). For the purpose of the present research, it was reasoned that wider use of risk assessment can usefully be promoted, in part because this permits such individuals to come forward and be recognised and rewarded for their proactivity. Nonetheless, many authors also assert that clear lines of risk ownership are essential, and ideally, consistent with enlightened principles of risk allocation where relevant knowledge, expertise and empowerment are taken into account when making the allocations (Deloach, 2000, 150; Chapman and Ward, 2002, p. 18; ISO, 2009). Hall (1998, p.131) suggests that a process to track such accountabilities should be defined, along with the techniques, metrics and any triggering devices used. To a large extent, these concerns can be handled through routine use of risk registers, which not only document the outputs of risk assessment, but can also specify risk ownerships and contingencies where risk owners are expected to take action. The promotion of risk assessment across the firm, we reasoned, would be more likely to leverage enthusiastic participation where risk registers are used to record risk assessment participation and any delegated risk ownerships, alongside assessment outputs, so that this information can then be used to assist performance appraisal and promotion decisions.

Innovative Recommendations: Smarter Use of a Broader Range of Risk Assessment Techniques

The action research drew upon the foregoing theoretical assumptions regarding risk communication and co-ordination by scoping, at interview, respondent opinions and suggestions regarding the ERM developmental opportunities that can be seized through more and better broadly participative use of risk assessment techniques across the firm. We had in mind the following assessment techniques, which were explained to the interview respondents (similarly to how we explain them below) and piloted to varying extents as opportunities arose during the period of research.

Scenario Modelling

We chose scenario modelling as one of our techniques, in part due to its fundamental requirement for intense co-working between diverse participants, and also in recognition of the importance of forecasting for internally complex risks, over and above estimating for simple risks which is the more traditional subject matter for risk management. The following phase-by-phase representation of the scenario modelling process, which we used, is a composite from various sources (Clarke and Varma, 1999; Miller and Waller, 2003; Pike, 2010, p. 18):

1. Create a heterogeneous scenario-building team whose work can be mediated by the risk manager;
2. Agree on the scope and confirm participant understanding;
3. Decide upon and ensure common understanding of any model frameworks to be applied or adapted (business models, mathematical models, etc.);
4. Critically discuss the variables that are to comprise the model in its present application or adaptation;
5. Score the model variables by importance;
6. Outline the particular scenario and forecast outcomes through critical consideration of the variables deemed to be at play;
7. Create a simplifying contextualised description of the scenario and the associated forecast, sustaining critical challenge to its plausibility throughout the discussions;
8. Elaborate the final scenario narrative so that even people outside the scenario team are able to understand it and find it plausible.

We considered that this technique might often make a useful contribution to firm risk management, by immersing the team participants in very rich critical discussion so as to produce not just better planning protocols but also latent management networks that might activate in future within ERM activity. Following this reasoning, what matters most is that the social event enables participants to build trust and familiarity with the total pool of roles, knowledge, skills, perspectives and resources that are being brought together.

Business Wargaming

Business wargaming is a decision-making tool stemming from military wargaming, which is useful for capturing risk management in its element of adversarial social interaction. Hence it is especially useful for understanding business competition risks through predictive simulation of social interaction between business competitors

(Kurtz, 2003; Oriesek and Schwarz, 2016, p. 7). The technique is highly immersive and social in character, involving iterative decision-making interactions between four main teams (Oriesek and Schwarz, 2016, p. 22):

- **Company Team:** This is usually formed by senior leaders within the organisation, so that the wargame may provide an opportunity to test strategic options;
- **Competitor Team:** This is also formed by senior leaders within the organisation. A "gamebook" is given to them with basic facts about the company they are now representing.
- **Market Team:** This comprises inside and/or outside market experts who judge the attractiveness of company and competitor team decisions from the customer insight perspective. They re-allocate market share based on their judgments.
- **Control Team:** This may be formed by wargame and industry experts as well as by the CEO or senior leaders within the organisation. They give structure to the simulation, assure rule enforcement and mediate between the other three teams. They may also inject more realism into the proceedings by introducing "disruptions" to make participants change direction or explore an issue. When required they can also play the role of other stakeholders who are not being explicitly represented.

Following the method presented by Oriesek and Schwarz, wargames are usually performed in three cycles, with each representing a particular period of time (2016, p. 25). The first cycle tends to begin in the present time (Ibid, 2016, p. 25). Decisions taken by the Company and Competitor team are annotated and given to the Market and Control teams so they can use them as inputs to make a movement (Ibid, 2016, p. 26). Following this, the Market team will provide feedback and award market share (Ibid, 2016, p. 26). After consolidating all soft and hard data, the control team can provide the previously decided quantitative indexes and Key Performance Indicators' status up to that point in time (Ibid, 2016, p. 26). This Control team response defines the preamble for the next round (Ibid, 2016, p. 26). All information exchanged between the Company and Competitor should be sent by email copying in the Control team, as they should not be collaborating or working on the same room (Ibid, 2016, p. 26). In a plenary session after a complete round, the current state and lessons learned are shared (Ibid, 2016, p. 27). Sharing the key insights learned from each team is one of the major benefits of the game (Ibid, 2016, p. 28). Hence, what is likely to emerge among managers is a broader and more realistic set of perspectives on competition risk and related marketing issues.

Intelligence Management

Generally speaking, looking at risk management through an intelligence analysis lens entails adapting risk management to become less sedentary by incorporating that proactive focus on intelligence gathering and use which is the hallmark of military intelligence, marketing intelligence, competitive intelligence and business intelligence practices (Marshall, 2017; Marshall and Ceylan, 2020; Costa Sperb and Marshall, 2020). Focusing this practice more narrowly towards a concern for developing early warnings, a simple methodology for risk intelligence can be pieced together from various sources (e.g. Arad, 2008, p. 66; Dash et al., 2014) as follows:

1. Collect and validate data pertaining to the broad issues of concern;
2. Set indicators to follow and define a way to update the data routinely from the chosen sources;
3. Define an index to aggregate the indicators and define an early warning level for triggering specified management responses.

However, we chose this risk assessment technique, partly in recognition of the importance of various more detailed team activities that can usefully take place to support the general process. What these various team activities have in common is that taken together they help guard against various misperceptions of objective reality, involving various forms of prejudice, groupthink or social-political bias that can easily interfere with evaluation of intelligence information and its sources. The team activities which we have in mind here, are those proposed by Heuer (2005, p. 61) as follows:

- **Group A and B:** either two groups are asked to analyze a topic at the same time or one before the other. In the latter option, the second group analyses based on the conclusions of the first group. The idea is to have different centers of thought and ensure redundancy.
- **Red Cell Analysis:** this tool focuses on a type of role-play in which the analyst is constantly trying to understand the opposing point of view.
- **"What if" Analysis:** focused on low probability events, this method looks at unlikely steps that might be taken by actors in the social world, possible indicators and model development for possible consequences.
- **Analysis of Competing Hypotheses (ACH):** this technique begins by brainstorming causal assessments of some past, present or future risk event. Following this, a matrix is produced mapping explanatory hypotheses against relevant available evidence so that hypotheses can be ranked by explanatory power.

- **Key Assumptions Check:** this technique pays critical attention to the causal-sequential understandings that are important within risk management. It entails paying attention to the main assumptions of the causal assessment, looking for example at what events might need to happen for the main assumptions to be correct.

These various supportive practices can all be considered as ways to create or strengthen communication links between the participants and the risk management team. Although each in its own way focuses on intelligence and its sources, it is also apparent that each can support not just intelligence management but also scenario modelling, business wargaming, and indeed forecasting planning for complex risk in general. We chose them because, taken together, they can all help risk management participants achieve a much richer understanding of the nature of both risk itself, and of how it can be discussed and managed on a collective basis. In other they supply means to deliver that more complex risk ontology which we theorised earlier as enabling effective ERM communication and co-ordination that can span cultural distance while dealing with high levels of complexity in risk environments.

From Theory to Practice: Options for a Risk Management Communication and Co-ordination Infrastructure at Proeza

As reported by the interviewees, currently, there is no formal process to communicate risk-related information (aside from the Internal Control efforts to report findings). Regarding existing provisions for co-ordination, these involve simple linear sequencing on a per risk basis. Specifically, if an employee finds a risk, they would have to report it to the SBU (Strategic Business Unit) risk management team, who will then communicate it to the corporate risk management team. The risk management of the SBU is responsible for building action plans and establishing risk ownerships for following up as necessary. The information is then sent to the corporate risk management team which consolidates the information from the different SBUs and presents it to the audit committee or board of directors.

Of particular note, however, is the fact that the corporate risk management team had started to encourage brainstorm teams comprising various directors of the organisation, especially where there are shared risks which justify their being drawn together. Added to that, action plans and further follow-ups are now routinely considered. Crucially, we reasoned, growing interest in brainstorming practice seemed to set a solid foundation for incorporating more and better risk assessment techniques that can further leverage the improved risk communication and coordination that are required within systems of enterprise risk management. Reflecting upon the nature of the benefits arising from the risk assessment practices we have set out above, it became clear that the best way to conceive of these, and to explain and promote them within the firm, was in terms of *risk culture*. Indeed, one of the most common comments when interviewing the risk management team was that there is a need to build a risk culture in the organisation. By 'risk culture', interviewees seemed to be referring, at the very least, to an ideal where every employee in the organisation is aware of the relevance of the risk management process and its benefits. Nonetheless, some interviewees considered a healthy risk culture to also include elements of motivation, empowerment, and critical reflection on how risk is perceived, as well as on what is meant by 'risk' wherever it is discussed. The 'footprint' of the risk management team was also regarded as an important consideration for risk culture. It was felt that, overall, the risk management team must remain visible and help to build and maintain trust among participating stakeholders. One suggestion from within the team was that they could do so by sharing regular risk insights via email or in a dedicated webpage on the firm intranet – and also by providing education on risk management topics of interest among employees. Furthermore, the risk management team appreciated that they could do much to incentivise risk management participation by ensuring that participants are very publicly recognised and credited for any risk insights and proactive contributions that demonstrate their excellence.

Risk culture building via smarter use of risk management techniques was also recognised by interviewees as a viable and indeed highly efficient means to bridge current communication and co-ordination gaps across the organisation, whilst also allowing these practices to become more dynamic, iterative, non-routine, and spontaneous in character. It was also felt that elements of creative opportunism could be introduced, for example by taking advantage of staff away days and other training events that were currently being planned, or run periodically, as opportunities to foster networking and team spiritedness through the introduction of novel risk management activities. The techniques were also recognised as highly effective for eliciting that 'tone at the top' (i.e. senior management participation which leads by example) which is frequently regarded as a key attribute of risk culture. Take business wargaming, for example, which relies explicitly on senior management participation – or indeed any other technique we have listed. In each case, participants can be chosen by varying seniority to create diagonal slices through the firm, with enormous potential to build and complexify informal networks of communication and co-ordination. In other words, it was felt that more widespread use of the various risk assessment techniques could do much to build risk culture in its management climate aspect, which is to say through human contact, with trust and relationship building happening where previously there is likely to have been little or no contact.

The case for wider use of the various risk assessment techniques, then, seemed compelling. Hence, over the course of the period of research there were efforts made to experiment with them. This allowed the risk management team to test their hopes and expectations regarding the benefits sketched out above. The team were then in a stronger position to participate in the final briefing and feedback session which collated the overall findings.

Final Presentation to Proeza and Feedback Received

The aim of the final presentation to the risk management team and various other participants from across the firm, being deeply integrated within the action research, was to explain and initiate what would be an ongoing process of developing risk communication and coordination infrastructure. Regarding the means of communication, the team had considered it appropriate to prepare for handling more complex and voluminous information by adopting a risk management information system. Hence the current state of plans for this was discussed. Interestingly, when these discussions came to focus on the overall team member allocations of accountability, roles and responsibilities for risk management activity that would be required, it was realised with enthusiasm that the proposed change would fit neatly with existing role structures.

In response to the agreed desirability of making more extensive use of the broader range of risk assessment techniques, the team balanced enthusiasm with a recognition that this would need to happen gradually and in line with the current resources of the firm, not least of which are the time resources of senior managers and the risk management team members. Nonetheless, there was agreement that the elements of creativity and novelty associated with using a broader range of risk assessment techniques would itself attract participants. It was also felt that the networking opportunities would be greatly valued. The team was also positive on the clarification provided, whereby the SBU's risk management team would be considered responsible for dealing with all associated issues relating to risk ownership/accountability, for example pertaining to any follow-up action plans that might be required.

Specific opportunities for using new risk assessment techniques, and also for reflecting on their significance for the firm's ongoing risk culture dynamic, were discussed. It was clarified that this may happen, for example, at some quarterly communication meetings. Another decision was to take advantage of the "*Ponte la Camiseta*" event. This is an annual team integration event in which all the headquarters employees spend a day out of the office participating in various activities to strengthen bonds with members of other working teams. It was recognised that this would be an ideal opportunity for experimenting with more novel techniques of risk assessment in particular.

CONCLUSION

A succinct conclusion arises from the foregoing research: developing enterprise risk management in its crucial risk communication and coordination aspect can be very straightforward; a simple matter, in fact, of promoting widespread use of diverse risk assessment techniques. Through such simple means, it is also possible to build an excellent risk culture, especially atop cultural foundations which already emphasise the importance of widespread human-centred stakeholder collaboration.

Arguably, *Proeza's* experience in both of these regards, shows that risk management can mature within a firm, in such a way that its nature, scope and significance always remain clear to all who are drawn in as participants. For any employee seeking to understand ERM, or risk culture, their attention need not be sunk within lengthy guidance documents that deal with elaborate architectures that relate risk management to performance and strategy, or within the burgeoning risk culture literature that has generated countless risk culture definitions and taxonomies of attributes. Instead, they can *learn by doing*, in what is effectively both a human focused participative experience, and an experience whose meaningfulness is always immediately apparent by calling attention to some real risk to the firm which must be managed.

We would conclude that the present action research illustrates an efficient means which any firm within an emerging economy might pursue, if it seeks to accelerate that virtuous cycle of growth, innovation and organisational complexity we introduced at the start of the chapter. More than that, however, it can also be used more generally by firms that already have a high level of ERM development – especially where this is felt to have been constructed from the top down with guidelines and checklists, while lacking the human centeredness that it needs most of all. Future research should certainly focus, we would urge, on understanding the heterogeneous benefits that can arise from fostering broader participation in more and better risk management processes that reflect more imaginative understandings of what risk management processes can comprise. Indeed this might arguably be considered both as a key driver, and as a key indicator, for risk management maturity within organisations.

REFERENCES

Ang, S., & Van Dyne, L. (2009). *Handbook of Cultural Intelligence Theory, Measurement, and Applications*. Routledge.

Arad, U. (2008). Intelligence Management as Risk Management. In P. Bracken, I. Bremmer, & D. Gordon (Eds.), *Managing Strategic Surprise. Lessons from Risk Management and Risk Assessment*. Cambridge University Press. doi:10.1017/CBO9780511755880.003

Astrum. (n.d.). *About Us*. Available at: https://www.astrum.com.mx/eng/about-us/

Bauer, J., & Gruber, H. (2007). Workplace Changes and Workplace Learning: Advantages of an Educational Micro Perspective. *International Journal of Lifelong Education*, *26*(6), 675–688. doi:10.1080/02601370701711364

Besley, T., & Ghatak, M. (2005). Incentives, Risk and Accountability in Organizations. In B. Hutter & M. Power (Eds.), *Organizational Encounters with Risk*. Cambridge University Press. doi:10.1017/CBO9780511488580.006

Butler, B. S., & Gray, P. H. (2006). Reliability, Mindfulness, and Information Systems. *Management Information Systems Quarterly*, *30*(2), 211–224. doi:10.2307/25148728

Centre for Risk Research. (2016). *Directing Risk Management in Organizations: Guidance from the Centre for Risk Research*. Centre for Risk Research, University of Southampton.

Chapman, C., & Ward, S. (2002). *Managing Project Risk and Uncertainty*. John Wiley and Sons.

Citrofrut. (2012). *Our Company*. Available at: https://www.citrofrut.com/eng/empresa.html

Clarke, C. J., & Varma, S. (1999). Strategic Risk Management: The New Competitive Edge. *Long Range Planning*, *32*(4), 414–424. doi:10.1016/S0024-6301(99)00052-7

COSO. (2017). *Enterprise Risk Management: integrating with strategy and performance*. COSO.

Costa Sperb, L. F., & Marshall, A. (2020). *The Risk Radar and the View of Risk: a Centre for Risk Research Discussion Document*. Centre for Risk Research, University of Southampton.

Dash Wu, D., Chen, S. H., & Olson, D. L. (2014). Business Intelligence in Risk Management: Some Recent Progresses. *Information Sciences*, *256*, 1–7. doi:10.1016/j.ins.2013.10.008

Deal, T., & Kennedy, A. (1982). *Corporate Cultures: The Rites and Rituals of Corporate Life*. Penguin Group.

Deloach, J. W. (2000). *Enterprise-Wide Risk Management. Strategies for Linking Risk and Opportunity*. Pearson Education.

French, S., Maule, A. J., & Mythen, G. (2005). Soft Modelling in Risk Communication and Management: Examples in Handling Food Risk. *The Journal of the Operational Research Society*, *53*(8), 879–888. doi:10.1057/palgrave.jors.2601901

Gigerenzer, G., & Edwards, A. (2003). Simple Tools for Understanding Risks: From Innumeracy to Insight. *British Medical Journal*, *327*(7417), 741–744. doi:10.1136/bmj.327.7417.741 PMID:14512488

Giles, J., & Middleton, T. (1999). *Studying Culture*. Blackwell.

Hall, E. M. (1998). *Managing Risk. Methods for Software Systems Development*. Addison-Wesley.

Harris-Jones, J., & Bergin, L. (1998). *The Management of Corporate Risk-a Framework for Directors*. The Association of Corporate Treasurers.

Heuer, J. R. J. Jr. (2005). Limits of Intelligence Analysis. *Orbis*, *49*(1), 75–94. doi:10.1016/j.orbis.2004.10.007

Hopkin, P. (2010). *Fundamentals of Risk Management. Understanding, Evaluating and Implementing Effective Risk Management*. Kogan Page.

ISO. (2009). International Organization for Standardization., ISO 31000.

Jardine, C.G., & Hurdey, S.E. (1997). Mixed Messages in Risk Communication. *Risk Analysis: An International Journal*, *17*(4), 489-498.

Jenks, C. (2005). *Culture* (2nd ed.). Routledge.

Johansen, W., Aggerholm, H. K., & Frandsen, F. (2012). Entering New Territory: A Study of Internal Crisis Management and Crisis Communication in Organizations. *Public Relations Review*, *38*(2), 270–279. doi:10.1016/j.pubrev.2011.11.008

Keller, C., Siegrist, M., & Gutscher, H. (2006). The Role of the Affect and Availability Heuristics in Risk Communication. *Risk Analysis: An International Journal*, *26*(3), 631-639.

Kuper, A., & Kuper, J. (2007). Culture. In *The Social Science Encyclopedia* (2nd ed., pp. 683–691). Routledge.

Kurtz, J. (2003). "Business Wargaming": Simulations Guide Crucial Strategy Decisions. *Strategy and Leadership*, *31*(6), 12–21. doi:10.1108/10878570310505550

Langer, E. J., & Moldoveanu, M. (2000). The Construct of Mindfulness. *The Journal of Social Issues*, *56*(1), 1–9. doi:10.1111/0022-4537.00148

Lipkus, I. M., & Hollands, J. G. (1999). The Visual Communication of Risk. *Journal of the National Cancer Institute. Monographs*, *1999*(25), 149–163. doi:10.1093/oxfordjournals.jncimonographs.a024191 PMID:10854471

Marshall, A. (2017). *Risk Intelligence: a Centre for Risk Research Discussion Document. Centre for Risk Research.* University of Southampton.

Marshall, A., & Ceylan, S. (2020). *Risk Intelligence Production on Complex Projects: practical discussion points. Centre for Risk Research.* University of Southampton.

Marsick, V. J., & Watkins, K. E. (2003). Demonstrating the Value of an Organization's Learning Culture: The Dimensions of the Learning Organization Questionnaire. *Sage (Atlanta, Ga.)*, *5*(2), 132–151. doi:10.1177/1523422303005002002

Maule, A. J. (2008). Risk Communication in Organizations. In G. P. Hodgkinson & W. H. Starbuck (Eds.), *The Oxford Handbook of Organizational Decision Making*. Oxford University Press.

Metalsa. (2019). *Identity.* Available at: https://www.metalsa.com/about-metalsa

Miller, K. D., & Waller, H. G. (2003). Scenarios, Real Options and Integrated Risk Management. *Long Range Planning*, *36*(1), 93–107. doi:10.1016/S0024-6301(02)00205-4

Oriesek, D., & Schwarz, J. O. (2016). *Business Wargaming: Securing Corporate Value.* Available at: https://www.taylorfrancis.com/books/9781315570648

Ott, J. S. (1989). *The Organizational Culture Perspective*. Brooks/Cole Publishing Company.

Pike, R. (2010). Scenario-Building Techniques for Improved Risk Management. In J. Reuvid (Ed.), *Managing Business Risk. A Practical Guide to Protecting Your Business*. Kogan Page.

Proeza. (n.d.). *Areya.* Available at: http://www.proeza.com.mx/en/areya/

Reason, J. (1997). *Managing the Risks of Organizational Accidents.* Ashgate Publishing Limited.

Renooija, S., & Witteman, C. (1999). Talking Probabilities: Communicating Probabilistic Information with Words and Numbers. *International Journal of Approximate Reasoning*, *22*(3), 169–194. doi:10.1016/S0888-613X(99)00027-4

Ruff, P., & Aziz, K. (2003). *Managing Communications in a Crisis*. Gower Publishing Limited.

Schein, E. H., & Schein, P. (2017). *Organizational Culture and Leadership* (5th ed.). John Wiley and Sons.

Seeger, M. W. (2006). Best Practices in Crisis Communication: An Expert Panel Process. *Journal of Applied Communication Research*, *34*(3), 232–244. doi:10.1080/00909880600769944

Slocum, J. W. J., & Hellriegel, D. (2009). *Principles of Organizational Behavior* (12th ed.). South-Western Cengage Learning.

Theil, M. (2002). The Role of Translations of Verbal into Numerical Probability Expressions in Risk Management: A Meta-Analysis. *Journal of Risk Research*, *5*(2), 177–186. doi:10.1080/13669870110038179

Thompson, K.M. (2002). Variability and Uncertainty Meet Risk Management and Risk Communication. *Risk Analysis: An International Journal, 22*(3), 647-654.

Waring, A., & Glendon, I. A. (1998). *Managing Risk*. Thomson Learning.

Weick, K. E., & Sutclliffe, K. M. (2001). *Managing the Unexpected*. Jossey-Bass.

Chapter 8
Innovation of SMEs and Their Effect on Productivity in Jalisco

José G. Vargas-Hernández
https://orcid.org/0000-0003-0938-4197
University Center for Economic and Managerial Sciences, University of Guadalajara, Mexico

ABSTRACT

Small and medium enterprises (SMEs) in Jalisco represent one of the main entities of economic activity that supports the bulk of the population living in the state; using statistics as a fundamental tool for conducting studies in the economic, natural, health sciences, among others, allows one to have proactive foundations for decision making within companies by senior executives and in the field public by officials responsible for promoting the growth of the industry in the State of Jalisco. This research tries to represent, under a statistical scheme, the use and disposition of information and communication technologies (ICTs) as a tool to increase average productivity levels within companies and under the Cobb production function. Douglas determines the ICT impact.

INTRODUCTION

In Mexico as in the State of Jalisco, the economic effects of the economic crisis suffered in 2008, as a result of excessive spending by Americans due to low interest rates, triggering an imbalance in the mortgage sector, is identified as the main cause of this crisis. For the country of Mexico as well as the State of Jalisco, the effects were evidenced in the real economy when our exports and remittances from the

DOI: 10.4018/978-1-7998-4195-1.ch008

Copyright © 2021, IGI Global. Copying or distributing in print or electronic forms without written permission of IGI Global is prohibited.

United States contracted, together with the reduction of confidence in the Mexican economy by entities that promoted the increase in R & D (Research and Development).

From these consequences the economy seems to have consolidated its stagnation in different areas of the economic activity, such as: mining, electricity, construction, manufacturing, commerce, services, transportation and communications. The strategic sectors are determined by the National Institute of the Entrepreneur (INADEM), for the state of Jalisco on12, and are grouped in the key and futures. The key sectors are the products for construction, agro industrial (Gourmet), electronic (Electronics and communications), travel services, and chemical products. The futures are the logistic services, medical services (medical tourism), information technology, green and alternative technologies, research and technological development services, wood products (Furniture and decoration), textile and clothing (Paz, 2020).

Electronic (Electronics and communications): Activities derived from the aluminum, iron and steel industry, manufacture of wire and springs, manufacture of cables for conducting electrical energy, plugs, contacts and fuses, rigid plastic laminates, industrial glass articles, manufacture of signal transmission and reception equipment, radio and wireless communication, manufacture of computers and peripheral equipment, measuring instruments, control, navigation, and electronic medical equipment, manufacture of audio and video equipment, Manufacture of other machinery and equipment for trade and services (Paz, 2020).

These activities represent the sectors that mostly absorb the Economically Active Population (PEA: Population aged 15 and over) through small and medium enterprises (SMEs). In Jalisco, micro, small, and medium-sized enterprises (MSMEs) are of great importance in public policies, and the State Government makes an important effort to promote them with training, advice, and financing (IIEG, 2018). The medium-sized companies represent 1% of the total of the companies of the state and support 22% of the Aggregate value. 77% of medium-sized companies are registered in the Central Area of the State, mainly in the municipalities of Guadalajara, Zapopan, Tlaquepaque and Tlajomulco de Zúñiga (Paz, 2020).

Compared with national performance, the percentage of medium-sized companies in Jalisco with access to financing is greater than that of the national economy. The medium-sized company faces a problem of access to financial financing that is very different from the Micro and Small company. The company mediated access to formal or institutional financing sources such as the Commercial Bank (its main financing source), suppliers and partner contributions (Paz, 2020). The market financing is practically null. Only 0.2% of the medium-sized companies of the medium-sized companies of Jalisco have access to this type of financing, in the national plan only 0.4% of the financing.

As for the financing of the Median companies of Jalisco, we can appreciate that these are in a better position than the national media. Companies mediate access to different sources of financing such as the suppliers and the own contribution of the partners. They have enough profit margin to self-finance their growth, a situation that could affect its market competitiveness at any time with new competitors (Paz, 2020). However, this situation varies according to each strategic sector of the state. The industry has access to financial support, followed by trade and finally services. Recently, the Jalisco government announced last Friday an Emergent Economic Support Plan with a 1,000-million-peso bag for micro, small and medium-sized enterprises (MSMEs), corn producers and self-employed people who are affected by the social isolation measures adopted in the state to deal with the Covid-19 pandemic (Romo, 2020).

With regard to the income from oil exports for December 2015, these prices are down, due to pressure from the member countries of the Organization of Petroleum Exporting Countries (OPEC) to promote the supply of crude oil. If this trend continues for the fourth quarter of 2016, an oil surplus is expected (El Economista, 2015). All these factors that limit the dynamism of the Mexican economy cause the deepening of the weakening of economic activities, negatively impacting the activities carried out by SMEs of Jalisco in the quest to absorb as much of the EAP as possible. Table 1 shows the concentration areas of MSMEs in México.

Table 1.

Zone	Percentage	Concentration	Porcentage
North	48%	Nuevo León	20%
Center	42%	Cd. De México y Estado de México	11%
South	10%	Jalisco	3%

Table 1 shows that Jalisco concentrates the 3% of MSMEs of the national total.

One of the challenges for companies of Jalisco is to be at the forefront of current technological systems. Mexico as a developing economy is subject to the imitation of technologies from central countries such as the United States, Germany, Japan, France and the United Kingdom (G5). As Myro points out in 2010: in economies with a low level of development, [...], technical progress should be more based on imitation than on one's own technological effort, so that cases such as Mexico's and Jalisco´s policies on technological innovation should focus on imitation to achieve the technical progress sought by SMEs in the State of Jalisco.

This is how Jalisco bases its innovative activity through reactive strategies that follow and imitate organizations. Pioneer nations such as Germany, Japan, the United States, among other developed nations, follow reactive strategies, since they are pioneers in technological innovations. Among the main results that Mexico in general and Jalisco in specific, have in terms of Science, Technology and Industry in a study that was carried out by the Organization for Economic Cooperation and Development (OECD) in 2013, are summarized those:

1. Mexico, including Jalisco suffers the consequences of a weak innovation environment, and investment in science and technology remains at a low level by OECD standards.
2. Among the main obstacles are: patterns of industrial specialization, high prevalence of micro-enterprises, skill gaps and an ICT infrastructure insufficiently developed and high cost.
3. Linkages between the research base and the underdeveloped economy, which translates into few scientific publications (OECD, 2013).

These characteristics, which currently prevail in conjunction with the low quality of educational services, make it difficult to build a solid technological base in the much sought-after technical progress, even though imitation. In this same report, it is mentioned that Mexico, including the state of Jalisco, also faces a series of challenges due to the weaknesses of its ICT infrastructure, which include low penetration of broadband (both fixed and wireless), low average speeds of broadband connection and high prices (OECD, 2013).

Information and Communication Technologies (ICTs) play in business logistics a fundamental role in the praxis of economic subjects. Because of the importance that these tools have among the relations of the global economies, keeping them up to date is fundamental for the capitalist system. It can be appreciated that there is a large difference between the access to the information technologies between the medium-sized companies and the micro-companies. According to the antiquity of the company, the companies between 3 and 5 years (Young) are the ones with the greatest access to information technologies, up to 30%. The main one that gives the company the information technologies are the search for information. In the measure that the company is larger, the use of the Internet is intensified, this is many marked in the banking and financial operations (Paz, 2020).

The following pages of the document describe the general aspects of the methodology used, the statistical design in which the basic statistics are calculated, at first about the stratification carried out by INEGI, followed by the segmentation proposed in this research. At the end of the methodology section establishes the relevance of using the average productivity and the Cobb-Douglas production model.

In the results section, the general statistics for the stratification of INEGI and the proposal formed by small, large and medium-sized companies are presented, the description of the type of activity they perform, the distribution of their income, the items to the that allocate their investment. This section also describes the use of traditional communication media, as well as the impacts of ICTs. In this same section we present the impacts of ICTs such as email, the Internet, social networks and the website in aspects of competitiveness. The results of the two regression models are also presented. Finally, in the last section, the conclusions and a series of recommendations are presented.

BACKGROUND OF THE PROBLEM

In the reconfiguration of productive paradigms, SMEs use sciences and techniques for the reconstruction of new technologies. Technology is understood as the sum of knowledge about the means and methods of production of goods and services (Luter, 1998), this same technology plays an important role in economic theory. The adoption of new technological tools, both to make their processes more efficient and to grow their markets, has allowed micro, small and medium-sized companies (MSMEs) in Jalisco not only to subsist, but to develop and conquer even international markets (Romo, 2019).

To define innovation, it is necessary to differentiate between invention and innovation (Galindo, 2012 pp.53). Invention as the idea of a person about a product or process and innovation as the first attempt to put it into practice. Galindo (2012) also considers that for an invention to become an innovation, the company must combine different elements, such as: knowledge, skills, abilities and resources.

In neoclassical economic theory, innovations are understood as exogenous phenomena in the equation that seeks the equilibrium between supply and demand while the current of the positive school that interprets the economy as a dynamic system considers innovation as a variable endogenous (Hernández, 2009). The positive theory makes reference that although the human being could not create the matter, if it can create his utility, to increase it or to diminish it, in this it consists precisely the innovation. With this, it assumes the importance of the reasoning of the human being, the capacity to invent and to create new forms from subjects.

Schumpeter being one of the modern authors, distinguishes the innovations themselves and technical innovations in the studies on growth and economic development. Hernández, (2009) distinguishes these two types of innovations, the first referring to the systemic search for general explanations of a phenomenon and technical innovation as an original solution resulting from the synthesis of information about needs or desires, and information about the technical means by which they can be satisfied (Utterback, 1971, p.77 in Hernández, 2009). This appreciation previously noted, where the human being seeks welfare through the least effort, the invention of the wheel, the steam engine and the innumerable instruments we use in our lives reflect the technical progress we have made to meet "n" human needs. Innovation is therefore an economic phenomenon that serves to create wealth and satisfy needs.

In this context, Hernández (2009) states that the variables that explain innovation are: entrepreneurial profits or the reduction of production costs, intentional research and development efforts, accumulation of human capital, exploitation of new inventions or in the application of mature technologies or new uses. For the company innovation is an important factor from any point in which it is considered, since it frees the market pressure in the creation or improvement of new products.

However, regulatory and fiscal barriers, or lack of revenue and business planning, remain factors that dictate failure in local and national companies. In Mexico, 75 to 80 percent of startups fail and die within two years. Of those that survive that barrier, 10 percent die each year, over a period of three to eight years El Informador (25 de Septiembre de 2017). According to estimates from Nacional Financiera, eight out of 10 SMEs in the country fail before the age of five due to business management problems (Romo, 2019).

Many companies that integrate markets base their innovations on scientific knowledge and technological developments measuring the innovation in number of patents for a certain period. Hernández, 2009 indicates that independent variables have to do with intensity or investment in research and development (Mansfield, 1963, Koeller, 1995, Gatti, 1998); with the provision of human capital according to the proportion of scientists and engineers in relation to company personnel, as well as the number of workers with the ability to execute changes or learn new skills (Koeller, 1995, Gatti, 1998, Afuah, 2002).

Companies being the primary entities of economic activities, innovation is a competitive advantage that allows them to extend their life in the market. Small and medium-sized companies (SMEs) born or located in Jalisco, have an average life of eight years, which places the state in seventh place in this category, above the national average of 7.8 years, according to data from the National Institute of Statistics, Geography and Informatics (INEGI). El Informador (25 de Septiembre de 2017). Innovation and technological change serve each other so that the company that produces them obtains better returns. Cantú, 2006 classifies the innovations according to the magnitude of the change they imply, mentioning the following typology (Cantú, 2006 in Dussage, Hart and Ramanantsoa, 1992, p.14-15):

1. **Incremental:** The articulation between concepts and components or architecture of the product is not changed, only some of its components or concepts are reinforced or improved.
2. **Radical:** Both the architecture and the components are altered, in fact it is a new product.

3. **Modular:** The modular components of a product are radically changed but its architecture remains unchanged; the change from analogue to digital telephones is an example of this type of technological innovation. Jalisco does not escape the behavior of the other states of the country where the adoption of technological solutions and the concept of digital transformation "is going to start speed up" (Romo, 2019).
4. **Architectural:** Modifies the way in which the components and concepts of the product are articulated but the components and concepts only reinforce or remain without change, examples of these changes occur in personal computers and are not easily identifiable by consumers because they are at the system level.

In this way, innovations are transformations made by the human being of the goods provided by nature with the purpose of facilitating the activities carried out and obtaining some benefits when exchanging them with other individuals, not limited to exclusively technological concepts, but rather to find also innovations in the economic, social, organizational, strategic areas of the companies.

The SMEs are the economic units by excellence that train the individuals, that when realizing a physical activity exchange this effort for an economic remuneration, this in order to solve their physical needs and those of their dependents. Since small and medium-sized companies are responsible for absorbing this population stratum, it is necessary to analyze the use of ICTs as an alternative to growth. That is why one of the main problems faced by SMEs is the lag in technological equipment that causes competitive asymmetries and disadvantages compared to foreign companies established in the State of Jalisco.

The process of equipping companies in their different dimensions when settling in defined geographical areas causes economic growth in the region. The study of this process is necessary to determine the effects it has on human capital, both in the average productivity, and the effect of ICTs on production levels in the company.

This investigation seeks to analyze this process and the influence on the living conditions of the State of Jalisco. Companies in Jalisco represent a great source of employment that encourage economic growth and social welfare. Jalisco contributes 7.4% to employed personnel at companies at the national level (Paz, 2020). Despite the fact that micro, small and medium-sized companies represent 99.8% of Jalisco's economic units and generate between 50 and 60% of employment, they barely contribute a third of the state's productivity (IIEG, 2018). Thus, statistics supports the operational alternatives in the decision making of the company in order to promote growth and with it the living conditions of workers.

REVIEW OF THE EMPIRICAL LITERATURE

In an investigation on the technological innovation of the network of suppliers of the electronic industry of Jalisco, mainly maquiladoras located in the Metropolitan Zone of Guadalajara, Basulto Castillo and Medina Ortega, (2006) reported the development of a pattern of peculiar behavior in the formation of supplier networks in the horizontal articulation of productive processes. Dutrénit (2009) found that depending of the nature of innovation activities, the type of linkages and the organizational capabilities of SMEs located in the area of Guadalajara, as factors supporting the levels of absorptive capacities of SMEs, when these are higher, it is more likely that they benefit from spillovers. A theoretical methodological proposal is formulated by Arce Rodríguez (2009) to assess the competitiveness factors of internationalized SMEs in Jalisco.

In a study carried out by Robles Estrada, (2009) the factors that lead to competitiveness are detected and analyzed and a theoretical methodological model is designed to assess the degree of competitiveness of internationalized SMEs in the State of Jalisco. Among the variables analyzed, the internal characteristics of the company and the relationships with its environment that generate greater competitiveness are considered. A study conducted in small enterprises in Jalisco by Ramirez Ruiz (2013), identified that the lack of capacities in human capital is one of the main inhibitors of innovation.

In another work by Amado Sánchez and Pico González (2013) the elements of innovation, collaborative processes and business networks that have driven the innovation of rubber and plastic manufacturing SMEs in the States of Jalisco, Estado de México and Nuevo León. The authors present empirical evidence of innovation variables, business networks and collaborative processes.

The main deficiencies of the constituent elements of the Regional Innovation System are identified by Ortiz-Cantú and Pedroza-Zapata (2013), who also point out that the logic of basic scientific research predominates. In the technological environment, they emphasize its importance to facilitate productive companies support in their innovation processes and its purpose is to boost the technological innovation of companies. In the productive environment, the industrial chambers carry out the tasks of raising awareness of business innovation. The effects of agglomeration and tax incentives for innovation have not been exploited, so the regional innovation system is characterized as incipient.

In the financial environment, the main one, the main funder of innovation is still the Ministry of Economy and Innovation for economic development, COECYTJAL, CONACYT and SEPROE. Ortiz-Cantú and Pedroza-Zapata (2013) conclude that the financial resources destined to foster innovation are meager. The persistence of institutional logic prevents the impulse to the creation of innovation capacities. These limitations make inescapable the strengthening of the institutions whose function is the promotion of business innovation in Jalisco. Among other recommendations, the authors ask for a support policy to boost innovation in clusters, integrate innovation in science and technology, as well as develop a business culture that supports the generation of innovation.

Camacho Sotelo, Hernández Cotón, Mayorga Salamanca, (2014) made a diagnosis of innovation and its interrelation with the competitiveness of manufacturing companies in the Guadalajara Metropolitan Area (ZMG) and demonstrated that there is a positive correlation between these two variables. Some of the areas that offer opportunities for improvement for competitiveness are financial issues and the use of technology. With regard to innovation, the use of information on the needs and recommendations of those is required to radically improve their products and services.

Vázquez Ávila, Núñez Moreno, Sánchez Gutiérrez, and Mejía Trejo (2015) confirm the correlation between the knowledge management and innovation variables using structural equations to determine the direct influence that these variables have with the competitiveness of the manufacturing companies in the Metropolitan Area of Guadalajara. The innovation factors analyzed are innovation barriers and changes implementation. They conclude that innovation activities that in addition to research and development include production and distribution activities, organization and marketing methods, knowledge and capital acquisition, among others.

In a paper published by Calle Medrano and Vargas Hernández, (2015) an index is determined and analyzed to measure the innovation capacity of companies in the Jalisco software industry, based on a survey of the companies that make up the Center for State software. In addition, the influence that the capacity of innovation has on its competitiveness is evaluated, looking for the empirical evidence that allows to answer the question asked.

Vázquez Ávila, Núñez Moreno, Sánchez Gutiérrez, and Mejía Trejo (2015) confirm the correlation between the knowledge management and innovation variables using structural equations to determine the direct influence that these variables have with the competitiveness of the manufacturing companies in the Metropolitan Area of Guadalajara. The innovation factors analyzed are innovation barriers and changes implementation. They conclude that innovation activities that in addition to research and development include production and distribution activities, organization and marketing methods, knowledge and capital acquisition, among others.

In the paper published by Calle Medrano and Vargas Hernández, (2015) an index is determined and analyzed to measure the innovation capacity of companies in the Jalisco software industry, based on a survey of the companies that make up the Software State Center. In addition, the influence that the capacity of innovation has on its competitiveness is evaluated, looking for the empirical evidence that allows to answer the question asked.

The research carried out by Calle Medrano and Vargas Hernández (2015) is based on the hypothesis that the ability to innovate is a factor that positively affects the performance of companies in the software industry, which is reflected in the competitiveness of the sector The methods used in this research are three: innovation capacity index (ICI), linear regression model with ordinary least squares and soft computing with application of evolutionary algorithms: Fuzzy Cesar; The latter is something very new that puts us on the frontier of knowledge in terms of methods.

The analysis of Pedroza-Zapata and Ortiz-Cantú (2015) describes the structure of the Jalisco State Innovation System, its governance, actors, programs and performance to assess the innovation capabilities of the State, which they consider are meager despite their growth because it is a decisive factor in the promotion of the State's R+D+I. The analysis identifies the minimum existence of constituent elements and the weakness of innovation capacities in characteristic productive environments with a low culture of competitiveness for innovation coupled with the lack of clarity of an industrial development policy.

A diagnosis of the organizational culture of 40 health SMEs located in Guadalajara, Jalisco, Mexico, carried out by Moyano Martínez (2016), and based on the instrument designed by Cameron and Quinn (2006), it was found that the type of organizational culture called clan is the one that promotes innovation and internationalization of these SMEs. The analysis and proposal of ergonomic innovations that promote the competitiveness and permanence of SMEs in the food sector in the downtown area of the city of Guadalajara, is the objective of the case study of Vázquez Ávila, Sánchez Gutiérrez and Núñez Moreno (2017). The case study focuses on food trucks located in the northern zone of Zapopan, Jalisco and concludes that small businesses have ambition and show a proactive attitude in their management.

The authors Arellano - Rodríguez, Sánchez Gutiérrez and Mejía - Trejo (2018) propose the administration of knowledge for the generation of innovation under the focus of the dynamic capacities of SMEs seeking better positions in the global value chain. They are based on empirical evidence based on studies of innovation in software companies in the city of Guadalajara (Mejía-Trejo et al. 2014). The analysis of the diagnosis and organizational intervention in MIPYMO`s del Sur de Jalisco conducted by Ramírez Lira, Rivera Espinoza, Azpeitia Torres, Amezcua Luján and Barajas Pérez (2018) consider that for organizations to have a culture of competitiveness, leadership must be articulated of managers among the owners, the leader and the workers.

THEORETICAL APPROACH

To solve the changes that our global environment demands of different societies is through knowledge, the different economic, political and social facts rethink the solution of problems through new and sustainable techniques. The promotion and development that governments make regarding managing knowledge is directly linked to the work of enterprises, to increase profitability, generate regional growth, improve living conditions and other promoting environmental care.

In this quest for knowledge management, companies create new and better products, improve their production systems, utopian looking solving major social and economic problems such as health, education, poverty, quality of life, etc., claiming that these new improvements do not compromise environmental conditions. In this way, companies, universities and the government are responsible for responding with solutions, using different strategies, mechanisms and policies that contribute to the improvement of current conditions. The conception of economy, the knowledge that is currently developed and involved in the tasks of companies to achieve higher returns, has to do with analyzing the situation, setting the objectives and finally optimizing knowledge.

Among the main features of this global knowledge economy, as stated by ECLAC, in its report "Innovating to grow", it must be:

1. Greater codification of knowledge.
2. A Closer relationship between technology and science, with higher innovation rates and shorter product life cycles.
3. A Growing importance of innovation in GDP growth, as well as education and continuous learning.
4. Greater investment in intangible elements (research and development, education, software, among others) than in fixed capital, and
5. Substantial changes in the demand for qualifications in the labor market (Figueroa, 2015)

These characteristics that foster the emergence of technological innovations imply a process to reach a final product or technological improvement. The process to follow can be clearly understood through the following funnel, (Figueroa, 2015).

Figure 1.

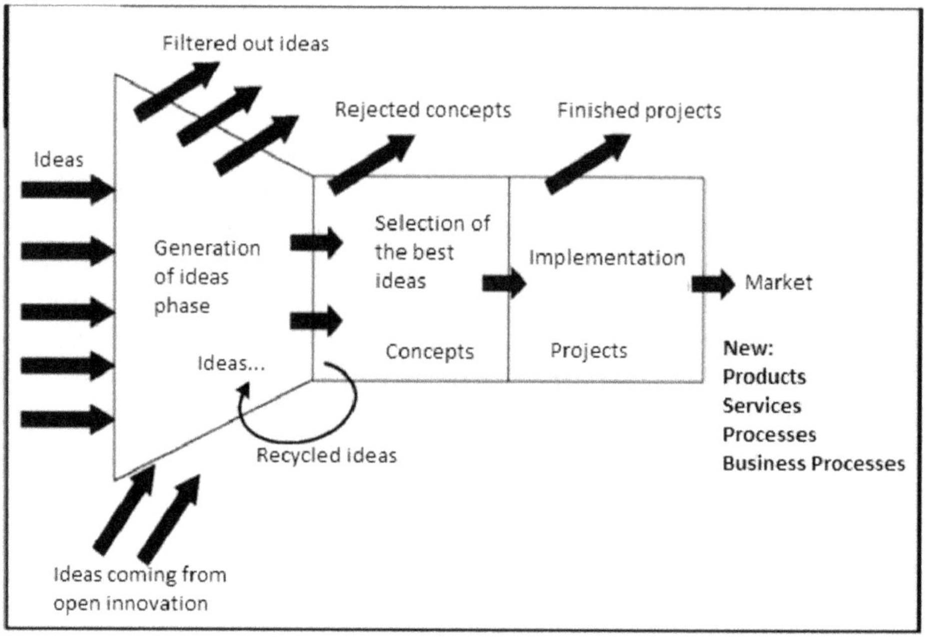

In this funnel, all ideas are filtered by ideas that are feasibly applied and that respond to a market need, so its implementation results in new products, services, processes and business processes. The importance of working under this scheme is reflected in the decrease in costs of the companies. Finally, to ensure the success of any technological innovation as Figueroa (2015) mentions, a social need, social resources and a receptive social concept have to be combined.

RESEARCH METHOD

General Aspects

The use of Information and Communication Technologies (ICTs) by companies in the State of Jalisco has seen considerable growth in recent years. The use of computers, landlines, mobile phones, internet, among other technological resources, has become essential for the operation of any company.

The following pages analyze the situation for 2013 of the use of ICTs by companies with a staff of more than 10 people. These companies are carrying out activities such as: mining, electricity, construction, manufacturing, commerce, services, transportation and communications, according to the classification made by the North American Industrial Classification System 2007 (SCIAN2007). This analysis is done taking the Survey on Information Technologies and Communications 2013 (ENTIC, 2013) conducted by the National Institute of Statistics and Geography (INEGI).

In Jalisco, there has been a growth in the adoption of information technologies and the myth that these tools were accessible only to large transnational companies has been banished (Romo, 2019). Among the companies from Jalisco that have adopted information technologies, the dairy group Sello Rojo (Lechera Guadalajara) that adopted the s4 Hana platform and they are close to implementing what distribution to the final customer is with SAP solutions.

Another of the success stories that the IT solutions company highlights is the Jalisco company Cloe, which through SAP Business One, has managed to emerge as an international company with 5,000 different fashion products and, according to its managers, every 30 seconds markets one of their items. Business One is the star SAP solution for the General Business segment that groups small and medium-sized companies and that in 2016 reported 10,000 clients in Latin America ... Therefore, cases like Cloe's that strengthens its business thanks to digitization, show that Growing companies can improve their performance and face the obstacles to reverse the statistics (Romo, 2019).

The survey was designed under a probabilistic scheme so that the results obtained can be generalized for the total population. The population of companies that integrate with 10 workers and more gives a total of 157, 611 and the total sample selected is 6, 941 companies. The available results are those presented for 42 companies.

It is worth mentioning that in this descriptive research, it had a limited sample of the results of the ENTIC, 2013 published by INEGI within its website, which is a mere approximation as an exercise that it intends to do as a research work at the international level. mastery with the complete survey. This is a cross-sectional study since the survey deals with the use of ICTs in 2013.

Statistical Design

The design used to carry out this research was an observational study, in which the ENTIC, 2013 is taken with the 42 companies that make up the database published by INEGI on its website. When carrying out this research it was decided to take all the companies as it was a limited database, so the results represent an exercise for the calculation of the final results that is proposed as thesis for the master's level.

The new stratification was carried out according to the size of the number of employees working in the company, so 3 groups were consolidated consisting of small companies that have a number of workers ranging from 1 to 50 employees, the medians of 51 to 250 employees and large companies that have more than 250 people employed.

Table 2.

	Estrata of personnel employed	Sample of companies
	Total	42
1.	More than 751	10
2.	251 a 750	6
3.	51 a 250	14
4.	21 a 50	5
5.	10 a 20	5
6.	1 a 9	2

Statistical Analysis

In the statistical analysis are the basic statistics of the original stratification presented by the INEGI according to the employed personnel, which includes data on the investment in fixed assets of the companies that allow identifying the items with greater influence on average productivity, the availability of the media in which the behavior of companies is identified with the media to position their products and services. These same basic statistics were also determined for the impacts of the use of ICTs in the productivity of companies. This as an alternative to promote competitive advantages over larger national companies as well as foreign companies established in the State of Jalisco that represent a potential competition.

In the proposal that is made to restructure the sample in 3 new groups, the structure of their income, the disposition of the means of communication, the use of computer equipment and the impact of ICTs, are finally proposed. 2 regression models to determine the average productivity and a modification to the production model using the Cobb-Douglas model using the Minitab statistical program.

ANALYSIS OF RESULTS

INEGI performs a stratification according to the employed or employed personnel, classifying the companies based on this criterion.

The results presented by INEGI, stratum 3 absorbs 33% of companies, followed by Stratum 1 with 24%, this stratum being large companies in terms of personnel, with more than 751 employed persons. The turn of the activities carried out by these companies are: television monitors, electric power commercialization, clothing retail trade, personnel transport service, crude oil, to name a few, this explains in some way the amount of personnel they require to develop their activities.

Figure 2.

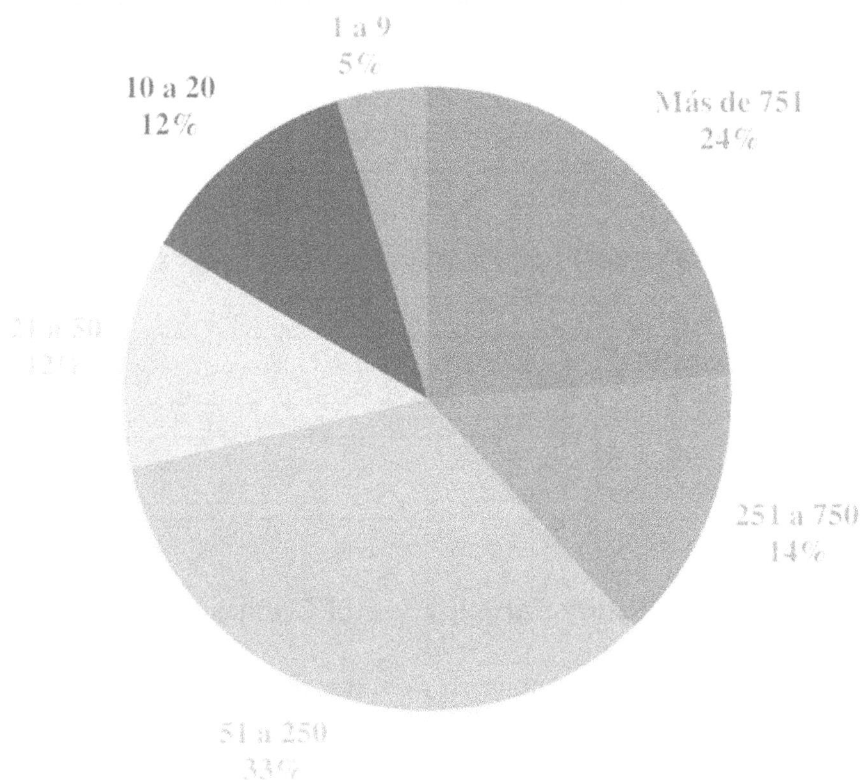

The business of the companies is presented in table 3. this classification is carried out by the OECD, with a total of 23 branches. The shift that predominates in the results presented by INEGI are the wholesale and retail sales and the complements of the service.

Table 3.

Branch of activity OCDE	Description OCDE	Companies
2	Mining	2
8	Textile	1
9	Clothing and leather	1
13	Pulp, paper and paper products	1
14	Publications, printers and reproduction of recording media	1
19	Chemical (pharmaceutical)	1
20	Rubber and plastic products	1
23	Ferrous basic metals	1
25	Products made of metal	2
28	Office, accounting and computer machinery	1
32	TV, radio and communications equipment	1
34	Motor vehicles	1
37	Aircraft	1
40	Furniture	1
41	Other manufactures not specified elsewhere	1
43	Electricity	1
46	Wholesales	5
48	Transportation and storage	3
53	Real estate, income and business activities	1
59	Community, social and personal services	3
SER	Complement services	4
46b	Retail sales	7

Investment and Equity Participation of Companies

Throughout economic history, talk about investment involves the injection of current assets to promote and reactivate some economic activity in order to grow this type of asset through yields. Within companies and any organization investments are made through direct injections of capital, for example the payment of wages and salaries, purchases of different inputs to make labor productive as the same production process, ICT equipment, among others. In the case of the study companies, it can be observed the distribution that is made of this investment being the items in machinery and equipment and the investment in computer equipment and peripherals that concentrate the largest amount of capital invested.

Figure 3.

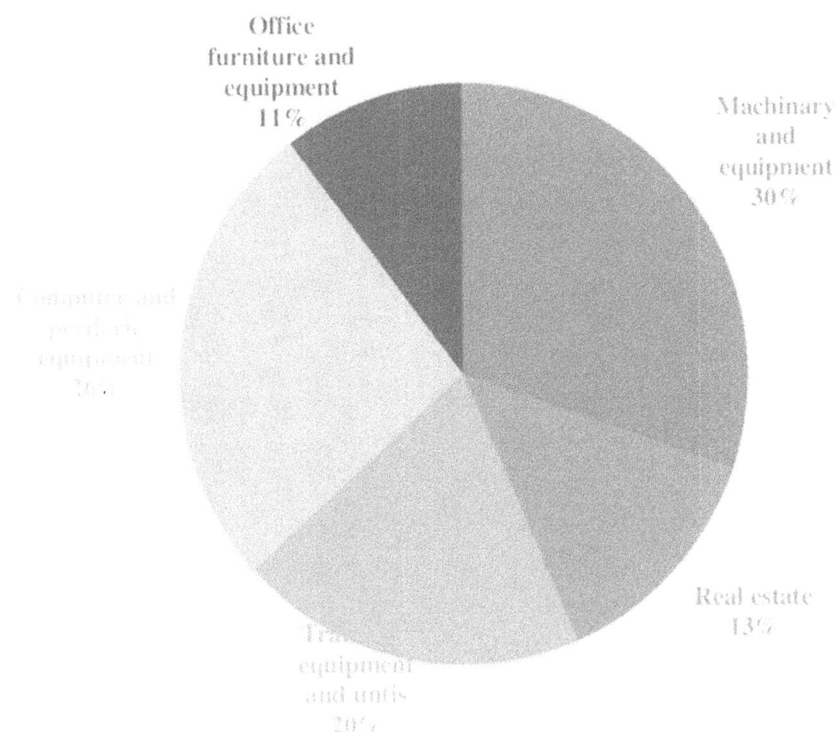

The information presented about the amounts of investment in fixed assets that companies make results with a large variance. In this way, through ranges it can

Table 4.

Rank	Investment	Total companies	% of investment rank
1	De $0 a 99	13	30.95
2	De $100 a 999	10	23.81
3	De $1,000 a 9,999	10	23.81
4	De $10,000 a 99,999	5	11.90
5	More than $100,000	4	9.52
Total		42	100.00

be have a clearer vision. It can be seen that 54.76% of companies invest less than $ 999.00 pesos. This investment ratio is a function of the size of the companies that for this research has been stratified in terms of the staff they have occupied.

Continuing with the formation of the participation of the social capital of these companies, of the 42, 78.57% is 100% national capital, then we have 19.05% with participation of foreign capital and a public company. Within companies with foreign capital participation (8 companies), 3 have 99% of foreign capital and 2 companies have 100% of this same type of capital.

Figure 4.

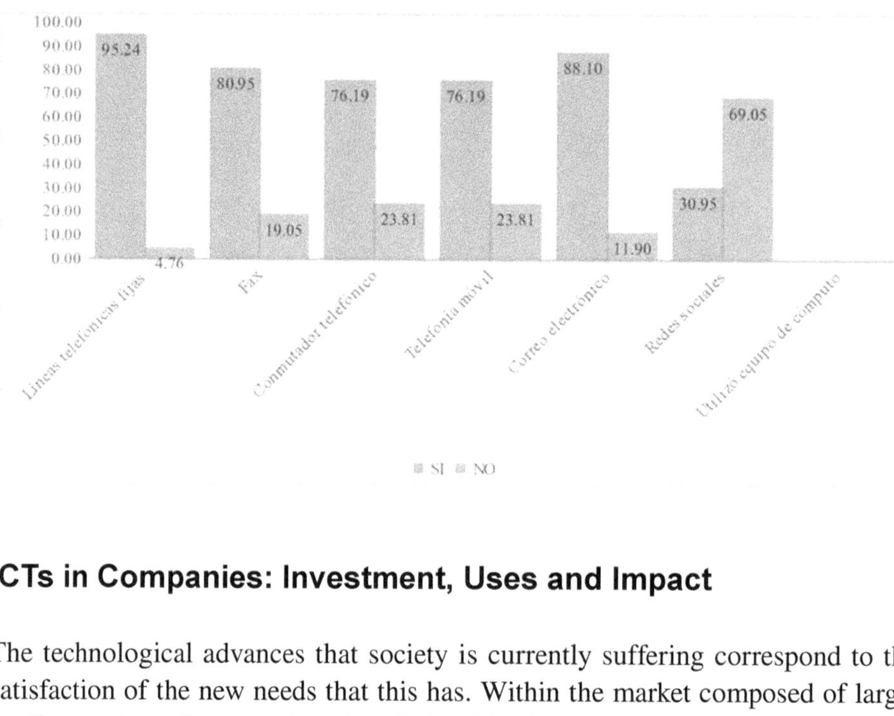

ICTs in Companies: Investment, Uses and Impact

The technological advances that society is currently suffering correspond to the satisfaction of the new needs that this has. Within the market composed of large, medium and small companies, the relationships between them have become closer. They link such simple matters as the purchase and sale of articles of daily commercial use, to the movement of large capitals that would, in short, impact the living conditions of the residents of any place or country where these movements occur.

In this way the use of ICTs is a tool within companies to make large and small movements of capital, to perform the administrative and operational tasks of the company, understood here the operability from inputs - outputs of goods until its commercialization and arrival to the final consumer.

The situation that predominates in the companies analyzed through the following graph, show that the companies which responded through a dichotomous variable (yes, no) about the resources with which they had at their disposal in the year immediately prior to the publication of the survey, the results are presented below:

The provision of means of communication such as telephone lines, fax, switch, mobile, email and social networks by companies involves multiple internal and external tasks. The companies, as shown in figure 4, represent the use of the traditional means of communication par excellence, such as fixed telephones, a strong percentage, 80.95 and 76.19% in fax and commutator, respectively. The provision of mobile telephony is on par with the same percentage of a traditional means of communication such as fax (76.19%). The email with 88.10% of the companies, proves to be only below the traditional landline phone the importance that has for the companies to have this ICT tool in the operation of their activities. On the other hand, it is seen that only 30.95% of these companies have social networks. Denote here the importance of the rise of social networks in recent years as they currently represent a niche of opportunity for the positioning and sales of companies.

The investments made by companies in the ICT category, are in the acquisition of computer equipment that includes: desktop computers (PC), mobile phones or laptops (laptop, notebook, netbook, tablet), workstations, servers, minicomputers, mainframes, supercomputers. In the results that INEGI presents, it is identified that on average each person employed within these companies has .35 computation equipment as media to perform the assigned activities.

Within the use of these equipment 92.85% that declare percentages in stock, it is noted that 63.67% of that 92.85%, is older than two years and only 17.62% of this equipment is less than one year. Taken into account the speed at which they depreciate (30% each year) this represents for companies a signal to be updated with new products that allow them to increase their productivity.

Another important aspect to highlight in the use, management and acquisition of computer equipment by companies of Jalisco are the support that the Mexican and State governments have to productive economic activities of companies. One of these programs is the PROSOFT 3.0 that supports companies with low levels of development for the adoption and development of new ICTs. Even within their calls, the innovations of companies are encouraged, all with the objective of increasing productivity levels in the strategic sectors of the economy (SE, 2016).

For the results presented by the ENTIC (2013), 93% of the companies did not receive any government support for these purposes. In the theoretical framework on the advances in the use of information technologies by companies, this use would imply significant advantages in the progress of the activities they carry out. When analyzing the situation of these 42 companies, it can be observed in the year of study, that the use of internet and email have impacts on the reduction of time of the processes of the companies.

The information collected by INEGI when applying its questionnaire on the impact of ICTs in the increase of sales and customers, reduction of time and costs, quality of services and market expansion is proposed based on the opinion of the person in charge of responding the survey, so it is a yes and no answer.

Although we do not count on the percentages of these increases or decreases to make specific estimates, this information helps to later consider the probabilities that these items have in decreasing or increasing productivity and production by making use of the internet, website, email or social networks. The most used instruments to increase sales were email and the Internet, which predominated in most of the categories: cost reduction, quality of services and customer growth.

Regarding the use of the website, it only impacts more or less significantly on the increase of customers. The issue of social networks turns out to be the one with less weight in these categories, having its greatest impact with 20.51% of companies that have social networks in the geographic expansion of their market.

In broad terms, these results represent the delay of companies in the use of ICTs to increase their productivity, since they are the tools we have in this century and mean the possibility of promoting competitiveness and growth in each of them. Stopping to observe the impact that the electronic mail is having within the operations of the companies in the period of surveying, it is noted that on average companies have .97 units of computer equipment to use with Internet access. Because the Internet network conditions the use of electronic mail, the people who used computer equipment with Internet access reach an average of 1.45 email accounts.

Electronic and digital technologies have already gone from the part of standardizing processes to how to win the market, how to incorporate technology to satisfy customers. In terms of solutions is the area called customer experience that help generate income for customers not only in e-commerce but also marketing, automation of sales, and experience management (Romo, 2019).

The average of email accounts combined with computer equipment with Internet access introduce, among other variables, the electronic commerce of goods and services offered by companies, which it will be analyzed later. Electronic commerce (digital economy) is not highly accepted by companies (Paz, 2020). In figure 5 we can observe these behaviors.

Figure 5.

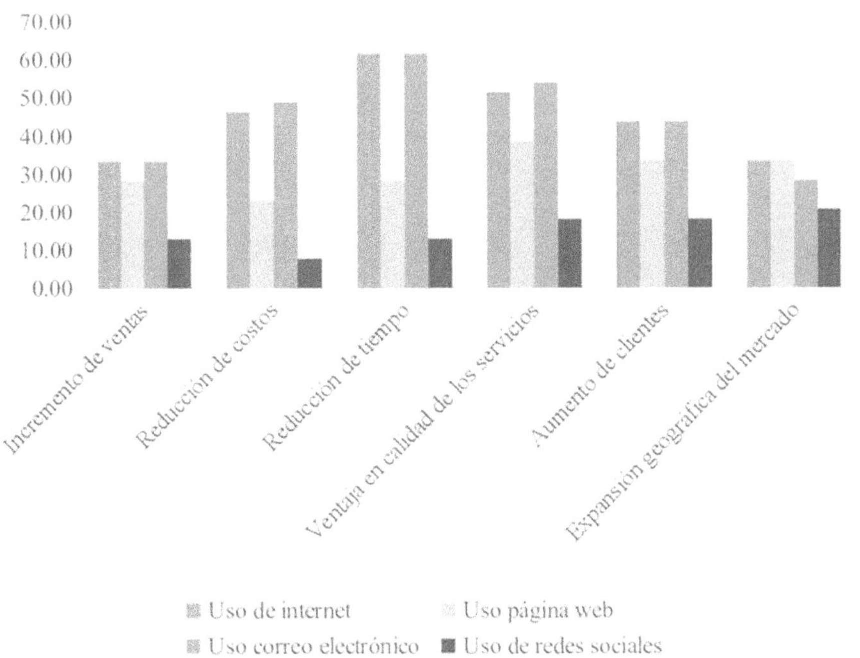

The increase due to the intensive use of ICTs would be a key factor together with the increase in productivity in the increase of yields, although as previously indicated, yields may increase due to the increase in prices, without this meaning an increase in the productivity of the company. These market forces are not very controllable by SMEs.

One aspect in which SMEs can have interference is in the training of their workers when using ICTs, since by keeping them trained they can update their knowledge of the factors that affect their market. Of the results presented by INEGI, only seven companies trained personnel taking between 2 to 100 courses in this period, a figure that shows information asymmetry due to the size of the company according to its personnel.

The Structure of the Market of Companies

The outputs direction of companies made up of goods and services that they produce in the form of manufacturing, mining, energy and services in the construction and sales branches, among others, determine the capacity of companies to determine the final consumer.

Figure 6.

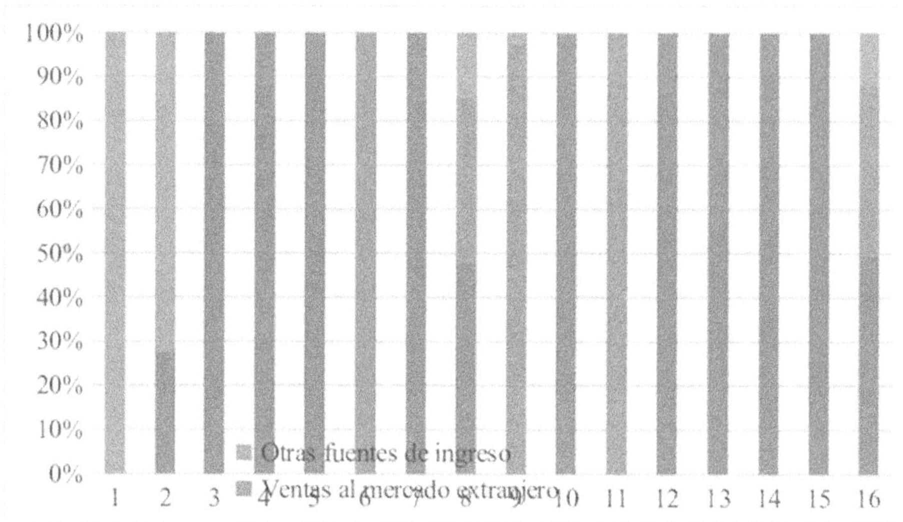

Figure 7.

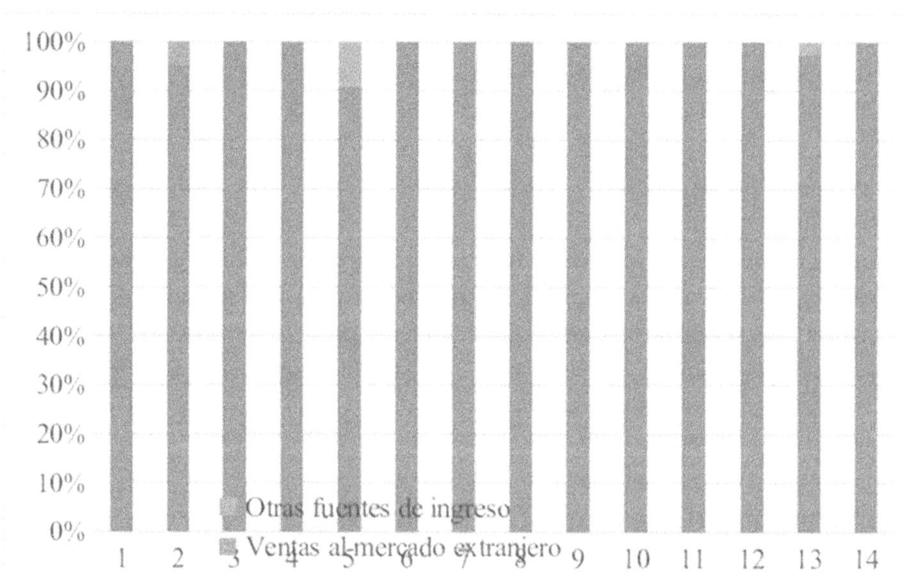

In this way, large companies, due to the magnitude they represent, are external to the national market, while small and medium-sized companies have a more or less local scope, with the exception of one company for each group, who export part of their products to the market. Externally, these sales contribute very little to their total income.

It is also the case of companies that do not sell either inside or outside the local market. So, it is about companies that obtain their income from other sources, their field therefore are the communal, social and personal services. In the following graphs it can be observed how the sales in the national market and the sales abroad (exports) as well as other sources of income, contribute to the total income of the companies.

Figure 8.

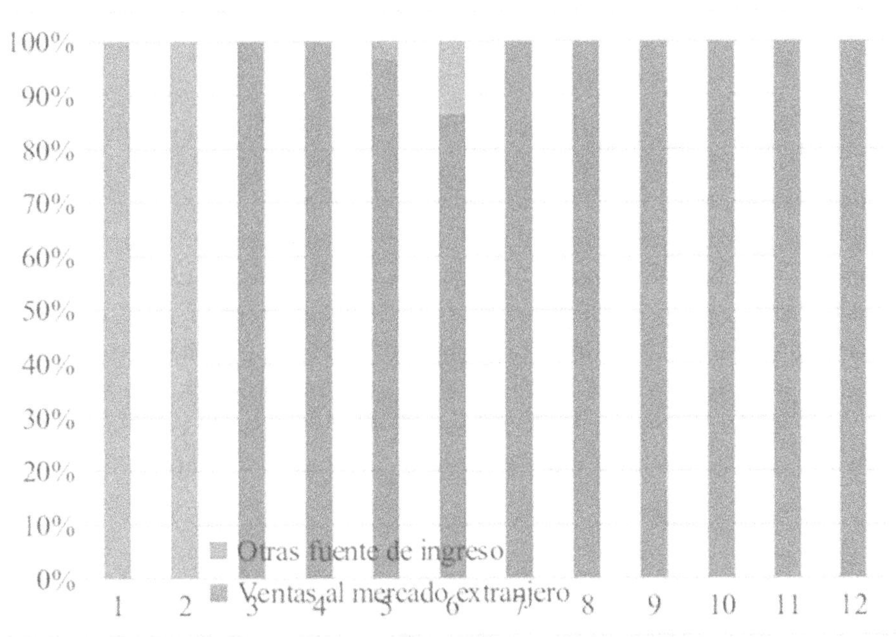

When classifying the companies in these 3 groups according to the size as mentioned above, it is a function of the total number of personnel employed. It is analyzed the disposition of the means of communication. It can be seen that the results are similar between medium and large companies. The large companies to be hypothetically consolidated within the market, their technological equipment is also, a situation that shares with medium-sized companies. Companies classified

Figure 9.

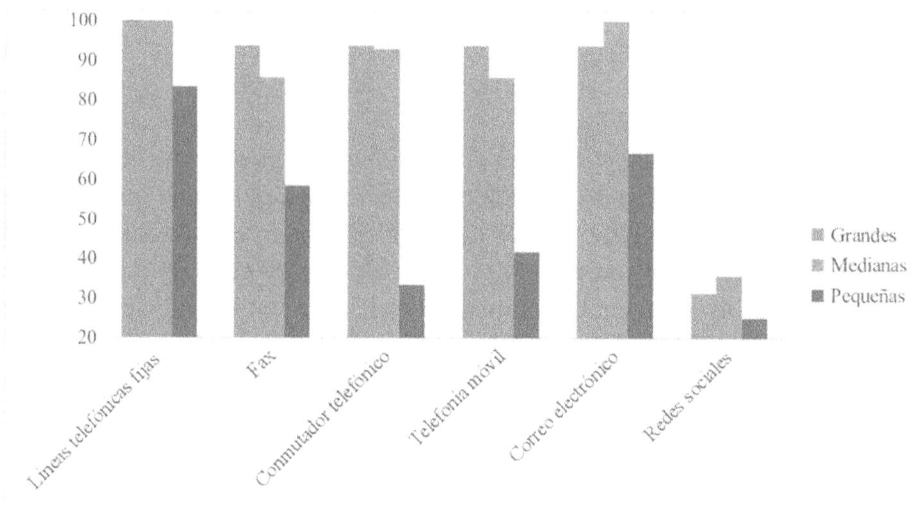

as large achieve in this way 100% provision in fixed telephone lines and email and only 31.25% of the total of companies in social networks, percentage below the medians that report a 35.71% of the total of companies.

On the other hand, there is a considerable gap between small companies with these two groups (medium and large), although they share a low use of social networks and a high percentage in telephone lines. Being the group of small companies which represents 84.18% of the total population, according to the methodological document presented by INEGI for the ENTIC (2013) represents a central issue to guide policies for the use of ICTs by the bodies of competent governments. The following graph details the use of the media by companies in the classified groups:

Table 5.

		Age of computer equipment %		
Type of company	Computer equipment *per capita*	Under 1 year	1 to 2 years	More than 2 years
Large	0.35	29.33	23.07	47.60
Medium	0.38	13	24	63
Small	0.31	6.5	4.3	89.2

Figure 10.

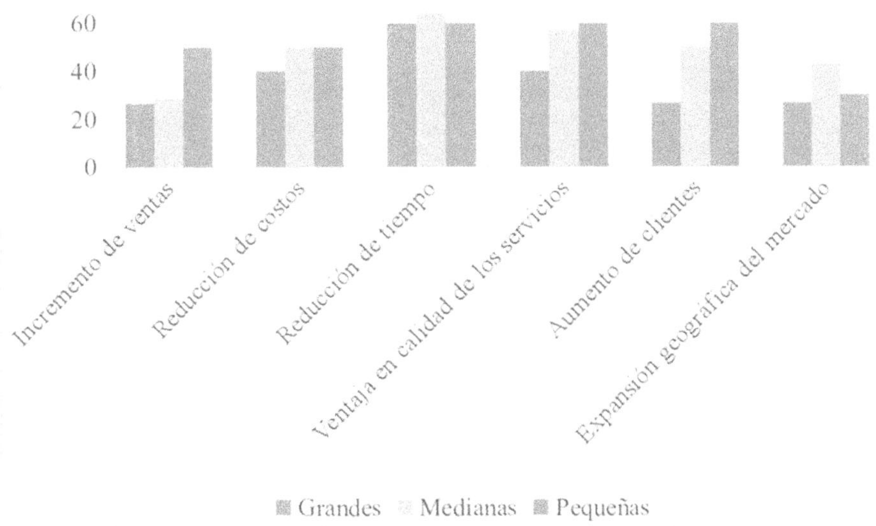

Differentiating the size of the companies to perform the analysis allows to identify the technical and technological advantages of medium and large companies in terms of cutting edge and acquisition of computer equipment. In terms of equipment per worker, medium-sized companies have a .38 computer equipment greater than the average of the whole (.35). Large companies are in the middle and small businesses, as expected, are below the average half.

The high percentage of obsolescence of the computer equipment of small companies is evident, which results in a disadvantage when competing with medium and large companies. Because of this, small businesses have a market to gain and equipping can be a powerful measure to achieve this goal. We see this information summarized in the following table 5:

Regarding the use of ICTs to create competitive advantages within the market, it is found a more or less uniform behavior among the groups of companies. On the one hand, 50% of small businesses saw their sales favored with the use of the internet and 60% of these same companies increased their customer base. This speaks of a significant use of the internet. In the case of medium-sized companies, their time of processes and administrative activities was reduced with the significant use of the internet with 64.29% of the companies that declare using these ICTs for their operations.

Figure 11.

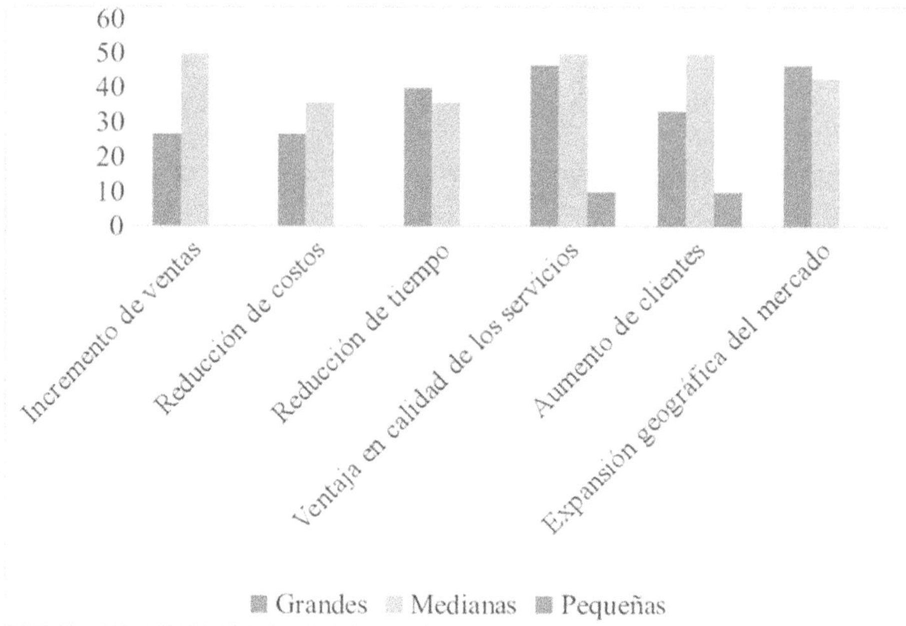

Figure 12.

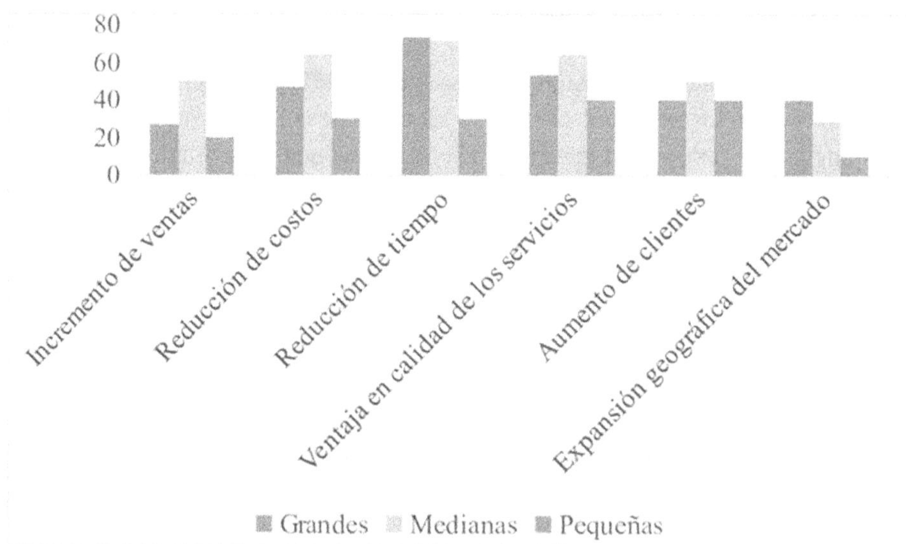

Figure 13.

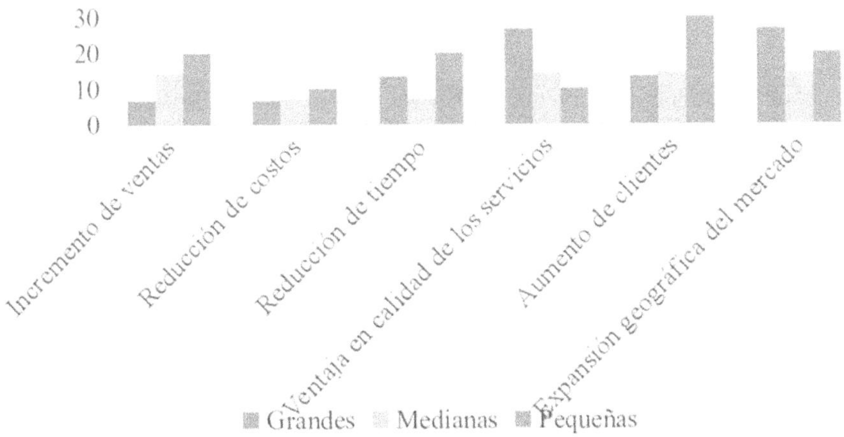

With this indicator, it can be spoken at a first moment that medium-sized companies are more productive with respect to small and large companies. The results of the large companies are mainly due to the field of their activities highlighting manufacturing as predominant, in the medium-sized manufactures and services and small businesses services. It can be seen this in the following figure 10:

The advantages provided by having an official website for each of the companies would represent an image positioning. The results presented for the web pages of the companies highlight the little use by small companies, having the biggest impacts for medium-sized companies, which is a more effective use to increase sales, offer quality services and a geographical expansion of the market. Large companies again fall short of the effects that medians could have, with web pages being a website where the characteristics are captured and the magnitude of these companies would expect these results. It can be seen this below:

E-mail is another tool of ICT for the realization of the activities of companies and in view of its impact on promoting the skills seen in its prevalence for medium-sized companies in the points on the increase in sales, cost reduction, improvements in the quality of their products as well as increases in the client portfolio.

For medium-sized companies, it is a tool for brand expansion and positioning. The benefits that the medium companies declare in the ENTIC (2013) because they have emails with considerable percentages in these items show the importance of the adoption of this ICT.

On this point large companies were favored by the use of mail in a slightly longer time reduction on medium-sized companies with 73.33% over 71.43%, while 40% of these same companies saw their market expanded geographically. In relation to small businesses, the percentages in terms of the impact of the use of electronic mail do not indicate a significantly beneficial trend, as shown below:

Finally, there are social networks as an ICT in which most of the companies have insignificant impacts as seen jointly and strengthen this thesis according to size. There seems to be a complementarity between large and small companies on the benefits of this ICT. The limited exploitation of ICTs by companies limits them to take advantage of benefits that would allow them to increase their sales through the positioning of their product, increase their customers and through these networks can be made known and achieve greater expansion of its national market and on a smaller state or regional scale.

Summarizing small companies are those who obtain advantages over social networks to increase their sales and increase the number of customers, although this tool is not the most remarkable of the analysis, this behavior can be reviewed in the following graph.

In this general outline, it can be identified that the use of ICTs to create competitive advantages, according to the size of the companies, the medians are those that are favored most, followed by small and large companies. What can be said about the low level of updating and investment that large companies have to operate through the use of ICTs.

Efforts in the adoption of ICT should be and is, as shown by this detailed analysis, by small and medium enterprises, since they are the entities that are obligated to invest in order to grow. In the case of large companies, the effort turns out to be less since they have reached a degree of maturity and consolidation within their market, they already have a client portfolio and their market is national and foreign.

The undoubted importance of technical and technological equipment for the disposition and use of ICTs by companies in any of its dimensions accompanied by users of these technologies: human capital converges in higher or lower revenues for companies.

For the analysis it is taken the total income of companies, presented previously and made up of sales to the domestic market, sales abroad and other types of income as an indicator of productivity that depends on the level of ICT equipment in this case is the investment in computer equipment and labor factor as the number of total personnel employed. The model to make the approximation to the productivity of the company would be represented by the following expression:

Average productivity model

$$lnP_{MEi} = \alpha + \beta lnI_{TICi} + \gamma lnI_{NOTICi} + \delta Tam + \varepsilon_i$$

Figure 14.

General Regression Analysis: LN de la pro versus LN I TIC x t, LN I en Mob , ..

```
Regression Equation

NVO_ESTRATO
1            LN de la productividad media  =  6.58481 + 0.183428 LN I TIC x
                                               trabajador + 0.259564 LN I en Mob
                                               y Equipo x trabajad

2            LN de la productividad media  =  5.83628 + 0.183428 LN I TIC x
                                               trabajador + 0.259564 LN I en Mob
                                               y Equipo x trabajad

3            LN de la productividad media  =  5.25229 + 0.183428 LN I TIC x
                                               trabajador + 0.259564 LN I en Mob
                                               y Equipo x trabajad


Coefficients

Term                                    Coef   SE Coef        T      P
Constant                             5.89113  0.286289  20.5776  0.000
LN I TIC x trabajador                0.18343  0.298885   0.6137  0.543
LN I en Mob y Equipo x trabajad      0.25956  0.120802   2.1487  0.038
NVO_ESTRATO
  1                                  0.69368  0.374024   1.8546  0.072
  2                                 -0.05485  0.358887  -0.1528  0.879


Summary of Model

S = 1.57328       R-Sq = 24.53%        R-Sq(adj) = 16.37%
PRESS = 114.072   R-Sq(pred) = 6.00%
```

Where:

α = intercept

lnP_{MEi} = lnProductivity average per worker of the company i

βI_{TICi} = ln Investment in ICT per company worker i

γlnI_{NOTICi} = ln Investment in NOTIC equipment per company worker i

δTam = Dummy of the size of the company

ε_i = random error

Certain characteristics acquired by companies according to capital, personnel, type of activities they develop, size, administrative and production processes, among others, make them adopt working mechanisms, decision making about the distribution of functions, tools to be used. Thus, in the search for increasing returns, technical and technological tools are provided with which the times of the processes can be minimized and generally optimizing the company's human and material resources.

Through the general linear model of double logarithm to determine the average productivity of the workers through elasticities that show the increases that have the increase in 1% plus the ICT equipment or the non-ICT. The results of the model by stratum show a significance of 24.53% (R).

The constants by strata, 6.58 for the large ones, 5.83 for the medium ones and 5.25 for the small companies shows the level of equipment that each group has. These results are to be expected since large companies by size would have to have a fixed capital greater than medium and small companies.

In the coefficients of the general model, it is identified that the investment in ICTs increased by 1% through computer equipment, the average productivity per worker increases by 0.18%, while by doing so in non-ICT investments (investment in furniture and equipment) the average productivity of workers grows by 0.25%. These significant differences correspond to a low intensive use of ICTs by small companies of Jalisco that, as indicated before, represent 84.18% of the total population of the ENTIC, 2013.

By strata of companies, it is observed that for large companies the average productivity is 0.64% higher than the average productivity of small and medium enterprises. Being a linear regression statistical model it is referred to the characteristics of the data to validate the assumptions, so we find that the data come from a normal distribution.

Production Model

Starting from the function of production mostly used and exposed by Cobb and Douglas in 1948, it is determined the relationship between the product with labor and the capital in which technology remains constant (Sánchez, 2016), in this way we will have:

$$Q = AL^{\alpha}K^{\beta}$$

Where:

$$Q = Product$$

$$L = Labor\left(Employed\ personnel\right)$$

$$K = Stock\ of\ Capital$$

Figure 15.

Regression Analysis: LN Ing Tot versus LN Total perso, NVO_ESTRATO, ...

```
The regression equation is
LN Ing Tot = 4.40 + 1.11 LN Total perso + 0.03 NVO_ESTRATO + 0.787 LN Stock


Predictor          Coef  SE Coef     T      P
Constant          4.401    1.920  2.29  0.028
LN Total perso   1.1058   0.2628  4.21  0.000
NVO_ESTRATO       0.031    1.147  0.03  0.979
LN Stock         0.7871   0.3432  2.29  0.027


S = 1.55822   R-Sq = 76.9%   R-Sq(adj) = 75.1%


Analysis of Variance

Source          DF      SS      MS      F      P
Regression       3  307.96  102.65  42.28  0.000
Residual Error  38   92.27    2.43
Total           41  400.22


Source          DF  Seq SS
LN Total perso   1  295.02
NVO_ESTRATO      1    0.17
LN Stock         1   12.78
```

α = Work participation in the generation of added value or product

β = Share of capital in the generation of added value or product

A = Factor scale or efficiency parameter, which reflects the level of technology

Finally introducing the double logarithm, we will have:

$$lnIN_i = lnA_i + \alpha lnL_i + \beta lnK_i$$

Under this model scheme it is obtained the elasticities of the product of labor and capital. In this sense we take Q as the total income of the company, a referring to a scale factor or parameter of technological efficiency and supported by the regression analysis where we calculate average productivity, where large companies are intensive in ICTs use, medium-sized companies to a lesser degree and finally to small ones such as those that make the best use of ICT. It will be used this same classification or parameters, where 1 uses the most technology, 2 uses medium technology and 3 uses less technology.

For L we will take the total of employed personnel and for K that represents the stock of capital, we take the total variable of investment in fixed assets 2012. In the first stage where we calculate the relations that have the product taken as the income of the companies of the sample with the explanatory variables, in this case of the total staff, the stock of capital and the level of technology, where stratum 1 is intensive companies, 2 medium-intensity companies and 3 those that use less technology, we have as a result that this model is adjusted by 76.9%.

By increasing the 1% employed personnel, the product increases by 1.10% as the most relevant variable, followed by stock of capital that increases by 0.78% in the same percentage. In the case of the strata that represent the intensity of the use of technology as a parameter, increasing one stratum to another results in a weight of 0.031%, remembering that this is a classification variable, which is the result of moving from one stratum to another.

In the following figure, we can find the results of the regression, the normality graphs are presented to fulfill the assumptions of distribution of the data of the sample.

CONCLUSIONS AND RECOMMENDATIONS

The delay that companies of Jalisco present in their technological equipment allows them to be placed at a disadvantage compared to multinational companies established in the State. The companies collected for this analysis place most of their sales in the national market, so it is of significant importance the decision making by the top managers to rethink investment efforts aimed at Information and Communication Technologies.

These results are preliminary and represent an exercise so it is recommended to conduct future studies thoroughly and with the entire sample. The efforts made by companies in their investments are based on the purchase of machinery and equipment (30%), followed by computer equipment and peripherals (26%), which means the importance in the operation of the companies the use of TIC's.

The companies studied continue to use traditional means of communication such as fixed telephone lines, fax and commutator. On the other hand, by making use of e-mail and the Internet, companies benefited from reducing their costs, increasing the quality of their services and increasing their client base.

In the results of the regression model in the coefficients identified that the increase in 1% investment in TIC's through computer equipment average productivity per worker increases by 0.18%, while doing so in non-ICT investments (investment in furniture and equipment) the average productivity of workers grows by 0.25%.

It should also be noted that by increasing the 1% employed personnel, the product increases by 1.10% as the most relevant variable, followed by stock of capital that increases by 0.78% in the same percentage, in the case of the strata that represent the intensity of the use of technology as a parameter, increasing one stratum to another results in a weight of 0.031%, remembering that this is a classification variable, which is the result of moving from one stratum to another.

The positioning of the companies in the Mexican market does not turn out to be simultaneous, but it raises a series of actions that guide the companies in the growth and permanence, within the actions that these companies carry out, the product of the realization of this research is a low investment with less than $ 999.00.

The companies under study, mainly national capital (78%) have to increase the training of their staff to make use of ICTs, programs such as PROSOFT 3.0 created to promote innovation and for the adoption and development of new ICT's must be exploited since 93% of companies do not receive support of this type.

Another point that should be noted is the necessary update of the computer equipment used by companies, since 63.67% of companies have equipment greater than two years old and taking into account depreciation per year (30%) is relevant to take measures for replacement.

The medium and large companies to have consolidated their market their efforts do not have to be comparable to those that have to do small businesses, so it is necessary to formulate strategies through subsidy ways of taxes, strengthening of government programs for the small business, so that this gap is shortened. This obsolescence in small businesses represents a significant obstacle since they have a market to win.

It is important to mention that the low equipment in computer equipment (.35 per capita of the total of the companies) responds to a circumstance of disadvantage. The employed personnel are limited to the development of their activities through these technologies that would allow them to limit their efforts and minimize times and costs.

Finally, electronic commerce should be encouraged among companies, since this way marks the future of a new virtual generation that is friendly to the environment, which would allow cost reduction and meet human needs simultaneously.

REFERENCES

Amado Sánchez, B., & Pico González, B. (2013). *Desarrollo de redes empresariales a través de procesos colaborativos para impulsar la innovación y lograr la satisfacción de los clientes en las SMEs manufactureras de hule y plástico de México.* Sexto Coloquio Interdisciplinario de Doctorado –Universidad Popular Autónoma del Estado de Puebla. Disponible en https://upaep.mx/micrositios/coloquios/coloquio2013/ memorias/Mesa%201%20PEyDT/Desarrollo%20de%20Redes%20 Empresariales%20a%20trav%C3%A9s%20de%20procesos%20colaborativos %20 para%20impulsar%20la.pdf

Arce Rodríguez, L. M. (2009). Competitividad de las SMES industriales internacionalizadas del Estado de Jalisco, México: agenda para una investigación empírica. *InterScience Place, 2*(4).

Arellano-Rodríguez J. B., Sánchez Gutiérrez J., Mejía-Trejo J. (2018). El cliente como proveedor de innovación. un enfoque de capacidades dinámicas en PyME. *Hitos de Ciencias Económico Administrativas, 24*(69), 476-485.

Basulto Castillo, A. & Medina Ortega, J. (2006). Innovación tecnológica en la red de proveedores de la industria electrónica de Jalisco. *Carta Económica Regional, 18*(95).

Calle Medrano, M. J., & Vargas Hernández, J. G. (2015). Capítulo 10: Enfoques teóricos para el análisis de la capacidad de innovación como factor que incide en la competitividad de la industria de software de Jalisco. In Gestión competitiva organizacional: un enfoque interdisciplinario. Universidad Autónoma de Querétaro.

Camacho Sotelo, C. K., Hernández Cotón, S. G., & Mayorga Salamanca, P. I. (2014) La innovación y su interrelación con la competitividad. Sector manufacturero de la zona metropolitana de Guadalajara. *Red Internacional de Investigadores en Competitividad Memoria del VIII Congreso, 8*(1).

Cameron, K. S., & Quinn, R. E. (2006). Diagnosing and changing organizational culture: based on the competing values framework. Jossey-Bass.

Cantú, S. O. (2006). ¿Qué es la gestión de la innovación y la tecnología (GInnT)? *Journal of Technology Management & Innovation, 1*(2), 64-82.

Dutrénit, G. (2009). *Sistemas regionales de innovación: un espacio para el desarrollo de las SMES. El caso de la industria de maquinados industriales.* MPRA_paper_31984. Munich Personal RePEc Archive.

El Economista. (2015). *Precios de Petróleo son de alto riesgo.* Goldman Sachs.

El Informador. (2017). PyMEs jaliscienses viven ocho año Las barreras regulatorias o la falta de ingresos y planeación dictaminan el fracaso de éstas. Periódico el Informador.

ENTIC. (2013). *Encuesta sobre Tecnologías de la Información y las Comunicaciones (ENTIC 2013)*. Disponible en: https://www.inegi.org.mx/programas/entic/2013/

Figueroa, G. M. (2015). El proceso de gestión de Innovación Tecnológica: sus etapas e indicadores relacionados. *Revista Venezolana de Análisis de Coyuntura, 21*(1), 59-90.

Galindo Martín, M. A., Ribeiro, D., & Méndez Picazo, M. T. (2012). Innovación y crecimiento económico: Factores que estimulan la innovación. Cuadernos de Gestión, 12, 51-58.

Hernández, L. M. (2009). Una revisión de la interpretación económica sobre la innovación. *Journal of Technology Management & Innovation*, *4*(4), 139-149.

IIEG. (2018). *Empresas por actividad y entidad federativa*. Instituto de Información, Estadística y Geografía. Gobierno del Estado de Jalisco. Guadalajara.

Luter, R. R. (1998). Desarrollo regional e innovación y desarrollo tecnológico. In Investigación y vinculación tecnológica: un enfoque regional (pp. 139-162). Culiacán Rosales, Sinaloa: BUAP, UAS.

Mejía-Trejo, J., Sanchez-Gutiérrez, J., & Haro-Beas, J. F. (2014). Customer Knowledge to Improve the Innovation: The Relationship in México. In *The 13th International conference of the Society for Global Business & Economic development. Managing the "Intangibles": Business and Entrepreneurship Perspectives in a Global Context.* Universitá Politecnica delle Marche.

Moyano Martínez, M. G. (2016). *La cultura organizacional: factor promotor de la innovación para el crecimiento e internacionalización de las SMEs de la salud ubicadas en Guadalajara, Jalisco, México*. Ponencia. XVIII Congreso de AECA. Disponible en http://www.aeca1.org/pub/on_line/comunicaciones_xviiicongresoaeca/cd/30c.pdf

Myro, R. (2010). Economic Growth And Innovation: A Short Note About The Empirical Evidence. Revista Galega de Economía, 19.

OCDE. (2013). *Indicadores de Ciencia, Tecnología e Industria de la OCDE 2013*. OCDE.

Ortiz-Cantú, S. J., & Pedroza-Zapata, Á. R. (2013). Innovación para el desarrollo económico de Jalsico. In M. T. Ballesca-Ramírez (Ed.), *Desarrollo económico de Jalisco: retrospectiva y retos* (pp. 295–318). Secretaría de Promoción Económica, Gobierno del Estado de Jalisco.

Paz Gómez, E. (2020). Estudio Sectorial y Regional de las Empresas Medianas en el Estado de Jalisco. Táctica informática. Guadalajara, Jalisco.

Pedroza-Zapata, A. R., & Ortiz-Cantú, S. J. (2015) Estructura, gobernanza, actores, programas y desempeño del sistema nacional y regional de innovación: avances del caso México-Jalisco. *XVI Congreso Latino-Iberoamericano de Gestión de la Tecnología*, Porto Alegre, Brasil.

RAE. (2016). Recuperado el 11 de 01 de 2016, dehttp://lema.rae.es/drae/srv/search?id=wCP3BlIJRDXX2uYFygrz

Ramírez Lira, E., Rivera Espinoza, M. P., Azpeitia Torres, E., Amezcua Luján, M. K., & Barajas Pérez, J. S. (2018). Análisis del diagnóstico e intervención organizacional en MIPYMO's del Sur de Jalisco: Una revisión desde el desarrollo organizacional. *Revista Global de Negocios*, *6*(4), 51–65.

Ramírez Ruiz, A. J. (2013). Capacidades del capital humano para la innovación tecnológica en pequeñas empresas de Jalisco, México. *Econ: teor. Práct*, *38*, 83-110.

Robles Estrada, C. (2009). Competitividad de las SMEs industriales internacionalizadas del estado de Jalisco: agenda para una investigación empírica. *Red Internacional de Investigadores en Competitividad Memoria del III Congreso, 3*(1).

Romo, P. (2019). Pymes de Jalisco aceleran adopción de soluciones tecnológicas A través de Innovation Tour, la firma alemana SAP muestra a empresas jaliscienses beneficios de herramientas tecnológicas. El Economista.

Romo, P. (2020). *Jalisco destinará 1,000 mdp para apoyar mipymes y autoempleados. La entidad descarta adquirir deuda de largo plazo* [Popup plan Jalisco will allocate 1,000 mp to support MSMEs and the self-employed The entity rules out acquiring long-term debt]. El Economista, Estados.

Sánchez, A. M. (2016). *Universidad del Cauca*. Obtenido de http://www.unicauca.edu.co/porik_an/imagenes_3noanteriores/No.9porikan/porikan_7.pdf

Vázquez Ávila, G., Núñez Moreno, T. E., Sánchez Gutiérrez, J., & Mejía Trejo, J. (2015). Gestión de conocimiento e innovación impulsores de la competitividad en las SMEs manufactureras de Guadalajara. In Sustentabilidad e innovación como detonantes de la competitividad. Universidad de Guadalajara.

Vázquez Ávila, G., Sánchez Gutiérrez, J., & Núñez Moreno, T. M. (2017). *Innovación en las operaciones con énfasis en la ergonomía para fomentar la competitividad en las SMES.* Memoria del XI Congreso de la Red Internacional de Investigadores en Competitividad.

KEY TERMS AND DEFINITIONS

ENTIC: Survey on Information Technologies and Communications.

Information and Communication Technologies (ICTs): Information and communication technologies, also known as ICT, are the set of technologies developed to manage information and send it from one place to another.

Innovation: Innovation is a change action that is a novelty.

Productivity: Productivity is an economic measure that calculates how many goods and services have been produced for each factor used (worker, capital, time, costs, etc.) during a given period.

R&D: R&D is an abbreviation for research and development and refers to the research and development work or department within a large company or organization.

SMEs: Small or medium-sized company in terms of volume of income, value of assets and number, and workers.

Chapter 9
Developing the First Digital Bank of Africa:
The Steps Towards the Creation of a Digital Bank in a Very Challenging Environment

Konstantinos Tsanis
Hult International Business School, Greece

Vasilios Stouraitis
Glasgow Caledonian University, UK

ABSTRACT

The following case study overviews the steps followed to develop the first Digital Bank in Africa. Following a case study method, the crucial decisions made over a 2-year period is analyzed. The challenges of each different phase are described, as well as the outcomes and the impact they had in the bank's digital transformation journey. The case study is accompanied by illustrative strategy tools used during development to make the reader more familiar with the decision made. The case study concludes by highlighting success and failures in digital transformation and lessons for other banks.

DOI: 10.4018/978-1-7998-4195-1.ch009

Copyright © 2021, IGI Global. Copying or distributing in print or electronic forms without written permission of IGI Global is prohibited.

INTRODUCTION

The banking industry is under an accelerated digital transformation route globally, despite being a relative laggard in this area. Whilst a large number of industries went digital starting from the 1990s as it can be seen from diagram 1, the banks have been able to resist. As Bill Gates quoted in the 1990s1, banks are like 'dinosaurs': They are powerful, and somehow slow moving, so they are still able to resist to technological change. This however changed in the last decade: The global Financial crisis of 2009 resulted on diminished trust to the banks from the customers (Lane and Feretti, 2018). Simultaneously, the expansion of internet users, and the technological developments, enabled start ups to focus on providing services that only the banks had previously offered. The regulators viewed these development quite positively, which altogether resulted in the creation of the so-called 'FinTech' industry.

Figure 1. Waves of digital disruption

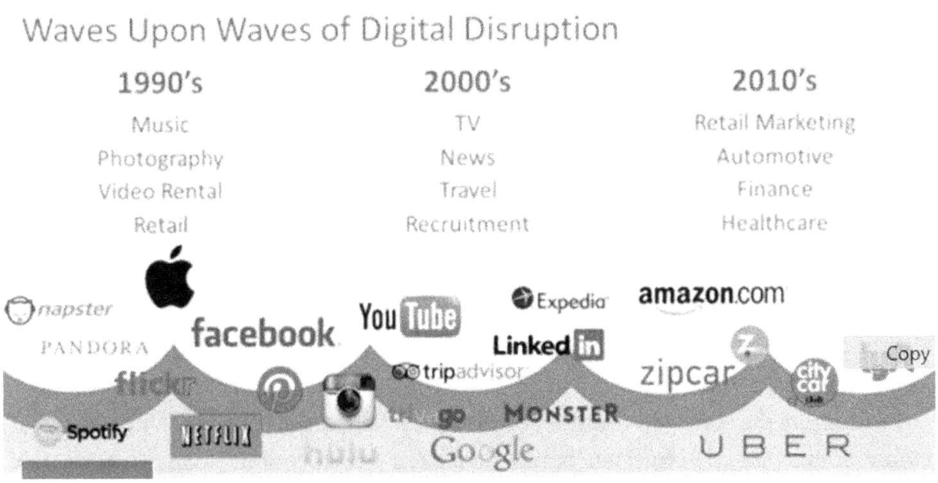

These developments have obliged banks from both emerging and developed economies to realize the imperative for Digital Transformation (Malar, Arvidsson, and Holmstrom, 2011). And, contrary to what would be expected, banks from emerging markets seem to have some strategic 'wins' in this sector, compared to banks from developed countries (Govindarajan and Ramamurti, 2011). Specific examples include the dominance of M-Pesa in Mobile Money (Foster and Heeks, 2013) firstly developed in Kenya, the highest number of digital banks per capita in the United Arab Emirates, and the worlds first traditional bank turned to fully

Digital Bank from Singapore2. Within this environment, the oldest indigenous bank in Nigeria, WEMA Bank, decided to pursue a brave Digital Strategy in 2016, aiming to digitalize its operations and change its overall business model, while at the same time strengthening its retail presence.

STRATEGIC CHOICES IN THE WAKE OF DIGITAL BANKING

As mentioned earlier, WEMA bank had been the longest surviving bank in Nigeria. Its situation back in 2015 wasn't the best however: Profits were heavily affected from the depreciation of the oil price, the IT infrastructure was quite old, and the word on the street was that 'this is a bank that our grandfathers were using and it has remained old itself'. The 250% depreciation of the Nigerian currency had created further performance issues, resulting on the regulator calling all banks of the country to transform their operations3.

The engagement in a digital transformation journey had 4 strategic implications for the bank. Firstly, the bank should aim to decrease its operational costs. Back in 2015, the bank had the highest cost to income ration in the industry within Nigeria. The pressure to cut down costs was clear. The lower profits of this year, because of the oil price drop, had brought in the spotlight of the regulator the operational inefficiencies of the bank.

Furthermore, the bank was an urgent need of cultural change. As a previously regional bank, which had been state owned for a large number of years4, a large number of employees had ''public sector'' attitude, ignoring the digital wave, and the renewed importance of the customer, in a world dominated by FinTechs. As a resulted, the bank was constantly ranking among the lowest in KPMGs' customer perception surveys (KPMG, 2018). All these facts where highlighting the urgent need for a cultural change.

In addition, the bank was in urgent need for new sources of revenue. The traditional revnue source for all Nigerian banks had been the corporate loans, where they had been able to charge 40-50% interest rates, allowing them to remain profitable without focusing on offering other products and services. This had resulted in a very large number of individuals without access to finance: as per diagram 2 below, in 2015, out of a population of 200 mn, there were almost 80 million Nigerians who were unbanked (and around 40 million underbanked), making the country with the highest number of unbanked persons in the world (Mathieu, Pani, Chen and Maino, 2019). This meant that an expansion to retail operations could potentially be a good opportunity, in order to create new revenue channels and hopefully increase revenues and profits

Figure 2. Unbanked population in Nigeria (Data from World Bank)

One more strategic reason highlighting the urgent need for digital engagement had to do with overall branding and the image of the bank: Albeit resilient, as the oldest bank in the country, it was considered as highly inefficient, a ''bank for the older people'', within the market. This was a result of its old infrastructure, and the fact that it had kept a few loyal customers over the years, without the need to engage in intensive competition with the rest banks.

With the strategic rationale behind the engagement highlighted, the imperative for a stronger digital focus was clear. The next and most challenging was to persuade the top management of the oldest Nigerian bank, over this imperative.

DIGITAL BANKING: "ITS ALL GREEK TO ME"

It has been widely document that one of the most important factors for successful digital transformations is the management buy-in (Broeders and Khanna, 2015). However, most of the transformations used in previous cases have happened within Western/Developed countries, where the executives had exposure and familiarity to advanced technological infrastructures and the emerging tech trends. The much less developed tech infrastructure of Nigeria implied clearly that the average banking executive would have much less knowledge on the potential of Financial Technology.

The top management background was a very important factor on engaging in digital discussions. Contrary to what could be expected, two out of the seven board members had an IT degree and working knowledge. This is quite uncommon, even for banks of the developed world. Their background however enabled them to have a much deeper understanding of the potential of digitalization, across the bank operations. Given their depth of understanding, it was then decided that the rest board members and senior management should also get the buy in, in order to engage in a digital journey.

The initial engagement consisted of multiple in house training on FinTech and its potential for different bank departments and process. These session had a very practical focus, referring to specific departments and alternative potential tech solutions that could be developed. As a result, the sessions that were initially focused 'training and selling the potential of digital transformation'', ended up being ''strategy sessions'', were, following the training on different trends and tech solutions within different departments, the discussions would focus on executing specific solutions within specified timelines.

Despite the training-turned-to-strategy sessions, the banks executives still couldn't really sense the way the technologies were implemented, and they were also somehow uncertain on their benefits. In order to solve that, an Executive trip was scheduled, for one week, in one of the banks that are having the largest digital transformation worldwide. This meant that the bank executives were exposed for one week to different organizational set ups and to different technologies, and were able to see themselves their potential. The conclusion of these trainings sessions was very positive: The banks' managed had concluded that this was the best time to engage in a digital journey, and that the management should focus on strategizing towards this route, in order to implement in the following 3 years.

Developing a Digital Strategy in a Very Traditional Environment

Whilst the top management was persuaded, the actual planning would involve a lot of middle management staff that had no particular exposure on financial technology. The first step to create a more digital mind was to establish ''FinTech sessions'' across the whole organization, where people could see how FinTech could help them do their jobs better. This was assisted from the creation of an internal ''Idea bank'', where people could upload their ideas, and vote on their potential. Last, a series of events focusing on start up engagement took place. Within these sessions, the bank employees could exchange ideas with the start ups on how they would go to solve the same problems. All of these enabled the bank staff to be much more eager to hear how innovation and digital transformation can help improve their work flows.

On the top management level, there was the need for continuous engagement in order to develop a coherent Digital Strategy. In order to ensure their active engagement, there was a series of weekend strategy retreats organized, where executives would be mandated to explore different business models in order to engage in successful digital transformation. This was further facilitated by the invitation of key international speakers on the FinTech area, as well as the CEO of the then fastest growing Digital Bank in Europe. At the end of the weekend retreats, where the future Digital Strategy was established a critical decision was made: The best way to engage in the tech transformation journey, would be to launch the first digital bank of Africa.

Next step was to create coherent plans on how to develop the digital bank. In order to develop it, the executives spent numerous weeks and weekends in strategizing. This was enhanced with engagements and site visits of other entities that had undergone successful digital transformation. Picture 3 provided below presents the initial timeline that would be used to execute the full digital strategy.

Figure 3. Timeline for the execution of the Digital Transformation strategy

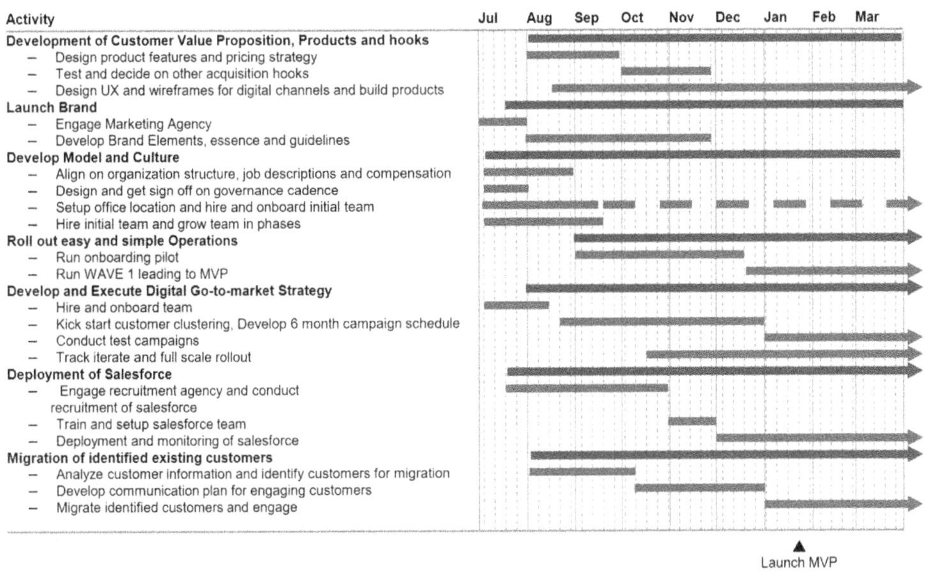

The Criticality of the Execution Muscle

Having developed a full digital strategy, the next step was to focus on its execution. The management however was familiar with the fact that beautiful strategies can go wrong because of loose execution, and that ''Strategy eats Culture for breakfast'' (Oliver, 2019). This meant that extra attention would be given on crafting out the pillars which would ensure a strong 'execution muscle'.

The first step had to do with the creation of a robust IT architecture. The bank hired the head of IT of one of the largest start ups in Africa to focus on this area.

Figure 4. Initial Customer Forecasts

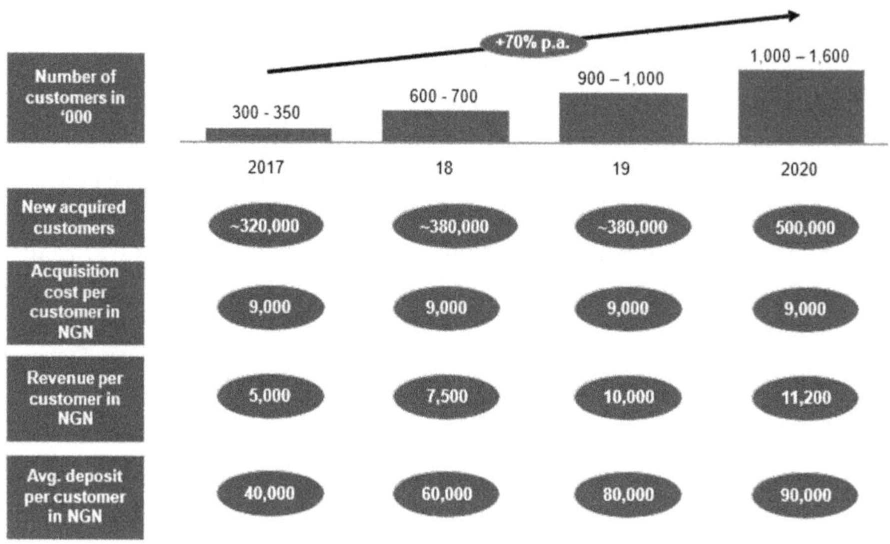

This helped the bank establish a roadmap for its tech refresh. Beyond this obvious deliverable however, the CIO was able to bring start up ideas and solutions within the whole tech architecture. This enabled the bank to have exposure to solution which were never thought of before, while also keeping an 'experimental' attitude on the potential of new technologies.

The next critical area for the strategy execution was the establishment of a data architecture. This was largely missing in all regional companies, and most of the global ones. Ultimately, a proper data architecture, would help the bank leverage data in its operations, in both internal and external levels. In the internal level, the bank would be enabled to use data to assess performance and make decisions, while in the external, the bank would be able to leverage data in order to ultimately increase its sales.

This enabled the digital bank to have proper sales capability from its inception. Whilst most banks didn't have a customer relationship management in place at this time, the digital bank would be able to have an actual sales strategy, with the ability to measure results, from its inception. This resulted in very impressive sales numbers: as per diagram 4 below, the bank had very aggressive plans for their Digital Banking operation, aiming to increase its new customer base by 70% within 4 years. Following the strategy execution, the digital infrastructure enabled the bank to be among the first in the whole continent focusing on ''sales discipline''. Impressively, the bank had been able to acquire in 1 year 1.000.000 new customers. The previous 1.000.000 customers had taken 75 years to be acquired!

The last act taken to ensure successful execution of the digital strategy had to do with the wide adoption of a start up/lean logic. A specific training curriculum was created focusing on how employees could take part in ''innovating at scale''. Furthermore, there was targeting hiring in specific roles, focusing on attracting young employees, from specific universities and schools, that would help upscale the rest workforce as well. The bank established weekly innovation hours for its employees, the dress code was relaxed, and the employees were incentivized to bring ideas and participate in growing the digital bank.

ESTABLISHING AN INNOVATION CULTURE ACROSS THE COMPANY

The innovation function was regarded as crucial for the successful implementation of its digital transformation. In order to create a fully innovative culture, several critical steps were steps were made. The innovation function would be based in the Innovation lad, which would be the go-to place for all things digital within the bank. The innovation lad became the center managing all strategic changes happening in the organization. This enabled a new, ''out of the box'' way of thinking towards solution, while at the same time allowing ideas and a fresh energy to be diffused in the company. The innovation culture was further strengthened through the use of ''Innovation Coaches'', the creation of an Idea Bank, and constant engagement with the banks employees through digital means. This enabled the creation of digital mindset in different departments. These department then were regarded as having different levels of ''readiness'' for transformation, as it can be seen in Diagram 5.

Figure 5. Phasing out Data Transformation

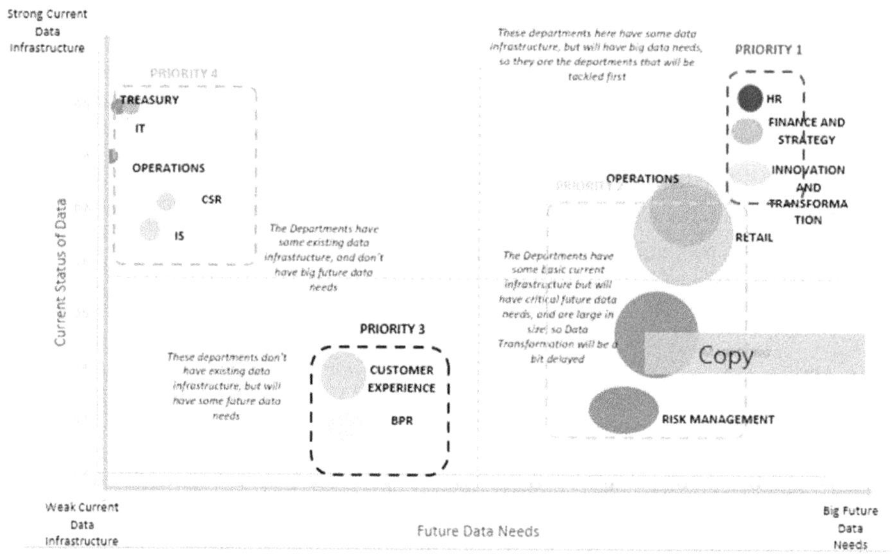

ALAT: Reaching New Heights

The correct approach to execution, resulted in multiple successes for the bank: not only the bank had been able to double its customers in one year of operation, but it was also able to do so in geographies that previously it had no presence at all! And, the underbanked population of 100 million Nigerians, only appeared to be a very attractive opportunity. This was because most banks and branches didn't have any presence at all in these areas, which meant that Mobile (or as called within WEMA Bank ''Selfie'') Banking had a great potential for the country. And we were the first and only bank in the continent ready to reap these profits!

The establishment of a fresh retail base, had clear strategic implications for the bank: It was time to stop being called ''the bank of the grandfathers'', and try to rebrand itself to the younger customers, who tend to be more eager to use online and digital services. This meant that the appropriate marketing channels (ie social media, events with young artists etc) were used to reach them out. A new bank was emerging; When people on the street were hearing that the new Digital Bank, ALAT, was actually a project of the oldest bank in Nigeria, WEMA Bank, they wouldn't believe it!

The successful launch of the digital bank resulted on multiple considerations of its business model. The Digital bank, contrary to the tradition bank, would focus on generating its revenue from transactions, and from the traditional fees, that most of the banks base their income. Furthermore, the bank would focus on having an ''open banking strategy'', where partnering with other start ups would be a major area of future growth. Rather than operating as a bank, the organization had decided to operate as a platform: customers should register and use the app for multiple transactions, and not only whenever need their banking service. Customer was a king again, and Innovation and Design Thinking would be the only way to attract and retain them.

Recognition the Potential of the Digital Bank

The performance of the digital entity was applauded from the market. The launch of the First Digital Bank of Africa was impressive itself. Beyond the launch itself, the bank had also been able to double the number of its customers, within one year! Furthermore, the digital onboarding meant that the bank could expand in virtually any area of the country, and, given that there are still areas in Nigeria that they don't have bank branches within the radius of 100 miles, the opportunity to capture the unbanked market share was clear. As a result, the bank received multiple national and international awards5, as one of the ''Most Innovative Banks'' in the continent. The Central Bank of Nigeria, which is the main regulatory authority for the banking sector requested our active role in drafting the legislation for the creation and development of Digital Banks in the country. A further important recognition came from the African Development Bank: Having recognized the success of our Digital Innovation for Financial Inclusion, they provided the bank with a special funding of $50 million for loans, which would be disbursed to previously underbanked areas and population groups6! The potential of the Digital Bank started being clear locally and internationally!

When Innovation-At-Scale Becomes your Daily Job Duty

The launch of the bank had been very successful. The customer base was growing, the customers were satisfied with the products offered, and this was also reflected to the performance metrics of the bank as well, with the bank having had the highest earnings growth compared to the rest banks, at the second year of the operations of the digital bank. The next critical step was to Innovate at scale, where the Digital and Innovation logic would be transplanted to all departments of the organization. In order to achieve that, a series of activities took place.

The first act was to establish an Innovation Lab. This would ultimately be the place where new ideas are being discussed, and problems are solved through innovative approaches. Beyond Ideation and problem solving, this place would also act as the training academy, where the bank employees would come to acquire digital skills.

The launch of the Innovation lab was very successful, and it was the first innovation lab for a lab in the country.

Following the launch of the innovation lab, a series of community engagements with start ups were expected to take place, in order to strengthen the 'lean' profile of the bank. The first act was a Hackathon. Specifically, the first corporate Hackathon in the country! This event was received with very much enthusiasm, and received almost 600 applications, which was a really good number, even for Western standards. The selected start ups were working on actual bank problems, enabling the bank employees to expose themselves in the benefits of ''start up attitude'' and ''agility''.

In order to strengthen the cultural learning from the start up engagements, the bank decided to establish a full incubator program, where some selected start ups would get funding to work closely with specific bank departments in problem solving. This was proven very beneficial for the bank: The older employees of the bank were able to partner with start ups, and work together in developing digital solutions in order to optimize their workflows. At the end of the development, the bank actually invested in these start ups, and one of them has grown so much in its valuation, making it the most successful investment in terms of ROI in the history of the bank!

A last area where active engagement took place in order to help to scale an Innovation mindset was the Banks' partnerships. Specifically, the bank decided that an efficient way to become more ''digital'' was to develop a 'platform' strategy, were partnerships of different nature would enable the bank to either improved operations or new revenue areas. The bank was among the first in the continent to take the ''partnerships'' function seriously. Multiple strategic partnerships were established, with both traditional and tech companies. The success of this strategy was two-fold: On the one hand, the corporate culture was changing, as the bank employees had large exposure to the agility that characterizes start ups. On the other hand, the whole profit mixed was changing as well: The bank's revenue didn't come 100% from bank fees. Instead, at the end of the first year of the establishment of the Platform strategy, 18% of the revenue was now coming from customer transactions, within the phone app! The cultural and commercial aspects of the whole Digital Transformation were being achieved. The success was further clarified from the interest of multiple Pan African banking groups to provide them the know how to our Digital Transformation, or to actually partner with us for the provision of banking services.

WHEN TECHNOLOGY IS ENABLING YOU TO ENTER NEW MARKETS

The successful operationalization of the Digital Banking confirmed to the bank that the best way to go was digital. The decision made at this point was to ensure that technology is fully leveraged to enable expansions in our operations. The first area to be developed, as a new market for the bank, was SME lending. With almost 18 million unbanked SMEs within Nigeria, the opportunity was clear (PWC, 2018). As done in the development of the initial app, the new service was developed in agile ways, incorporating design thinking and using scrum methodologies for product development. The launch of the service was successful: Within 3 months, the bank had acquired more customers than it had acquired over the previous 76 years!

A strong digital infrastructure also enabled the bank to develop some of the first alternative credit scoring models in the country. Contrary to the Western countries, most African countries neither have credit bureaus, nor they have the ability to centrally manage and track credit profiles (IFC, 2011). As the individuals were using the app however, the ability to track the data and leverage it was clear. So the outcome of that was first the development of credit profiles. These were essentially among the first alternative credit scoring models developed in the country. Beyond the development of these models, the bank was the first in the country that would be able to offer automated loans within ten minutes; ''selfie banking'' had arrived.

The next critical area for growth and development was the development of an overall ''platform strategy'', in the likes of Amazon and Google. This implied a business model where the customer would not only come when they need a banking service, but instead they would use the bank as a platform to engage in multiple transactions. The platform strategy consistent of three pillars: The development of an online ecosystem (named ''OUTLET by ALAT'') and the engagement of multiple partners, who would offer their services, in revenue-sharing agreements. As mentioned earlier, the overall platform strategy was successful from the very beginning, as this was reflected from the altered revenue model of the bank, where 18% of its revenue would now come from the platform transaction. The success of the Digital bank was also highlighted from the international partnerships requests received, were, among others, the fastest growing digital bank of Europe, as we ll as well the largest African bank in terms of assets, were actually requesting to strengthen our relations in a strategic levels.

THE FUTURE IS HERE

The substantial investments in the area of technology in order to build strong foundations for growth seemed to be paying for WEMA bank. The bank was having the highest earnings growth in the country, and had enjoyed 13 consecutive quarters of revenue and profit growth. The bank share price also had almost tripled from its price at the end of 2014, during a period which was characterized from a bad economic environment within Nigeria, because of the low oil prices. At the same time, a large number of the bank employees had transformed to tech savvy employees, who were able to leverage their knowledge and approach work issues as opportunities for innovation. Of course, there were also lessons learned, in all the different areas of the digital journey: From the IT and Data architecture, to the different products and services required from the banks customers. However, the fast growth of the bank, due to technological enablement, aspired the banks management to set up the next targets: To ''Double in Two'', in terms of profits, customers, and in overall performance.

REFERENCES

Broeders, H., & Khanna, S. (2015). *Strategic choices for banks in the digital age.* McKinsey & Company.

Foster, C., & Heeks, R. (2013). Innovation and scaling of ICT for the bottom-of-the-pyramid. *Journal of Information Technology, 28*(4), 296–315. doi:10.1057/jit.2013.19

Govindarajan, V., & Ramamurti, R. (2011). Reverse innovation, emerging markets, and global strategy. *Global Strategy Journal, 1*(3-4), 191–205. doi:10.1002/gsj.23

IFC Advisory Services. (2011). *Access To Credit Among Micro, Small, And Medium Enterprises.* http://www.ifc.org/wps/ wcm/connect/1f2c968041689903950bb79e78015671/AccessCreditMSME-Brochure-Final.pdf?MOD=AJPERES

KPMg. (2018). *Annual Banking Industry Satisfaction Survey.* Accessible on: https://home.kpmg/ng/en/home/insights/2018/07/KPMG%E2%80%99s-Annual-Banking-Industry-Customer-Satisfaction-Survey.html

Lane, P. R., & Milesi-Ferretti, G. M. (2018). The external wealth of nations revisited: International financial integration in the aftermath of the global financial crisis. *IMF Economic Review, 66*(1), 189–222. doi:10.105741308-017-0048-y

Malar, D. A., Arvidsson, V., & Holmstrom, J. (2019). Digital transformation in banking: Exploring value co-creation in online banking services in India. *Journal of Global Information Technology Management*, *22*(1), 7–24. doi:10.1080/1097198X.2019.1567216

Mathieu, M. P. H., Pani, M. M., Chen, S., & Maino, M. R. (2019). *Drivers of Cross-Border Banking in Sub-Saharan Africa*. International Monetary Fund. doi:10.5089/9781498321549.001

McKinsey. (2017). *Digital Banking in the Gulf. McKinsey Special Report*. UAE.

Oliver, J. J. (2019). *Culture also eats innovation for breakfast!* Strategic Direction. doi:10.1108/SD-07-2019-0135

PWC. (2018). *Assessing current market conditions and business growth prospects PWC Surveys*. Accessible on https://www.pwc.com/ng/en/events/nigeria-sme-survey.html

ENDNOTES

1. https://www.americanbanker.com/news/is-microsofts-bill-gates-right-when-he-says-banks-are-technology
2. https://www.euromoney.com/article/b18k8wtzv7v23d/world39s-best-digital-bank-2018-dbs
3. WEMA Bank annual report 2018.
4. https://qz.com/africa/564513/a-not-so-brief-history-of-the-fall-and-fall-of-the-nigerian-naira/
5. https://www.wemabank.com/wema-bank-secures-35m-international-lenders-fund-smes/
6. https://punchng.com/wemas-alat-named-africas-best-digital-banking-app/ and https://techpoint.africa/2018/01/19/alat-wema-wins-best-digital-bank-award/

Chapter 10
Risk Management:
Minimizing the Triple Risks – Strategic, Financial, and Operational

Eman A. Zabalawi
https://orcid.org/0000-0003-4948-7684
Higher Colleges of Technology, Dubai, UAE

Abderazak Bakhouche
Higher Colleges of Technology, Dubai, UAE

Randa El Chaar
Higher Colleges of Technology, Dubai, UAE

ABSTRACT

The chapter covers practical risk managers' points during the planning stage of entrepreneurship to integrate into decision making and core business processes. The chapter includes three risks and how to improve the integration of risk management into organizational culture grouped into three high-level objectives. First, strategic risks include the study of competitors, macroeconomics with its industry changes. Second, financial risks such as the business return of investment and forecasting, customer payments, loan interest charges, and liquidity. Access to finance featured prominently in several studies as a constraint on SME development. The third is the operational risks and internal analysis that includes legal compliance, breakdown of essential equipment, employee mismatch, partnership, information technology, external events, and supply chain reliability. It is vital to establish an organizational culture where risk management is a daily component activity.

DOI: 10.4018/978-1-7998-4195-1.ch010

Copyright © 2021, IGI Global. Copying or distributing in print or electronic forms without written permission of IGI Global is prohibited.

INTRODUCTION

As Pavodani and Tugnoli (2005) mention, some elements can explain the current importance of the discipline of risk management. For example, the increasing volatility and competition that organizations have to face in this era have forced them to implement at least some risk awareness level. Risk management connects with planning in a systematic process of deciding how to approach, plan, and execute risk management activities throughout the business's life within an industry affected by the economic situation. Assessing startup as a project intends to maximize the beneficial outcome of the opportunities and minimize or eliminate adverse risk/ uncertain events.

Risk can be identified through both qualitative and quantitative analysis. Qualitative risk analysis involves Project teams assessing identified risks for the probability of occurrence and impact on project objectives. Teams can elicit assistance from subject matter experts or functional units to assess their respective fields' risks. Risks are measured by their "quality" in words rather than quantified in numbers. Quantitative risk analysis numerically estimates the probability that a project will meet its cost and time objectives. The response to risk involves developing options and determining actions to reduce threats or enhance project objectives. Effects are identified and assigned to parties that take responsibility for the risk response. This process ensures that each risk requiring an intervention has an "owner." The Project Manager and the project team identify the best strategy for each risk and then select specific actions to implement that strategy. Risk response is followed by monitoring and control to track and identify risks, monitor residual risks, and identify new risks—ensuring the execution of risk plans and evaluating their effectiveness in reducing risk. Risk monitoring and control is an ongoing process for the life of the project. After each risk log, an improvement and correction action must occur at an agreed time of the project closure.

Small and Medium Enterprises (SMEs) need to follow a structured process for selecting their project management practices. They need to identify their strategic objectives, appropriate success criteria and key performance indicators for their projects, and thus necessary success factors; and proper project management tools and techniques, which meet the requirements outlined above. Ledwith (2004) and Murphy and Ledwith (2007). Project risk management involves careful consideration and thought about the project and the associated uncertainties and risks such as uncertainty an entrepreneur faces with competitors, macroeconomics of the business industry that requires decision making where danger could be influenced. This knowledge emphasizes individual responsibility in making informed risk decisions an essential element for success on and off duty. More generally, entrepreneurs boost their success if they pick industries that align with the skills they excel with the passion to practice.

One can assume the entrepreneur's job is to think big thoughts and hire other people to do the actual work. One big reason that startups do not succeed is that the founders do not do what needs to be done to get the business up and running. Many tech startups fail because the CEO cannot code. Odds of success will increase if one brings world-beating sales skills and knowledge of the market. However, there still needs a strong relationship with a world-class coder. Do not start a company if the primary motivation is to make money. The reason is simple. To be successful, one will need to spend about 80 hours a week with very little pay to make the startup successful. It is impossible to work that hard and be valid unless one believes that life's mission is to make potential customers better off by providing them with the company's product. To avoid hitting this rhetorical iceberg, direct the startup at solving a problem that one cares about deeply. Research for *Hungry Start-up* Strategy revealed that people start companies most often because the founder had a problem that nobody else had solved.

Rhetorically, how does one know the risks involved in order to avoid? There are warning signs of individual risk that may be present, such as: when the person is confused, making errors, distracted, using improper procedures, lacks focus on both job responsibilities and overlapping of knowledge, has unclear goals that are not aligned with a business model, and overconfidence. Numerous influences affect the accomplishment of day to day activities; the most common and variable influence is human behavior. Behavior is vital to be embedded in the job description and on the job training. Human behavior includes the assertiveness of decision making. It is the behavior of being ready, willing, and able to participate, maintain, and improve the work actively. Human behavior's uncertainty is harmful to entrepreneurs due to its effect on both strategic and operational risks. Therefore, one must plan to avoid risks —understanding and mapping these behavioral skills in the business process improvement task and mission effectiveness.

STRATEGIC RISKS

Strategic Risk and Corporate Performance

"Risk Management" is the art and science of thinking about what could go wrong, and what should be done to mitigate those risks cost-effectively. SMEs generally experience a scarcity of resources (Wong, 2005) such as time, financial, and human resources. Areas of potential risk need to be aligned with business goals and success factors.

The **Iceberg Principle**, or **Iceberg Theory**, suggests that we cannot detect most of a situation's data. The theory, which we also call the '**Theory of Omission** 'or '**Iceberg Model**,' applies to systems and problems. As with an iceberg, the tip is visible, while its bulk is below the water's surface, or invisible. Competitive advantage as a theoretical subject is considered as a must for a successful and efficient company, yet, it is rarely visible in practice.

Common company practice is to choose one of M. Porter's defined competitive advantage routes as companies a competitive advantage, without a more in-depth investigation where the considered advantage is routed and linked with companies' operations and targets. Competitive advantage is a much more complicated decision. The company is grounded within the cost, innovation, differentiation leadership, or focusing on operational effectiveness and excellence. Well investigated and defined competitive advantage can guide a company more efficiently towards its strategic and tactical targets.

There are numerous sources of competitive advantage, including more efficient production techniques, brand image, consumer loyalty, and location. Possession of competitive advantage should deliver a higher level of profit than obtained by its rivals (Black, J., Hashimzade, N., Myles, G., 2012). An advantage over competitors is gained by offering consumers higher value, either utilizing lower prices or providing more significant benefits and better servicing facilities that could justify higher rates.

This advantage may be achieved in various ways, including increased product performance, superior distribution methods, or creative advertising. Most competitive advantage forms cannot be sustained in the long term because competitors will initiate or find substitutes for the innovations that created it. A company is said to have a sustainable competitive advantage (SCA) when it has resources that cannot readily be imitated or substituted (Oxford University Press, 2009).

The company can achieve above-average performance in an industry by implementing one of these three strategies (Porter M. E., 1998). Cost leadership strategy may be the clearest of the three generic strategies. It usually targets a broader aspect of the market is the low-cost producer in an industry for a particular level of quality and segment. The company that implements a cost leadership strategy sells its products at average industry prices to earn a profit higher than competitors, or even below the average industry prices to gain more significant market share. The company may also operate in other related industries implementing this strategy – the company's breadth is often essential to maintain its cost advantage.

According to Porter, in the occurrence of a price war, the company can still maintain profitability while its rivals suffer losses (Porter M. E., 1998). A company seeks to be unique in its industry along those dimensions that are important to buyers in a differentiation strategy. By implementing a differentiation strategy, a company aims to develop such a product or service that offers any type of unique attributes that are valued by customers and that customers perceive to be better than the competition. Differentiation can be based on the product itself, the delivery system, the marketing approach, and other factors (Porter M. E., 1998).

While cost leadership differentiation strategies seek competitive advantage in a broad range of industry segments, the plan aims at cost advantage (cost focus) or differentiation (differentiation focus) in a narrow section. This is the most significant difference between the focus strategy and the other two strategies. The premise is that the target audience's needs can be better serviced by focusing entirely on it (Porter M. E., 1998).

The generic strategies are not by premise compatible with one another. If a company attempts to achieve an advantage in cost leadership and differentiation, it may achieve no advantage. For example, the benefits of optimizing the company's strategy for one specific segment (focus) cannot be gained if a company simultaneously serves a broad range of segments (i.e., adapts the main elements of cost leadership and differentiation strategies) (Porter M. E., 1998). Every venture has more competitors and fewer competitive advantages than it thinks. Money is to be made by satisfying a pressing need in the marketplace, and one can be sure that plenty of others are gunning for that same consumer dollar.

Business is a contact sport, and some of the competitors will play rough. They will copy a business model. They will try to out-innovate current existing competitors. They will try to out-spend on marketing. They will start price wars or enhance existing trade secrets. To stay ahead of one's competition, one must continuously ask what others might do to try to win and then develop appropriate defenses. Thus, it is crucial to know the strengths, weaknesses, opportunities, threats, or SWOT analyses. Figure out what the startup can do better than all competitors – whether it be price, features, quality, or some other advantage – and focus on maintaining leadership.

How to Integrate Risk Management Into Strategic Planning

Mission analysis. It can develop short-term, long term, and contingency plans, including the coordination, allocation, and monitoring for changes to the policies while they are occurring.

Leadership in a startup aims to direct and coordinate other team members' activities and take responsibility for how plans are expected. It includes the duties and characteristics of the leader and how work is delegated to the team. Leadership is not limited to the rank of position. It is required at various job tasks across the business in order to support mission attainment at different stages of the business growth or project. Leadership is connected to situational awareness. It is the perception of what is in practice and how it affects the tasks or mission carried on with the projection of what is seen the future. It is based on life experience and knowledge. It is gaining situational awareness to reduce behavioral influence through adaptability and flexibility. This behavior refers to the ability to alter a course of action when the situation changes, how to recognize and acknowledge the change is communicated vital. As communication, it is the ability to clear and accurately send and understand information and instructions and provide useful feedback. Communication requires two ways of interaction to convey information accurately and concisely and avoid uncertain information. Personal characteristics and skills are fundamental in operational risk management to guide the employees' decision making. The risk management process provides an understanding of communicating intentions and style.

Risk management is a continuous process integral from the strategic level planning through the tactical level execution. It is a tool to help improve mission readiness and mission accomplishment. The team is a factor relative to each one, but it is not "defined primary." These controls become resources that need to be planned for execution by having the leaders provide the equipment, training, and guidance for operations and deliberate execution with ample time.

What factors impact decision making? Level of training, experience, attitudes, and personality. These factors influence business operations' risk encounters, and they vary depending on the role and the task performed. An iceberg model that sinks startups is when a leader cannot recruit the most talented people for the work needed. The simple reality is that learning to become a success is hard if one is not a great leader. Moreover, the leadership skills are different from a company with less than ten employees than a 100-person or 1,000-person company requires.

At the startup stage, a great leader has the charisma and track record to conjure up a compelling vision for the company and recruit top talent for the ride to realize that vision. Controls developed at a strategic level for each task aim to build layers of protection that are available to assist leaders with risk management. Different categories such as

- Policies, procedures, and routines are red block and high-risk control documents. These resources speed up decision making and increase predictable through the standardized operation.
- Checklists are the instructions and maintenance instruction manuals. These resources decrease the potential for error and improve coordination.
- Automation such as alarms and reminders provides another opportunity to reduce risk by providing a faster interpretation of information, providing warnings, and distributing the workload.
- Briefing and external resources transfer situational awareness among the team. Briefing establishes expectations and improves situational awareness.

- Knowledge, skill, and techniques are resources such as training, practice, and the individual bringing drills to the task or mission. Besides, it improves situational awareness and the ability to make informed decisions.

The critical risk is to manage when time and resources are limited, which is the case of a startup. It is primarily used in the planning stages of a task. Since most business personnel are not involved in the planning process, the most relevant process is deliberate.

Workforce Inputs and Outputs

Any kind of risk analysis should start by taking a high-level objective and breaking it down into more tactical, operational key performance indicators (KPIs) and targets. Following the McKinsey MECE principle (ME-Mutually Exclusive, CE-Collectively Exhaustive) helps avoid unnecessary duplication and overlap. Most of the time, strategic objectives are broken down into more tactical KPIs and targets by the strategy department or HR, saving the risk manager much time. This is a critical step to make sure that risk managers understand each objective's business logic and make risk analysis more focused.

Important note, while it should be management's responsibility to identify and assess risks, the business reality in a company may be that sometimes the risk manager should take responsibility for performing risk assessment on strategic objectives and take the lead to actions needed.

Turning Risk Analysis into Actions

Risk managers should discuss risk analysis outcomes with the executive team to see whether the results are reasonable, realistic, and actionable. If the risk analysis results are significant, the management with the help from the risk manager may need to:

- Revise the assumptions used in the strategy.
- Consider sharing risks with third parties by using hedging, outsourcing, or insurance mechanisms.
- Consider reducing risk by adopting alternative approaches or implementing control measures.
- Accept risk and develop a business continuity/improvement plan to minimize risks in the long term.
- Alternatively, perhaps, change the strategy altogether. The management may be required to review or update the entire strategy or just elements of it. This

is one reason why it is highly recommended to perform risk analysis before the strategy is finalized.

At a later stage, the risk manager should work with the internal audit to determine whether the risks identified during the risk analysis are controlled, and the agreed risk mitigations are implemented.

FINANCIAL RISKS

Financials lead us to another vast iceberg. More so than larger organizations, SMEs require adopting a risk management (RM) strategy and methodology. They lack the resources to respond promptly to internal and external threats, leading to potentially huge losses that seriously threaten their survival.

A further motivation to push the implementation of RM in SMEs is to protect innovative projects, which are fundamental to gain competitive advantage and succeed in the market, but necessarily involve risky decisions and activities (Vargas-Hernandez, 2011). The days are past when Baumol (2004) asserted that product innovation is the core challenge for firms, particularly SMEs, to survive in today's highly competitive economic environment. The firm's competitive advantage and higher chance for survival were necessarily dictated by the innovative streak the organization harbored, thus ensuring the capacity for more innovation in the future (Twiss, 1993). On the one hand, innovation is not without financial risk as resources are used up to fuel organizational productivity and growth. On the other hand, an innovation strategy should consider the values of the returns from the innovative process to recover the firm's stakeholders' economic efforts. (Nogueira et al., 2018) and (Montejo and Bravo, 2010).

Nogueira et al. (2018) advocate that innovation is critical to survival; it gives rise to higher financial risk levels, causing the firm's failure. According to them, the literature on firm failure suggests that the firms' financial risk mainly depends on their financial performance and other firm-specific characteristics. While the literature on innovation has generally considered some firm-specific attributes such as firm size and age, it has ignored firms' financial performance. In their research study, however, they offered analysis combining the influence of innovation, firm financial performance, and firm-specific characteristics on the survival of 146 Spanish SMEs between 2010 and 2012. (Nogueira et al., 2018)

Buddelmeyer et al. (2009) arrived at a similar conclusion and asserted that although innovation and survival are positively correlated, change involves a degree of uncertainty. Investments in product innovation have a higher tendency to fail because of the financial risk associated with the innovation process. In their firm survival model, Nogueira et al. (2018), studied the effect of financial rates such as profitability, liquidity, leverage, and efficiency on the firm's capacity to survive. Closer analysis of the model's variables revealed how the innovation process in its four categories of product innovation, process innovation, marketing innovation, and organizational innovation contributes to its financial risk. Innovation variables like product innovation, process innovation, and commercial innovation, if managed properly, will increase profitability and operational efficiency. Product innovation entails introducing a new product on the market or significantly improving an existing product with the objective that the value of the innovative products will increase the competitiveness of the firm. Process innovation involves installing machinery and new equipment to improve production methods and enables firms to become more efficient. It generates a competitive advantage over the competition as it allows anticipating technological developments, an important factor when operating in highly dynamic sectors (Nogueira et al., 2018). Both innovative processes and products require substantial investments typically financed by permanent capital, equity, and long-term bonds. So is commercial innovation, where the focus is on effective marketing policies involving changes in the 4Ps, namely product, price, promotion, and positioning.

SMEs and Banks

Now that we have identified the importance of access to funding, it is worth re-visiting the literature for risk models in the application by banks when testing SMEs' eligibility for funding. SMEs are perceived as highly risky, and with the lack of proper collateral, their access to finance is made more challenging. The main characteristic of the relationship between banks and SMEs is the lack of understanding of the customer's nature and the details of the lending request, which can result in recommending the wrong product to the customer. For instance, the SME might not recover the debt because the lender was unaware of the legal implications of lending to that particular customer type. The relationship, per se, needs to be addressed from two different points of view. One related to the financial risk inherent in the operations of any SME and another related to the lender's contribution to the financial risks encountered by the SME. While the nature of lending does mean that occasionally the lender will incur debt, it is through an appreciation of the risks involved in lending, and an ability to reduce those risks, that the lender can make better decisions. A full understanding of the lending cycle undoubtedly reduces the risks. The lending cycle starts with the lending decision, including an analysis of financial information and includes monitoring and control plus the ability to detect early warning signals before ultimately passing the debt over for recovery.

That is for considering the role of banks in financing SMEs. The SMEs who are developed and have robust internal operating systems and risk management techniques can make it to the stage of approaching banks for working capital and longer-term finance. The question remains, while financial institutions like banks take a corporate view of lending principles, particularly corporate risk and responsibility, at the shop floor level. Do individual lenders understand the framework in which they are lending and the basic tenets by which they must act? Is the structure in use the most appropriate to follow when testing SMEs' eligibility to tap into the sources of banks for financing their innovative operations? Are banks required to come up with more innovative tools to help SMEs on their growth journey?

In response to this gap, diverse funding platforms emerged to harvest the opportunities available for early-stage innovators. Seed money, sometimes known as seed funding or seed capital, is a form of a securities offering. An investor invests capital in a startup company in exchange for an equity stake or convertible note stake in the company before it grows into an SME. Venture capitalists also showed up. This is a type of financing provided by firms or funds to small, early-stage, emerging firms that are deemed to have high growth potential or have demonstrated high growth and are expected to become potential SMEs.

SME's Ecosystem

In its 2010 report, the International Financial Corporation (IFC), addressed the challenges leading to this gap of SMEs' ability to access financing. Comprehensive approaches must include the most significant number of SMEs operating in national markets so that economies can build on microfinance approaches. This includes up-scaling existing microfinance institutions, if they have any, to serve small businesses. As in the case of expanding credit to more established SMEs, this will need to be combined with enhancements to the enabling environment for SME lending, including improvements to the financial infrastructure of credit reporting and collateral registries.

The report points out that the SME finance gap results from a mismatch between the needs of the small firms and the supply of financial services, which are typically more relaxed for larger firms to access. The SME bank relationship, in which providers of funding can meet their expected return on capital while serving client needs, can be severely limited. This is due to SME intrinsic weaknesses, flaws in provider delivery models and, most importantly, lingering deficiencies in the enabling environment for financial services: financial infrastructure (accounting and auditing standards, credit reporting systems, collateral and insolvency regimes), and the legal and regulatory framework for financial institutions and instruments.

The report sheds light on how business models aimed at providing financial services to SMEs in a cost-effective manner are arising. From microfinance up-scaling to bank down-scaling, including community banks, these models share common characteristics: they reduce the cost to serve through intensive use of technology and the adoption of cost-effective client-relationship models; they combine offering of savings, transactional, and credit products, to increase generated income; they use advanced risk management technology to maximize the risk/reward balance; and, they achieve strong focus on the small and medium enterprise segment, to help implement excellent execution capabilities in the above areas.

Effective SME financing models can be implemented in different country and market environments, but greater outreach is achieved in the most developed financial sector environments. Financial information and the ability to enforce collateral are seen as critical by major SME banks operating in developed markets. Weaknesses in these areas appear to impede more aggressive financial services growth in developing markets.

The Financial Inclusion Experts Group (FIEG), on another front, focused on developing a supportive legal and regulatory framework, strengthening the financial information infrastructure, building consistent and reliable data sources on SME finance; and, building the capacity of the financial institutions.

With the options available to SMEs to fund the investments that fuel their growth and increase their profitability, managing their financial risk has not been resolved. While we can identify a deficiency in the financial ecosystem hosting SMEs, their responsibility to establish and maintain an internal control and audit system to manage their financial risk remains essential. Of particular importance is following their cash flows and managing the short term liquidity needed to survive in the short term and later achieve sustainable growth in the long term.

SME's Lending Framework and Financial Risks

The lending framework defining SME's financial risks, thus depriving them of financing and hindering their organic growth under increased uncertainty resides in the lack of governance.

SMEs need to build and set their internal control processes to manage financial risk to change lenders' view towards financial risk.

First, on the list of the lending framework and with increased uncertainty arising from financial risk comes the need for corporate governance. To state that risk management is the responsibility of the board of directors alone is a misconception. In practice, the burden of risk management, especially in larger firms, is often delegated by the corporate governance committee to either the audit, finance or compliance committee of the board or a risk management officer called the chief risk officer or a risk management group headed by a risk management officer. Thus, the discussion starts with the four key risk management processes: risk identification, risk assessment, risk mitigation, and risk transfer. The method of risk management involves determining which risks to accept, which to neutralize, and which to transfer.

When a company is exposed to an event that can cause a shortfall in a targeted financial measure or value, it is called financial risk. The financial measure or value could be earnings per share (EPS), return on equity (ROE), or cash flows, to name some important ones. Financial risks include market risk, credit risk, market liquidity risk, operational risk, and legal risk.

The traditional process of risk management focuses on managing the risks of only parts of the business (products, departments, or divisions), ignoring the implications these risks have for the firm's value. The management process organized only on parts of a business is referred to as a "silo structure." What is needed is an Enterprise Risk Management (ERM) process that management can employ to handle uncertainty effectively and evaluate how the risks and opportunities that a firm faces can either create destroy or preserve a firm's value. The process should help management to align the risk appetite and strategies across the firm, improve the quality of the firm's risk-response decisions, identify and manage the risks across the firm. Internal controls provide a mechanism for mitigating risks and increase the likelihood that a firm can achieve its financial objective.

An ERM exceeds internal controls in three significant ways. First, when establishing its strategy for the firm, ERM requires that the board consider risks. Second, ERM requires the board to identify what level of risk it is willing to accept. Finally, the ERM requires that risk management decisions be made throughout the firm to be consistent with the risk policy established. The most popular definition of ERM has been proposed by the Committee of Sponsoring Organizations of the Treadway Commission (COSO). COSO defines ERM as a "… process, effected by an entity's board of directors, management and other personnel, applied in strategy setting and across the enterprise, designed to identify potential events that may affect the entity, and manage risk to be within its risk appetite, to provide reasonable assurance regarding the achievement of entity objectives."

The Casualty Actuarial Society (CAS), provides a broader definition of ERM by describing it as:

…the discipline by which an organization in any industry assesses, controls, exploits, finances, and monitors risk from all sources to increase the organization's short- and long-term value to its stakeholders.

Both COSO and CAS definitions of ERM do converge. (Fabozzi et al., 2008) ERM is an ongoing process that provides a structured method to reduce the adverse consequences of events due to natural catastrophes, terrorism, changes in the economic, political and legal environments, tax litigation, failure of a firm's corporate governance, and product and financial market volatility. (Fabozzi et al., 2008) They continue to focus on the fact that an effective ERM starts at the board level, meaning that corporate governance is critical. The Society of Actuaries (SOA) argues that the term enterprise can have many definitions. The one description of interest to our discussion has an Auditing/Process control trace in that it is a process that is used consistently and effectively throughout the firm. Within the context of process control, ERM is linked to strategic planning and organizational objectives.

Other definitions focus on the fact that it is not stand-alone risk that is key within the capital budgeting context, but the entire firm's risk. The risk profile can be altered using derivative instruments and other risk transfer products and strategies such as retaining the risk or transferring it, or even neutralizing it.

In line with the COSO framework, the four risk objectives are summarized by the following: strategic goals, operations performance measures to safeguard against loss, reporting by providing reliable financial and operational data and reports internally and externally, and compliance that is complying with laws and regulations at all levels, local, state, national and in other countries where the firm operates. Although there are common risks shared by all firms, and there are risks specific to some firms, the building blocks for ERM process are common to all firms. ERM is chiefly concerned with evaluating the firm's risk processes and identifying and quantifying risk exposures. All firm risks are treated as a portfolio of risks and managed on a portfolio or firm level. The risk context is the firm and not the individual products, departments, or divisions.

However, corporate risk management relies heavily on the firm to attract high-value expertise to help it plan and strategize. Younger startups and SMEs can hardly sustain the experts' expenses, provided they could reach them. Not to mention, this process is built around a business case. Managers describe a potential investment or other strategic action in great detail and then build a fact-based case to estimate its expected economic return. Since the return to any strategy depends on how it impacts future cash flows, the process is naturally forward-looking- and thus reliant on sound forecasts of variables such as market size and share, prices, and productivity. Foresight-an accurate view of the future is essential in generating the best forecasts and making the right strategic choices. The typical process assumes that the strategists possess the foresight to translate their knowledge of the future into point forecasts of key value drivers. These point forecasts allow for accurate estimates of net present value (NPV) and other financial measures, which, in turn, determine which strategy will deliver the highest return. The typical process further assumes that a deep analytical understanding of today's market environment and today's company capabilities are the keys to developing foresight. This can be reasonable in relatively stable market environments – environments characterized by limited uncertainty.

As such, SMEs are believed to operate in economic environments of high uncertainty. Their financial risk is amplified. Their success factors are highly reliant on investors willing to take up the chances they exude and have the personally vested incentive to support them to grow and become profitable.

Though startups and SMEs have less access to resources that can help them adapt to the proper governance structure, the need for corporate governance has favorable implications for all stakeholders involved. The role of SME management is essential in instilling the proper internal controls and culture in the firm. With the growing importance of the role of SMEs worldwide and their contribution to national economies, the regulators, federal governments, and standard setters have collaborated to establish the grounds for a growth conducive ecosystem for these firms. In what follows, we discuss these players' roles in addressing some of the obstacles and challenges facing SMEs worldwide.

Reporting Requirements for Non-Publicly Accountable Entities

The European Union (EU), national governments, and standard setters have realized that the numerous small and medium-sized businesses (SMEs) do not raise funds on the stock exchange and do not prepare general-purpose financial statements for external users. Countries adopting International Financial Reporting Standards (IFRS) for publicly accountable entities have been able to issue their national standards for non-publicly responsible entities. Part of the exercise followed in reporting is to help these smaller entities organize their "inner house" and set in control factors that contribute to mitigating financial risk.

In the UK, companies have a statutory obligation to submit accounts annually to shareholders and file a copy with the Registrar of Companies. In recognition of the cost implications and need for different privacy levels, there was provision for small and medium-sized companies to file abbreviated accounts and adopt Financial Reporting Standards for Smaller Entities (FRSSE). This standard follows the top-down approach to the standard-setting by reducing some of the disclosures required by standards applicable to listed companies – such as disclosing earnings per share figure. The FRSSE was withdrawn from 1 January 2016 and replaced by either FRS 105, *The Financial Reporting Standard for the Micro-entities Regime,* or Section 1A of FRS 102 *The Financial Reporting Standard.* Whereas the UK has FRS 105, the International Accounting Standards Board (IASB), which among other things, has the responsibility for preparing and issuing international and financial reporting standards, has issued the *IFRS for SMEs.*

The International Accounting Standards Board "IASB" issued IFRS for SMEs in July 2009. The standards focus on the information needs of lenders, creditors, and other users of SME financial statements who are interested primarily in information about cash flows, liquidity, and solvency. Some topics, such as earnings per share, operating segments, interim financial reporting, and assets held for sale and insurance contracts, can be omitted. Additional requirements can be requested, such as producing a statement of cash flows and more information on related party transactions. The more straightforward options allowed included expensing rather than capitalizing borrowing costs, simpler recognition, included allowing for an amortization (with a maximum life of 10 years) rather than annual impairment review of goodwill, as well as more straightforward measurement methods such as using the historical cost depreciation model for property, plant, and equipment. The EU Commission rejected the option to adopt IFRS for SMEs because it did not meet the objective of reducing the administrative burden. After investigating the differences among national standard-setting bodies, the main factors influencing the development of financial reporting are: the national legal system, the methods in which the industry is financed, the relationship of the tax and reporting systems, the influence and status of the accounting profession, and the extent to which accounting theory is developed.

In the UAE, research by Beehive, a peer-to-peer finance platform serving SMEs and providing more available finance for them, has revealed that SME owners have limited resources to take advantage of innovative opportunities. Only 2% of business owners are currently trying to access finance to fund it, and 48% of SMEs hiring a manager under 25 with no experience. The reason cited maybe that salaries are generally high, and very experienced employees can be cost-prohibitive for SMEs to employ on a full-time basis. Cultural predispositions of investors were also an influencing factor. Investors are more likely to invest in proven concepts, not brand-new ideas that have not yet delivered proof of concept in other markets. This makes dedicating resources to provide more advanced innovation, more challenging, and riskier for smaller businesses.

Financial risk by UAE SMEs has been dictated by the meager sources available for funding and the culturally entrenched "cash-society" attitude of the UAE entrepreneurs. Their major obstacles culminate in challenges such as late payments, affecting managing cash flow, and delivering sustainable growth. Flexible and fast access to finance remains a crucial need for SMEs, be it short term finance to help cash flow or longer-term fund expansion. Liquidity has been managed through short-term finance solutions such as invoice financing and accounts receivables factoring. According to Beehive, 66% of SME respondents stated late payments as the biggest challenge for growth. Access to finance has always proved challenging, but most importantly, substantial working capital is always required to enable the business's everyday running. A creditworthy company can still struggle to plan and grow due to unpredictable cash flow effectively. Their plans include mitigating the impact of late payments, and fast and alternative finance sources continue to be required to bridge the time gap between invoice and payment. Market expansion is the main focus for SMEs; this can be more achievable with proper management of financial risks and access to funding.

OPERATIONAL RISKS

Operational risk is defined as the risk of loss resulting from inadequate or failed internal processes, people, and systems or external events.

Business/operational risk relates to activities carried out within an entity, arising from the structure, systems, people, products, or processes. CIMA Official Terminology, 2005

This definition clarifies operation key risk indicators such as legal compliance, the industry's essential equipment, employee mismatch, partnership, information technology, external events, and supply chain reliability.

Operational risks associated with business and operation risk relate to less visible aspects and are often difficult to pin down. Operational risks range from the minimal, for example, the risk of loss errors or omissions by employees, risk of bankruptcy due to fraud, product failure, health and safety, failure of IT systems, loss of key people, and loss of suppliers. Operational risk can occur at every level in an organization that must be in control through risk assessment and risk management practices, including internal control and insurance, to mitigate risk obstacles.

For example, in a project's execution stage, teams finalize the product design from a basic research and development budget. Will the production outcome be as intended? With primary research and development partnerships and outsources could it yield unreliable vendors who will affect the manufacturing stage. Therefore the evaluation of a useful product in a stable operation will provide a high-risk assessment.

Another example of using information systems is to prevent hackers from accessing customer credit card numbers that could lead to legal risk. On the other hand, the risk of having a backup plan upon accident destroys some essential equipment in the production line. During the execution, there is no substitute for risk management. Mistakes are inevitable. However, it is all about careful planning with transparent processes and procedures to minimize individual intervention due to a lack of written processes.

Gompers, Kovner, Lerner, and Scharfstein Harvard Business School, 2008 suggest in the paper of Performance Persistence entrepreneurs with a track record of success have a much higher probability of future success. Each level of risk controls and resources improves the business probability of goal attainment and progress. These controls and resources make it easier to manage risk in all business activities. Operation risk management is dealing with the risk associated with business operations, implementation of adequate controls. By providing a framework to define who is responsible during internal controls and assist in simplified risk reporting, train those in charge of using their experience to risk categories—categorization of risk help to identify related risks and recognize which risks are inter-related with its causes. Internal controllers should be trained on the use of risk reporting techniques to cause and effect or gap analysis techniques generated by the careful study of resources, processes, and technology.

Failure to identify risk followed by cause and effect analysis will mean that no action is taken to manage that risk or develop an improvement to the risk. This can be applied at different levels of the organization and can identify a large number of risks. Thus, to keep causes flowing, it is vital to identify causes of risks and not to move on to evaluate the risks that will conclude to lack of trust of the execution team and delay improvement efforts. When **time** and resources are limited, risk factors rise. Processes and procedures include highlights to such difficult to accomplish tasks that require error-free within a tight time frame and lack of support of information. Such operational risk is assessed with a high-risk stage, which requires high collaboration and communication built-in with in the process followed.

The critical success factors of implementing high-risk processes require a senior management team to support the operation team. A senior management existence should then adopt a framework for risk management that is transparent actively monitored and regularly reviewed, and fully embedded in the management process and consistently applied among communication with all staff and linked to the achievement of objectives.

Operational readiness starts with a focus on customers' added value, stakeholders, and regulators. By measuring to improve, challenge to innovate, and exceed business objectives, understanding that people will change their behavior based on unintended consequences could lead to loss of experts within the organization or lack of trust to leaders. *Human factors and behavioral* skills which impact decision making are a vital point in each process that is mapped clearly to key performance indicators. People are, at the same time, the most crucial and least predictable element of any business. Failure to recruit, motivate, and retain the right partners is risky.

As an entrepreneur or strategic leader, one of the essential responsibilities is establishing a clear vision and culture that the entire team can rally. The team needs to grow, tolerate each other, manage strong egos, mediate personality clashes and disagreements, and rein in rogue team members.

CONCLUSION

Some risk is inevitable in business. Entrepreneurs learn to accept those risks that are unavoidable and mitigate those that can be managed. The best safeguards against risk are a good core team, a business-friendly government, diversified marketing channels, and prudent financial management.

To get a business off the ground, one needs money. Whether one has savings in the bank, sells assets in preparation, takes out a loan, or acquires funding from external investors, committing these funds to a new business is a gamble. The risk is even higher if one leaves current employment to dedicate time to the new business, as this will inevitably put a pause on one's regular cash flow.

Relations between risk and performance are highly related, given the three types of risk factors identified. In examining those relations, we used measures to explain risk and performance in period two, a procedure that greater confidence that we could assign causality than we would with cross-sectional analysis. Using the risk measures developed estimated (1) the influence of risk on subsequent performance and liability of that influence across industries and performance levels influence of performance on subsequent risk and the stability across performance levels.

REFERENCES

Alexander, C. (2003). *Operational risk: regulation, analysis, and management.* Pearson Education.

Barlow & Gilbert. (Eds.). (2000). *Risk management for accountants.* London: ABG Professional Information.

Baumol, W. J. (2004). Entrepreneurial cultures and countercultures. *Academy of Management Learning & Education, 3*(3), 316–326. doi:10.5465/amle.2004.14242240

Buddelmeyer, H., Jensen, P. H., & Webster, E. (2009). *Innovation and the Determinants of Company Survival.* Oxford Economic Papers. http://oep.oxfordjournals.org/content/ early/2009/05/15/oep.gpp012

Davis, E. (2006). *The advanced measurement approach to operational risk.* Risk Books.

Davis, E. L. (2005). *Operational risk: practical approaches to implementation.* Risk Books.

DeLoach, J. (2000). *Enterprise-wide risk management: strategies for linking risk and opportunity.* Harlow: Financial Times/Prentice Hall.

Dowd, K. (1998). Beyond value at risk: the new science of risk management. Chichester: Wiley.

Enterprise risk management: an integrated framework. (2004). *Committee of Sponsoring Organisations of the Treadway Commission (COSO)*. Available from: http://digbig.com/4xeqm

Fontana, R., & Nesta, L. (2009). Product innovation and survival in a high-tech industry. *Review of Industrial Organization*, *34*(4), 287–306. doi:10.100711151-009-9210-7

Hoffman, D. (2002). *Managing operational risk: 20 firmwide best practice strategies*. John Wiley and Sons.

Kaiser, T. (2006). *An introduction to operational risk: a practitioner guide*. Risk Books.

Loader, D. (2006). *Operations risk: managing a key component of operational risk*. Elsevier.

McNeill, I. (2003). Business continuity. In A. Jolly (Ed.), *Managing Business Risk*. Kogan Page.

Montejo, M. J., & Bravo, A. (2010). *La innovación en sentido amplio: Un modelo empresarial*. Colección Innovación Práctica, Fundación Cotec.

Nash, T. (Ed.). (2003). Risk management: helping directors to identify and control business risks effectively. London: Director Publications.

Beehive Report. (2019). *State of the Nation-SMEs in MENA Report 2019*. Academic Press.

Reuvid, J. (Ed.). (2007). *Managing business risk: a practical guide to protecting your business* (4th ed.). Kogan Page.

Rodeiro Pazos, D., Calvo, N., Nogueira, M., & Fernández López, S. (2018). Firm characteristics, financial variables, and types of innovation: Influence in Spanish firms' survival. *International Journal of Entrepreneurship and Innovation Management*, *22*(1/2), 57. doi:10.1504/IJEIM.2018.10010670

Scandizzo, S. (2007). The operational risk manager's guide: how to understand methodologies, policies and procedures. London: Risk Books Summit for Financial Inclusion Experts Group.

Twiss, B. C. (1993). *Managing Technological Innovation*. Pitman Publishing.

Vargas-Hernández, J. G. (2011). Modeling Risk and Innovation Management. *Advances in Competitiveness Research, 19*(3-4), 45–57.

Vinella, P., & Jin, J. (2006). Corporate governance and operational risk: a practical guide. New York: Wiley.

Compilation of References

Abzug, R., & Webb, N. J. (1996). Rational and extra-rational motivations for corporate giving: Complementing economic theory with organization science. *New York Law School Law Review. New York Law School, 41*, 1035.

Accenture. (2005). What Makes Innovation Successful? In *Accenture Report on European Companies*. Accenture Publishing.

Acemoglu, D., Johnson, S., & Robinson, J. A. (2005). Institutions as a fundamental cause of long-run growth. In P. Aghion & S. D. Durlauf (Eds.), *Handbook of economic growth* (pp. 385–472). North-Holland.

Agarchand, N., & Laishram, B. (2017). Sustainable infrastructure development challenges through PPP procurement process: Indian perspective. *International Journal of Managing Projects in Business, 10*(3), 642–662. doi:10.1108/IJMPB-10-2016-0078

Agénor, P. R. (2017). Caught in the middle? The economics of the middle-income traps. *Journal of Economic Surveys, 31*(3), 771–791. doi:10.1111/joes.12175

Aghion, P., & Akcigit, U. (2017). Innovation and Growth. The Schumpeterian Perspective. In Economics without Borders, Economic Research for European Policy Challenges (pp. 29-72). Cambridge University Press. doi:10.1017/9781316636404.003

Aghion, P., David, P. A., & Foray, D. (2009). Science, technology and innovation for economic growth: Linking policy research and practice in 'STIG Systems'. *Research Policy, 38*(4), 681–693. doi:10.1016/j.respol.2009.01.016

Ahmad, N., Abdul Halim, H., Ramayah, T., & Rahman, S. A. (2015). Green Entrepreneurship inclination among Generation Y: The road towards a green economy. *Problems and Perspectives in Management, 13*(2).

Alexander, C. (2003). *Operational risk: regulation, analysis, and management*. Pearson Education.

Allen, M. M. C. (2009). Germany's National Innovation System. In *Encyclopaedia of Technology & Innovation* (pp. 375–389). Basil Blackwell Ltd.

Amabile, T (1998). How to kill creativity. *Harvard Business Review, 76*, 77-87.

Amado Sánchez, B., & Pico González, B. (2013). *Desarrollo de redes empresariales a través de procesos colaborativos para impulsar la innovación y lograr la satisfacción de los clientes en las SMEs manufactureras de hule y plástico de México.* Sexto Coloquio Interdisciplinario de Doctorado –Universidad Popular Autónoma del Estado de Puebla. Disponible en https://upaep.mx/micrositios/coloquios/coloquio2013/ memorias/Mesa%201%20PEyDT/Desarrollo%20de%20Redes%20Empresariales%20a%20trav%C3%A9s%20de%20procesos%20colaborativos %20para%20impulsar%20la.pdf

Amankwah-Amoah, J. (2016). The evolution of science, technology and innovation policies: A review of the Ghanaian experience. *Technological Forecasting and Social Change*, *110*, 134–142. doi:10.1016/j.techfore.2015.11.022

Aminulla, E., & Gammeltoft, P. (2006). *The Indonesian Innovation System at a Crossroads, Research papers in economics.* http://www.dieas.repec.org

Andic, S. (2016). The Composition of Growth Matters: South Korea vs. Turkey (No. 1629). Research and Monetary Policy Department, Central Bank of the Republic of Turkey.

Ang, S., & Van Dyne, L. (2009). *Handbook of Cultural Intelligence Theory, Measurement, and Applications*. Routledge.

Anokhin, S., & Schulze, W. S. (2009). Entrepreneurship, innovation, and corruption. *Journal of Business Venturing*, *24*(5), 465–476. doi:10.1016/j.jbusvent.2008.06.001

Arad, U. (2008). Intelligence Management as Risk Management. In P. Bracken, I. Bremmer, & D. Gordon (Eds.), *Managing Strategic Surprise. Lessons from Risk Management and Risk Assessment.* Cambridge University Press. doi:10.1017/CBO9780511755880.003

Arce Rodríguez, L. M. (2009). Competitividad de las SMES industriales internacionalizadas del Estado de Jalisco, México: agenda para una investigación empírica. *InterScience Place*, *2*(4).

Arellano-Rodríguez J. B., Sánchez Gutiérrez J., Mejía-Trejo J. (2018). El cliente como proveedor de innovación. un enfoque de capacidades dinámicas en PyME. *Hitos de Ciencias Económico Administrativas*, *24*(69), 476-485.

Astrum. (n.d.). *About Us*. Available at: https://www.astrum.com.mx/eng/about-us/

Atiyas, İ., & Bakis, O. (2015). Structural change and industrial policy in Turkey. *Emerging Markets Finance & Trade*, *51*(6), 1209–1229. doi:10.1080/1540496X.2015.1080523

Aubert, J. E. (2004). *Promoting innovation in developing countries: a conceptual framework.* The World Bank.

Baird, R., Bowles, L., & Lall, S. (2013). *Bridging the pioneer gap: The role for accelerators in launching high-impact enterprises. Innovations, 8(3/4).*

Barlow & Gilbert. (Eds.). (2000). *Risk management for accountants*. London: ABG Professional Information.

Barro, R. J. (2013). Inflation and Economic Growth. *Annals of Economics and Finance. Society for AEF*, *14*(1), 121–144.

Basulto Castillo, A. & Medina Ortega, J. (2006). Innovación tecnológica en la red de proveedores de la industria electrónica de Jalisco. *Carta Económica Regional*, *18*(95).

Bauer, J., & Gruber, H. (2007). Workplace Changes and Workplace Learning: Advantages of an Educational Micro Perspective. *International Journal of Lifelong Education*, *26*(6), 675–688. doi:10.1080/02601370701711364

Baumol, W. J. (2004). Entrepreneurial cultures and countercultures. *Academy of Management Learning & Education*, *3*(3), 316–326. doi:10.5465/amle.2004.14242240

Beehive Report. (2019). *State of the Nation-SMEs in MENA Report 2019*. Academic Press.

Bergmann. (2005). Jesu Ein and Alles. *Brandeius, 9*, 94-99.

Berle, G. (1991). The Green Entrepreneur: Business Opportunities that can Save the Earth and Make You Money. *Journal of Business Venturing*, *32*(5), 461–475.

Besley, T., & Ghatak, M. (2005). Incentives, Risk and Accountability in Organizations. In B. Hutter & M. Power (Eds.), *Organizational Encounters with Risk*. Cambridge University Press. doi:10.1017/CBO9780511488580.006

Betz, F., Carayannis, E., Jetter, A., Min, W., Phillips, F., & Shin, D. W. (2016). Modeling an innovation intermediary system within a helix. *Journal of the Knowledge Economy*, *7*(2), 587–599. doi:10.100713132-014-0230-7

Bhattacharya, A., & Pangestu, M. (1993). *The Lessons of East Asia. Indonesian Development, Transformation and Public Policy*. The World Bank.

Bierly, P. E., & Daly, P. S. (2007). Alternative knowledge strategies, competitive environment, and organizational performance in small manufacturing firms. *Entrepreneurship Theory and Practice*, *31*(4), 493–516. doi:10.1111/j.1540-6520.2007.00185.x

Blind, K. (2012). The influence of regulations on innovation: A quantitative assessment for OECD countries. *Research Policy*, *41*(2), 391–400. doi:10.1016/j.respol.2011.08.008

Bloom, N., Van Reenen, J., & Williams, H. (2019). A toolkit of policies to promote innovation. *The Journal of Economic Perspectives*, *33*(3), 163–184. doi:10.1257/jep.33.3.163

Booz Allen Hamilton. (2005). *How Companies Turn Customer's Big Ideas into Innovation*. Strategy & Business. http/:www.strategy-business.com/sbkw article/sbkw050112/pg=3&id=230(status.06.12.2005

Bowen, G. A. (2009). Document analysis as a qualitative research method. *Qualitative Research Journal*, *9*(2), 27–40. doi:10.3316/QRJ0902027

Brands, R. F. (2015). *The Key to Successful Innovation is Proper Implementation*. The Chief Executive. http://www.chiefeexcutive.net

Breen. (2004). *The 6 Myths of Creativity*. Fast Company. https://www.fastcompany.com/magazine/89/creativity.html

Broeders, H., & Khanna, S. (2015). *Strategic choices for banks in the digital age*. McKinsey & Company.

Buddelmeyer, H., Jensen, P. H., & Webster, E. (2009). *Innovation and the Determinants of Company Survival*. Oxford Economic Papers. http://oep.oxfordjournals.org/content/ early/2009/05/15/oep.gpp012

Burgelman, R. A., & Sayles, L. R. (1988). *Inside corporate innovation*. Simon and Schuster.

Burkus, D. (2013, July 23). *Innovation Isn't an Idea Problem*. Retrieved June 04, 2020, from Harvard Business Review: https://hbr.org/2013/07/innovation-isnt-an-idea-proble

Burns, T., & Stalker, G.M. (1061). *The management of Innovation*. Tavistock.

Butler, B. S., & Gray, P. H. (2006). Reliability, Mindfulness, and Information Systems. *Management Information Systems Quarterly*, *30*(2), 211–224. doi:10.2307/25148728

Bylund, P., & McCaffrey, M. (2017). A theory of entrepreneurship and institutional uncertainty. *Journal of Business Venturing*, *32*(5), 461–475. doi:10.1016/j.jbusvent.2017.05.006

Cabezas, H., & Diwekar, U. (2012). Sustainability: Multi-disciplinary perspectives. Sharjah, UAE: Bentham Science Publishers Ltd. doi:10.2174/97816080510381120101

Calle Medrano, M. J., & Vargas Hernández, J. G. (2015). Capítulo 10: Enfoques teóricos para el análisis de la capacidad de innovación como factor que incide en la competitividad de la industria de software de Jalisco. In Gestión competitiva organizacional: un enfoque interdisciplinario. Universidad Autónoma de Querétaro.

Camacho Sotelo, C. K., Hernández Cotón, S. G., & Mayorga Salamanca, P. I. (2014) La innovación y su interrelación con la competitividad. Sector manufacturero de la zona metropolitana de Guadalajara. *Red Internacional de Investigadores en Competitividad Memoria del VIII Congreso*, *8*(1).

Cameron, K. S., & Quinn, R. E. (2006). Diagnosing and changing organizational culture: based on the competing values framework. Jossey-Bass.

Campsie, A. (2017 August 6). Indian chefs enlisted in climate change battle. *Scotland on Sunday*, 28.

Cantú, S. O. (2006). ¿Qué es la gestión de la innovación y la tecnología (GInnT)? *Journal of Technology Management & Innovation*, *1*(2), 64-82.

Cao, X., & Yuan, Z. (2019). Overview of the important science and technology policies of new China in 70 years. *Science & Technology Review*, *37*(18), 20–30.

Carbon Masters Ltd. (2011). *Carbon Masters*. Retrieved from http://www.carbonmasters.co.uk/

Carroll, A. B. (1979). A three-dimensional conceptual model of corporate performance. *Academy of Management Review*, *4*(4), 497–505. doi:10.5465/amr.1979.4498296

Cassiolato, J. E., & Vitorino, V. (Eds.). (2009). *BRICS and development alternatives: innovation systems and policies* (Vol. 1). Anthem Press.

Centre for Risk Research. (2016). *Directing Risk Management in Organizations: Guidance from the Centre for Risk Research.* Centre for Risk Research, University of Southampton.

Chakraborty, S. (2018). Carbon Masters: Fueling new possibilities. *Forbes India.* Retrieved from http://www.forbesindia.com/article/social-impact-special-2017/carbon-masters-fuelling new-possibilities/49105/1

Chapman, C., & Ward, S. (2002). *Managing Project Risk and Uncertainty.* John Wiley and Sons.

Cheng. (2008). The evolution of China's science and technology strategy and policy of international cooperation in the past 30 years. *Forum on Science and Technology in China*, *2008*(7), 7-11.

Cheng, H., & Qian, F. (2013). Research on the relationship between innovation performance and the power, stability and instruments of policy—Empirical analysis based on 2000-2009 industry panel data. *Science Research Management*, *34*(10), 103–108.

Chesbrough, H., Vanhaverbeke, W., & West, J. (Eds.). (2006). Open Innovation: Researching a new Paradigm. Oxford University Press.

Chesbrough, H. W. (2006). *Open Innovation.* Harvard Business School Press.

Choi, D. Y., & Gray, E. R. (2008). Socially responsible entrepreneurs: What do they do to create and build their companies? *Business Horizons*, *51*(4), 341–352. doi:10.1016/j.bushor.2008.02.010

Chung, S. (2011). Innovation, competitiveness, and growth: Korean experiences. In J.Y. Lin & B. Pleskovic (Eds.), *Lessons from East Asia and the global financial crisis: Annual World Bank Conference on Development Economics- Global* (pp. 333-357). Washington, DC: World Bank.

Citrofrut. (2012). *Our Company.* Available at: https://www.citrofrut.com/eng/empresa.html

Clarke, C. J., & Varma, S. (1999). Strategic Risk Management: The New Competitive Edge. *Long Range Planning*, *32*(4), 414–424. doi:10.1016/S0024-6301(99)00052-7

Cohen, S. (2013). *What do accelerators do? Insights from incubators and angels. Innovations, 8(3/4).*

Coleman, J. S., Katz, E., & Menzel, H. (1966). *Medical innovation: A diffusion study.* Bobbs-Merrill Co.

Coleman, J., Katz, E., & Menzel, H. (1957). The diffusion of an innovation among physicians. *Sociometry*, *20*(4), 253–270. doi:10.2307/2785979

Collier, P. (2007). *The Bottom Billion: Why the Poorest Countries are Failing and What Can Be Done About It.* OUP.

Cooper & Kleinshmidt. (1992). Stage Gate System for New Product Success. Marketing Management, 7, 20-29.

COSO. (2017). *Enterprise Risk Management: integrating with strategy and performance*. COSO.

Costa Sperb, L. F., & Marshall, A. (2020). *The Risk Radar and the View of Risk: a Centre for Risk Research Discussion Document*. Centre for Risk Research, University of Southampton.

D'Cunha, S. D. (2017 June 21). This Start-up Is Making India's Garbage Its Business. *Forbes*. Retrieved from https://www.forbes.com/sites/suparnadutt/2017/06/21/this-startup-is- making-indias-garbage-its-business/#78beb8e55124

Dahlander, L., & Gann, D. (2010). *How Open is Innovation?* http://www.sciencedirect.com

Dash Wu, D., Chen, S. H., & Olson, D. L. (2014). Business Intelligence in Risk Management: Some Recent Progresses. *Information Sciences*, *256*, 1–7. doi:10.1016/j.ins.2013.10.008

Davis, E. (2006). *The advanced measurement approach to operational risk*. Risk Books.

Davis, E. L. (2005). *Operational risk: practical approaches to implementation*. Risk Books.

Day, J. (2016), *Overcoming 10 Barriers to Innovation*. http://www.ideascale.com

Deal, T., & Kennedy, A. (1982). *Corporate Cultures: The Rites and Rituals of Corporate Life*. Penguin Group.

Dejong. (2003). *Innovation in Service Firms explored: What, How and Why?* EIM Business Policy Research. http://www.eim.net/pdf-ez/B200205

DeLoach, J. (2000). *Enterprise-wide risk management: strategies for linking risk and opportunity*. Harlow: Financial Times/Prentice Hall.

Deloach, J. W. (2000). *Enterprise-Wide Risk Management. Strategies for Linking Risk and Opportunity*. Pearson Education.

Deloitte. (2005). *Glittering Price, How Financial Institution can drive growth through process and service innovation*. Author.

Department of Drinking Water & Sanitation. (2020, June 9). *Swachh Bharat Mission – Gramin*. Retrieved from https://swachhbharatmission.gov.in/sbmcms/index.htm

Desjardins, J. (2018, February 15). *The Future of Automotive Innovation*. Retrieved June 04, 2020, from Visual capitalist: https://www.visualcapitalist.com/future-automobile-innovation/

Devadula, S., Gurumoorthy, B., & Chakrabarti, A. (2015). Design for sustainability: Case of designing an urban household organic waste management system. *Current Science*, *109*(9), 1622–1629.

Dewangan, D. K., Agarwal, R., & Sharma, V. (2015). Enablers for Competitiveness of Indian Manufacturing Sector: An ISM-Fuzzy MICMAC Analysis. *Procedia: Social and Behavioral Sciences*, *189*, 416–432. doi:10.1016/j.sbspro.2015.03.200

Dirk, D., Leva, R., & Barnhorn, R. (2017). Open Innovation Generates Great Ideas, So Why aren't Companies adopting them? *Harvard Business Review*. http://hbr.org.org

Dodgson, M. (2000a). Innovation policies in East Asia. *Science, technology and innovation Policy: Opportunities and Challenges for the Knowledge Economy*, (8), 399.

Dodgson, M. (2000b). Policies for science, technology and innovation in Asian newly industrializing economies. *Technology, learning, and innovation: Experiences of newly industrializing economies*, 229-268.

Dorobantu, S., Kaul, A., & Zelner, B. (2017). Nonmarket strategy research through the lens of new institutional economics: An integrative review and future directions. *Strategic Management Journal, 38*(1), 114–140. doi:10.1002mj.2590

Dowd, K. (1998). Beyond value at risk: the new science of risk management. Chichester: Wiley.

Du, B., & Zhang, H. (2018). An Analysis of the Policy System for the Transformation of Scientific and Technological Achievements in China Based on the 'Three-Dimensional'. *Perspective. Science of Science and Management of S.& T., 39*(9), 36–49.

Dushnitsky, G., & Lenox, M. J. (2005). When do incumbents learn from entrepreneurial ventures? *Research Policy, 34*(5), 615–639. doi:10.1016/j.respol.2005.01.017

Dutrénit, G. (2009). *Sistemas regionales de innovación: un espacio para el desarrollo de las SMES. El caso de la industria de maquinados industriales.* MPRA_paper_31984. Munich Personal RePEc Archive.

Easterly, W., & Rebelo, S. (1993). Fiscal policy and economic growth: An empirical investigation. *Journal of Monetary Economics, 32*(3), 417–458. doi:10.1016/0304-3932(93)90025-B

Economist. (2010, Oct. 2). A Bumpier but Freer Road. *The Economist,* 58-60.

Editorial. (2019, August 17). Crisis in the Automobile Industry. *Economic and Political Weekly, 54*(33), 8.

Eichengreen, B., Park, D., & Shin, K. (2014). Growth Slowdown redux. *Japan and the World Economy, 32*, 65–84. doi:10.1016/j.japwor.2014.07.003

Eisenhardt, K. M. (1989). Making Fast Strategic Decisions in High-Velocity Environments. *Academy of Management Journal, 32*(September), 543–576.

El Economista. (2015). *Precios de Petróleo son de alto riesgo*. Goldman Sachs.

El Informador. (2017). PyMEs jaliscienses viven ocho año Las barreras regulatorias o la falta de ingresos y planeación dictaminan el fracaso de éstas. Periódico el Informador.

Elkington, J. (1998). Cannibals With Forks: The Triple Bottom Line. In 21st *Century Business*. Stony Creek, CT: New Society Publishers.

Elliott, L. (2017, August 15). IMF warns China over 'dangerous' growth in debt. *The Guardian*. Retrieved from https://www.theguardian.com/business/2017/aug/15/imf-warns-china-debt-slowdown-financialcrisis

Enterprise risk management: an integrated framework. (2004). *Committee of Sponsoring Organisations of the Treadway Commission (COSO)*. Available from: http://digbig.com/4xeqm

ENTIC. (2013). *Encuesta sobre Tecnologías de la Información y las Comunicaciones (ENTIC 2013)*. Disponible en: https://www.inegi.org.mx/programas/entic/2013/

EVPA. (2019). *Policy Brief. Incubators and Accelerators: Bridging the Gap for New Impact Ventures in Europe*. Accessed 20th March 2020 at https://evpa.eu.com/knowledge-centre/publications/incubators-and-accelerators-bridging-the-gap-for-new-impact-ventures-in-europe

Eyring, M. (2011, January 11). *Learning from Tata's Nano Mistakes*. https://hbr.org/2011/01/learning-from-tatas-nano-mista?registration=success

Fan, B., Duan, Z., & Jiang, L. (2012). Literature Review on Innovation Policy. *China Soft Science*, *26*(11), 43–47.

Farinelli, F., Bottini, M., Akkoyunlu, S., & Aerno, P. (2011). Green Entrepreneurship: The Missing Link Towards a Greener Economy. *ATDF Journal, 8*(3/4).

Figueroa, G. M. (2015). El proceso de gestión de Innovación Tecnológica: sus etapas e indicadores relacionados. *Revista Venezolana de Análisis de Coyuntura, 21*(1), 59-90.

Flanagan, K., & Uyarra, E. (2016). Four dangers in innovation policy studies–and how to avoid them. *Industry and Innovation*, *23*(2), 177–188. doi:10.1080/13662716.2016.1146126

Fontana, R., & Nesta, L. (2009). Product innovation and survival in a high-tech industry. *Review of Industrial Organization*, *34*(4), 287–306. doi:10.100711151-009-9210-7

Foster, C., & Heeks, R. (2013). Innovation and scaling of ICT for the bottom-of-the-pyramid. *Journal of Information Technology*, *28*(4), 296–315. doi:10.1057/jit.2013.19

Freeman, C., & Soete, L. (1982). *The Economics of Industrial Innovation*. Routledge.

Freeman, C., & Soete, L. (2009). Developing science, technology and innovation indicators: What we can learn from the past. *Research Policy*, *38*(4), 583–589. doi:10.1016/j.respol.2009.01.018

Freeman, C., & Soete, L. (Eds.). (1987). *Technical Change and Full Employment*. Basil Blackwell.

French, S., Maule, A. J., & Mythen, G. (2005). Soft Modelling in Risk Communication and Management: Examples in Handling Food Risk. *The Journal of the Operational Research Society*, *53*(8), 879–888. doi:10.1057/palgrave.jors.2601901

Galindo Martín, M. A., Ribeiro, D., & Méndez Picazo, M. T. (2012). Innovación y crecimiento económico: Factores que estimulan la innovación. Cuadernos de Gestión, 12, 51-58.

Gartner, W. B. (1990). What Are We Talking About When We Talk About Entrepreneurship? *Journal of Business Venturing*, *5*(1), 15–28. doi:10.1016/0883-9026(90)90023-M

Gautier, A., & Pache, A.-C. (2015). Research on corporate philanthropy: A review and assessment. *Journal of Business Ethics*, *126*(3), 343–369. doi:10.100710551-013-1969-7

Gerhard, D., Brem, A., & Voigt, K.-I. (2008). Product development in the automotive industry: Crucial success drivers for technological innovations. *International Journal of Technology Marketing*, *2*(2), 203–222. doi:10.1504/IJTMKT.2008.019922

Gerpott. (1999). *Strategie-Technologie-und Innovation Management*. Auflage.

Gigerenzer, G., & Edwards, A. (2003). Simple Tools for Understanding Risks: From Innumeracy to Insight. *British Medical Journal*, *327*(7417), 741–744. doi:10.1136/bmj.327.7417.741 PMID:14512488

Giles, J., & Middleton, T. (1999). *Studying Culture*. Blackwell.

GIPA. (2019). *Understanding Indonesia's Innovation system*. GIPA.

Global Green Growth Institute. (2015). *Green Growth and Sustainable Development in India: Towards the 2030 Development Agenda*. Retrieved from https://www.teriin.org/projects/green/pdf/National_SPM.pdf

Global Innovation Index. (2007-2018). Retrieved April 4,2019 from https://www.globalinnovationindex.org/Home

Govindarajan, V., & Ramamurti, R. (2011). Reverse innovation, emerging markets, and global strategy. *Global Strategy Journal*, *1*(3-4), 191–205. doi:10.1002/gsj.23

Grossman, G. M., & Helpman, E. (1991). *Innovation and Growth in the Global Economy*. MIT press.

Guerrero, L. A., Maas, G., & Hogland, W. (2013). Solid waste management challenges for cities in developing countries. *Waste Management (New York, N.Y.)*, *33*(1), 220–232. doi:10.1016/j.wasman.2012.09.008 PMID:23098815

Gupta, M. (2017). *How to Overcome Barriers to Innovation in Your Organization*. Customer Think. http://www.customerthink.com

Gupta, A. (1994). *Indian Entrepreneurial Culture: Its Many Paradoxes*. Wishwa Prakshan.

Gupta, S., Mohan, K., Prasad, R., Gupta, S., & Kansal, A. (1998). Solid waste management in India: Options and opportunities. *Resources, Conservation and Recycling*, *24*(2), 137–154. doi:10.1016/S0921-3449(98)00033-0

Hackett, S., & Dilts, D. M. (2004). A systematic review of business incubation research. *The Journal of Technology Transfer*, *29*(1), 55–82. doi:10.1023/B:JOTT.0000011181.11952.0f

Hadjimanolis, A., & Dickson, K. (2001). Development of national innovation policy in small developing countries: The case of Cyprus. *Research Policy*, *30*(5), 805–817. doi:10.1016/S0048-7333(00)00123-2

Haldar, S. (2019). Green entrepreneurship in the renewable energy sector – a case study of Gujarat. *Journal of Science and Technology Policy Management*, *10*(1), 234–250. doi:10.1108/JSTPM-12-2017-0070

Hall, B. H., & Lerner, J. (2010). *Handbook of the Economics of Innovation*. North-Holland.

Hall, E. M. (1998). *Managing Risk. Methods for Software Systems Development*. Addison-Wesley.

Hardford, T. (2011). *Adapt: Why success always starts with failure*. Macmillan.

Harris-Jones, J., & Bergin, L. (1998). *The Management of Corporate Risk-a Framework for Directors*. The Association of Corporate Treasurers.

Hartono, A. (2017). What Hampers Innovation of Indonesian Manufacturing Firms? Insight from the Indonesian Innovation Survey, In *CIE 2017-Proceedings of the 5th International Conference on Innovation and Entrepreneurship* (p. 33). Academic Conferences and Publishing Ltd.

Hendrickson, L., & Tuttle, D. B. (1997). Dynamic management of the environmental enterprise: A qualitative analysis. *Journal of Organizational Change Management*, *10*(4), 363–382. doi:10.1108/09534819710175875

Hernández, L. M. (2009). Una revisión de la interpretación económica sobre la innovación. *Journal of Technology Management & Innovation*, *4*(4), 139-149.

Heuer, J. R. J. Jr. (2005). Limits of Intelligence Analysis. *Orbis*, *49*(1), 75–94. doi:10.1016/j.orbis.2004.10.007

Hippel, E. V. (2005). The Sources of Innovation. Oxford University Press.

Hoffman, D. (2002). *Managing operational risk: 20 firmwide best practice strategies*. John Wiley and Sons.

Hopkin, P. (2010). *Fundamentals of Risk Management. Understanding, Evaluating and Implementing Effective Risk Management*. Kogan Page.

Hu, C. (2009). Review of the development of China's Science and Technology Policy since the Reform and Opening Up. *Productivity Research*, *2009*(12), 5-8.

Huang, C., Zhao, P., & Li, J. (2015). Research on China's Science and Technology Policy Changes based on Co-word Cluster Analysis. *Chinese Public Administration*, *363*(9), 115–122.

Hutton, J. (2018). *Corruption 101: An Insider's guide to graft in Indonesia*. http://www.international.the news.com

IEA. (2020). India 2020. *IEA*. Retrieved from https://www.iea.org/reports/india-2020

IFC Advisory Services. (2011). *Access To Credit Among Micro, Small, And Medium Enterprises*. http://www.ifc.org/wps/ wcm/connect/1f2c968041689903950bb79e78015671/AccessCreditMSME-Brochure-Final.pdf?MOD=AJPERES

IIEG. (2018). *Empresas por actividad y entidad federativa*. Instituto de Información, Estadística y Geografía. Gobierno del Estado de Jalisco. Guadalajara.

Imhausen. (2005). *Haus-Peta-Herausfor derung und Zeid*. PFIF 2005. http://www.pfif.de/herausfordeng.html

ISO. (2009). International Organization for Standardization., ISO 31000.

Jain, A. K. (2019, August 20). Demand for transportation is falling first. *The Business Line*, p. 7.

Jardine, C.G., & Hurdey, S.E. (1997). Mixed Messages in Risk Communication. *Risk Analysis: An International Journal*, *17*(4), 489-498.

Jenks, C. (2005). *Culture* (2nd ed.). Routledge.

Jensen, M. C., & Meckling, W. H. (1976). Theory of the firm: Managerial behavior, agency costs and ownership structure. *Journal of Financial Economics*, *3*(4), 305–360. doi:10.1016/0304-405X(76)90026-X

Johansen, W., Aggerholm, H. K., & Frandsen, F. (2012). Entering New Territory: A Study of Internal Crisis Management and Crisis Communication in Organizations. *Public Relations Review*, *38*(2), 270–279. doi:10.1016/j.pubrev.2011.11.008

John, R. (2015). *Asia's impact angels: How business angel investing can support social enterprises in Asia*. Entrepreneurial social finance in Asia: Working paper no. 4. Singapore: Asia Centre for Social Entrepreneurship & Philanthropy, NUS Business School.

John, R., Chia, A., & Ito, K. (2017). *Corporate Philanthropy in Asia*. Entrepreneurial social finance in Asia: Working paper no. 5. Singapore: Asia Centre for Social Entrepreneurship & Philanthropy, NUS Business School.

Jung, J. (2019). The Fourth Industrial Revolution, Knowledge Production and Higher Education in South Korea. *Journal of Higher Education Policy and Management*, *42*(2), 134–156. doi:10.1080/1360080X.2019.1660047

Kaiser, T. (2006). *An introduction to operational risk: a practitioner guide*. Risk Books.

Karslberg, R., & Adler, J. (2005). *Strategies for Sustained Innovation*. http://www.innovationtools.com/Articles/EnterpriseDetails.asap?a=185

Kearney, A. T. (2005). *European Best innovators, in: The New frontiers*. http://www.atkearney.com/shared.pdf/European-Bestinnovator.pdf

Keller, C., Siegrist, M., & Gutscher, H. (2006). The Role of the Affect and Availability Heuristics in Risk Communication. *Risk Analysis: An International Journal, 26*(3), 631-639.

Kohli, R. (2019, August 20). What to do about the slowdown? *The Financial Express*, p. 8.

KPMg. (2018). *Annual Banking Industry Satisfaction Survey*. Accessible on: https://home.kpmg/ng/en/home/insights/2018/07/KPMG%E2%80%99s-Annual-Banking-Industry-Customer-Satisfaction-Survey.html

Kramer, E., & Maharajh, R. (2010). *Innovation Strategies in Developing Countries*. https://www.resarchgate.net/publications/1231182504

Kripalani, J. (2019, August 15). Auto stocks lose favor among FIIs, fund houses. *The Business Standard*, p. 9.

Kumar, R. (2019 May 9). Waste controlling in India – Is it really happening? *Business Today India*. Retrieved from https://www.businesstoday.in/opinion/columns/waste- controlling-india-waste-management-plastic-recycling/story/344945

Kuper, A., & Kuper, J. (2007). Culture. In *The Social Science Encyclopedia* (2nd ed., pp. 683–691). Routledge.

Kurtz, J. (2003). "Business Wargaming": Simulations Guide Crucial Strategy Decisions. *Strategy and Leadership*, *31*(6), 12–21. doi:10.1108/10878570310505550

Lakitan, B. (2013). *Connecting all the dots: Identifying the "actor level" Challenges in establishing effective Innovation System in Indonesia*. Science Direct. http://www.elservier.com/locate/techsoc35

Lall, S., & Pietrobelli, C. (2005). National technology systems in sub-Saharan Africa. *International Journal of Technology and Globalisation*, *1*(3/4), 311. doi:10.1504/IJTG.2005.008746

Lam, I. (2013). *Social Enterprise: Mission Analysis and Practice of Value Creation*. Dissertation of Doctor of Business Administration, United Business Institute (UBI), Belgium.

Lane, P. R., & Milesi-Ferretti, G. M. (2018). The external wealth of nations revisited: International financial integration in the aftermath of the global financial crisis. *IMF Economic Review*, *66*(1), 189–222. doi:10.105741308-017-0048-y

Langer, E. J., & Moldoveanu, M. (2000). The Construct of Mindfulness. *The Journal of Social Issues*, *56*(1), 1–9. doi:10.1111/0022-4537.00148

Laranja, M., Uyarra, E., & Flanagan, K. (2008). Policies for science, technology and innovation: Translating rationales into regional policies in a multi-level setting. *Research Policy*, *37*(5), 823–835. doi:10.1016/j.respol.2008.03.006

Laursen, K., & Salter, A. (2006). Open for Innovation: The role of Openness in Explaining Innovation Performances among UK Manufacturing Firms. *Strategic Management Journal*, *27*(2), pp131–pp150. doi:10.1002mj.507

Lemola, T. (2002). Convergence of national science and technology policies: The case of Finland. *Research Policy*, *31*(8-9), 1481–1490. doi:10.1016/S0048-7333(02)00077-X

Lin, J., Wan, G., & Morgan, P. J. (2016). Prospects for a re-acceleration of economic growth in the PRC. *Journal of Comparative Economics*, *44*(4), 842–853. doi:10.1016/j.jce.2016.08.006

LIPI. (2010). *Current Conditions, Research and Development of State University survey R and D of Higher Education Sector in 2010.* http://www.Pappiptek.lipi.go.id/id/node/48

Lipkus, I. M., & Hollands, J. G. (1999). The Visual Communication of Risk. *Journal of the National Cancer Institute. Monographs*, *1999*(25), 149–163. doi:10.1093/oxfordjournals.jncimonographs.a024191 PMID:10854471

List, F. (1841). *The National System of Political Economy*. Routledge.

Liu, L. (2008). Four milestones of China's science and technology policy since the reform and opening up. *Forum on Science and Technology in China*, *2008*(10), 3-5.

Liu, F., & Sun, Y. (2007). The Course of, Trend in and Proposal for Evolution from S&T Policies to Innovation Policies—Based on the Empirical Analysis of China's 289 Innovation Policy Documents. *China Soft Science*, *2007*(5), 34–42.

Liu, X., & Liu, J. (2011). *Science and technology and innovation policy in China*. Anthem Press.

Liu, Y. (2013). Sustainable competitive advantage in turbulent business environments. *International Journal of Production Research*, *51*(10), 2821–2841. doi:10.1080/00207543.2012.720392

Liu, Y. (2014). The evolution of technology policy in Britain, France and Germany and their inspiration to our count. *Scientific Management Research*, *32*(4), 113–116.

Liu, Y., Fu, Z., & Liu, Z. (2012). Evolution of Technology Policy in the United States, Japan, Korea and their Inspiration to our Count. *Science and Technology Management Research*, *2013*(2), 31–35.

Loader, D. (2006). *Operations risk: managing a key component of operational risk*. Elsevier.

London, T., & Hart, S. (2010). *Next Generation Business Strategies for the Base of the Pyramid: New Approaches for Building Mutual Value* (1st ed.). FT Press.

Lu, L., & Etzkowitz, H. (2008). Strategic challenges for creating knowledge-based innovation in China. *Journal of Technology management in China*.

Lundvall, B. Å., & Borrás, S. (2005). Science, technology and innovation policy. The Oxford handbook of innovation, 599-631.

Lundvall, B. A. (2016). *The Learning Economy and the Economics of Hope*. Anthem Press. doi:10.26530/OAPEN_626406

Lundvall, B. A. (Ed.). (1992). *National Systems of Innovation: Towards a Theory of Innovation and Interactive learning*. Anthem Press.

Luter, R. R. (1998). Desarrollo regional e innovación y desarrollo tecnológico. In Investigación y vinculación tecnológica: un enfoque regional (pp. 139-162). Culiacán Rosales, Sinaloa: BUAP, UAS.

Luthria, M. (2002). Supporting technology generation and diffusion at the firm level. *Building Competitive Firms*, 98.

Mahendra, S., & Goyel, A. (2019, August 21). GDP measurement and the slowdown. *The Business Standard*, p. 9.

Majumder, A. (2019, August 22). Maruti seeks better terms of lending for dealers. *The Business Standard*, p. 3.

Malar, D. A., Arvidsson, V., & Holmstrom, J. (2019). Digital transformation in banking: Exploring value co-creation in online banking services in India. *Journal of Global Information Technology Management*, *22*(1), 7–24. doi:10.1080/1097198X.2019.1567216

Marshall, A. (2017). *Risk Intelligence: a Centre for Risk Research Discussion Document. Centre for Risk Research*. University of Southampton.

Marshall, A., & Ceylan, S. (2020). *Risk Intelligence Production on Complex Projects: practical discussion points. Centre for Risk Research*. University of Southampton.

Marsick, V. J., & Watkins, K. E. (2003). Demonstrating the Value of an Organization's Learning Culture: The Dimensions of the Learning Organization Questionnaire. *Sage (Atlanta, Ga.)*, *5*(2), 132–151. doi:10.1177/1523422303005002002

Martin, M. (2014). *Driving innovation through corporate impact venturing: A primer on business transformation*. Impact Economy Primer Series, Vol. 3. The Italian language version can be downloaded for free at https://www.impacteconomy.com/en/primer3.php

Martin, B. R. (2012). The evolution of science policy and innovation studies. *Research Policy*, *41*(7), 1219–1239. doi:10.1016/j.respol.2012.03.012

Mathieu, M. P. H., Pani, M. M., Chen, S., & Maino, M. R. (2019). *Drivers of Cross-Border Banking in Sub-Saharan Africa*. International Monetary Fund. doi:10.5089/9781498321549.001

Maule, A. J. (2008). Risk Communication in Organizations. In G. P. Hodgkinson & W. H. Starbuck (Eds.), *The Oxford Handbook of Organizational Decision Making*. Oxford University Press.

McKinsey. (2017). *Digital Banking in the Gulf. McKinsey Special Report*. UAE.

McNeill, I. (2003). Business continuity. In A. Jolly (Ed.), *Managing Business Risk*. Kogan Page.

Mehrotra, S. (2010). India and the global economic crisis. *Journal of Asian Public Policy*, *3*(2), 122–134. doi:10.1080/17516234.2010.504326

Mehrotra, S., & Delamonica, E. (2007). *Eliminating human poverty. Macro-economic and social policies for equitable growth*. Zed Press.

Mejía-Trejo, J., Sanchez-Gutiérrez, J., & Haro-Beas, J. F. (2014). Customer Knowledge to Improve the Innovation: The Relationship in México. In *The 13th International conference of the Society for Global Business & Economic development. Managing the "Intangibles": Business and Entrepreneurship Perspectives in a Global Context*. Universitá Politecnica delle Marche.

Menna, A., Walsh, P. R., & Ekhtari, H. (2019). Identifying enablers of innovation in developed economies: A National Innovation Systems approach. *Journal of Innovation Management*, *7*(1), 108–128. doi:10.24840/2183-0606_007.001_0007

Menzies, G., Simpson, T., Hay, D., & Vines, D. (2019). Restoring Trust in Finance: From Principal–Agent to Principled Agent. *The Economic Record*, *95*(311), 497–509. doi:10.1111/1475-4932.12494

Metalsa. (2019). *Identity.* Available at: https://www.metalsa.com/about-metalsa

Miglani, S. (2019). The Growth of the Indian Automobile Industry: Analysis of the Roles of Government Policy and Other Enabling Factors. In Innovation, Economic Development, and Intellectual Property in India and China. Springer.

Millar, C. C., Choi, C. J., & Chu, R. T. (2005). The state in science, technology and innovation districts: Conceptual models for China. *Technology Analysis and Strategic Management*, *17*(3), 367–373. doi:10.1080/09537320500211722

Miller, K. D., & Waller, H. G. (2003). Scenarios, Real Options and Integrated Risk Management. *Long Range Planning*, *36*(1), 93–107. doi:10.1016/S0024-6301(02)00205-4

Monitor Deloitte. (2015). *Accelerating impact: Exploring best practices, challenges and innovations in impact enterprise acceleration.* New York, NY: Rockefeller Foundation. Retrieved September 21, 2016, from https://www.rockefellerfoundation.org/report/accelerating-impact-exploring-best-practices-challenges-and-innovations-in-impact-enterprise-acceleration/

Montejo, M. J., & Bravo, A. (2010). *La innovación en sentido amplio: Un modelo empresarial.* Colección Innovación Práctica, Fundación Cotec.

Morlacchi, P., & Martin, B. R. (2009). *Emerging challenges for science, technology and innovation policy research: a reflexive overview.* Academic Press.

Moyano Martínez, M. G. (2016). *La cultura organizacional: factor promotor de la innovación para el crecimiento e internacionalización de las SMEs de la salud ubicadas en Guadalajara, Jalisco, México.* Ponencia. XVIII Congreso de AECA. Disponible en http://www.aeca1.org/pub/on_line/comunicaciones_xviiicongresoaeca/cd/30c.pdf

Myro, R. (2010). Economic Growth And Innovation: A Short Note About The Empirical Evidence. Revista Galega de Economía, 19.

Narasimhan, T. E. (2019, August 8). Carmakers drive market disruption for growth. *The Business Standard*, p. 8.

Nash, T. (Ed.). (2003). Risk management: helping directors to identify and control business risks effectively. London: Director Publications.

Nawaz, S. (2015). Growth effects of institutions: A disaggregated analysis. *Economic Modelling*, *45*(1), 118–126. doi:10.1016/j.econmod.2014.11.017

Ndubisi, N., & Nair, S. (2009). Green entrepreneurship (GE) and Green Value Added (GVA): A conceptual framework. *International Journal of Entrepreneurship*, *13*, 21–34.

Nesta. (2019). *Understanding Policymakers in Indonesia*. http:/www.nesta.org.uk

Nhargava, Y. (2019, August 18). Why is the auto industry facing trouble? *The Hindu*, p. 2.

Norman, W., & MacDonald, C. (2004). Getting to the bottom of "Triple Bottom Line.". *Business Ethics Quarterly*, *14*(2), 243–262. doi:10.5840/beq200414211

OCDE. (2013). *Indicadores de Ciencia, Tecnología e Industria de la OCDE 2013*. OCDE.

OECD & Eurostat. (2005). Oslo Manual: Guidelines for Collecting & Interpreting Innovation data (3rd Ed). Paris: Author.

OECD. (1997). *National Innovation Systems*. Retrieved March 20,2019 from https://www.oecd.org/science/inno/2101733.pdf

OECD. (2014). *Industry and Technology Policies in Korea*. Retrieved from https://read.oecd-ilibrary.org/industry-and-services/industry-and-technology-policies-in-korea_9789264213227-en#page1

OECD. (2016). Indonesia. In *SMEs, Entrepreneurship and Innovation*. OECD Publishing.

Oguzturk, S. (2017). The Role of Innovation in Growth Process of South Korea: An Econometric Analysis. *Suleyman Demirel University The Journal of Faculty of Economics and Administrative Sciences*, *22*(4), 1203–1222.

Okamoto, Y., & Sjoholm, F. (2001). *Technological Development in Indonesia*. ELJS. (Working paper no: 124)

Okumu, I. M., Bbaale, E., & Guloba, M. M. (2019). Innovation and employment growth: Evidence from manufacturing firms in Africa. *Journal of Innovation and Entrepreneurship*, *8*(7), 1–27. doi:10.118613731-019-0102-2

Oliver, J. J. (2019). *Culture also eats innovation for breakfast!* Strategic Direction. doi:10.1108/SD-07-2019-0135

Onsel Ekici, S., Kabak, O., & Ulengin, F. (2019). Improving logistics performance by reforming the pillars of Global Competitiveness Index. *Transport Policy*, *81*, 197–207. doi:10.1016/j.tranpol.2019.06.014

Oriesek, D., & Schwarz, J. O. (2016). *Business Wargaming: Securing Corporate Value*. Available at: https://www.taylorfrancis.com/books/9781315570648

Ortiz-Cantú, S. J., & Pedroza-Zapata, Á. R. (2013). Innovación para el desarrollo económico de Jalsico. In M. T. Ballesca-Ramírez (Ed.), *Desarrollo económico de Jalisco: retrospectiva y retos* (pp. 295–318). Secretaría de Promoción Económica, Gobierno del Estado de Jalisco.

Ott, J. S. (1989). *The Organizational Culture Perspective*. Brooks/Cole Publishing Company.

Oura, H. (2007). *Wild or tamed? India's potential growth.* IMF Working Paper WP/07/224.

Padilla-Pérez, R., & Gaudin, Y. (2014). Science, technology and innovation policies in small and developing economies: The case of Central America. *Research Policy, 43*(4), 749–759. doi:10.1016/j.respol.2013.10.011

Palepu, K. G., Bullock, R. J., & Khanna, T. (2001). *Winning in Emerging Markets: A Road Map for Strategy and Execution.* Harvard Business Press.

Panda, S. (2019, August 4). Auto slowdown hits insurers. *The Business Standard*, p. 3.

Pangestu, M., & Hrianto, F. (1999). *Corporate Governance in Indonesia. Prognosis and Way Ahead.* Submitted for International Conference on Democracy, Market Economy and Development, Feb 1999, Soeul, South Korea.

Patrinos, H. A., & Sosale, S. (Eds.). (2007). *Mobilizing the private sector for public education. A view from the trenches.* World Bank. doi:10.1596/978-0-8213-7199-2

Paz Gómez, E. (2020). Estudio Sectorial y Regional de las Empresas Medianas en el Estado de Jalisco. Táctica informática. Guadalajara, Jalisco.

Pedroza-Zapata, A. R., & Ortiz-Cantú, S. J. (2015) Estructura, gobernanza, actores, programas y desempeño del sistema nacional y regional de innovación: avances del caso México-Jalisco. *XVI Congreso Latino-Iberoamericano de Gestión de la Tecnología*, Porto Alegre, Brasil.

Pelz, D. C., & Andrews, F. M. (1966). *Scientists in organizations: Productive climates for research and development.* Academic Press.

Pence, I., Kalkan, A., & Cesmeli, M. S. (2019). Estimation of the Country Ranking Scores on the Global Innovation Index 2016 Using the Artificial Neural Network Method. *International Journal of Innovation and Technology Management, 16*(4), 1940007. doi:10.1142/S0219877019400078

Peng, J., Sun, W., & Zhong, W. (2008). The evolution of Chinese technological and innovational policies and the empirical research on the performance (1978 -2006). *Science Research Management, 29*(4), 134–150.

Pike, R. (2010). Scenario-Building Techniques for Improved Risk Management. In J. Reuvid (Ed.), *Managing Business Risk. A Practical Guide to Protecting Your Business.* Kogan Page.

Pisano, G. P. (2015). You Need an Innovation Strategy. *Harvard Business Review.* http://www.hbr.org

Poddar, T., & Yi, E. (2007). *India's rising growth potential.* Goldman Sachs Global Economics Paper No. 152. https.gs.com

Porter, M. (1996). *America's green strategy. In Business and the Environment.* Earthscan.

Powers. (2004). *What Innovation Can't Do.* Business 2.0. http://www.business2.com/b2/web articles/0.17863,68312300.html

Prahalad, C. K. (2004). *The Fortune at the Bottom of the Pyramid: Eradicating Poverty Through Profits*. Wharton School Publishing.

Prahalad, C. K., & Bettis, R. A. (1995). The Dominant Logic: A New Linkage Between Diversity and Performance. *Strategic Management Journal*, *16*, 5–14.

Prahalad, C. K., & Hammond, A. (2002). Serving the World's Poor, profitably. *Harvard Business Review*, (September), 4–11. PMID:12227146

Prahalad, C. K., & Mashelkar, R. A. (2010). Innovation's Holy Grail. *Harvard Business Review*, (July-August), 1–10.

Pritchett, L. (2000). Understanding patterns of economic growth: Searching for hills among plateaus, mountains and plains. *The World Bank Economic Review*, *14*(2), 221–250. doi:10.1093/wber/14.2.221

Proeza. (n.d.). *Areya*. Available at: http://www.proeza.com.mx/en/areya/

PTI. (2019 August 23). India to achieve most of COP21 climate change goals in next 1.5 years: Modi. *The Economic Times of India*. Retrieved from https://economictimes.indiatimes.com/news/politics-and-nation/india-to-achieve-most-of- cop-21-climate-change-goals-in-next-1-5-years- modi/articleshow/70809788.cms?from=mdr

PTI. (2020, January 6). *Tata Nano ends 2019 with zero production; sales of 1 unit*. https://timesofindia.indiatimes.com/business/india-business/tata-nano-ends-2019-with-zero-production-sales-of-1-unit/articleshow/73119753.cms

PWC. (2018). *Assessing current market conditions and business growth prospects PWC Surveys*. Accessible on https://www.pwc.com/ng/en/events/nigeria-sme-survey.html

RAE. (2016). Recuperado el 11 de 01 de 2016, dehttp://lema.rae.es/drae/srv/search?id=wCP3BlIJRDXX2uYFygrz

Rakas, M., & Hain, D. S. (2019). The state of innovation system research: What happens beneath the surface? *Research Policy*, *48*(9), 103787. doi:10.1016/j.respol.2019.04.011

Ram Mohan, T. T. (2019, August 23). Fix credit growth to fix the slowdown. *The Business Standard*, p. 9.

Ramírez Lira, E., Rivera Espinoza, M. P., Azpeitia Torres, E., Amezcua Luján, M. K., & Barajas Pérez, J. S. (2018). Análisis del diagnóstico e intervención organizacional en MIPYMO's del Sur de Jalisco: Una revisión desde el desarrollo organizacional. *Revista Global de Negocios*, *6*(4), 51–65.

Ramírez Ruiz, A. J. (2013). Capacidades del capital humano para la innovación tecnológica en pequeñas empresas de Jalisco, México. *Econ: teor. Práct*, *38*, 83-110.

Ranjan, R., Jain, R., & Dhal, S. C. (2007). India's potential economic growth, measurement issues and policy implications. *Economic and Political Weekly*, *28*(April).

Raposo, J. (1970, Jan. 20). Bein' Green. [Recorded by Jim Henson as Kermit the Frog]. On Sesame Street [television]. Los Angeles, US: Jonico Music Inc.

Rattani, V., Venkatesh, S., Pandey, K., Kukreti, I., Somvanshi, A., & Sangomla, A. (2018 October 18). India's National Action Plan on Climate Change needs desperate repair. *DownToEarth*. Retrieved from https://www.downtoearth.org.in/news/climate- change/india-s-national-action-plan-on-climate-change-needs-desperate-repair-61884

Ravichandran, R. (2019, July 27). 3-wheeler sales dip 11.64% in first quarter. *The Financial Express*, p. 7.

Reason, J. (1997). *Managing the Risks of Organizational Accidents*. Ashgate Publishing Limited.

Rehn, D., & Simon, D. F. (1988). *Technological Innovation in China: The Case of the Shanghai Semiconductor Industry*. Ballinger.

Renooija, S., & Witteman, C. (1999). Talking Probabilities: Communicating Probabilistic Information with Words and Numbers. *International Journal of Approximate Reasoning*, *22*(3), 169–194. doi:10.1016/S0888-613X(99)00027-4

Republic of Turkey Ministry of Industry and Trade. (2010). *Turkish industrial strategy document (towards EU membership) 2011-2014*. Retrieved from https://www.sanayi.gov.tr/Files/Documents/TurkiyeSanayiStratejisiIngilizce.pdf

Reuvid, J. (Ed.). (2007). *Managing business risk: a practical guide to protecting your business* (4th ed.). Kogan Page.

Revathy, L. N. (2020 January 30). Renewable energy start-up Carbon Masters receives second round of funding. *The Hindu*. Retrieved from https://www.thehindubusinessline.com/companies/renewable-energy-start-up-carbon masters-receives-second-round-of-funding/article30685467.ece#

Riederer. (2005). *Innovation Management- An Overview and some Best Practices* (Report volume 4, No 3). Paderborn University.

Robles Estrada, C. (2009). Competitividad de las SMEs industriales internacionalizadas del estado de Jalisco: agenda para una investigación empírica. *Red Internacional de Investigadores en Competitividad Memoria del III Congreso, 3*(1).

Rodeiro Pazos, D., Calvo, N., Nogueira, M., & Fernández López, S. (2018). Firm characteristics, financial variables, and types of innovation: Influence in Spanish firms' survival. *International Journal of Entrepreneurship and Innovation Management*, *22*(1/2), 57. doi:10.1504/IJEIM.2018.10010670

Romo, P. (2019). Pymes de Jalisco aceleran adopción de soluciones tecnológicas A través de Innovation Tour, la firma alemana SAP muestra a empresas jaliscienses beneficios de herramientas tecnológicas. El Economista.

Romo, P. (2020). *Jalisco destinará 1,000 mdp para apoyar mipymes y autoempleados. La entidad descarta adquirir deuda de largo plazo* [Popup plan Jalisco will allocate 1,000 mp to support MSMEs and the self-employed The entity rules out acquiring long-term debt]. El Economista, Estados.

Rothwell, R. (1992). Industrial innovation and government environmental regulation: Some lessons from the past. *Technovation*, *12*(7), 447–458. doi:10.1016/0166-4972(92)90050-R

Roy, R. (2019, August 9). Structural slowdown and home market demand. *The Business Standard*, p. 11.

Roy, S. (2018, July 17). *Tata Nano – Why Did the People Not Want the People's Car?* Retrieved June 04, 2020, from The Wire: https://thewire.in/business/tata-nano-why-did-the-people-not-want-the-peoples-car

Ruff, P., & Aziz, K. (2003). *Managing Communications in a Crisis*. Gower Publishing Limited.

Salazar, M., & Holbrook, A. (2007). Canadian science, technology and innovation policy: The product of regional networking? *Regional Studies*, *41*(8), 1129–1141. doi:10.1080/00343400701530865

Salter. (2005). *Whirlpool finds its Cool*. Fast Company. http://www.fast company.com/magazine/95/open-design-Jones-html

Sánchez, A. M. (2016). *Universidad del Cauca*. Obtenido de http://www.unicauca.edu.co/porik_an/imagenes_3noanteriores/No.9porikan/porikan_7.pdf

Scandizzo, S. (2007). The operational risk manager's guide: how to understand methodologies, policies and procedures. London: Risk Books Summit for Financial Inclusion Experts Group.

Schein, E. H., & Schein, P. (2017). *Organizational Culture and Leadership* (5th ed.). John Wiley and Sons.

Schmookler, J. (1966). *Invention and Economic Growth*. Harvard University Press. http://www.philpapers.org

Schumpeter, J. (1912). Theorie der Wirtschaftlichen Ent Wickhng. Academic Press.

Schumpeter, J.A. (1934). The theory of economic development: an inquiry into profits, capital, credit, interest and the business cycle. *Harvard Economic Studies, 46*.

Schumpeter, J. (1947). The Creative Response in Economic History. *The Journal of Economic History*, *7*(2), 149–159. doi:10.1017/S0022050700054279

Seeger, M. W. (2006). Best Practices in Crisis Communication: An Expert Panel Process. *Journal of Applied Communication Research*, *34*(3), 232–244. doi:10.1080/00909880600769944

Sen, P. (2019, August 10). Rural investment best way to revive economy. *The Business Standard*, p. 6.

Shapiro, M. A., So, M., & Woo Park, H. (2010). Quantifying the national innovation system: Inter-regional collaboration networks in South Korea. *Technology Analysis and Strategic Management*, *22*(7), 845–857. doi:10.1080/09537325.2010.511158

Shaw, S., Elston, J., & Abbott, S. (2004). Comparative analysis of health policy implementation: The use of documentary analysis. *Policy Studies*, *25*(4), 259–266. doi:10.1080/0144287042000288451

Sherman. (2005). *The Innovative Organization; Lessons from Most Admired Companies*. Hay Insight Selection. http://www.haygroup.com/mediafiles/downloads/Hay_Insight_selection_April_2005

Shin, J., & Park, Y. (2007). Building the national ICT frontier: The case of Korea. *Information Economics and Policy*, *19*(2), 249–277. doi:10.1016/j.infoecopol.2007.01.003

Shleifer, A., & Vishny, R. W. (1993). Corruption. *The Quarterly Journal of Economics*, *108*(3), 599–617. doi:10.2307/2118402

Silverthorne, S. (2011). The Untold Story of 'Green' Entrepreneurs. *HBS Working Knowledge*. Retrieved from https://hbswk.hbs.edu/item/6561.html

Singh, R. K., Luthra, S., Mangla, S. K., & Uniyal, S. (2019). Applications of information and communication technology for sustainable growth of SMEs in India food industry. *Resources, Conservation and Recycling*, *147*, 10–18. doi:10.1016/j.resconrec.2019.04.014

Sloane, P. (2020). *Recessions, Innovation and Survival- A Lesson from Kellogg's*. http//www.innovationmanagement.se

Slocum, J. W. J., & Hellriegel, D. (2009). *Principles of Organizational Behavior* (12th ed.). South-Western Cengage Learning.

Soekarno. (2009). Technology transfer Challenges in Indonesia; An experience from Industry Turbine Overhaul. *Asian Journal of Technology Management*, *2*(1), 2009.

Soenarso, W. S., & Saderno, H. (2014). *A Strategy to Increase Indonesian Private R and D Investment*. Asia Pacific Tech Monitor.

Soesastro, H., & Pengestu, M. (1988). Indonesia's Electronic Industry. In The Effects of Liberalization in Asia's Textiles, Clothings and Electronics Industries. Australian Pacific economic Cooperation Committee.

Soleas, E. K. (2020). Leader strategies for motivating innovation in individuals: A systematic review. *Journal of Innovation and Entrepreneurship*, *9*(9), 1–28. doi:10.118613731-020-00120-w PMID:32685342

Solow, R. M. (1956). A contribution to the theory of economic growth. *The Quarterly Journal of Economics*, *70*(1), 65–94. doi:10.2307/1884513

Sun, Y., & Du, D. (2010). Determinants of industrial innovation in China: Evidence from its recent economic census. *Technovation*, *30*(9-10), 540–550. doi:10.1016/j.technovation.2010.05.003

Swink, M. (2006). Building collaborative innovation capability. *Research Technology Management*, *49*(2), 37–47. doi:10.1080/08956308.2006.11657367

Temple, J. (1999). A positive effect of human capital on growth. *Economics Letters*, *65*(1), 131–134. doi:10.1016/S0165-1765(99)00120-2

The World Bank. (2018a). *GDP (current US $) of Korea and Turkey: 1980-2017*. Retrieved from https://data.worldbank.org/indicator/NY.GDP.MKTP.CD?end=2017&locations=KR-TR&start=1980&view=chart

The World Bank. (2018b). *High-tech export % of manufactured good of South Korea and Turkey: 1980-2017*. Retrieved from https://data.worldbank.org/indicator/TX.VAL.TECH.MF.ZS?locations=KR-TR&view=chart

The World Bank. (2018c). *Researchers in R&D per million people of South Korea and Turkey: 1980-2017*. Retrieved from https://data.worldbank.org/indicator/SP.POP.SCIE.RD.P6?end=2018&locations=KR-TR&start=1980

The World Bank. (2018d). *Patent applications, residents of South Korea and Turkey: 1980-2017*. Retrieved from https://data.worldbank.org/indicator/IP.PAT.RESD?end=2016&locations=KR-TR&start=1980&view=chart

The World Bank. (2018e). *Patent applications, nonresidents of South Korea and Turkey: 1980-2017*. Retrieved from https://data.worldbank.org/indicator/IP.PAT.NRES?end=2016&locations=KR-TR&start=1980&view=chart

The World Bank. (2018f). *Government expenditure on education (%GDP) of South Korea and Turkey: 1980-2017*. Retrieved from https://data.worldbank.org/indicator/SE.XPD.TOTL.GD.ZS?end=2018&locations=KR-TR&start=1980

The World Bank. (2018g). *Scientific and technical journal articles (thousand) of South Korea and Turkey: 1980-2017*. Retrieved from https://data.worldbank.org/indicator/IP.JRN.ARTC.SC?locations=KR-TR&view=chart

Theil, M. (2002). The Role of Translations of Verbal into Numerical Probability Expressions in Risk Management: A Meta-Analysis. *Journal of Risk Research*, *5*(2), 177–186. doi:10.1080/13669870110038179

Thompson, K.M. (2002). Variability and Uncertainty Meet Risk Management and Risk Communication. *Risk Analysis: An International Journal, 22*(3), 647-654.

Tomizawa, A., Zhao, L., Bassellier, G., & Ahlstrom, D. (2020). Economic growth, innovation, institutions, and the Great Enrichment. *Asia Pacific Journal of Management*, *37*(1), 7–31. doi:10.100710490-019-09648-2

Tressel, T., & Scarpetta, S. (2004). *Boosting productivity via innovation and adoption of new technologies: any role for labor market institutions?* Retrieved from https://documents.worldbank.org/curated/en/101151468762892644/Boosting-productivity-via-innovation-and-adoption-of-new-technologies-any-role-for-labor-market-institutions

Turpin, T., & Liu, X. (2000). Balanced Development: The Challenge for Science, Technology and Innovation Policy. In Contemporary Developments and Issues in China's Economic Transition (pp. 191-211). Palgrave Macmillan.

Turrell, M., & Lindow, Y. (2003). *The innovation Pipeline*. Imginatik Research White paper.

Twiss, B. C. (1993). *Managing Technological Innovation*. Pitman Publishing.

UNDP. (2018a). *Mean years of schooling*. Retrieved from http://hdr.undp.org/en/data

UNDP. (2018b). *Expected years of schooling*. Retrieced from http://hdr.undp.org/en/data

UNRISD. (2012). United Nations Research Institute for Social Development. In Social Dimensions of Green Economy. UNRISD.

Uzo, U., & Mair, J. (2014). Source and patterns of organizational defiance of formal institutions: Insights from Nollywood, the Nigerian movie industry. *Strategic Entrepreneurship Journal*, *8*(1), 56–74. doi:10.1002ej.1171

Vahs, D., & Burmester, R. (2005). *Vahs, Dietmari; Burmester, Ralf: Innovation Management,Auflage, Scahaeffer*. Poeschel.

Valery. (1999). Innovation in Industry: Industry Gets Religion. *Economist*, *350*(8107).

Van Geenhuizen, M., & Indarti, N. (2005). Knowledge as a Critical Resource in Innovation among Small Furniture Companies in Indonesia. *Gadjah Mada International Journal of Business*, *7*(3), 371–390. doi:10.22146/gamaijb.5581

Vargas-Hernández, J. G. (2011). Modeling Risk and Innovation Management. *Advances in Competitiveness Research*, *19*(3-4), 45–57.

Vázquez Ávila, G., Núñez Moreno, T. E., Sánchez Gutiérrez, J., & Mejía Trejo, J. (2015). Gestión de conocimiento e innovación impulsores de la competitividad en las SMEs manufactureras de Guadalajara. In Sustentabilidad e innovación como detonantes de la competitividad. Universidad de Guadalajara.

Vázquez Ávila, G., Sánchez Gutiérrez, J., & Núñez Moreno, T. M. (2017). *Innovación en las operaciones con énfasis en la ergonomía para fomentar la competitividad en las SMES*. Memoria del XI Congreso de la Red Internacional de Investigadores en Competitividad.

Verworn. (2000). *Innovation Management in Kleinen und Mittleren*. Academic Press.

Viki, T. (2017). Why Companies must align Innovation Strategy with Business Strategy. *Innovation as a Corporate Mission/Business Goals*. http://www.forbes.com

Vinella, P., & Jin, J. (2006). Corporate governance and operational risk: a practical guide. New York: Wiley.

Vitta, P. B. (1990). Technology policy in sub-Saharan Africa: Why the dream remains unfulfilled. *World Development*, *18*(11), 1471–1480. doi:10.1016/0305-750X(90)90037-X

Volans. (2014). *Investing in breakthrough: Corporate venture capital.* Retrieved March 7, 2016, from http://volans.com/project/investing-in-breakthrough-corporate-venture-capital/

Vyas, M. (2019, July 30). Worry about informal employment. *The Business Standard*, p. 8.

Wadhwa, P., & Koorgaonkar, D. (2019, July 20). Auto indices hit 3-year low. *The Business Standard*, p. 10.

Walker, J. L. (1969). The diffusion of innovations among the American states. *The American Political Science Review*, *63*(3), 880–899. doi:10.1017/S0003055400258644

Wamae, W. (2009). Enhancing the role of knowledge and innovation for Development. *International Journal of Technology Management & Sustainable Development*, *8*(3), 199–228. doi:10.1386/ijtm.8.3.199/1

Waring, A., & Glendon, I. A. (1998). *Managing Risk.* Thomson Learning.

Webb, H., & Liu, S. (2020). The Sustainable Falcon: Dubai's Path to Becoming a Green Economic Leader. In H. C. Webb & H. A. Al Numairy (Eds.), *Entrepreneurial Innovation and Economic Development in Dubai and Comparisons to Its Sister Cities* (pp. 1–16). IGI Global. doi:10.4018/978-1-5225-9377-5.ch001

Weick, K. E., & Sutclliffe, K. M. (2001). *Managing the Unexpected.* Jossey-Bass.

Wilson, S., Maharaj, C. S., & Maharaj, R. (2020). Formalising the National Innovation System in a Developing Country. *The West Indian Journal of Engineering*, *42*(2), 4–16.

Woodward, J. (1958). *Management and technology* (No. 3). HM Stationery Off.

World Economic Forum. (2018). *Global Competitiveness Report.* Retrieved March 20,2019 from https://www.weforum.org/reports/the-global-competitveness-report-2018

Wright, M. (2001). Creating and growing wealth: Sue Birley on entrepreneurship and wealth creation. *The Academy of Management Executive*, *15*(1).

Yilmaz, G., & Saracoglu, D. S. (2016). Technological change, human capital, and absorptive capacity: Can Turkey escape the Middle Income Trap? *ODTÜ Gelisme Dergisi*, *43*(1), 391–424.

Yose Damuri, R., Aswicahyona, H., & Christian, D. (2018). *Innovation Policy in Indonesia.* Innovation Policy in ASEAN. http://www.sematic.sch

Zhang, J., Huang, C., Ye, X., Shi, K., & Su, J. (2016). Study on China's Public Policy Diffusion Based on the Quantitative Analysis of Policy Documents: A Case Study on Policies Promoting Commercialization of Scientific and Technological Achievements. *China Soft Science*, *2016*(2), 145–155.

Zhang, Y. (2019). Evolution of China's Science and Technology Policy since the Reform and Opening Up. *Forum on Science and Technology in China*, *2019*(4), 1–7.

Zhang, Y., & Chen, R. (2012). The Convergence Trend of Science and Technology Policy in Technological Power and Its Countermeasure. *Science & Technology Progress and Policy*, *30*(2), 108–111.

Zhu, P. (2020). Five Innovation Practices for Building and Managing all Innovation Program. *Collaborative Innovation- Leadership, Organization Culture, Strategies, Support for SMEs*. http://www.innovationmanagement.se

Zimmermann, V. (2020). Innovation and Investment Finance in Comparison. In *Contemporary Developments in Entrepreneurial Finance* (pp. 59–79). Springer. doi:10.1007/978-3-030-17612-9_3

Zyman, S., & Brott, A. (2004). *Renovate Before You Innovate: Why doing New Thing Might Not be the Right thing*. Penguin Group USA.

Related References

To continue our tradition of advancing information science and technology research, we have compiled a list of recommended IGI Global readings. These references will provide additional information and guidance to further enrich your knowledge and assist you with your own research and future publications.

Abtahi, M. S., Behboudi, L., & Hasanabad, H. M. (2017). Factors Affecting Internet Advertising Adoption in Ad Agencies. *International Journal of Innovation in the Digital Economy*, *8*(4), 18–29. doi:10.4018/IJIDE.2017100102

Agrawal, S. (2017). The Impact of Emerging Technologies and Social Media on Different Business(es): Marketing and Management. In O. Rishi & A. Sharma (Eds.), *Maximizing Business Performance and Efficiency Through Intelligent Systems* (pp. 37–49). Hershey, PA: IGI Global. doi:10.4018/978-1-5225-2234-8.ch002

Alnoukari, M., Razouk, R., & Hanano, A. (2016). BSC-SI: A Framework for Integrating Strategic Intelligence in Corporate Strategic Management. *International Journal of Social and Organizational Dynamics in IT*, *5*(2), 1–14. doi:10.4018/IJSODIT.2016070101

Alnoukari, M., Razouk, R., & Hanano, A. (2016). BSC-SI, A Framework for Integrating Strategic Intelligence in Corporate Strategic Management. *International Journal of Strategic Information Technology and Applications*, *7*(1), 32–44. doi:10.4018/IJSITA.2016010103

Altındağ, E. (2016). Current Approaches in Change Management. In A. Goksoy (Ed.), *Organizational Change Management Strategies in Modern Business* (pp. 24–51). Hershey, PA: IGI Global. doi:10.4018/978-1-4666-9533-7.ch002

Alvarez-Dionisi, L. E., Turner, R., & Mittra, M. (2016). Global Project Management Trends. *International Journal of Information Technology Project Management, 7*(3), 54–73. doi:10.4018/IJITPM.2016070104

Anantharaman, R. N., Rajeswari, K. S., Angusamy, A., & Kuppusamy, J. (2017). Role of Self-Efficacy and Collective Efficacy as Moderators of Occupational Stress Among Software Development Professionals. *International Journal of Human Capital and Information Technology Professionals, 8*(2), 45–58. doi:10.4018/IJHCITP.2017040103

Aninze, F., El-Gohary, H., & Hussain, J. (2018). The Role of Microfinance to Empower Women: The Case of Developing Countries. *International Journal of Customer Relationship Marketing and Management, 9*(1), 54–78. doi:10.4018/IJCRMM.2018010104

Arsenijević, O. M., Orčić, D., & Kastratović, E. (2017). Development of an Optimization Tool for Intangibles in SMEs: A Case Study from Serbia with a Pilot Research in the Prestige by Milka Company. In M. Vemić (Ed.), *Optimal Management Strategies in Small and Medium Enterprises* (pp. 320–347). Hershey, PA: IGI Global. doi:10.4018/978-1-5225-1949-2.ch015

Aryanto, V. D., Wismantoro, Y., & Widyatmoko, K. (2018). Implementing Eco-Innovation by Utilizing the Internet to Enhance Firm's Marketing Performance: Study of Green Batik Small and Medium Enterprises in Indonesia. *International Journal of E-Business Research, 14*(1), 21–36. doi:10.4018/IJEBR.2018010102

Atiku, S. O., & Fields, Z. (2017). Multicultural Orientations for 21st Century Global Leadership. In N. Baporikar (Ed.), *Management Education for Global Leadership* (pp. 28–51). Hershey, PA: IGI Global. doi:10.4018/978-1-5225-1013-0.ch002

Atiku, S. O., & Fields, Z. (2018). Organisational Learning Dimensions and Talent Retention Strategies for the Service Industries. In N. Baporikar (Ed.), *Global Practices in Knowledge Management for Societal and Organizational Development* (pp. 358–381). Hershey, PA: IGI Global. doi:10.4018/978-1-5225-3009-1.ch017

Ávila, L., & Teixeira, L. (2018). The Main Concepts Behind the Dematerialization of Business Processes. In M. Khosrow-Pour, D.B.A. (Ed.), Encyclopedia of Information Science and Technology, Fourth Edition (pp. 888-898). Hershey, PA: IGI Global. doi:10.4018/978-1-5225-2255-3.ch076

Bartens, Y., Chunpir, H. I., Schulte, F., & Voß, S. (2017). Business/IT Alignment in Two-Sided Markets: A COBIT 5 Analysis for Media Streaming Business Models. In S. De Haes & W. Van Grembergen (Eds.), *Strategic IT Governance and Alignment in Business Settings* (pp. 82–111). Hershey, PA: IGI Global. doi:10.4018/978-1-5225-0861-8.ch004

Bashayreh, A. M. (2018). Organizational Culture and Organizational Performance. In W. Lee & F. Sabetzadeh (Eds.), *Contemporary Knowledge and Systems Science* (pp. 50–69). Hershey, PA: IGI Global. doi:10.4018/978-1-5225-5655-8.ch003

Bedford, D. A. (2018). Sustainable Knowledge Management Strategies: Aligning Business Capabilities and Knowledge Management Goals. In N. Baporikar (Ed.), *Global Practices in Knowledge Management for Societal and Organizational Development* (pp. 46–73). Hershey, PA: IGI Global. doi:10.4018/978-1-5225-3009-1.ch003

Benmoussa, F., Nakara, W. A., & Jaouen, A. (2016). The Use of Social Media by SMEs in the Tourism Industry. In I. Lee (Ed.), *Encyclopedia of E-Commerce Development, Implementation, and Management* (pp. 2159–2170). Hershey, PA: IGI Global. doi:10.4018/978-1-4666-9787-4.ch155

Berger, R. (2016). Indigenous Management and Bottom of Pyramid Countries: The Role of National Institutions. In U. Aung & P. Ordoñez de Pablos (Eds.), *Managerial Strategies and Practice in the Asian Business Sector* (pp. 107–123). Hershey, PA: IGI Global. doi:10.4018/978-1-4666-9758-4.ch007

Bharwani, S., & Musunuri, D. (2018). Reflection as a Process From Theory to Practice. In M. Khosrow-Pour, D.B.A. (Ed.), Encyclopedia of Information Science and Technology, Fourth Edition (pp. 1529-1539). Hershey, PA: IGI Global. doi:10.4018/978-1-5225-2255-3.ch132

Bhatt, G. D., Wang, Z., & Rodger, J. A. (2017). Information Systems Capabilities and Their Effects on Competitive Advantages: A Study of Chinese Companies. *Information Resources Management Journal*, *30*(3), 41–57. doi:10.4018/IRMJ.2017070103

Bhushan, M., & Yadav, A. (2017). Concept of Cloud Computing in ESB. In R. Bhadoria, N. Chaudhari, G. Tomar, & S. Singh (Eds.), *Exploring Enterprise Service Bus in the Service-Oriented Architecture Paradigm* (pp. 116–127). Hershey, PA: IGI Global. doi:10.4018/978-1-5225-2157-0.ch008

Bhushan, S. (2017). System Dynamics Base-Model of Humanitarian Supply Chain (HSCM) in Disaster Prone Eco-Communities of India: A Discussion on Simulation and Scenario Results. *International Journal of System Dynamics Applications*, *6*(3), 20–37. doi:10.4018/IJSDA.2017070102

Biswas, A., & De, A. K. (2017). On Development of a Fuzzy Stochastic Programming Model with Its Application to Business Management. In S. Trivedi, S. Dey, A. Kumar, & T. Panda (Eds.), *Handbook of Research on Advanced Data Mining Techniques and Applications for Business Intelligence* (pp. 353–378). Hershey, PA: IGI Global. doi:10.4018/978-1-5225-2031-3.ch021

Bücker, J., & Ernste, K. (2018). Use of Brand Heroes in Strategic Reputation Management: The Case of Bacardi, Adidas, and Daimler. In A. Erdemir (Ed.), *Reputation Management Techniques in Public Relations* (pp. 126–150). Hershey, PA: IGI Global. doi:10.4018/978-1-5225-3619-2.ch007

Bureš, V. (2018). Industry 4.0 From the Systems Engineering Perspective: Alternative Holistic Framework Development. In R. Brunet-Thornton & F. Martinez (Eds.), *Analyzing the Impacts of Industry 4.0 in Modern Business Environments* (pp. 199–223). Hershey, PA: IGI Global. doi:10.4018/978-1-5225-3468-6.ch011

Buzady, Z. (2017). Resolving the Magic Cube of Effective Case Teaching: Benchmarking Case Teaching Practices in Emerging Markets – Insights from the Central European University Business School, Hungary. In D. Latusek (Ed.), *Case Studies as a Teaching Tool in Management Education* (pp. 79–103). Hershey, PA: IGI Global. doi:10.4018/978-1-5225-0770-3.ch005

Campatelli, G., Richter, A., & Stocker, A. (2016). Participative Knowledge Management to Empower Manufacturing Workers. *International Journal of Knowledge Management, 12*(4), 37–50. doi:10.4018/IJKM.2016100103

Căpusneanu, S., & Topor, D. I. (2018). Business Ethics and Cost Management in SMEs: Theories of Business Ethics and Cost Management Ethos. In I. Oncioiu (Ed.), *Ethics and Decision-Making for Sustainable Business Practices* (pp. 109–127). Hershey, PA: IGI Global. doi:10.4018/978-1-5225-3773-1.ch007

Carneiro, A. (2016). Maturity in Health Organization Information Systems: Metrics and Privacy Perspectives. *International Journal of Privacy and Health Information Management, 4*(2), 1–18. doi:10.4018/IJPHIM.2016070101

Chan, R. L., Mo, P. L., & Moon, K. K. (2018). Strategic and Tactical Measures in Managing Enterprise Risks: A Study of the Textile and Apparel Industry. In K. Strang, M. Korstanje, & N. Vajjhala (Eds.), *Research, Practices, and Innovations in Global Risk and Contingency Management* (pp. 1–19). Hershey, PA: IGI Global. doi:10.4018/978-1-5225-4754-9.ch001

Chandan, H. C. (2016). Motivations and Challenges of Female Entrepreneurship in Developed and Developing Economies. In N. Baporikar (Ed.), *Handbook of Research on Entrepreneurship in the Contemporary Knowledge-Based Global Economy* (pp. 260–286). Hershey, PA: IGI Global. doi:10.4018/978-1-4666-8798-1.ch012

Charlier, S. D., Burke-Smalley, L. A., & Fisher, S. L. (2018). Undergraduate Programs in the U.S: A Contextual and Content-Based Analysis. In J. Mendy (Ed.), *Teaching Human Resources and Organizational Behavior at the College Level* (pp. 26–57). Hershey, PA: IGI Global. doi:10.4018/978-1-5225-2820-3.ch002

Chaudhuri, S. (2016). Application of Web-Based Geographical Information System (GIS) in E-Business. In U. Panwar, R. Kumar, & N. Ray (Eds.), *Handbook of Research on Promotional Strategies and Consumer Influence in the Service Sector* (pp. 389–405). Hershey, PA: IGI Global. doi:10.4018/978-1-5225-0143-5.ch023

Choudhuri, P. S. (2016). An Empirical Study on the Quality of Services Offered by the Private Life Insurers in Burdwan. In U. Panwar, R. Kumar, & N. Ray (Eds.), *Handbook of Research on Promotional Strategies and Consumer Influence in the Service Sector* (pp. 31–55). Hershey, PA: IGI Global. doi:10.4018/978-1-5225-0143-5.ch002

Dahlberg, T., Kivijärvi, H., & Saarinen, T. (2017). IT Investment Consistency and Other Factors Influencing the Success of IT Performance. In S. De Haes & W. Van Grembergen (Eds.), *Strategic IT Governance and Alignment in Business Settings* (pp. 176–208). Hershey, PA: IGI Global. doi:10.4018/978-1-5225-0861-8.ch007

Damnjanović, A. M. (2017). Knowledge Management Optimization through IT and E-Business Utilization: A Qualitative Study on Serbian SMEs. In M. Vemić (Ed.), *Optimal Management Strategies in Small and Medium Enterprises* (pp. 249–267). Hershey, PA: IGI Global. doi:10.4018/978-1-5225-1949-2.ch012

Daneshpour, H. (2017). Integrating Sustainable Development into Project Portfolio Management through Application of Open Innovation. In M. Vemić (Ed.), *Optimal Management Strategies in Small and Medium Enterprises* (pp. 370–387). Hershey, PA: IGI Global. doi:10.4018/978-1-5225-1949-2.ch017

Daniel, A. D., & Reis de Castro, V. (2018). Entrepreneurship Education: How to Measure the Impact on Nascent Entrepreneurs. In A. Carrizo Moreira, J. Guilherme Leitão Dantas, & F. Manuel Valente (Eds.), *Nascent Entrepreneurship and Successful New Venture Creation* (pp. 85–110). Hershey, PA: IGI Global. doi:10.4018/978-1-5225-2936-1.ch004

David, F., van der Sijde, P., & van den Besselaar, P. (2016). Enterpreneurial Incentives, Obstacles, and Management in University-Business Co-Operation: The Case of Indonesia. In J. Saiz-Álvarez (Ed.), *Handbook of Research on Social Entrepreneurship and Solidarity Economics* (pp. 499–518). Hershey, PA: IGI Global. doi:10.4018/978-1-5225-0097-1.ch024

David, R., Swami, B. N., & Tangirala, S. (2018). Ethics Impact on Knowledge Management in Organizational Development: A Case Study. In N. Baporikar (Ed.), *Global Practices in Knowledge Management for Societal and Organizational Development* (pp. 19–45). Hershey, PA: IGI Global. doi:10.4018/978-1-5225-3009-1.ch002

Delias, P., & Lakiotaki, K. (2018). Discovering Process Horizontal Boundaries to Facilitate Process Comprehension. *International Journal of Operations Research and Information Systems*, *9*(2), 1–31. doi:10.4018/IJORIS.2018040101

Denholm, J., & Lee-Davies, L. (2018). Success Factors for Games in Business and Project Management. In *Enhancing Education and Training Initiatives Through Serious Games* (pp. 34–68). Hershey, PA: IGI Global. doi:10.4018/978-1-5225-3689-5.ch002

Deshpande, M. (2017). Best Practices in Management Institutions for Global Leadership: Policy Aspects. In N. Baporikar (Ed.), *Management Education for Global Leadership* (pp. 1–27). Hershey, PA: IGI Global. doi:10.4018/978-1-5225-1013-0.ch001

Deshpande, M. (2018). Policy Perspectives for SMEs Knowledge Management. In N. Baporikar (Ed.), *Knowledge Integration Strategies for Entrepreneurship and Sustainability* (pp. 23–46). Hershey, PA: IGI Global. doi:10.4018/978-1-5225-5115-7.ch002

Dezdar, S. (2017). ERP Implementation Projects in Asian Countries: A Comparative Study on Iran and China. *International Journal of Information Technology Project Management*, *8*(3), 52–68. doi:10.4018/IJITPM.2017070104

Domingos, D., Martinho, R., & Varajão, J. (2016). Controlled Flexibility in Healthcare Processes: A BPMN-Extension Approach. In M. Cruz-Cunha, I. Miranda, R. Martinho, & R. Rijo (Eds.), *Encyclopedia of E-Health and Telemedicine* (pp. 521–535). Hershey, PA: IGI Global. doi:10.4018/978-1-4666-9978-6.ch040

Domingos, D., Respício, A., & Martinho, R. (2017). Reliability of IoT-Aware BPMN Healthcare Processes. In C. Reis & M. Maximiano (Eds.), *Internet of Things and Advanced Application in Healthcare* (pp. 214–248). Hershey, PA: IGI Global. doi:10.4018/978-1-5225-1820-4.ch008

Dosumu, O., Hussain, J., & El-Gohary, H. (2017). An Exploratory Study of the Impact of Government Policies on the Development of Small and Medium Enterprises in Developing Countries: The Case of Nigeria. *International Journal of Customer Relationship Marketing and Management*, *8*(4), 51–62. doi:10.4018/IJCRMM.2017100104

Durst, S., Bruns, G., & Edvardsson, I. R. (2017). Retaining Knowledge in Smaller Building and Construction Firms. *International Journal of Knowledge and Systems Science*, *8*(3), 1–12. doi:10.4018/IJKSS.2017070101

Edvardsson, I. R., & Durst, S. (2017). Outsourcing, Knowledge, and Learning: A Critical Review. *International Journal of Knowledge-Based Organizations*, *7*(2), 13–26. doi:10.4018/IJKBO.2017040102

Edwards, J. S. (2018). Integrating Knowledge Management and Business Processes. In M. Khosrow-Pour, D.B.A. (Ed.), Encyclopedia of Information Science and Technology, Fourth Edition (pp. 5046-5055). Hershey, PA: IGI Global. doi:10.4018/978-1-5225-2255-3.ch437

Ejiogu, A. O. (2018). Economics of Farm Management. In *Agricultural Finance and Opportunities for Investment and Expansion* (pp. 56–72). Hershey, PA: IGI Global. doi:10.4018/978-1-5225-3059-6.ch003

Ekanem, I., & Abiade, G. E. (2018). Factors Influencing the Use of E-Commerce by Small Enterprises in Nigeria. *International Journal of ICT Research in Africa and the Middle East*, *7*(1), 37–53. doi:10.4018/IJICTRAME.2018010103

Ekanem, I., & Alrossais, L. A. (2017). Succession Challenges Facing Family Businesses in Saudi Arabia. In P. Zgheib (Ed.), *Entrepreneurship and Business Innovation in the Middle East* (pp. 122–146). Hershey, PA: IGI Global. doi:10.4018/978-1-5225-2066-5.ch007

El Faquih, L., & Fredj, M. (2017). Ontology-Based Framework for Quality in Configurable Process Models. *Journal of Electronic Commerce in Organizations*, *15*(2), 48–60. doi:10.4018/JECO.2017040104

El-Gohary, H., & El-Gohary, Z. (2016). An Attempt to Explore Electronic Marketing Adoption and Implementation Aspects in Developing Countries: The Case of Egypt. *International Journal of Customer Relationship Marketing and Management*, *7*(4), 1–26. doi:10.4018/IJCRMM.2016100101

Entico, G. J. (2016). Knowledge Management and the Medical Health Librarians: A Perception Study. In J. Yap, M. Perez, M. Ayson, & G. Entico (Eds.), *Special Library Administration, Standardization and Technological Integration* (pp. 52–77). Hershey, PA: IGI Global. doi:10.4018/978-1-4666-9542-9.ch003

Faisal, M. N., & Talib, F. (2017). Building Ambidextrous Supply Chains in SMEs: How to Tackle the Barriers? *International Journal of Information Systems and Supply Chain Management, 10*(4), 80–100. doi:10.4018/IJISSCM.2017100105

Fernandes, T. M., Gomes, J., & Romão, M. (2017). Investments in E-Government: A Benefit Management Case Study. *International Journal of Electronic Government Research, 13*(3), 1–17. doi:10.4018/IJEGR.2017070101

Fouda, F. A. (2016). A Suggested Curriculum in Career Education to Develop Business Secondary Schools Students' Career Knowledge Management Domains and Professional Thinking. *International Journal of Technology Diffusion, 7*(2), 42–62. doi:10.4018/IJTD.2016040103

Gallardo-Vázquez, D., & Pajuelo-Moreno, M. L. (2016). How Spanish Universities are Promoting Entrepreneurship through Your Own Lines of Teaching and Research? In L. Carvalho (Ed.), *Handbook of Research on Entrepreneurial Success and its Impact on Regional Development* (pp. 431–454). Hershey, PA: IGI Global. doi:10.4018/978-1-4666-9567-2.ch019

Gao, S. S., Oreal, S., & Zhang, J. (2018). Contemporary Financial Risk Management Perceptions and Practices of Small-Sized Chinese Businesses. In I. Management Association (Ed.), Global Business Expansion: Concepts, Methodologies, Tools, and Applications (pp. 917-931). Hershey, PA: IGI Global. doi:10.4018/978-1-5225-5481-3.ch041

Garg, R., & Berning, S. C. (2017). Indigenous Chinese Management Philosophies: Key Concepts and Relevance for Modern Chinese Firms. In B. Christiansen & G. Koc (Eds.), *Transcontinental Strategies for Industrial Development and Economic Growth* (pp. 43–57). Hershey, PA: IGI Global. doi:10.4018/978-1-5225-2160-0.ch003

Gencer, Y. G. (2017). Supply Chain Management in Retailing Business. In U. Akkucuk (Ed.), *Ethics and Sustainability in Global Supply Chain Management* (pp. 197–210). Hershey, PA: IGI Global. doi:10.4018/978-1-5225-2036-8.ch011

Giacosa, E. (2016). Innovation in Luxury Fashion Businesses as a Means for the Regional Development. In L. Carvalho (Ed.), *Handbook of Research on Entrepreneurial Success and its Impact on Regional Development* (pp. 206–222). Hershey, PA: IGI Global. doi:10.4018/978-1-4666-9567-2.ch010

Giacosa, E. (2018). The Increasing of the Regional Development Thanks to the Luxury Business Innovation. In L. Carvalho (Ed.), *Handbook of Research on Entrepreneurial Ecosystems and Social Dynamics in a Globalized World* (pp. 260–273). Hershey, PA: IGI Global. doi:10.4018/978-1-5225-3525-6.ch011

Gianni, M., & Gotzamani, K. (2016). Integrated Management Systems and Information Management Systems: Common Threads. In P. Papajorgji, F. Pinet, A. Guimarães, & J. Papathanasiou (Eds.), *Automated Enterprise Systems for Maximizing Business Performance* (pp. 195–214). Hershey, PA: IGI Global. doi:10.4018/978-1-4666-8841-4.ch011

Gianni, M., Gotzamani, K., & Linden, I. (2016). How a BI-wise Responsible Integrated Management System May Support Food Traceability. *International Journal of Decision Support System Technology*, *8*(2), 1–17. doi:10.4018/IJDSST.2016040101

Glykas, M., & George, J. (2017). Quality and Process Management Systems in the UAE Maritime Industry. *International Journal of Productivity Management and Assessment Technologies*, *5*(1), 20–39. doi:10.4018/IJPMAT.2017010102

Glykas, M., Valiris, G., Kokkinaki, A., & Koutsoukou, Z. (2018). Banking Business Process Management Implementation. *International Journal of Productivity Management and Assessment Technologies*, *6*(1), 50–69. doi:10.4018/IJPMAT.2018010104

Gomes, J., & Romão, M. (2017). The Balanced Scorecard: Keeping Updated and Aligned with Today's Business Trends. *International Journal of Productivity Management and Assessment Technologies*, *5*(2), 1–15. doi:10.4018/IJPMAT.2017070101

Gomes, J., & Romão, M. (2017). Aligning Information Systems and Technology with Benefit Management and Balanced Scorecard. In S. De Haes & W. Van Grembergen (Eds.), *Strategic IT Governance and Alignment in Business Settings* (pp. 112–131). Hershey, PA: IGI Global. doi:10.4018/978-1-5225-0861-8.ch005

Grefen, P., & Turetken, O. (2017). Advanced Business Process Management in Networked E-Business Scenarios. *International Journal of E-Business Research*, *13*(4), 70–104. doi:10.4018/IJEBR.2017100105

Haider, A., & Saetang, S. (2017). Strategic IT Alignment in Service Sector. In S. Rozenes & Y. Cohen (Eds.), *Handbook of Research on Strategic Alliances and Value Co-Creation in the Service Industry* (pp. 231–258). Hershey, PA: IGI Global. doi:10.4018/978-1-5225-2084-9.ch012

Haider, A., & Tang, S. S. (2016). Maximising Value Through IT and Business Alignment: A Case of IT Governance Institutionalisation at a Thai Bank. *International Journal of Technology Diffusion*, *7*(3), 33–58. doi:10.4018/IJTD.2016070104

Hajilari, A. B., Ghadaksaz, M., & Fasghandis, G. S. (2017). Assessing Organizational Readiness for Implementing ERP System Using Fuzzy Expert System Approach. *International Journal of Enterprise Information Systems*, *13*(1), 67–85. doi:10.4018/IJEIS.2017010105

Haldorai, A., Ramu, A., & Murugan, S. (2018). Social Aware Cognitive Radio Networks: Effectiveness of Social Networks as a Strategic Tool for Organizational Business Management. In H. Bansal, G. Shrivastava, G. Nguyen, & L. Stanciu (Eds.), *Social Network Analytics for Contemporary Business Organizations* (pp. 188–202). Hershey, PA: IGI Global. doi:10.4018/978-1-5225-5097-6.ch010

Hall, O. P. Jr. (2017). Social Media Driven Management Education. *International Journal of Knowledge-Based Organizations*, *7*(2), 43–59. doi:10.4018/IJKBO.2017040104

Hanifah, H., Halim, H. A., Ahmad, N. H., & Vafaei-Zadeh, A. (2017). Innovation Culture as a Mediator Between Specific Human Capital and Innovation Performance Among Bumiputera SMEs in Malaysia. In N. Ahmad, T. Ramayah, H. Halim, & S. Rahman (Eds.), *Handbook of Research on Small and Medium Enterprises in Developing Countries* (pp. 261–279). Hershey, PA: IGI Global. doi:10.4018/978-1-5225-2165-5.ch012

Hartlieb, S., & Silvius, G. (2017). Handling Uncertainty in Project Management and Business Development: Similarities and Differences. In Y. Raydugin (Ed.), *Handbook of Research on Leveraging Risk and Uncertainties for Effective Project Management* (pp. 337–362). Hershey, PA: IGI Global. doi:10.4018/978-1-5225-1790-0.ch016

Hass, K. B. (2017). Living on the Edge: Managing Project Complexity. In Y. Raydugin (Ed.), *Handbook of Research on Leveraging Risk and Uncertainties for Effective Project Management* (pp. 177–201). Hershey, PA: IGI Global. doi:10.4018/978-1-5225-1790-0.ch009

Hassan, A., & Privitera, D. S. (2016). Google AdSense as a Mobile Technology in Education. In J. Holland (Ed.), *Wearable Technology and Mobile Innovations for Next-Generation Education* (pp. 200–223). Hershey, PA: IGI Global. doi:10.4018/978-1-5225-0069-8.ch011

Hassan, A., & Rahimi, R. (2016). Consuming “Innovation” in Tourism: Augmented Reality as an Innovation Tool in Digital Tourism Marketing. In N. Pappas & I. Bregoli (Eds.), *Global Dynamics in Travel, Tourism, and Hospitality* (pp. 130–147). Hershey, PA: IGI Global. doi:10.4018/978-1-5225-0201-2.ch008

Hawking, P., & Carmine Sellitto, C. (2017). Developing an Effective Strategy for Organizational Business Intelligence. In M. Tavana (Ed.), *Enterprise Information Systems and the Digitalization of Business Functions* (pp. 222–237). Hershey, PA: IGI Global. doi:10.4018/978-1-5225-2382-6.ch010

Hawking, P., & Sellitto, C. (2017). A Fast-Moving Consumer Goods Company and Business Intelligence Strategy Development. *International Journal of Enterprise Information Systems, 13*(2), 22–33. doi:10.4018/IJEIS.2017040102

Hawking, P., & Sellitto, C. (2017). Business Intelligence Strategy: Two Case Studies. *International Journal of Business Intelligence Research, 8*(2), 17–30. doi:10.4018/IJBIR.2017070102

Haynes, J. D., Arockiasamy, S., Al Rashdi, M., & Al Rashdi, S. (2016). Business and E Business Strategies for Coopetition and Thematic Management as a Sustained Basis for Ethics and Social Responsibility in Emerging Markets. In M. Al-Shammari & H. Masri (Eds.), *Ethical and Social Perspectives on Global Business Interaction in Emerging Markets* (pp. 25–39). Hershey, PA: IGI Global. doi:10.4018/978-1-4666-9864-2.ch002

Hee, W. J., Jalleh, G., Lai, H., & Lin, C. (2017). E-Commerce and IT Projects: Evaluation and Management Issues in Australian and Taiwanese Hospitals. *International Journal of Public Health Management and Ethics, 2*(1), 69–90. doi:10.4018/IJPHME.2017010104

Hernandez, A. A. (2018). Exploring the Factors to Green IT Adoption of SMEs in the Philippines. *Journal of Cases on Information Technology, 20*(2), 49–66. doi:10.4018/JCIT.2018040104

Hernandez, A. A., & Ona, S. E. (2016). Green IT Adoption: Lessons from the Philippines Business Process Outsourcing Industry. *International Journal of Social Ecology and Sustainable Development, 7*(1), 1–34. doi:10.4018/IJSESD.2016010101

Hollman, A., Bickford, S., & Hollman, T. (2017). Cyber InSecurity: A Post-Mortem Attempt to Assess Cyber Problems from IT and Business Management Perspectives. *Journal of Cases on Information Technology, 19*(3), 42–70. doi:10.4018/JCIT.2017070104

Igbinakhase, I. (2017). Responsible and Sustainable Management Practices in Developing and Developed Business Environments. In Z. Fields (Ed.), *Collective Creativity for Responsible and Sustainable Business Practice* (pp. 180–207). Hershey, PA: IGI Global. doi:10.4018/978-1-5225-1823-5.ch010

Ilahi, L., Ghannouchi, S. A., & Martinho, R. (2016). A Business Process Management Approach to Home Healthcare Processes: On the Gap between Intention and Reality. In M. Cruz-Cunha, I. Miranda, R. Martinho, & R. Rijo (Eds.), *Encyclopedia of E-Health and Telemedicine* (pp. 439–457). Hershey, PA: IGI Global. doi:10.4018/978-1-4666-9978-6.ch035

Iwata, J. J., & Hoskins, R. G. (2017). Managing Indigenous Knowledge in Tanzania: A Business Perspective. In P. Jain & N. Mnjama (Eds.), *Managing Knowledge Resources and Records in Modern Organizations* (pp. 198–214). Hershey, PA: IGI Global. doi:10.4018/978-1-5225-1965-2.ch012

Jabeen, F., Ahmad, S. Z., & Alkaabi, S. (2016). The Internationalization Decision-Making of United Arab Emirates Family Businesses. In N. Zakaria, A. Abdul-Talib, & N. Osman (Eds.), *Handbook of Research on Impacts of International Business and Political Affairs on the Global Economy* (pp. 1–22). Hershey, PA: IGI Global. doi:10.4018/978-1-4666-9806-2.ch001

Jain, P. (2017). Ethical and Legal Issues in Knowledge Management Life-Cycle in Business. In P. Jain & N. Mnjama (Eds.), *Managing Knowledge Resources and Records in Modern Organizations* (pp. 82–101). Hershey, PA: IGI Global. doi:10.4018/978-1-5225-1965-2.ch006

Jamali, D., Abdallah, H., & Matar, F. (2016). Opportunities and Challenges for CSR Mainstreaming in Business Schools. *International Journal of Technology and Educational Marketing*, *6*(2), 1–29. doi:10.4018/IJTEM.2016070101

James, S., & Hauli, E. (2017). Holistic Management Education at Tanzanian Rural Development Planning Institute. In N. Baporikar (Ed.), *Management Education for Global Leadership* (pp. 112–136). Hershey, PA: IGI Global. doi:10.4018/978-1-5225-1013-0.ch006

Janošková, M., Csikósová, A., & Čulková, K. (2018). Measurement of Company Performance as Part of Its Strategic Management. In R. Leon (Ed.), *Managerial Strategies for Business Sustainability During Turbulent Times* (pp. 309–335). Hershey, PA: IGI Global. doi:10.4018/978-1-5225-2716-9.ch017

Jean-Vasile, A., & Alecu, A. (2017). Theoretical and Practical Approaches in Understanding the Influences of Cost-Productivity-Profit Trinomial in Contemporary Enterprises. In A. Jean Vasile & D. Nicolò (Eds.), *Sustainable Entrepreneurship and Investments in the Green Economy* (pp. 28–62). Hershey, PA: IGI Global. doi:10.4018/978-1-5225-2075-7.ch002

Jha, D. G. (2016). Preparing for Information Technology Driven Changes. In S. Tiwari & L. Nafees (Eds.), *Innovative Management Education Pedagogies for Preparing Next-Generation Leaders* (pp. 258–274). Hershey, PA: IGI Global. doi:10.4018/978-1-4666-9691-4.ch015

Joia, L. A., & Correia, J. C. (2018). CIO Competencies From the IT Professional Perspective: Insights From Brazil. *Journal of Global Information Management, 26*(2), 74–103. doi:10.4018/JGIM.2018040104

Juma, A., & Mzera, N. (2017). Knowledge Management and Records Management and Competitive Advantage in Business. In P. Jain & N. Mnjama (Eds.), *Managing Knowledge Resources and Records in Modern Organizations* (pp. 15–28). Hershey, PA: IGI Global. doi:10.4018/978-1-5225-1965-2.ch002

K., I., & A, V. (2018). Monitoring and Auditing in the Cloud. In K. Munir (Ed.), *Cloud Computing Technologies for Green Enterprises* (pp. 318-350). Hershey, PA: IGI Global. doi:10.4018/978-1-5225-3038-1.ch013

Kabra, G., Ghosh, V., & Ramesh, A. (2018). Enterprise Integrated Business Process Management and Business Intelligence Framework for Business Process Sustainability. In A. Paul, D. Bhattacharyya, & S. Anand (Eds.), *Green Initiatives for Business Sustainability and Value Creation* (pp. 228–238). Hershey, PA: IGI Global. doi:10.4018/978-1-5225-2662-9.ch010

Kaoud, M. (2017). Investigation of Customer Knowledge Management: A Case Study Research. *International Journal of Service Science, Management, Engineering, and Technology, 8*(2), 12–22. doi:10.4018/IJSSMET.2017040102

Kara, M. E., & Fırat, S. Ü. (2016). Sustainability, Risk, and Business Intelligence in Supply Chains. In M. Erdoğdu, T. Arun, & I. Ahmad (Eds.), *Handbook of Research on Green Economic Development Initiatives and Strategies* (pp. 501–538). Hershey, PA: IGI Global. doi:10.4018/978-1-5225-0440-5.ch022

Katuu, S. (2018). A Comparative Assessment of Enterprise Content Management Maturity Models. In N. Gwangwava & M. Mutingi (Eds.), *E-Manufacturing and E-Service Strategies in Contemporary Organizations* (pp. 93–118). Hershey, PA: IGI Global. doi:10.4018/978-1-5225-3628-4.ch005

Khan, M. A. (2016). MNEs Management Strategies in Developing Countries: Establishing the Context. In M. Khan (Ed.), *Multinational Enterprise Management Strategies in Developing Countries* (pp. 1–33). Hershey, PA: IGI Global. doi:10.4018/978-1-5225-0276-0.ch001

Khan, M. A. (2016). Operational Approaches in Organizational Structure: A Case for MNEs in Developing Countries. In M. Khan (Ed.), *Multinational Enterprise Management Strategies in Developing Countries* (pp. 129–151). Hershey, PA: IGI Global. doi:10.4018/978-1-5225-0276-0.ch007

Kinnunen, S., Ylä-Kujala, A., Marttonen-Arola, S., Kärri, T., & Baglee, D. (2018). Internet of Things in Asset Management: Insights from Industrial Professionals and Academia. *International Journal of Service Science, Management, Engineering, and Technology*, *9*(2), 104–119. doi:10.4018/IJSSMET.2018040105

Klein, A. Z., Sabino de Freitas, A., Machado, L., Freitas, J. C. Jr, Graziola, P. G. Jr, & Schlemmer, E. (2017). Virtual Worlds Applications for Management Education. In L. Tomei (Ed.), *Exploring the New Era of Technology-Infused Education* (pp. 279–299). Hershey, PA: IGI Global. doi:10.4018/978-1-5225-1709-2.ch017

Kożuch, B., & Jabłoński, A. (2017). Adopting the Concept of Business Models in Public Management. In M. Lewandowski & B. Kożuch (Eds.), *Public Sector Entrepreneurship and the Integration of Innovative Business Models* (pp. 10–46). Hershey, PA: IGI Global. doi:10.4018/978-1-5225-2215-7.ch002

Kumar, J., Adhikary, A., & Jha, A. (2017). Small Active Investors' Perceptions and Preferences Towards Tax Saving Mutual Fund Schemes in Eastern India: An Empirical Note. *International Journal of Asian Business and Information Management*, *8*(2), 35–45. doi:10.4018/IJABIM.2017040103

Lassoued, Y., Bouzguenda, L., & Mahmoud, T. (2016). Context-Aware Business Process Versions Management. *International Journal of e-Collaboration*, *12*(3), 7–33. doi:10.4018/IJeC.2016070102

Lavassani, K. M., & Movahedi, B. (2017). Applications Driven Information Systems: Beyond Networks toward Business Ecosystems. *International Journal of Innovation in the Digital Economy*, *8*(1), 61–75. doi:10.4018/IJIDE.2017010104

Lazzareschi, V. H., & Brito, M. S. (2017). Strategic Information Management: Proposal of Business Project Model. In G. Jamil, A. Soares, & C. Pessoa (Eds.), *Handbook of Research on Information Management for Effective Logistics and Supply Chains* (pp. 59–88). Hershey, PA: IGI Global. doi:10.4018/978-1-5225-0973-8.ch004

Lederer, M., Kurz, M., & Lazarov, P. (2017). Usage and Suitability of Methods for Strategic Business Process Initiatives: A Multi Case Study Research. *International Journal of Productivity Management and Assessment Technologies*, *5*(1), 40–51. doi:10.4018/IJPMAT.2017010103

Lee, I. (2017). A Social Enterprise Business Model and a Case Study of Pacific Community Ventures (PCV). In V. Potocan, M. Üngan, & Z. Nedelko (Eds.), *Handbook of Research on Managerial Solutions in Non-Profit Organizations* (pp. 182–204). Hershey, PA: IGI Global. doi:10.4018/978-1-5225-0731-4.ch009

Lee, L. J., & Leu, J. (2016). Exploring the Effectiveness of IT Application and Value Method in the Innovation Performance of Enterprise. *International Journal of Enterprise Information Systems*, *12*(2), 47–65. doi:10.4018/IJEIS.2016040104

Lee, Y. (2016). Alignment Effect of Entrepreneurial Orientation and Marketing Orientation on Firm Performance. *International Journal of Customer Relationship Marketing and Management*, *7*(4), 58–69. doi:10.4018/IJCRMM.2016100104

Leon, L. A., Seal, K. C., Przasnyski, Z. H., & Wiedenman, I. (2017). Skills and Competencies Required for Jobs in Business Analytics: A Content Analysis of Job Advertisements Using Text Mining. *International Journal of Business Intelligence Research*, *8*(1), 1–25. doi:10.4018/IJBIR.2017010101

Leu, J., Lee, L. J., & Krischke, A. (2016). Value Engineering-Based Method for Implementing the ISO14001 System in the Green Supply Chains. *International Journal of Strategic Decision Sciences*, *7*(4), 1–20. doi:10.4018/IJSDS.2016100101

Levy, C. L., & Elias, N. I. (2017). SOHO Users' Perceptions of Reliability and Continuity of Cloud-Based Services. In M. Moore (Ed.), *Cybersecurity Breaches and Issues Surrounding Online Threat Protection* (pp. 248–287). Hershey, PA: IGI Global. doi:10.4018/978-1-5225-1941-6.ch011

Levy, M. (2018). Change Management Serving Knowledge Management and Organizational Development: Reflections and Review. In N. Baporikar (Ed.), *Global Practices in Knowledge Management for Societal and Organizational Development* (pp. 256–270). Hershey, PA: IGI Global. doi:10.4018/978-1-5225-3009-1.ch012

Lewandowski, M. (2017). Public Organizations and Business Model Innovation: The Role of Public Service Design. In M. Lewandowski & B. Kożuch (Eds.), *Public Sector Entrepreneurship and the Integration of Innovative Business Models* (pp. 47–72). Hershey, PA: IGI Global. doi:10.4018/978-1-5225-2215-7.ch003

Lhannaoui, H., Kabbaj, M. I., & Bakkoury, Z. (2017). A Survey of Risk-Aware Business Process Modelling. *International Journal of Risk and Contingency Management*, *6*(3), 14–26. doi:10.4018/IJRCM.2017070102

Li, J., Sun, W., Jiang, W., Yang, H., & Zhang, L. (2017). How the Nature of Exogenous Shocks and Crises Impact Company Performance?: The Effects of Industry Characteristics. *International Journal of Risk and Contingency Management*, *6*(4), 40–55. doi:10.4018/IJRCM.2017100103

Lu, C., & Liu, S. (2016). Cultural Tourism O2O Business Model Innovation-A Case Study of CTrip. *Journal of Electronic Commerce in Organizations*, *14*(2), 16–31. doi:10.4018/JECO.2016040102

Machen, B., Hosseini, M. R., Wood, A., & Bakhshi, J. (2016). An Investigation into using SAP-PS as a Multidimensional Project Control System (MPCS). *International Journal of Enterprise Information Systems*, *12*(2), 66–81. doi:10.4018/IJEIS.2016040105

Malega, P. (2017). Small and Medium Enterprises in the Slovak Republic: Status and Competitiveness of SMEs in the Global Markets and Possibilities of Optimization. In M. Vemić (Ed.), *Optimal Management Strategies in Small and Medium Enterprises* (pp. 102–124). Hershey, PA: IGI Global. doi:10.4018/978-1-5225-1949-2.ch006

Malewska, K. M. (2017). Intuition in Decision-Making on the Example of a Non-Profit Organization. In V. Potocan, M. Ünğan, & Z. Nedelko (Eds.), *Handbook of Research on Managerial Solutions in Non-Profit Organizations* (pp. 378–399). Hershey, PA: IGI Global. doi:10.4018/978-1-5225-0731-4.ch018

Maroofi, F. (2017). Entrepreneurial Orientation and Organizational Learning Ability Analysis for Innovation and Firm Performance. In N. Baporikar (Ed.), *Innovation and Shifting Perspectives in Management Education* (pp. 144–165). Hershey, PA: IGI Global. doi:10.4018/978-1-5225-1019-2.ch007

Martins, P. V., & Zacarias, M. (2017). A Web-based Tool for Business Process Improvement. *International Journal of Web Portals*, *9*(2), 68–84. doi:10.4018/IJWP.2017070104

Matthies, B., & Coners, A. (2017). Exploring the Conceptual Nature of e-Business Projects. *Journal of Electronic Commerce in Organizations*, *15*(3), 33–63. doi:10.4018/JECO.2017070103

McKee, J. (2018). Architecture as a Tool to Solve Business Planning Problems. In M. Khosrow-Pour, D.B.A. (Ed.), Encyclopedia of Information Science and Technology, Fourth Edition (pp. 573-586). Hershey, PA: IGI Global. doi:10.4018/978-1-5225-2255-3.ch050

McMurray, A. J., Cross, J., & Caponecchia, C. (2018). The Risk Management Profession in Australia: Business Continuity Plan Practices. In N. Bajgoric (Ed.), *Always-On Enterprise Information Systems for Modern Organizations* (pp. 112–129). Hershey, PA: IGI Global. doi:10.4018/978-1-5225-3704-5.ch006

Meddah, I. H., & Belkadi, K. (2018). Mining Patterns Using Business Process Management. In R. Hamou (Ed.), *Handbook of Research on Biomimicry in Information Retrieval and Knowledge Management* (pp. 78–89). Hershey, PA: IGI Global. doi:10.4018/978-1-5225-3004-6.ch005

Mendes, L. (2017). TQM and Knowledge Management: An Integrated Approach Towards Tacit Knowledge Management. In D. Jaziri-Bouagina & G. Jamil (Eds.), *Handbook of Research on Tacit Knowledge Management for Organizational Success* (pp. 236–263). Hershey, PA: IGI Global. doi:10.4018/978-1-5225-2394-9.ch009

Mnjama, N. M. (2017). Preservation of Recorded Information in Public and Private Sector Organizations. In P. Jain & N. Mnjama (Eds.), *Managing Knowledge Resources and Records in Modern Organizations* (pp. 149–167). Hershey, PA: IGI Global. doi:10.4018/978-1-5225-1965-2.ch009

Mokoqama, M., & Fields, Z. (2017). Principles of Responsible Management Education (PRME): Call for Responsible Management Education. In Z. Fields (Ed.), *Collective Creativity for Responsible and Sustainable Business Practice* (pp. 229–241). Hershey, PA: IGI Global. doi:10.4018/978-1-5225-1823-5.ch012

Muniapan, B. (2017). Philosophy and Management: The Relevance of Vedanta in Management. In P. Ordóñez de Pablos (Ed.), *Managerial Strategies and Solutions for Business Success in Asia* (pp. 124–139). Hershey, PA: IGI Global. doi:10.4018/978-1-5225-1886-0.ch007

Muniapan, B., Gregory, M. L., & Ling, L. A. (2016). Marketing Education in Sarawak: Looking at It from the Employers' Viewpoint. In B. Smith & A. Porath (Eds.), *Global Perspectives on Contemporary Marketing Education* (pp. 112–130). Hershey, PA: IGI Global. doi:10.4018/978-1-4666-9784-3.ch008

Murad, S. E., & Dowaji, S. (2017). Using Value-Based Approach for Managing Cloud-Based Services. In A. Turuk, B. Sahoo, & S. Addya (Eds.), *Resource Management and Efficiency in Cloud Computing Environments* (pp. 33–60). Hershey, PA: IGI Global. doi:10.4018/978-1-5225-1721-4.ch002

Mutahar, A. M., Daud, N. M., Thurasamy, R., Isaac, O., & Abdulsalam, R. (2018). The Mediating of Perceived Usefulness and Perceived Ease of Use: The Case of Mobile Banking in Yemen. *International Journal of Technology Diffusion, 9*(2), 21–40. doi:10.4018/IJTD.2018040102

Naidoo, V. (2017). E-Learning and Management Education at African Universities. In N. Baporikar (Ed.), *Management Education for Global Leadership* (pp. 181–201). Hershey, PA: IGI Global. doi:10.4018/978-1-5225-1013-0.ch009

Naidoo, V., & Igbinakhase, I. (2018). Opportunities and Challenges of Knowledge Retention in SMEs. In N. Baporikar (Ed.), *Knowledge Integration Strategies for Entrepreneurship and Sustainability* (pp. 70–94). Hershey, PA: IGI Global. doi:10.4018/978-1-5225-5115-7.ch004

Nayak, S., & Prabhu, N. (2017). Paradigm Shift in Management Education: Need for a Cross Functional Perspective. In N. Baporikar (Ed.), *Management Education for Global Leadership* (pp. 241–255). Hershey, PA: IGI Global. doi:10.4018/978-1-5225-1013-0.ch012

Ndede-Amadi, A. A. (2016). Student Interest in the IS Specialization as Predictor of the Success Potential of New Information Systems Programmes within the Schools of Business in Kenyan Public Universities. *International Journal of Information Systems and Social Change, 7*(2), 63–79. doi:10.4018/IJISSC.2016040104

Nedelko, Z., & Potocan, V. (2016). Management Practices for Processes Optimization: Case of Slovenia. In G. Alor-Hernández, C. Sánchez-Ramírez, & J. García-Alcaraz (Eds.), *Handbook of Research on Managerial Strategies for Achieving Optimal Performance in Industrial Processes* (pp. 545–561). Hershey, PA: IGI Global. doi:10.4018/978-1-5225-0130-5.ch025

Nedelko, Z., & Potocan, V. (2017). Management Solutions in Non-Profit Organizations: Case of Slovenia. In V. Potocan, M. Üngan, & Z. Nedelko (Eds.), *Handbook of Research on Managerial Solutions in Non-Profit Organizations* (pp. 1–22). Hershey, PA: IGI Global. doi:10.4018/978-1-5225-0731-4.ch001

Nedelko, Z., & Potocan, V. (2017). Priority of Management Tools Utilization among Managers: International Comparison. In V. Wang (Ed.), *Encyclopedia of Strategic Leadership and Management* (pp. 1083–1094). Hershey, PA: IGI Global. doi:10.4018/978-1-5225-1049-9.ch075

Nedelko, Z., Raudeliūnienė, J., & Črešnar, R. (2018). Knowledge Dynamics in Supply Chain Management. In N. Baporikar (Ed.), *Knowledge Integration Strategies for Entrepreneurship and Sustainability* (pp. 150–166). Hershey, PA: IGI Global. doi:10.4018/978-1-5225-5115-7.ch008

Nguyen, H. T., & Hipsher, S. A. (2018). Innovation and Creativity Used by Private Sector Firms in a Resources-Constrained Environment. In S. Hipsher (Ed.), *Examining the Private Sector's Role in Wealth Creation and Poverty Reduction* (pp. 219–238). Hershey, PA: IGI Global. doi:10.4018/978-1-5225-3117-3.ch010

Nycz, M., & Pólkowski, Z. (2016). Business Intelligence as a Modern IT Supporting Management of Local Government Units in Poland. *International Journal of Knowledge and Systems Science*, *7*(4), 1–18. doi:10.4018/IJKSS.2016100101

Obaji, N. O., Senin, A. A., & Olugu, M. U. (2016). Supportive Government Policy as a Mechanism for Business Incubation Performance in Nigeria. *International Journal of Information Systems and Social Change*, *7*(4), 52–66. doi:10.4018/IJISSC.2016100103

Obicci, P. A. (2017). Risk Sharing in a Partnership. In *Risk Management Strategies in Public-Private Partnerships* (pp. 115–152). Hershey, PA: IGI Global. doi:10.4018/978-1-5225-2503-5.ch004

Obidallah, W. J., & Raahemi, B. (2017). Managing Changes in Service Oriented Virtual Organizations: A Structural and Procedural Framework to Facilitate the Process of Change. *Journal of Electronic Commerce in Organizations*, *15*(1), 59–83. doi:10.4018/JECO.2017010104

Ojasalo, J., & Ojasalo, K. (2016). Service Logic Business Model Canvas for Lean Development of SMEs and Start-Ups. In N. Baporikar (Ed.), *Handbook of Research on Entrepreneurship in the Contemporary Knowledge-Based Global Economy* (pp. 217–243). Hershey, PA: IGI Global. doi:10.4018/978-1-4666-8798-1.ch010

Ojo, O. (2017). Impact of Innovation on the Entrepreneurial Success in Selected Business Enterprises in South-West Nigeria. *International Journal of Innovation in the Digital Economy*, *8*(2), 29–38. doi:10.4018/IJIDE.2017040103

Okdinawati, L., Simatupang, T. M., & Sunitiyoso, Y. (2017). Multi-Agent Reinforcement Learning for Value Co-Creation of Collaborative Transportation Management (CTM). *International Journal of Information Systems and Supply Chain Management*, *10*(3), 84–95. doi:10.4018/IJISSCM.2017070105

Ortner, E., Mevius, M., Wiedmann, P., & Kurz, F. (2016). Design of Interactional Decision Support Applications for E-Participation in Smart Cities. *International Journal of Electronic Government Research*, *12*(2), 18–38. doi:10.4018/IJEGR.2016040102

Pal, K. (2018). Building High Quality Big Data-Based Applications in Supply Chains. In A. Kumar & S. Saurav (Eds.), *Supply Chain Management Strategies and Risk Assessment in Retail Environments* (pp. 1–24). Hershey, PA: IGI Global. doi:10.4018/978-1-5225-3056-5.ch001

Palos-Sanchez, P. R., & Correia, M. B. (2018). Perspectives of the Adoption of Cloud Computing in the Tourism Sector. In J. Rodrigues, C. Ramos, P. Cardoso, & C. Henriques (Eds.), *Handbook of Research on Technological Developments for Cultural Heritage and eTourism Applications* (pp. 377–400). Hershey, PA: IGI Global. doi:10.4018/978-1-5225-2927-9.ch018

Parry, V. K., & Lind, M. L. (2016). Alignment of Business Strategy and Information Technology Considering Information Technology Governance, Project Portfolio Control, and Risk Management. *International Journal of Information Technology Project Management*, *7*(4), 21–37. doi:10.4018/IJITPM.2016100102

Pashkova, N., Trujillo-Barrera, A., Apostolakis, G., Van Dijk, G., Drakos, P. D., & Baourakis, G. (2016). Business Management Models of Microfinance Institutions (MFIs) in Africa: A Study into Their Enabling Environments. *International Journal of Food and Beverage Manufacturing and Business Models*, *1*(2), 63–82. doi:10.4018/IJFBMBM.2016070105

Patiño, B. E. (2017). New Generation Management by Convergence and Individual Identity: A Systemic and Human-Oriented Approach. In N. Baporikar (Ed.), *Innovation and Shifting Perspectives in Management Education* (pp. 119–143). Hershey, PA: IGI Global. doi:10.4018/978-1-5225-1019-2.ch006

Pawliczek, A., & Rössler, M. (2017). Knowledge of Management Tools and Systems in SMEs: Knowledge Transfer in Management. In A. Bencsik (Ed.), *Knowledge Management Initiatives and Strategies in Small and Medium Enterprises* (pp. 180–203). Hershey, PA: IGI Global. doi:10.4018/978-1-5225-1642-2.ch009

Pejic-Bach, M., Omazic, M. A., Aleksic, A., & Zoroja, J. (2018). Knowledge-Based Decision Making: A Multi-Case Analysis. In R. Leon (Ed.), *Managerial Strategies for Business Sustainability During Turbulent Times* (pp. 160–184). Hershey, PA: IGI Global. doi:10.4018/978-1-5225-2716-9.ch009

Perano, M., Hysa, X., & Calabrese, M. (2018). Strategic Planning, Cultural Context, and Business Continuity Management: Business Cases in the City of Shkoder. In A. Presenza & L. Sheehan (Eds.), *Geopolitics and Strategic Management in the Global Economy* (pp. 57–77). Hershey, PA: IGI Global. doi:10.4018/978-1-5225-2673-5.ch004

Pereira, R., Mira da Silva, M., & Lapão, L. V. (2017). IT Governance Maturity Patterns in Portuguese Healthcare. In S. De Haes & W. Van Grembergen (Eds.), *Strategic IT Governance and Alignment in Business Settings* (pp. 24–52). Hershey, PA: IGI Global. doi:10.4018/978-1-5225-0861-8.ch002

Perez-Uribe, R., & Ocampo-Guzman, D. (2016). Conflict within Colombian Family Owned SMEs: An Explosive Blend between Feelings and Business. In J. Saiz-Álvarez (Ed.), *Handbook of Research on Social Entrepreneurship and Solidarity Economics* (pp. 329–354). Hershey, PA: IGI Global. doi:10.4018/978-1-5225-0097-1.ch017

Pérez-Uribe, R. I., Torres, D. A., Jurado, S. P., & Prada, D. M. (2018). Cloud Tools for the Development of Project Management in SMEs. In R. Perez-Uribe, C. Salcedo-Perez, & D. Ocampo-Guzman (Eds.), *Handbook of Research on Intrapreneurship and Organizational Sustainability in SMEs* (pp. 95–120). Hershey, PA: IGI Global. doi:10.4018/978-1-5225-3543-0.ch005

Petrisor, I., & Cozmiuc, D. (2017). Global Supply Chain Management Organization at Siemens in the Advent of Industry 4.0. In L. Saglietto & C. Cezanne (Eds.), *Global Intermediation and Logistics Service Providers* (pp. 123–142). Hershey, PA: IGI Global. doi:10.4018/978-1-5225-2133-4.ch007

Pierce, J. M., Velliaris, D. M., & Edwards, J. (2017). A Living Case Study: A Journey Not a Destination. In N. Silton (Ed.), *Exploring the Benefits of Creativity in Education, Media, and the Arts* (pp. 158–178). Hershey, PA: IGI Global. doi:10.4018/978-1-5225-0504-4.ch008

Radosavljevic, M., & Andjelkovic, A. (2017). Multi-Criteria Decision Making Approach for Choosing Business Process for the Improvement: Upgrading of the Six Sigma Methodology. In J. Stanković, P. Delias, S. Marinković, & S. Rochhia (Eds.), *Tools and Techniques for Economic Decision Analysis* (pp. 225–247). Hershey, PA: IGI Global. doi:10.4018/978-1-5225-0959-2.ch011

Radovic, V. M. (2017). Corporate Sustainability and Responsibility and Disaster Risk Reduction: A Serbian Overview. In M. Camilleri (Ed.), *CSR 2.0 and the New Era of Corporate Citizenship* (pp. 147–164). Hershey, PA: IGI Global. doi:10.4018/978-1-5225-1842-6.ch008

Raghunath, K. M., Devi, S. L., & Patro, C. S. (2018). Impact of Risk Assessment Models on Risk Factors: A Holistic Outlook. In K. Strang, M. Korstanje, & N. Vajjhala (Eds.), *Research, Practices, and Innovations in Global Risk and Contingency Management* (pp. 134–153). Hershey, PA: IGI Global. doi:10.4018/978-1-5225-4754-9.ch008

Raman, A., & Goyal, D. P. (2017). Extending IMPLEMENT Framework for Enterprise Information Systems Implementation to Information System Innovation. In M. Tavana (Ed.), *Enterprise Information Systems and the Digitalization of Business Functions* (pp. 137–177). Hershey, PA: IGI Global. doi:10.4018/978-1-5225-2382-6.ch007

Rao, Y., & Zhang, Y. (2017). The Construction and Development of Academic Library Digital Special Subject Databases. In L. Ruan, Q. Zhu, & Y. Ye (Eds.), *Academic Library Development and Administration in China* (pp. 163–183). Hershey, PA: IGI Global. doi:10.4018/978-1-5225-0550-1.ch010

Ravasan, A. Z., Mohammadi, M. M., & Hamidi, H. (2018). An Investigation Into the Critical Success Factors of Implementing Information Technology Service Management Frameworks. In K. Jakobs (Ed.), *Corporate and Global Standardization Initiatives in Contemporary Society* (pp. 200–218). Hershey, PA: IGI Global. doi:10.4018/978-1-5225-5320-5.ch009

Renna, P., Izzo, C., & Romaniello, T. (2016). The Business Process Management Systems to Support Continuous Improvements. In W. Nuninger & J. Châtelet (Eds.), *Handbook of Research on Quality Assurance and Value Management in Higher Education* (pp. 237–256). Hershey, PA: IGI Global. doi:10.4018/978-1-5225-0024-7.ch009

Rezaie, S., Mirabedini, S. J., & Abtahi, A. (2018). Designing a Model for Implementation of Business Intelligence in the Banking Industry. *International Journal of Enterprise Information Systems*, *14*(1), 77–103. doi:10.4018/IJEIS.2018010105

Riccò, R. (2016). Diversity Management: Bringing Equality, Equity, and Inclusion in the Workplace. In J. Prescott (Ed.), *Handbook of Research on Race, Gender, and the Fight for Equality* (pp. 335–359). Hershey, PA: IGI Global. doi:10.4018/978-1-5225-0047-6.ch015

Romano, L., Grimaldi, R., & Colasuonno, F. S. (2017). Demand Management as a Success Factor in Project Portfolio Management. In L. Romano (Ed.), *Project Portfolio Management Strategies for Effective Organizational Operations* (pp. 202–219). Hershey, PA: IGI Global. doi:10.4018/978-1-5225-2151-8.ch008

Rostek, K. B. (2016). Risk Management: Role and Importance in Business Organization. In D. Jakóbczak (Ed.), *Analyzing Risk through Probabilistic Modeling in Operations Research* (pp. 149–178). Hershey, PA: IGI Global. doi:10.4018/978-1-4666-9458-3.ch007

Rouhani, S., & Savoji, S. R. (2016). A Success Assessment Model for BI Tools Implementation: An Empirical Study of Banking Industry. *International Journal of Business Intelligence Research*, *7*(1), 25–44. doi:10.4018/IJBIR.2016010103

Ruan, Z. (2016). A Corpus-Based Functional Analysis of Complex Nominal Groups in Written Business Discourse: The Case of "Business". *International Journal of Computer-Assisted Language Learning and Teaching*, *6*(2), 74–90. doi:10.4018/IJCALLT.2016040105

Ruhi, U. (2018). Towards an Interdisciplinary Socio-Technical Definition of Virtual Communities. In M. Khosrow-Pour, D.B.A. (Ed.), Encyclopedia of Information Science and Technology, Fourth Edition (pp. 4278-4295). Hershey, PA: IGI Global. doi:10.4018/978-1-5225-2255-3.ch371

Ryan, J., Doster, B., Daily, S., & Lewis, C. (2016). A Case Study Perspective for Balanced Perioperative Workflow Achievement through Data-Driven Process Improvement. *International Journal of Healthcare Information Systems and Informatics*, *11*(3), 19–41. doi:10.4018/IJHISI.2016070102

Safari, M. R., & Jiang, Q. (2018). The Theory and Practice of IT Governance Maturity and Strategies Alignment: Evidence From Banking Industry. *Journal of Global Information Management*, *26*(2), 127–146. doi:10.4018/JGIM.2018040106

Sahoo, J., Pati, B., & Mohanty, B. (2017). Knowledge Management as an Academic Discipline: An Assessment. In B. Gunjal (Ed.), *Managing Knowledge and Scholarly Assets in Academic Libraries* (pp. 99–126). Hershey, PA: IGI Global. doi:10.4018/978-1-5225-1741-2.ch005

Saini, D. (2017). Relevance of Teaching Values and Ethics in Management Education. In N. Baporikar (Ed.), *Management Education for Global Leadership* (pp. 90–111). Hershey, PA: IGI Global. doi:10.4018/978-1-5225-1013-0.ch005

Sambhanthan, A. (2017). Assessing and Benchmarking Sustainability in Organisations: An Integrated Conceptual Model. *International Journal of Systems and Service-Oriented Engineering*, *7*(4), 22–43. doi:10.4018/IJSSOE.2017100102

Sambhanthan, A., & Potdar, V. (2017). A Study of the Parameters Impacting Sustainability in Information Technology Organizations. *International Journal of Knowledge-Based Organizations*, *7*(3), 27–39. doi:10.4018/IJKBO.2017070103

Sánchez-Fernández, M. D., & Manríquez, M. R. (2018). The Entrepreneurial Spirit Based on Social Values: The Digital Generation. In P. Isaias & L. Carvalho (Eds.), *User Innovation and the Entrepreneurship Phenomenon in the Digital Economy* (pp. 173–193). Hershey, PA: IGI Global. doi:10.4018/978-1-5225-2826-5.ch009

Sanchez-Ruiz, L., & Blanco, B. (2017). Process Management for SMEs: Barriers, Enablers, and Benefits. In M. Vemić (Ed.), *Optimal Management Strategies in Small and Medium Enterprises* (pp. 293–319). Hershey, PA: IGI Global. doi:10.4018/978-1-5225-1949-2.ch014

Sanz, L. F., Gómez-Pérez, J., & Castillo-Martinez, A. (2018). Analysis of the European ICT Competence Frameworks. In V. Ahuja & S. Rathore (Eds.), *Multidisciplinary Perspectives on Human Capital and Information Technology Professionals* (pp. 225–245). Hershey, PA: IGI Global. doi:10.4018/978-1-5225-5297-0.ch012

Sarvepalli, A., & Godin, J. (2017). Business Process Management in the Classroom. *Journal of Cases on Information Technology*, *19*(2), 17–28. doi:10.4018/JCIT.2017040102

Satpathy, B., & Muniapan, B. (2016). Ancient Wisdom for Transformational Leadership and Its Insights from the Bhagavad-Gita. In U. Aung & P. Ordoñez de Pablos (Eds.), *Managerial Strategies and Practice in the Asian Business Sector* (pp. 1–10). Hershey, PA: IGI Global. doi:10.4018/978-1-4666-9758-4.ch001

Saygili, E. E., Ozturkoglu, Y., & Kocakulah, M. C. (2017). End Users' Perceptions of Critical Success Factors in ERP Applications. *International Journal of Enterprise Information Systems*, *13*(4), 58–75. doi:10.4018/IJEIS.2017100104

Saygili, E. E., & Saygili, A. T. (2017). Contemporary Issues in Enterprise Information Systems: A Critical Review of CSFs in ERP Implementations. In M. Tavana (Ed.), *Enterprise Information Systems and the Digitalization of Business Functions* (pp. 120–136). Hershey, PA: IGI Global. doi:10.4018/978-1-5225-2382-6.ch006

Seidenstricker, S., & Antonino, A. (2018). Business Model Innovation-Oriented Technology Management for Emergent Technologies. In M. Khosrow-Pour, D.B.A. (Ed.), Encyclopedia of Information Science and Technology, Fourth Edition (pp. 4560-4569). Hershey, PA: IGI Global. doi:10.4018/978-1-5225-2255-3.ch396

Senaratne, S., & Gunarathne, A. D. (2017). Excellence Perspective for Management Education from a Global Accountants' Hub in Asia. In N. Baporikar (Ed.), *Management Education for Global Leadership* (pp. 158–180). Hershey, PA: IGI Global. doi:10.4018/978-1-5225-1013-0.ch008

Sensuse, D. I., & Cahyaningsih, E. (2018). Knowledge Management Models: A Summative Review. *International Journal of Information Systems in the Service Sector*, *10*(1), 71–100. doi:10.4018/IJISSS.2018010105

Sensuse, D. I., Wibowo, W. C., & Cahyaningsih, E. (2016). Indonesian Government Knowledge Management Model: A Theoretical Model. *Information Resources Management Journal*, *29*(1), 91–108. doi:10.4018/irmj.2016010106

Seth, M., Goyal, D., & Kiran, R. (2017). Diminution of Impediments in Implementation of Supply Chain Management Information System for Enhancing its Effectiveness in Indian Automobile Industry. *Journal of Global Information Management*, *25*(3), 1–20. doi:10.4018/JGIM.2017070101

Seyal, A. H., & Rahman, M. N. (2017). Investigating Impact of Inter-Organizational Factors in Measuring ERP Systems Success: Bruneian Perspectives. In M. Tavana (Ed.), *Enterprise Information Systems and the Digitalization of Business Functions* (pp. 178–204). Hershey, PA: IGI Global. doi:10.4018/978-1-5225-2382-6.ch008

Shaikh, A. A., & Karjaluoto, H. (2016). On Some Misconceptions Concerning Digital Banking and Alternative Delivery Channels. *International Journal of E-Business Research*, *12*(3), 1–16. doi:10.4018/IJEBR.2016070101

Shams, S. M. (2016). Stakeholder Relationship Management in Online Business and Competitive Value Propositions: Evidence from the Sports Industry. *International Journal of Online Marketing*, *6*(2), 1–17. doi:10.4018/IJOM.2016040101

Shamsuzzoha, A. (2016). Management of Risk and Resilience within Collaborative Business Network. In R. Addo-Tenkorang, J. Kantola, P. Helo, & A. Shamsuzzoha (Eds.), *Supply Chain Strategies and the Engineer-to-Order Approach* (pp. 143–159). Hershey, PA: IGI Global. doi:10.4018/978-1-5225-0021-6.ch008

Shaqrah, A. A. (2018). Analyzing Business Intelligence Systems Based on 7s Model of McKinsey. *International Journal of Business Intelligence Research*, *9*(1), 53–63. doi:10.4018/IJBIR.2018010104

Sharma, A. J. (2017). Enhancing Sustainability through Experiential Learning in Management Education. In N. Baporikar (Ed.), *Management Education for Global Leadership* (pp. 256–274). Hershey, PA: IGI Global. doi:10.4018/978-1-5225-1013-0.ch013

Shetty, K. P. (2017). Responsible Global Leadership: Ethical Challenges in Management Education. In N. Baporikar (Ed.), *Innovation and Shifting Perspectives in Management Education* (pp. 194–223). Hershey, PA: IGI Global. doi:10.4018/978-1-5225-1019-2.ch009

Sinthupundaja, J., & Kohda, Y. (2017). Effects of Corporate Social Responsibility and Creating Shared Value on Sustainability. *International Journal of Sustainable Entrepreneurship and Corporate Social Responsibility*, *2*(1), 27–38. doi:10.4018/IJSECSR.2017010103

Škarica, I., & Hrgović, A. V. (2018). Implementation of Total Quality Management Principles in Public Health Institutes in the Republic of Croatia. *International Journal of Productivity Management and Assessment Technologies*, *6*(1), 1–16. doi:10.4018/IJPMAT.2018010101

Smuts, H., Kotzé, P., Van der Merwe, A., & Loock, M. (2017). Framework for Managing Shared Knowledge in an Information Systems Outsourcing Context. *International Journal of Knowledge Management*, *13*(4), 1–30. doi:10.4018/IJKM.2017100101

Soares, E. R., & Zaidan, F. H. (2016). Information Architecture and Business Modeling in Modern Organizations of Information Technology: Professional Career Plan in Organizations IT. In G. Jamil, J. Poças Rascão, F. Ribeiro, & A. Malheiro da Silva (Eds.), *Handbook of Research on Information Architecture and Management in Modern Organizations* (pp. 439–457). Hershey, PA: IGI Global. doi:10.4018/978-1-4666-8637-3.ch020

Sousa, M. J., Cruz, R., Dias, I., & Caracol, C. (2017). Information Management Systems in the Supply Chain. In G. Jamil, A. Soares, & C. Pessoa (Eds.), *Handbook of Research on Information Management for Effective Logistics and Supply Chains* (pp. 469–485). Hershey, PA: IGI Global. doi:10.4018/978-1-5225-0973-8.ch025

Spremic, M., Turulja, L., & Bajgoric, N. (2018). Two Approaches in Assessing Business Continuity Management Attitudes in the Organizational Context. In N. Bajgoric (Ed.), *Always-On Enterprise Information Systems for Modern Organizations* (pp. 159–183). Hershey, PA: IGI Global. doi:10.4018/978-1-5225-3704-5.ch008

Steenkamp, A. L. (2018). Some Insights in Computer Science and Information Technology. In *Examining the Changing Role of Supervision in Doctoral Research Projects: Emerging Research and Opportunities* (pp. 113–133). Hershey, PA: IGI Global. doi:10.4018/978-1-5225-2610-0.ch005

Studdard, N., Dawson, M., Burton, S. L., Jackson, N., Leonard, B., Quisenberry, W., & Rahim, E. (2016). Nurturing Social Entrepreneurship and Building Social Entrepreneurial Self-Efficacy: Focusing on Primary and Secondary Schooling to Develop Future Social Entrepreneurs. In Z. Fields (Ed.), *Incorporating Business Models and Strategies into Social Entrepreneurship* (pp. 154–175). Hershey, PA: IGI Global. doi:10.4018/978-1-4666-8748-6.ch010

Sun, Z. (2016). A Framework for Developing Management Intelligent Systems. *International Journal of Systems and Service-Oriented Engineering*, *6*(1), 37–53. doi:10.4018/IJSSOE.2016010103

Swami, B., & Mphele, G. T. (2016). Problems Preventing Growth of Small Entrepreneurs: A Case Study of a Few Small Entrepreneurs in Botswana Sub-Urban Areas. In N. Baporikar (Ed.), *Handbook of Research on Entrepreneurship in the Contemporary Knowledge-Based Global Economy* (pp. 479–508). Hershey, PA: IGI Global. doi:10.4018/978-1-4666-8798-1.ch020

Tabach, A., & Croteau, A. (2017). Configurations of Information Technology Governance Practices and Business Unit Performance. *International Journal of IT/Business Alignment and Governance*, *8*(2), 1–27. doi:10.4018/IJITBAG.2017070101

Talaue, G. M., & Iqbal, T. (2017). Assessment of e-Business Mode of Selected Private Universities in the Philippines and Pakistan. *International Journal of Online Marketing*, *7*(4), 63–77. doi:10.4018/IJOM.2017100105

Tam, G. C. (2017). Project Manager Sustainability Competence. In *Managerial Strategies and Green Solutions for Project Sustainability* (pp. 178–207). Hershey, PA: IGI Global. doi:10.4018/978-1-5225-2371-0.ch008

Tambo, T. (2018). Fashion Retail Innovation: About Context, Antecedents, and Outcome in Technological Change Projects. In I. Management Association (Ed.), Fashion and Textiles: Breakthroughs in Research and Practice (pp. 233-260). Hershey, PA: IGI Global. doi:10.4018/978-1-5225-3432-7.ch010

Tambo, T., & Mikkelsen, O. E. (2016). Fashion Supply Chain Optimization: Linking Make-to-Order Purchasing and B2B E-Commerce. In S. Joshi & R. Joshi (Eds.), *Designing and Implementing Global Supply Chain Management* (pp. 1–21). Hershey, PA: IGI Global. doi:10.4018/978-1-4666-9720-1.ch001

Tandon, K. (2016). Innovative Andragogy: The Paradigm Shift to Heutagogy. In S. Tiwari & L. Nafees (Eds.), *Innovative Management Education Pedagogies for Preparing Next-Generation Leaders* (pp. 238–257). Hershey, PA: IGI Global. doi:10.4018/978-1-4666-9691-4.ch014

Tantau, A. D., & Frăţilă, L. C. (2018). Information and Management System for Renewable Energy Business. In *Entrepreneurship and Business Development in the Renewable Energy Sector* (pp. 200–244). Hershey, PA: IGI Global. doi:10.4018/978-1-5225-3625-3.ch006

Teixeira, N., Pardal, P. N., & Rafael, B. G. (2018). Internationalization, Financial Performance, and Organizational Challenges: A Success Case in Portugal. In L. Carvalho (Ed.), *Handbook of Research on Entrepreneurial Ecosystems and Social Dynamics in a Globalized World* (pp. 379–423). Hershey, PA: IGI Global. doi:10.4018/978-1-5225-3525-6.ch017

Trad, A., & Kalpić, D. (2016). The E-Business Transformation Framework for E-Commerce Architecture-Modeling Projects. In I. Lee (Ed.), *Encyclopedia of E-Commerce Development, Implementation, and Management* (pp. 733–753). Hershey, PA: IGI Global. doi:10.4018/978-1-4666-9787-4.ch052

Trad, A., & Kalpić, D. (2016). The E-Business Transformation Framework for E-Commerce Control and Monitoring Pattern. In I. Lee (Ed.), *Encyclopedia of E-Commerce Development, Implementation, and Management* (pp. 754–777). Hershey, PA: IGI Global. doi:10.4018/978-1-4666-9787-4.ch053

Trad, A., & Kalpić, D. (2018). The Business Transformation Framework, Agile Project and Change Management. In M. Khosrow-Pour, D.B.A. (Ed.), Encyclopedia of Information Science and Technology, Fourth Edition (pp. 620-635). Hershey, PA: IGI Global. doi:10.4018/978-1-5225-2255-3.ch054

Trad, A., & Kalpić, D. (2018). The Business Transformation and Enterprise Architecture Framework: The Financial Engineering E-Risk Management and E-Law Integration. In B. Sergi, F. Fidanoski, M. Ziolo, & V. Naumovski (Eds.), *Regaining Global Stability After the Financial Crisis* (pp. 46–65). Hershey, PA: IGI Global. doi:10.4018/978-1-5225-4026-7.ch003

Turulja, L., & Bajgoric, N. (2018). Business Continuity and Information Systems: A Systematic Literature Review. In N. Bajgoric (Ed.), *Always-On Enterprise Information Systems for Modern Organizations* (pp. 60–87). Hershey, PA: IGI Global. doi:10.4018/978-1-5225-3704-5.ch004

van Wessel, R. M., de Vries, H. J., & Ribbers, P. M. (2016). Business Benefits through Company IT Standardization. In K. Jakobs (Ed.), *Effective Standardization Management in Corporate Settings* (pp. 34–53). Hershey, PA: IGI Global. doi:10.4018/978-1-4666-9737-9.ch003

Vargas-Hernández, J. G. (2017). Professional Integrity in Business Management Education. In N. Baporikar (Ed.), *Management Education for Global Leadership* (pp. 70–89). Hershey, PA: IGI Global. doi:10.4018/978-1-5225-1013-0.ch004

Vasista, T. G., & AlAbdullatif, A. M. (2017). Role of Electronic Customer Relationship Management in Demand Chain Management: A Predictive Analytic Approach. *International Journal of Information Systems and Supply Chain Management, 10*(1), 53–67. doi:10.4018/IJISSCM.2017010104

Vergidis, K. (2016). Rediscovering Business Processes: Definitions, Patterns, and Modelling Approaches. In P. Papajorgji, F. Pinet, A. Guimarães, & J. Papathanasiou (Eds.), *Automated Enterprise Systems for Maximizing Business Performance* (pp. 97–122). Hershey, PA: IGI Global. doi:10.4018/978-1-4666-8841-4.ch007

Vieru, D., & Bourdeau, S. (2017). Survival in the Digital Era: A Digital Competence-Based Multi-Case Study in the Canadian SME Clothing Industry. *International Journal of Social and Organizational Dynamics in IT, 6*(1), 17–34. doi:10.4018/IJSODIT.2017010102

Vijayan, G., & Kamarulzaman, N. H. (2017). An Introduction to Sustainable Supply Chain Management and Business Implications. In M. Khan, M. Hussain, & M. Ajmal (Eds.), *Green Supply Chain Management for Sustainable Business Practice* (pp. 27–50). Hershey, PA: IGI Global. doi:10.4018/978-1-5225-0635-5.ch002

Vlachvei, A., & Notta, O. (2017). Firm Competitiveness: Theories, Evidence, and Measurement. In A. Vlachvei, O. Notta, K. Karantininis, & N. Tsounis (Eds.), *Factors Affecting Firm Competitiveness and Performance in the Modern Business World* (pp. 1–42). Hershey, PA: IGI Global. doi:10.4018/978-1-5225-0843-4.ch001

von Rosing, M., Fullington, N., & Walker, J. (2016). Using the Business Ontology and Enterprise Standards to Transform Three Leading Organizations. *International Journal of Conceptual Structures and Smart Applications, 4*(1), 71–99. doi:10.4018/IJCSSA.2016010104

von Rosing, M., & von Scheel, H. (2016). Using the Business Ontology to Develop Enterprise Standards. *International Journal of Conceptual Structures and Smart Applications, 4*(1), 48–70. doi:10.4018/IJCSSA.2016010103

Walczak, S. (2016). Artificial Neural Networks and other AI Applications for Business Management Decision Support. *International Journal of Sociotechnology and Knowledge Development, 8*(4), 1–20. doi:10.4018/IJSKD.2016100101

Wamba, S. F., Akter, S., Kang, H., Bhattacharya, M., & Upal, M. (2016). The Primer of Social Media Analytics. *Journal of Organizational and End User Computing, 28*(2), 1–12. doi:10.4018/JOEUC.2016040101

Wang, C., Schofield, M., Li, X., & Ou, X. (2017). Do Chinese Students in Public and Private Higher Education Institutes Perform at Different Level in One of the Leadership Skills: Critical Thinking?: An Exploratory Comparison. In V. Wang (Ed.), *Encyclopedia of Strategic Leadership and Management* (pp. 160–181). Hershey, PA: IGI Global. doi:10.4018/978-1-5225-1049-9.ch013

Wang, F., Raisinghani, M. S., Mora, M., & Wang, X. (2016). Strategic E-Business Management through a Balanced Scored Card Approach. In I. Lee (Ed.), *Encyclopedia of E-Commerce Development, Implementation, and Management* (pp. 361–386). Hershey, PA: IGI Global. doi:10.4018/978-1-4666-9787-4.ch027

Wang, J. (2017). Multi-Agent based Production Management Decision System Modelling for the Textile Enterprise. *Journal of Global Information Management, 25*(4), 1–15. doi:10.4018/JGIM.2017100101

Wiedemann, A., & Gewald, H. (2017). Examining Cross-Domain Alignment: The Correlation of Business Strategy, IT Management, and IT Business Value. *International Journal of IT/Business Alignment and Governance, 8*(1), 17–31. doi:10.4018/IJITBAG.2017010102

Wolf, R., & Thiel, M. (2018). Advancing Global Business Ethics in China: Reducing Poverty Through Human and Social Welfare. In S. Hipsher (Ed.), *Examining the Private Sector's Role in Wealth Creation and Poverty Reduction* (pp. 67–84). Hershey, PA: IGI Global. doi:10.4018/978-1-5225-3117-3.ch004

Wu, J., Ding, F., Xu, M., Mo, Z., & Jin, A. (2016). Investigating the Determinants of Decision-Making on Adoption of Public Cloud Computing in E-government. *Journal of Global Information Management, 24*(3), 71–89. doi:10.4018/JGIM.2016070104

Xu, L., & de Vrieze, P. (2016). Building Situational Applications for Virtual Enterprises. In I. Lee (Ed.), *Encyclopedia of E-Commerce Development, Implementation, and Management* (pp. 715–724). Hershey, PA: IGI Global. doi:10.4018/978-1-4666-9787-4.ch050

Yablonsky, S. (2018). Innovation Platforms: Data and Analytics Platforms. In *Multi-Sided Platforms (MSPs) and Sharing Strategies in the Digital Economy: Emerging Research and Opportunities* (pp. 72–95). Hershey, PA: IGI Global. doi:10.4018/978-1-5225-5457-8.ch003

Yusoff, A., Ahmad, N. H., & Halim, H. A. (2017). Agropreneurship among Gen Y in Malaysia: The Role of Academic Institutions. In N. Ahmad, T. Ramayah, H. Halim, & S. Rahman (Eds.), *Handbook of Research on Small and Medium Enterprises in Developing Countries* (pp. 23–47). Hershey, PA: IGI Global. doi:10.4018/978-1-5225-2165-5.ch002

Zanin, F., Comuzzi, E., & Costantini, A. (2018). The Effect of Business Strategy and Stock Market Listing on the Use of Risk Assessment Tools. In *Management Control Systems in Complex Settings: Emerging Research and Opportunities* (pp. 145–168). Hershey, PA: IGI Global. doi:10.4018/978-1-5225-3987-2.ch007

Zgheib, P. W. (2017). Corporate Innovation and Intrapreneurship in the Middle East. In P. Zgheib (Ed.), *Entrepreneurship and Business Innovation in the Middle East* (pp. 37–56). Hershey, PA: IGI Global. doi:10.4018/978-1-5225-2066-5.ch003

About the Contributors

Heather C. Webb is an Assistant Professor of Business at Higher Colleges of Technology, Dubai Men's College where she teaches strategy, entrepreneurship, strategic marketing, project management and other international business courses. She received both her PhD in Management and her MSc in International Business and Emerging Markets (IBEM) from the University of Edinburgh, and her BA in History from the University of Washington. Her research focuses on aspects of strategy, culture, innovation, sustainability, and artificial intelligence. She has successfully published research on fin tech, sectoral system of innovation, Internet of Things, green marketing and sustainable innovation. Heather is from Seattle, WA and has lived in Edinburgh, Scotland, and currently resides in Dubai, UAE.

* * *

Abderazak Bakhouche is assistant professor of Economics and Finance at Dubai Men's College (HCT, Dubai). He holds an BSc degree in Economics and Finance, MA and Ph.D. degrees in Banking and Finance from the University of Wales, UK. Prior to joining the HCT, Abderazak has taught several modules in economics, banking and finance at both the undergraduate and graduate levels in the UK and Oman, and supervised graduate students' research dissertations. His primary area of research interest covers issues related to financial systems, in particular structure, competition, and efficiency.

Serkan Ceylan is the Director for the Centre for Applied Science in Project Management (CentasPM). He is playing a key role in the field of project management within the Operations, Projects, Purchasing, and Supply (OPPS) group within the Department of Decision Analytics and Risk (DAR) at the University of Southampton Business School. Dr Serkan Ceylan is a published author of the book: AgileFrame® Understanding multifaceted project approaches for successful project management. Prior to joining the University of Southampton Business School, Dr Serkan Ceylan was a senior lecturer in economics and business. His qualifications include business management studies in Germany (University of Hamburg/ Leuphana University of Lüneburg), a BA (Hons) and an MBA. Dr Serkan Ceylan completed his PhD with Professor Steven Henderson in the area of competitive theory and strategy formulation, with his research title: Using Knowledge Transfer Partnership Projects to Reveal Latent Dynamics in the Knowledge-Based View of Strategy. He is also a certified trainer for several project management qualifications including AgileFrame, AgilePM and PRINCE2 trainer and a fellow of the Higher Education Academy. Serkan has been a programme director for ACCA and MSc Project Management. Serkan has experience in teaching various undergraduate, postgraduate as well as professional courses in the areas of project management, business, strategy and marketing. Dr Serkan Ceylan currently leads and collaborates on a number of high-profile national and international research grants which reflect his focus and research interests. He has secured well over £500,000 worth of funding as well as securing PhD Scholarships from EPSRC and ESRC. Serkan's inspiring business acumen and international communication skills have generated contacts and courses for countries such as Germany, Austria, Turkey, Nigeria and China.

Ilse de la Cruz was born in Monterrey, Nuevo Leon, Mexico in 1994. Graduated from the Universidad Autonoma de Nuevo Leon in Mexico her country of origin with honors in International Business and a Cum Laude recognition in her double degree in Business Administration from City University of Seattle in USA in 2015. Had a semester abroad during her studies in Fachhochschule Osnabrük in Germany in 2014. Recently graduated (2019) with distinction from her master's degree in risk and Finance from the University of Southampton in England. Has been part of Grupo Proeza from the last 7 years in roles finance related roles. Up to date she performs as the Enterprise Risk Management Specialist of the Group.

Rajat Deb, Assistant Professor, Department of Commerce, Tripura University (A Central University), Tripura, India; did M. Com. (Accounting), MBA (Finance) and Ph. D. in Accounting from the same institution. He is a UGC-NET qualifier and the recipient of three Gold Medals for top ranks in UG & PG examinations; stood First Class First in HS examination in Commerce from Tripura State Board. He has more than 12 years teaching experience in PG courses, 2 years experience in Government Audit & Accounting; is an academic counselor and project guide of IGNOU M. Com. & Management Programs, life member of six academic associations and has 46 publications in his credit including in the journals of IIM-Kozhikode, IIM-Lucknow, IIM-Indore, XLRI, IPE, Amity University, NMIMS, ICA, IAA, SCMHRD, Publishing India Group Journals and others.

Randa El Chaar joined the department of business at Higher Colleges of Technology – UAE, as business faculty in 2014. She has MSc in Money and Banking from the American University of Beirut. Prior to joining academia, Randa built up extensive experience in the financial industries raising awareness and representing shareholders' interests. Her research interests include compliance in banking and financial institutions, and the role of Small and Medium Enterprises (SMEs) in achieving economic stability.

Li He has become a PhD candidate in Department of Public Policy, City University of Hong Kong since 2019, after graduating from Beijing Normal University and working as a Research Assistant at Shenzhen Research Institute, City University of Hong Kong. Her research interests including urban development, economic development, policy studies, and science, technology and innovation.

Rob John (D.Phil) is an independent philanthropy researcher based in the U.K. Dr John was a senior visiting fellow at NUS Business School, Singapore from 2011 to 2017 and a visiting fellow at Said Business School, Oxford from 2005 to 2009. He was the founding executive director of the European Venture Philanthropy Association and co-founded the Asian Venture Philanthropy Network. He is an Associate of the Centre for the Study of Philanthropy and Public Good at the University of St Andrews.

Fatma Nur Karaman Kabadurmus (PhD) is currently working as an assistant professor at Yasar University, and got her Ph.D. in Economics from Southern Illinois University-Carbondale. Her main areas of research include antecedents of innovation and governance in developing countries.

Fenfang Lin is a lecturer in Marketing at the University of Southampton. She holds a PhD in Marketing from the University of Edinburgh with a number of years working experience in various industries. Her research interests lie in B2B marketing, SME branding and marketing strategies, marketing capability development. She is a fellow of the Higher Education Academy (FHEA) of the UK.

Alasdair Marshall has been a risk researcher within academia since 2003. He is currently an Associate Professor in Risk Management at the University of Southampton in the UK, where he has taught and researched risk management since 2008. Dr Marshall has published extensively in risk management and related disciplines such as project management, and has a particular research interest in the ongoing development of the risk profession.

Udechukwu (Udi) Ojiako is Professor of Engineering Management at the University of Sharjah, United Arab Emirates. He currently serves as an Associate Editor of Production Planning & Control. He is also Visiting Professor in Management at the Risk Institute, University of Hull. He has held prior academic positions in the UK, South Africa and now the United Arab Emirates. Udi holds a PhD in Project Management (2005, Northumbria University), a PhD in Business (2015, University of Hull), an LLB in Laws (2017, University of London) and an MPhil in Law (2019, Aberystwyth University).

Ceyda Şenses is continuing her Economics master's degree at Pamukkale University. She received her bachelor's degree from the Yaşar University Department of Economics.

Vasilios Stouraitis is a lecturer in International Business and Management at Glasgow Caledonian University in the UK and visiting lecturer in several institutions abroad including Italy and Panama. Specializing in small and medium-sized enterprises and with a background in International Business and Economics, he holds a PhD from Henley Business School/University of Reading, an Msc in Development studies from University College London and an MBA and Bsc from the University of Kent. He has worked on development issues (agribusiness and governance) for the United Nations (Food and Agriculture Organization and the International Fund for Agricultural Development) and European Commission (DG Enterprise and Industry) and is also a published author in international business strategy and entrepreneurship. Regarding academic work, he has taught in several institutions (Edinburgh Business School at Athens, The American University of Rome, Link Campus Rome, Swiss School of Management Rome) and supervised several BA/BSc and MA/MSc theses on International Business topics and Food Economics. He has published in journals such as the International Journal of Entrepreneurial Behavior and Research, Journal of Small Business and Enterprise Development and in United Nations working paper series. His academic interests include SMEs, entrepreneurship, internationalization, exporting and agri-business smallholders. He speaks Italian, Greek, French, English and Spanish. Regarding research, he collects data and publishes in academic journals regularly with many collaborations and pending projects including books. He is a member of the Africa Children and Bread-Action NGOs based in Rome and Athens, a board member of the GCU UHatch incubator and start-up advisor.

Konstantinos Tsanis is currently leading the innovation and transformation arm of the first digital bank of Africa, Alat, created by WEMA Bank. He is a seasoned financial technology and digitalization executive, with 12+ years hands of experience across different continents and industries [FinTech, Energy (Oil, Gas and Utilities), Consulting, High Tech, Academic, Military and Financial], having worked on several market wide FinTech projects such as the E-Bond or FX trading platforms in Nigeria, Ghana and Kenya, among others. He is also an Adjunct Professor at Hult International Business School in Entrepreneurship and Innovation. In his past roles he focused on the growth of the corporate incubator within Thomson Reuters, with a particular focus in FinTechs, Start Ups and SMEs across MENA, led the strategy and sales department of Bayzat, the highest funded FinTech start up in the Middle East, helped the business development of Bloomberg LP across the Middle East and Africa, advised multiple Fortune 500 companies with Kaiser Associates, worked as a strategic advisor on improving the performance of EDF Energy (now called UK Power Networks), while simultaneously having retained his academic engagement by delivering multiple lectures and conducting academic research at the same time. His work has been recognized by winning multiple awards in Entrepreneurship and Innovation, and by being published in leading newspapers and Journals, including the MIT Technology Review and Harvard Business Review. In addition, he is keynote speaker in major industry events in the areas of FinTech, Innovation, Data and Investment in Africa.

Buse Türkyılmaz graduated from Yaşar University, Department of Economics, where she currently is following her masters degree.

José G. Vargas-Hernández, M.B.A., Ph.D., Member of the National System of Researchers of Mexico and a research professor at University Center for Economic and Managerial Sciences, University of Guadalajara. Professor Vargas-Hernández has a Ph. D. in Public Administration and a Ph.D. in Organizational Economics. He has undertaken studies in Organisational Behaviour and has a Master of Business Administration, published four books and more than 200 papers in international journals and reviews (some translated to English, French, German, Portuguese, Farsi, Chinese, etc.) and more than 300 essays in national journals and reviews. He has obtained several international Awards and recognition.

Xukun Zhang received her PhD in public policy from the City University of Hong Kong in 2019. Since 2019, she started working as a Postdoc fellow at Shenzhen Research Institute, City University of Hong Kong. Her research interests including urban development, policy studies, and science, technology, and innovation.

Index

A

Accelerator 30-33, 45, 50
Angel Investing 26-27, 34-35, 52
Asia 26-27, 30, 32, 34, 39, 42, 44-45, 47, 52, 57, 69, 74-75, 102, 104-105, 129, 132
auto dealers 16-17, 19, 21
Automobile sector 16, 20

B

Business Process Outsourcing 26-27, 29, 46

C

China 18, 23-24, 39, 43, 45, 48, 55-63, 65-72, 76, 82
Co-creation 26-27, 29, 50, 205
competitiveness 18, 23, 64, 74, 77-78, 82-84, 95, 99-101, 106, 108-110, 112-114, 127, 129-130, 132, 157, 159, 162-164, 174, 214, 225
Corporate Philanthropy 26-29, 35, 47, 50, 52
Corporate Venture Capital 26-27, 29, 37-38, 43, 46, 50, 53

D

Digital Banking 84, 192, 194-195, 198, 203, 205
Digital Transformation 161, 192-194, 196-197, 199, 202, 205

E

enterprise risk management 133, 135, 137, 147, 150-151, 217, 224
ENTIC 167, 173, 178, 181, 184, 189, 191

F

FinTech 192-193, 196-197

G

Global Competitiveness Index 106, 109, 112, 130
Global Innovation Index 78, 106, 109, 112, 114, 129-130
green economy 1-4, 12, 15
green entrepreneur 1, 3, 12
Grupo Proeza 133-136

I

ICTs 155, 158-159, 161, 166-168, 172-175, 178-179, 182, 184-185, 187, 191
India 1-3, 5-7, 9-19, 22, 24-26, 31, 34-43, 45, 50, 131, 205
Indonesia 34, 74-84, 88, 90-91, 93, 95, 97-99, 101, 103-105
Information and Communication Technologies (ICTs) 155, 158, 166, 191
Innovation 2-8, 11-12, 14-15, 18, 20-21, 23-25, 32-33, 38, 43, 47, 53-74, 76-107, 109-110, 112, 114-117, 120, 123, 126-132, 134, 150, 155, 157-166,

187-191, 196, 199, 201-202, 204-205, 209, 213-214, 220, 223-225
Innovation Management 73, 77-79, 82-86, 90, 93, 95, 101, 103, 105, 130, 224-225
innovation policy 54, 56-57, 63, 69-74, 76, 78, 82, 96, 98, 105, 109

J

job cuts 16

M

Mexico 133-135, 139, 155, 157-158, 160, 164

N

National Innovation Systems 106-107, 109, 130

P

policy analysis 54, 59, 68
Productivity 70, 77-78, 110, 123, 132, 155, 158, 161, 168, 173-175, 182, 184-186, 191, 213, 218

R

R&D 20, 56-57, 73, 79-83, 85-86, 92-95, 98-100, 108, 111, 127, 131, 191
risk communication and coordination 135, 142, 147, 149-150
risk culture 135-136, 140, 148-150
risk management 133, 135-138, 140-144, 146-154, 206-208, 210-211, 213, 215-218, 221-224

S

slowdown 16-19, 22-25
SMEs 3, 94, 100-101, 104-105, 131, 155-157, 159-162, 164, 175, 188-191, 203, 207-208, 213-216, 218-221
Social Enterprise 26-27, 30-32, 46-49, 53
Social Value 26-27, 29, 33, 38, 50
South Korea 56, 104, 106, 108-110, 112-116, 118, 120-121, 123, 127-132
strategic risk management 151
sustainability 1-2, 4, 11-13, 22, 28, 36, 38, 46, 123
Sustainable Innovation 73

T

technology policy 13, 54, 56-57, 63, 67-68, 70, 72
Turkey 106, 108-118, 120-121, 123, 126-129, 131-132

W

waste management 1, 3, 6-7, 9, 11, 13, 36

Purchase Print, E-Book, or Print + E-Book

IGI Global's reference books can now be purchased from three unique pricing formats: Print Only, E-Book Only, or Print + E-Book.
Shipping fees may apply.

www.igi-global.com

Recommended Reference Books

ISBN: 978-1-5225-6201-6
© 2019; 341 pp.
List Price: $345

ISBN: 978-1-5225-7262-6
© 2019; 360 pp.
List Price: $215

ISBN: 978-1-5225-8003-4
© 2019; 216 pp.
List Price: $205

ISBN: 978-1-5225-5763-0
© 2019; 304 pp.
List Price: $205

ISBN: 978-1-5225-6980-0
© 2019; 325 pp.
List Price: $235

ISBN: 978-1-5225-7808-6
© 2019; 397 pp.
List Price: $215

Looking for free content, product updates, news, and special offers?
Join IGI Global's mailing list today and start enjoying exclusive perks sent only to IGI Global members.
Add your name to the list at **www.igi-global.com/newsletters.**

Publisher of Peer-Reviewed, Timely, and Innovative Academic Research

IGI Global
DISSEMINATOR OF KNOWLEDGE

www.igi-global.com Sign up at www.igi-global.com/newsletters facebook.com/igiglobal twitter.com/igiglobal

Ensure Quality Research is Introduced to the Academic Community

Become an IGI Global Reviewer for Authored Book Projects

The overall success of an authored book project is dependent on quality and timely reviews.

In this competitive age of scholarly publishing, constructive and timely feedback significantly expedites the turnaround time of manuscripts from submission to acceptance, allowing the publication and discovery of forward-thinking research at a much more expeditious rate. Several IGI Global authored book projects are currently seeking highly-qualified experts in the field to fill vacancies on their respective editorial review boards:

Applications and Inquiries may be sent to:
development@igi-global.com

Applicants must have a doctorate (or an equivalent degree) as well as publishing and reviewing experience. Reviewers are asked to complete the open-ended evaluation questions with as much detail as possible in a timely, collegial, and constructive manner. All reviewers' tenures run for one-year terms on the editorial review boards and are expected to complete at least three reviews per term. Upon successful completion of this term, reviewers can be considered for an additional term.

If you have a colleague that may be interested in this opportunity, we encourage you to share this information with them.

IGI Global Proudly Partners With eContent Pro International

Receive a 25% Discount on all Editorial Services

Editorial Services

IGI Global expects all final manuscripts submitted for publication to be in their final form. This means they must be reviewed, revised, and professionally copy edited prior to their final submission. Not only does this support with accelerating the publication process, but it also ensures that the highest quality scholarly work can be disseminated.

English Language Copy Editing

Let eContent Pro International's expert copy editors perform edits on your manuscript to resolve spelling, punctuaion, grammar, syntax, flow, formatting issues and more.

Scientific and Scholarly Editing

Allow colleagues in your research area to examine the content of your manuscript and provide you with valuable feedback and suggestions before submission.

Figure, Table, Chart & Equation Conversions

Do you have poor quality figures? Do you need visual elements in your manuscript created or converted? A design expert can help!

Translation

Need your documjent translated into English? eContent Pro International's expert translators are fluent in English and more than 40 different languages.

Hear What Your Colleagues are Saying About Editorial Services Supported by IGI Global

"The service was very fast, very thorough, and very helpful in ensuring our chapter meets the criteria and requirements of the book's editors. I was quite impressed and happy with your service."

– Prof. Tom Brinthaupt,
Middle Tennessee State University, USA

"I found the work actually spectacular. The editing, formatting, and other checks were very thorough. The turnaround time was great as well. I will definitely use eContent Pro in the future."

– Nickanor Amwata, Lecturer,
University of Kurdistan Hawler, Iraq

"I was impressed that it was done timely, and wherever the content was not clear for the reader, the paper was improved with better readability for the audience."

– Prof. James Chilembwe,
Mzuzu University, Malawi

Email: customerservice@econtentpro.com

www.igi-global.com/editorial-service-partners

IGI Global
DISSEMINATOR OF KNOWLEDGE
www.igi-global.com

Celebrating Over 30 Years of Scholarly Knowledge Creation & Dissemination

InfoSci®-Books

A Database of Over 5,300+ Reference Books Containing Over 100,000+ Chapters Focusing on Emerging Research

GAIN ACCESS TO **THOUSANDS** OF REFERENCE BOOKS AT **A FRACTION** OF THEIR INDIVIDUAL LIST **PRICE**.

InfoSci®-Books Database

The **InfoSci®-Books** database is a collection of over 5,300+ IGI Global single and multi-volume reference books, handbooks of research, and encyclopedias, encompassing groundbreaking research from prominent experts worldwide that span over 350+ topics in 11 core subject areas including business, computer science, education, science and engineering, social sciences and more.

Open Access Fee Waiver (Offset Model) Initiative

For any library that invests in IGI Global's InfoSci-Journals and/ or InfoSci-Books databases, IGI Global will match the library's investment with a fund of equal value to go toward **subsidizing the OA article processing charges (APCs) for their students, faculty, and staff** at that institution when their work is submitted and accepted under OA into an IGI Global journal.*

INFOSCI® PLATFORM FEATURES

- No DRM
- No Set-Up or Maintenance Fees
- A Guarantee of No More Than a 5% Annual Increase
- Full-Text HTML and PDF Viewing Options
- Downloadable MARC Records
- Unlimited Simultaneous Access
- COUNTER 5 Compliant Reports
- Formatted Citations With Ability to Export to RefWorks and EasyBib
- No Embargo of Content (Research is Available Months in Advance of the Print Release)

The fund will be offered on an annual basis and expire at the end of the subscription period. The fund would renew as the subscription is renewed for each year thereafter. The open access fees will be waived after the student, faculty, or staff's paper has been vetted and accepted into an IGI Global journal and the fund can only be used toward publishing OA in an IGI Global journal. Libraries in developing countries will have the match on their investment doubled.

To Learn More or To Purchase This Database:
www.igi-global.com/infosci-books
eresources@igi-global.com • Toll Free: 1-866-342-6657 ext. 100 • Phone: 717-533-8845 x100

IGI Global
DISSEMINATOR OF KNOWLEDGE
www.igi-global.com

IGI Global
DISSEMINATOR OF KNOWLEDGE
www.igi-global.com

Publisher of Peer-Reviewed, Timely, and Innovative Academic Research Since 1988

IGI Global's Transformative Open Access (OA) Model: **How to Turn Your University Library's Database Acquisitions Into a Source of OA Funding**

In response to the OA movement and well in advance of Plan S, IGI Global, early last year, unveiled their OA Fee Waiver (Read & Publish) Initiative.

Under this initiative, librarians who invest in IGI Global's InfoSci-Books (5,300+ reference books) and/or InfoSci-Journals (185+ scholarly journals) databases will be able to subsidize their patron's OA article processing charges (APC) when their work is submitted and accepted (after the peer review process) into an IGI Global journal. *See website for details.

How Does it Work?

1. When a library subscribes or perpetually purchases IGI Global's InfoSci-Databases and/or their discipline/subject-focused subsets, IGI Global will match the library's investment with a fund of equal value to go toward subsidizing the OA article processing charges (APCs) for their patrons.

   ***Researchers:* Be sure to recommend the InfoSci-Books and InfoSci-Journals to take advantage of this initiative.**
2. When a student, faculty, or staff member submits a paper and it is accepted (following the peer review) into one of IGI Global's 185+ scholarly journals, the author will have the option to have their paper published under a traditional publishing model or as OA.
3. When the author chooses to have their paper published under OA, IGI Global will notify them of the OA Fee Waiver (Read & Publish) Initiative. If the author decides they would like to take advantage of this initiative, IGI Global will deduct the US$ 2,000 APC from the created fund.
4. This fund will be offered on an annual basis and will renew as the subscription is renewed for each year thereafter. IGI Global will manage the fund and award the APC waivers unless the librarian has a preference as to how the funds should be managed.

Hear From the Experts on This Initiative:

"I'm very happy to have been able to make one of my recent research contributions, "Visualizing the Social Media Conversations of a National Information Technology Professional Association" featured in the *International Journal of Human Capital and Information Technology Professionals*, freely available along with having access to the valuable resources found within IGI Global's InfoSci-Journals database."

– **Prof. Stuart Palmer,**
Deakin University, Australia

For More Information, Visit: www.igi-global.com/publish/contributor-resources/open-access/read-publish-model or contact IGI Global's Database Team at eresources@igi-global.com.

ARE YOU READY TO **PUBLISH YOUR RESEARCH?**

IGI Global
DISSEMINATOR OF KNOWLEDGE

IGI Global offers book authorship and editorship opportunities across 11 subject areas, including business, computer science, education, science and engineering, social sciences, and more!

Benefits of Publishing with IGI Global:

- Free, one-on-one editorial and promotional support.
- Expedited publishing timelines that can take your book from start to finish in less than one (1) year.
- Choose from a variety of formats including: Edited and Authored References, Handbooks of Research, Encyclopedias, and Research Insights.
- Utilize IGI Global's eEditorial Discovery® submission system in support of conducting the submission and blind review process.
- IGI Global maintains a strict adherence to ethical practices due in part to our full membership with the Committee on Publication Ethics (COPE).
- Indexing potential in prestigious indices such as Scopus®, Web of Science™, PsycINFO®, and ERIC – Education Resources Information Center.
- Ability to connect your ORCID iD to your IGI Global publications.
- Earn royalties on your publication as well as receive complimentary copies and exclusive discounts.

Get Started Today by Contacting the Acquisitions Department at:
acquisition@igi-global.com

www.igi-global.com/infosci-ondemand

InfoSci®-OnDemand

Continuously updated with new material on a weekly basis, InfoSci®-OnDemand offers the ability to search through thousands of quality full-text research papers. Users can narrow each search by identifying key topic areas of interest, then display a complete listing of relevant papers, and purchase materials specific to their research needs.

Comprehensive Service

- Over 125,000+ journal articles, book chapters, and case studies.
- All content is downloadable in PDF and HTML format and can be stored locally for future use.

No Subscription Fees

- One time fee of $37.50 per PDF download.

Instant Access

- Receive a download link immediately after order completion!

"It really provides an excellent entry into the research literature of the field. It presents a manageable number of highly relevant sources on topics of interest to a wide range of researchers. The sources are scholarly, but also accessible to 'practitioners'."

- Lisa Stimatz, MLS, University of North Carolina at Chapel Hill, USA

"It is an excellent and well designed database which will facilitate research, publication, and teaching. It is a very useful tool to have."

- George Ditsa, PhD, University of Wollongong, Australia

"I have accessed the database and find it to be a valuable tool to the IT/IS community. I found valuable articles meeting my search criteria 95% of the time."

- Prof. Lynda Louis, Xavier University of Louisiana, USA

Recommended for use by researchers who wish to immediately download PDFs of individual chapters or articles.

www.igi-global.com/e-resources/infosci-ondemand

IGI Global
DISSEMINATOR OF KNOWLEDGE
www.igi-global.com

www.ingramcontent.com/pod-product-compliance
Lightning Source LLC
LaVergne TN
LVHW081331021026
849161LV00008BA/1934
* 9 7 8 1 7 9 9 8 4 1 9 5 1 *